WHAT PEOPLE AR

MOSES AND JESU!

CW00819349

*The author Dr Jones-Hunt, in her*
*reviews the mountainous evidence down the ages of personal inspiration*
*and communication from a higher spiritual dimension coupled with its*
*spiritually transformative consequences...a valuable insight into*
*the...cross-cultural nature of spiritual experiences...the author's extensive*
*research offers a new perspective which could aid the growth of ecumenical*
*and interfaith relations so badly needed in today's troubled climate.*
**Rev. Dr Michael Stanley**, author and former principal of the New
Church College (Swedenborgian)

*Although much of orthodox religion looks upon mediumship as the work of*
*the devil, a strong case can be made that messages received through*
*mediumship are the very foundation of organized religion. Jacqueline Jones-*
*Hunt PhD makes that case, offering an abundance of evidence suggesting*
*that what today is known as mediumship went by different names in earlier*
*times.*
**Michael Tymn**, author, member of the Academy of Spirituality and
Paranormal Studies, USA. www.lightlink.com

*This is a remarkable and revolutionary book which sheds a new light on*
*familiar religious traditions...comprehensive, thoroughly researched and*
*very though-provoking.*
**Professor Rupert Sheldrake**, British biochemist, Director of Perrott-
Warrwick Project, author, including *Telepathy, Psychic Pets & Other*
*Powers of Animals.*

*Looks great!...the information is pure gold...a lifetime reference book...a*
*very important book...*
**Victor J. Zammit**, Euro-Australian attorney-at-law, (retired),
psychical researcher, author, New South Wales, Australia.

*I recommend this thoroughly researched book to all those enquiring into knowledge about life after death. Based on my 50 years of personal experience with psycho-energetic phenomena and humans manifesting same, their origin is not in space-time though they yield correlates that have space-time manifestations...*
**Professor William A. Tiller,** Professor Emeritus, Stanford University, USA, Author & Founder of the Tiller Foundation.

*Jackie Jones-Hunt has written an exciting and fascinating book by taking some bold steps in her discussions about Jesus as a shaman. Her research and journeys into world religions and the history of mystics leads her in places few have gone. She is suggesting new ways of looking at very old beliefs. I commend her explorations and look forward to seeing where this research will lead us.*
**Diane Corcoran PhD,** President of the International Association for Near Death Studies Inc. (IANDS).

*I thoroughly endorse this excellent, original research and recommend it to all to read.*
**Rev. Dr. (Dean) Pat W. Fenske,**
Former Executive Director of the Spiritual Frontiers Fellowship International Inc: Former Trustee of the Academy of Spirituality & Paranormal Studies Inc: Former President of IANDS & Former Editor of IANDS Journal: Vital Signs.

*...well written, exceptionally well-researched...Dr Jones-Hunt takes us on a journey through history to decode evidence of mediumship...arguing that...mediumship...could be the foundation stone of the religious experience...clearly condensed knowledge gained through many, many years of research and experience...a highly recommended volume...one of the only textbooks on mediumship that combines an academic and scientific worldview with an understanding of spiritualism...*
**Robert Black,** Former Editor for Living Traditions Magazine, Australia. www.living traditions-magazine.com

*What I have read is exceedingly good and I am sure will be valued by all who read it…and trust that your hard work will be rewarded by the appeal it will have among those who are discerning!*
**Eric Hatton**, Minister & First & Only Honorary President of the Spiritualist National Union, UK.

*The author Dr J. Jones-Hunt,…I can thoroughly recommend this book as one of undoubted value to anyone who has an open mind…*
**Professor Archie E. Roy**, Former President of the Society for Psychical Research and Founding President of the Scottish SPR, UK.

*A comprehensive and well thought out work, correlating historical and biblical events with modern-day mediumship. A must for the serious student of psychic research.*
**Dr Robin Foy PhD**, spiritual scientist, psychic researcher & sitter including the Scole Experiment.

*This is an inspiring book that will enlighten all who have the good fortune to read it…fluid and absorbing…an enthralling read.*
**Simon Forsyth**, The Psychic Times www.thepsychictimes.com

*A valuable and original work and a major contribution to the understanding of the complex subject of mediumship, spirituality and religions. Dr Jones-Hunt's excellent book is likely to become a foundational resource….*
**Professor Abdul Hassam PhD, DSc (hon)**.

*This book is an encyclopaedic foundation stone providing vital knowledge …compiled painstakingly by the author…*
**Sonia Rinaldi**, Author, International Prize Winner & Director of the Advanced Research Institute on Instrumental Transcommunication (Brazil).

*This book takes a giant leap towards synthesising evidential aspects of psychical research with evidence, which would appear to indicate a spiritual*

*dimension. As someone who has researched these matters...for over 20 years I would thoroughly recommend this book... as almost compulsory reading.*
**Tricia Robertson**, Hon Secretary & former president of the Scottish Society for Psychical Research, UK, co-author with prof. Archie Roy on 3 papers on mediumship, DACE tutor, Glasgow University.

*This excellent, revolutionary...book should be read by everyone. They will learn many invaluable things including the many facets of mediumship, the origins of religions and evidence for the survival of the dead.*
**Crawford Knox PhD**. Author, Former Trustee & Hon. Treasurer of the Alistair Hardy (Psychical) Research Centre, & former council member of the SSPR, UK.

*A comprehensive survey of the history of relations between the psychic and the spiritual drawing on a vast rande of sources and culminating in an evaluation of the 18th century scientist and seer Swedenborg.*
**David Lorimer MA, PGCE, FRSA**, Author of 12 books, Programme Director of the Scientific & Medical Network, Executive Vice-President of the Wrekin Trust & Vice- President of the Swedenborg Society.

*...the author analyzes...evidence...from an interesting perspective seldom covered...an important addition to...literature on psychical research.*
**Thomas Jones**, Co-founder of www.SurvivalAfterDeath.org

*...a fascinating exploration of the main sources of ancient wisdom...*
**Dr Anabela Cardosso**, Author, Founder, Editor & Director of the ITC Research Centre, Spain.

*This remarkable book presents a vast array of evidence for the survival of all living creatures...excellent, stimulating, ...and most certainly inspired book.*
**Ann McCutcheon**, President of Langside and Cambuslang Spiritualist Churches and medium.

# Moses and Jesus: the Shamans

Jackie Jones-Hunt PhD

# Moses and Jesus:
# the Shamans

Jackie Jones-Hunt PhD

BOOKS

Winchester, UK
Washington, USA

First published by O-Books, 2011
O-Books is an imprint of John Hunt Publishing Ltd., Laurel House, Station Approach,
Alresford, Hants, SO24 9JH, UK
office1@o-books.net
www.o-books.com

For distributor details and how to order please visit the 'Ordering' section on our website.

Text copyright: Jackie Jones-Hunt 2010

www.jackiejoneshunt.co.uk

ISBN: 978 1 84694 471 0

A CIP catalogue record for this book is available from the British Library.

Design: Stuart Davies

Printed in the UK by CPI Antony Rowe
Printed in the USA by Offset Paperback Mfrs, Inc

We operate a distinctive and ethical publishing philosophy in all
areas of our business, from our global network of authors to
production and worldwide distribution.

# CONTENTS

This book is dedicated with great love to Tony my husband, my parents, Eric and Eileen, grandparents Elizabeth and Bob, and to our wonderful Jack Russell dogs: Jac, Sioux, Edward and Lizzie. They each give oceans of love, devotion, loyalty, fun and companionship, unreservedly and unconditionally.

A special dedication goes to Sioux our 16 year old dog who recently passed to spirit herself and wee Jac who passed to spirit some years before her. It is clear to see why they go to spirit long before us, as they are such innocent, vulnerable, emotional souls who have little to learn. Words cannot describe their love nor express our love for them. They are indeed spiritual teachers and it is a privilege to share our lives with them giving them contented dreams and happy lives.

*Lead me from death to life, from falsehood to truth*
*Lead me from despair to hope, from fear to trust*
*Lead me from hate to love, from war to peace*
*Let peace fill our heart, our world, our universe*
Satish Kumar (Indian writer, 1937–1981), 'Prayer for Peace',
adapted from the Upanishads

*Hurry to begin the slow process of healing this dying planet. Very*
*soon it will be too late. If not for ourselves, as we are the ones who*
*are killing her, save her for the innocents, the animals, who were left*
*in our care and keeping.*
Jackie Jones-Hunt PhD

# Foreword I

By Archie E. Roy, professor emeritus of astronomy, Department of Physics and Astronomy, Glasgow University, Glasgow, United Kingdom

We are told frequently that in the West we live in a post-religious age, that church attendances are diminishing yearly, and that for many people who still call themselves members of a church, it has essentially become a four-wheeler membership, in that they only come to church in a pram to be baptized, in a taxi to be married and in a hearse to be buried. A gross over-simplification, of course, but it neatly encapsulates the result of the legacy left us in the second half of the 19th century by Darwin and Wallace in their theory of the survival of species by natural selection, a legacy – unwelcome to many religious fundamentalists such as the 'creationist science group' – reinforced by the astronomers' awesome mapping of the gigantic size of the universe.

It is a universe in which, if on a suitable scale it was the size of Asia, the 200,000 million galaxies it contained would be grains of sand. If then the scale was enlarged and one of those grains of sand – our galaxy – was magnified to the size of Asia, its 100,000 million stars would themselves be grains of sand scattered a few hundred yards from each other. One of them, the star we call the sun, has a planetary system that would be covered on that scale by a penny centered on the sun's speck of celestial fire. If the scale was altered yet again with the penny expanded to the size of Asia, the earth would be a ball that would fit comfortably inside a modest-sized bungalow. The thin film of air, land and water in which life in all its varieties exists on our planet would on that last scale be less than one half-inch in thickness.

But the legacy has been modified yet again by those materialist reductionists who accept the widespread opinion that all evidence teaches that a human being's physical body contains everything that makes up that person. They believe that the brain of that person, by heredity and upbringing, ultimately holds the personality, the memory, the emotions and intelligence that provide the capability to face and respond to the problems life brings, the 'slings and arrows of outrageous fortune', the joys of human friendship and love, the numbing loss of loved ones. If that is so, then the logical deduction must be stoically accepted that death, that inescapable appointment we all must keep, brings total annihilation.

And it does seem that this bleak picture is supported by hard facts. We see birth, growth, maturity, decay and death in all their physical forms. The tremendous success of science in understanding and controlling the environment, the success of its handmaiden technology in fashioning the civilization in which we – the privileged ones of the planet – live, providing food, clothing, medicine, housing, television, video and a multitude of other material comforts, again conditions and orientates us to the physical world, persuading us that there is nothing else.

We therefore look back on the vague superstitions of past ages and congratulate ourselves wryly that we have been rescued by rational thought and the scientific method from such follies, comfort blankets we clung to in the childhood of the human race against a host of inexplicable natural disasters occurring in a strange and terrifying world. In our superior wisdom we smile pityingly at those who still clutch at the drifting matchwood raft of religion in all its many worldwide forms and dare not learn to swim stoically in the ocean of truth, accepting the reality that we are simply clever animals, our minds but the brain in action, struggling to survive in an aloof, uncaring physical world.

This sketch, simplistic though it is, is still a fair model of a large fraction of the intelligent West's world outlook. For most, it dictates an instant dismissal of any article or book on comparative religion. It is also somewhat similar to the attitude of a tourist who has had a boring, irritating, time-wasting sojourn in a strange, indeed alien, country with confusing, seemingly irrational customs. *Been there, done that, got the T-shirt – thrown it away.*

But it is more even than that. To the many who believe that science and technology are citadels against the onslaught of irrationality, constantly under siege by the ignorant and irrational, anything that threatens to undermine them must be resisted. There is a long list of *alleged* irrational, baseless pseudosciences that immediately raise the hackles of the skeptics when they are mentioned. Often the skeptics are justified in their dismay – to put it mildly – that a considerable fraction of the human race should still take astrology at all seriously in an age where the majestic scale of the universe compared to the infinitesimal size of the earth is known. In such a case skeptics may be forgiven for believing the old adage that while many drink of the waters of the fountain of knowledge, others merely gargle.

Where I take issue with skeptics is with those who insist that psychical research and parapsychology are to be listed among the pseudosciences. Not only do they dismiss the testimony from the beginnings of history of mystics, shamans, great philosophers and religious teachers such as the Buddha, Jesus of Nazareth, Lao Tse, Confucius, to name but a few, that there exists a spiritual dimension, but they also dismiss the wealth of evidence of more than a century of psychical research by hard-headed, initially skeptical but brilliant scientists, psychologists and others that genuine psychics and mediums have existed and still do whose abilities make a nonsense of the materialist theory that a human being is simply a complicated physico-chemico-electro mechanism.

The theory is embarrassingly inadequate, not to say downright wrong, in the light of the evidence from psychical research. There undoubtedly exist human abilities such as clairvoyance, telepathy, psychokinesis, precognition, the astonishing properties of mediumship, the ability to see apparitions, and so on, that indicate dimensions of reality other than the purely physical. As a scientist who has given sufficient attention in the study of and experiment in psychical research to recognize that the accumulated evidence for the existence of paranormal phenomena is overwhelming, I still find it hard to come to terms with the tendency of most scientists – who have absolutely no track record in the subject! – to dismiss it as delusion. I find such an attitude ignorant (they have no knowledge of the field), arrogant (but they know what is and is not possible in nature), incomprehensible (haven't they yet learned that a scientist's first step is to examine the evidence?) and downright exasperating.

The present book is one in which the phenomena of mediumship are explored in order to answer the question whether there is a relationship between the sensitive psychic faculty associated with mediumship and that of the spiritual experience. The subject is timely in our western society in that it may encourage the thoughtful reader to take seriously the view that a comparative study of the experiences – to put it no more strongly – of history's great psychic sensitives, be they mystics, shamans, biblical prophets, great teachers or avatars, is enlightening, enriching and made meaningful by considering them from the standpoint of the findings of psychical research.

The author, Dr J. Jones-Hunt, in her exhaustive survey of the literature concerning the world's psychic sensitives, has gathered together and discussed the most reliable studies made of every type of sensitive by a wide variety of careful and observant students. In their published work it is obvious that they have taken seriously the accounts given by the type of sensitive they have studied in that they have accepted that the genuine sensitive is striving to report not only what they believe they have experienced but also their subsequent attempts to interpret the experiences in a meaningful way.

One of the consequences of such a comparative study is that it highlights the 'family resemblances' in the phenomena and their interpretations over the types of sensitive to be found around the world. Inescapably, the situation in which the sensitive finds himself or herself reminds one of those 18th and 19th century attempts to describe the dark continent of Africa. Seemingly conflicting accounts of its landscapes, animals and peoples were given by explorers, traders and colonialists, their accounts colored by the facts that firstly they were landing in Africa in many different places, each giving its own bewildering and unfamiliar spectrum of experiences, and secondly the visitors were traveling with the luggage of their various motivations and prejudices. But that Africa – that colossal continent – was there could not be denied.

The attempts by sensitives to visit and explore and relate their experiences in dimensions other than the physical have of course been going on for much longer than the exploration by Europeans of Africa, certainly for many thousands of years, probably for a period stretching far into the impenetrable mists of prehistory. The total number of shamans, mystics, saints, prophets, spiritual teachers, mediums, and other sensitives who have ever lived is therefore impossible to estimate but it must run into tens of thousands.

Among them many are remembered by name and what we think they taught, for their teachings are often seen through the distorting lenses of their devoted followers' limited understanding and ability to accept. Nevertheless the purest unmuddied stream of those teachings – the perennial philosophy – can be discerned as a consensus given by the highest of those teachers and sensitives: love one another; do unto others as you would have done to yourself; as ye sow, so shall ye reap.

In her introduction to her book Dr J. Jones-Hunt cautions the reader by saying that

the research contained in this book cannot prove survival beyond physical death, nor the existence of non-physical inhabitants who dwell in domains beyond the physical, nor can this book seek to prove the existence of an Immortal, Divine, Creative Energy, permeating all creatures and life-forms, namely God. These issues will inevitably remain perennial questions and defy any wholly, comprehensive explanation.

That is of course true. Even so, I can thoroughly recommend this book as one of undoubted value.

Archie E. Roy

Archie E. Roy is a Fellow of the Royal Society of Edinburgh, the Royal Astronomical Society and the British Interplanetary Society and a member of the International Astronomical Union. He is the founding president of the Scottish Society for Psychical Research (SSPR), president of the Society for Psychical Research (SPR) 1993–1995 and ongoing vice-president of the SPR. In 2004 Roy was awarded the Myers Memorial Medal for his outstanding contributions to psychical research. This is not an annual award but given only when a suitable person has been found. The medal commemorates the work of Frederick Myers, one of the founders of the Society for Psychical Research in London. Myers' book *Human Personality and Its Survival of Bodily Death* is considered a classic today.

# Foreword II

This is a remarkable book. The author has drawn on a vast range of evidence from many ages, cultures and religions to show the pervasive implications on this world of other-world influences and communications, even when we do not recognise them as such. Few will be able to read this book without having their understanding of the world significantly changed and deepened. This book should be read by anyone interested in the many facets of mediumship and in particular, in evidence for the survival of the dead.

Crawford Knox PhD

Author of *Changing Christian Paradigms and Their Implications for Modern Thought* (Brill, 1993), former trustee and honorary treasurer of the Alistair Hardy (Psychical) Research Centre, Oxford, UK, and former council member of the Society for Psychical Research, London, UK

# Foreword III

'And in the Beginning'

We are all people of the present, with hopes for the future. That does not preclude the obligation we all have to look at the past – for in the past lies the basis of both the now and what will happen from here on. Sometimes, during a talk or lecture, I purposely provoke my audience by asking them when the psychical world of spirit began.

I tease, 'If we accept that it is with us now, did it begin, say, at 2pm on the afternoon of July 15th 1442? Or did it begin on the stroke of midnight in the year 4000 BC? Or when?'

I get the audience to work out for themselves that not only has the psychic world been around as long as the universe but, whether some of us like the idea or not, we and all creation must have been part and parcel of it from the earliest times. This book helps to illustrate to us that whatever philosophies we hold towards psychical science or religion, those thoughts and attitudes can only be the fruition of centuries and millennia of people of all nations, races and creeds wrestling with ideas concerning spiritual things. Dealing with solid and tangible items is easy compared to wrestling with abstract ideas and yet humankind has taken it upon itself to do both – and willingly.

The author leads us skillfully through many of those ideas, showing us, in a structured and scholarly way, the ongoing and sometimes diverse thought-patterns developed by various nations and groups down the ages as they grappled with spiritual matters in an attempt to make sense of things that were unseen, but that they positively knew were all around them.

Archibald A. Lawrie

Vice-president of the Scottish Society for Psychical Research, UK

# Introduction

This book will prove to you that Jesus was a spiritual shaman. Jesus was a deeply, spiritually evolved individual and these pages will reveal that he was a gifted psychic and medium. Today, medium's are alternatively known as channels. Jesus was not alone. Jesus' spiritual shamanism shared a place among many of the world's other highly respected spiritual leaders such as Moses. This will become clear as the following chapters clarify textual mistranslations that deliberately distort our understanding of the lives and mediumistic practices of a number of the world's mediumistic spiritual forebears.

Many of the world's famous spiritual teachers will be proven to have had mediumistic spiritual gifts. Some of the authentic prophetic lives that will be revealed include detailed proof of the spiritual mediumistic practices of a number of the world's famous religious leaders and founders of religions. Some of whom include Abraham, Isaac, Jacob, Joseph, Moses, the biblical Judges, Samuel, King Saul, King David, Ezekiel and Jesus.

This exciting revolutionary book delivers an astounding shock to rigid religious orthodoxy, which has lost touch with its roots, claiming that all mediumship is 'the work of the devil.' This factual research proves that many eminent, global, spiritual leaders known as prophets were in fact spiritual mediums, channels, chosen and guided by non-physical, spiritually elevated communicators.

Moses and Jesus the Shamans contains the results of research conducted by an author who is a spiritual historian and archaeologist, a comparatist of religion and psychical researcher. This book is the result of decades of both theoretical and observational research, delving into original religious teachings, the broad spectrum of psychical research and the fascinating multifaceted workings of mediumship. These pages represent the culmination of a unique blend of religious-historical, archaeological and psychical research into uncharted territories.

I would describe myself as a religious archaeologist in the deepest sense. My research includes, yet goes beyond researching the ancient scrolls, ruins and historical intrigues that distorted the authentic teachings of those prophetic individuals who founded world religions and furthered our spiritual knowledge. My unique blend of research has dug in and beyond, the ancient ruins and scripts, to the original paranormal angelic and spirit sources. It will be shown that these celestial communicators delivered spiritual teachings to gifted psychic sensitives from the most ancient of times throughout the millennia and across the globe, and indeed have not ceased.

I uncover the most ancient of celestial communicators, namely angels or spirit guides, who sought to take humankind spiritually forward as they delivered their messages, guidance and leadership. These messages were seen and heard due to the psychic and mediumistic gifts of our most ancient prophets, oracles and seers.

As a spiritual historian and psychical researcher, my research is crucially different to testing mediums for extrasensory perception in laboratory conditions as has traditionally been the case in the field of parapsychology. My observational research has involved working with countless recordings of unassuming, sincere genuine mediumistic individuals in altered states of consciousness.

In these direct-voice entranced states, these gifted individuals have clarified fact from fiction regarding the actual lives of many profoundly important historic personalities. They have also provided myriads of tantalizing insights into the importance of living a spiritual life. Unknown to each other, such mediums have corroborated one another's accounts regarding the repercussions of our thoughts and actions which draw to us the most fitting landscapes and companions in the after-death dimension.

Their descriptions of the metaphysical spheres experienced after the transition called 'death' have also been corroborated by near-death experiencers and the 18th-century writings of Emanuel

Swedenborg. This genius and inventor was the medium employed by Europe's royalty and governments. He was also a seasoned soul-journey traveler in durative, amplified, sacred time and space. These post-death dimensions are the 'geo-psychic' regions inhabited by all creatures after physical death. Swedenborg brought back descriptions of the many levels of existence in the meta-geographic realms which lie beyond the threshold of our ordinary circadian, mundane three-dimensional time and space.

Swedenborg taught us the concept that 'like attracts like' in these non-physical landscapes. These landscapes are brought to us as a result of our thoughts and actions during our earthly life time. This thought-responsive, post-death world of which no person can afford to remain ignorant is explained in later chapters.

My paradigm-shattering research uncovers the spiritual-mediumistic practices of history's great spiritual leaders,' proving that they were mediums. This research corrects biblical mistranslations and corruptions and unearths the spiritual mediumistic practices of prophetic mediums in the Bible. After correcting the mistranslations and corruptions of the biblical text, it becomes clear that Yahweh, the messenger of the lord, manifested and said to Moses: 'I am the celestial spirit guide of your ancestors, the celestial spirit guide of Abraham, Isaac and Jacob.'

My profound research convincingly proves that as a result of Moses' mediumistic gifts, Moses received the Ten Commandments. These commandments represented a new, improved ethical code of conduct. After a turning point in his life, Moses experienced regular sightings of, and communications with, the celestial communicator who came to be known as 'Yahweh'

I will show that God and Yahweh are two different entities and that this fact was deliberately suppressed. Subsequently, this knowledge was lost for all future generations. A large number of decoded, clarified biblical accounts testify to the fact that many generations of prophets, tribal leaders and their people witnessed Yahweh speak and manifest his presence. Physical manifestations occurred in particular in the 'holy of holies' over the Ark of the Covenant.

Celestial communicators are conclusively shown to have played a pivotal role throughout the whole of humankind's spiritual history. Readers are invited on an amazing journey revealing many millennia of spiritually transformative psychic history. Mediumship is proven to have been practiced by psychically sensitive individuals. They were guided to become spiritual leaders who founded and contributed to world religions.

This fascinating voyage of discovery uncovers a unifying, spiritual message for adherents to the religions of the world. This is of vital significance for all people who follow any particular religion. Consequently, this inspired research encourages a newfound respect and understanding for those of humankind's religious traditions which teach people to lead spiritually orientated lives. A human life which demonstrates compassion and the utmost respect for all living creatures is one that follows the powerful tenets of the First Commandment which bids us: 'Thou shalt not kill.'

Humanity, through interpretation, ever distorts the most ancient spiritual commands conveyed by varying celestial messengers. They have repeatedly taught the importance of doing no harm to any creature-member of God's family. Notably, heeding this vital prohibition is the crucial, first step on the ladder as an individual embarks on a personal spiritual journey seeking to attain spiritual growth. Throughout the ages this concept has been embodied in the vegetarianism of our spiritual forbears.

It must be remembembered that throughout the ages all prophetic mediums inevitably interpreted their received communications at the level of their individual spiritual understanding and evolution. These revelations were understood and further molded by the limited level of spiritual maturity of the historic epoch in which these communications were delivered. Each medium was also shaped by the social customs of their historic era.

Many from the broad-based spiritual grouping known as the

Essenes, of which it is believed Jesus was a member, were vegetarian. It is known that James the Just, the brother of Jesus, was a vegetarian since birth, confirming that Jesus' parents and indeed his whole compassionate family were vegetarian. They taught, in harmony with the earliest verses of the biblical Book of Genesis, that the true meaning of this First Commandment prohibited killing all animals, human and non-human alike.

My following book reveals the original, suppressed and later lost, spiritual communications and teachings that condemn humanity for committing harm to our fellow animals. These prohibitative commandments are found throughout many of the world's authentic, undistorted original religious texts. These profoundly wise, far-sighted and compassionate edicts have been increasingly fudged and lost by institutionalized religions over the millennia. This has had catastrophic consequences for all animals, human and non-human, and for the ecology of our planet.

The transformative spiritual mediumship of the world's highly esteemed prophets who communicated with variously spiritually elevated spirits or angels is proven in these pages to be the unifying factor amongst the world's religions. This brings all religious ideologies together. As a result of these transformative spiritual mediumistic experiences, the succession of mediumistic prophets throughout the ages founded and then subsequently developed different world religions. Communications from spiritually elevated celestial beings are proven to underlie many aspects of humankind's spiritual ebb and flow.

I will expose the religio-political intrigues and mistranslations of biblical texts which resulted in the erroneous condemnation of all mediumship and will conclusively restore the correct meaning. Accurate historic accounts of the beliefs and practices of many of the world's spiritual prophets are given, proving that the prophets not only came to live for their mediumistic communications but their whole lives were guided by their mediumship, their people were led by it, and religions were born as a result of it.

The biblical accounts are shown to be meaningless if not decoded in the way this research reveals. These pages make clear that mediumship has spanned the millennia and the globe encompassing humankind's whole existence as a universal spiritual phenomenon. This revolutionary book therefore empowers modern observers of mediumistic phenomena and enables them to perceive biblical accounts not as symbolic stories but rather as authentic experiences of celestial communications.

My research spans the entire globe from the beginning of time to the present day. It commences with ancient shamanic paranormal feats of consciousness, facets of mediumship and their metaphysical soul-journeys to geo-psychic realms beyond the boundaries of three-dimensional time and space. This pioneering research reveals examples of spiritual mediumship found in every century throughout the world. Ancient mediumistic practices are uncovered in Egypt, China, Japan, India and Greece. This is followed by an exhaustive survey of global mediumistic phenomena ranging from the 7th to the 21st century.

Included in this encyclopedic catalogue of examples of mediumship are the mediumistic experiences of Muhammad, the 7th-century prophet who founded the world religion of Islam, the 18th-century genius Emanuel Swedenborg, and the 19th-century American mediums Andrew Jackson Davis, Leonora Piper and the Fox sisters, who were catalysts for the paranormal Hydesville phenomena in America.

I will also discuss present-day spiritual mediumship, including clarifications of intriguing accompanying paranormal phenomena and scientific explanations regarding their authenticity. This book provides an impressive summary of the modern state of psychical research. It insightfully unravels the complexities involved in paranormal phenomena showing the differences between communicating with 'psychic or memory systems' and 'surviving dynamically alive intelligences.' The latter are known as non-physical spirit or angelic communicators.

These chapters explain many fascinating aspects of psychical research some of which include fraud, cryptomnesia, the game playing demon theory, possession, super ESP, clairvoyance, clairaudience, trance and the amazing proof of survival found in the cross-correspondence cases of automatic writing. Summaries of the salient theories used to explain psychic phenomena are given including the 'universal archive theory' and the 'holographic theory.'

*Moses and Jesus the Shamans* is a stimulating book for all ages, backgrounds and levels of knowledge. It goes a long way towards answering a number of vital perennial questions including: 'Is consciousness boundless and infinite?' 'Does the consciousness of all animals, human and non-human survive physical death?' 'Do soul-journeys out of the body and near-death experiences prove consciousness can separate from the physical body, proving post-death survival?'

My innovative research was conducted, firstly, in reaction to the present-day all-consuming materialist ethos which leaves no individual or society unscathed. The contemporary world is increasingly gripped by the ever encroaching western, materialist, reductionist understanding of the nature of life and death and the constitution of all living creatures. People are progressively, unwittingly conditioned, overtly and covertly, to believe that all creatures live and die and that is the simplistic end of the story.

This has resulted in a strange dichotomy: on one hand, the materialist, reductionist philosophy that we are taught to believe; and on the other hand, millions of global human testimonies of mediumistic and psychic experiences. This book proves that such experiences range from the beginning of time to present day and completely contradict the simplistic materialist view of this unfathomable limitless world. To combat the limitations of materialist science, its devotee scientists simplistically deny the obvious existence of millennia of multitudinous global psychic and mediumistic experiences. Thankfully, the latest advances in quantum physics are rescuing us from our current inadequate, traditional, non-quantum science, which cannot explain and therefore denies the authenticity of all psychic and mediumistic experiences. Quantum physics highlights this inadequate response and reveals the very real world of the paranormal.

It is unfortunate that as a result of materialism, many testimonies regarding transformative, spiritual mediumistic and psychic experiences are suppressed by the experiencers. They do this because they are unwilling to have their life-changing accounts ignored, ridiculed or reduced to nothing more than psychological or chemical aberrations and imaginings.

By contrast, my groundbreaking research provides a profoundly improved meaningful and comprehensive context for understanding mediumistic experiences of spirit and angelic communicators. This is done by showing the weight of the experiential evidence which has spanned the millennia and the globe from ancient times to present day.

Consequently, these pages give credibility to human testimonies of spiritually transformative psychic and mediumistic experiences. I accept the genuine accounts at face value due to the rich spiritual legacy the experiences have impacted on the lives of experiencers and mediumistic prophets alike. They are shown to be profoundly life-changing experiences that have affected all cultures since the dawn of time and cannot be simplistically reduced by contemporary materialist parapsychologists to a person's imagination.

It is certainly the case that if the source events that gave birth to our world religions occurred today and world religions were therefore born today, present day materialist parapsychologists would seek to explain all revealed religions away. They would dismiss them as mere imaginings.

This would be done despite the fact that such experiences have encompassed much of humanity's accumulated quest for evolving spirituality! This fact alone should alert the reader to the dangers and far-reaching scope of unbridled materialistic science. Fortunately, this traditional science is now being significantly supplemented by the findings of quantum physics.

Historic and present-day mediums believe that they progressively receive spiritual truths and information about the post-death dimension from variously spiritually elevated communicators. Arguably, this spiritual information is continually absorbed and becomes part of the ebb and flow of our religious knowledge. This indicates that the acquisition of spiritual knowledge from mediumistic teachers throughout the ages, is a dynamic process which at intervals is spiritually progressive. However, original teachings become assimilated, interpreted and often distorted by organized religions.

Ironically, however, present-day spiritual revelations and communications which by nature supplement and enrich the ever evolving composition of religions are rejected outright by most materialist parapsychologists. They cannot disallow the revealed world religions because religions were born in the days of antiquity prior to the days of reductionist science and materialist parapsychology.

However, materialist parapsychologists can significantly halt the stream of modern spirituality, by denying the authenticity of all transformative spiritual mediumistic experiences which access elevated spiritual communicators. Therefore, materialist parapsychologists can, in effect, stop the continued flow and growth of spirituality, stopping the development of religions in their tracks!

Current society reflects the sad consequences of materialism with its pitiless, industrialized, conveyor-belt genocide of billions of animals every year. These related earth-family members are shown little mercy. Sadly very few people give their pitiful lives of suffering and excruciatingly painful deaths a second thought.

Opposition to spiritual mediumship comes from a second, perhaps less expected quarter – that of institutionalized religion. As I will show, messages received from spirits and angels are the very foundation stone of organized religion, which has then ironically turned its back on the ongoing dynamic fountain, the source from which it came into being! Centuries of prejudiced mistranslations, combined with negativity and ignorance relating to spiritual mediumship, have caused religious orthodoxy to cut itself off from the very mediumistic faculty which gave birth to religion itself. Ironically, the compendium of ancient spiritual-mediumistic experiences has become fossilized into the rigid forms of institutionalized religion, with the result that any mediumistic messages that came later areexcluded.

There is a desperate need for this research to be disseminated to the wider world in order to clarify the correct context in which to fit spiritual mediumship and to encourage respect for spiritually elevatedteachings which are desperately needed for the protection of all life-forms and the planet herself. Ancient, on-going and contemporary mediumistic themes are synthesized throughout my book and shown to be a spiritually dynamic, continuous process.

It provides a vital bridge of understanding between the realm of the personal-experiential, the realm of the materialist reductionist investigators, and the realm of adversarial institutionalized religion. Ironically, the compendium of ancient spiritual mediumistic experiences have become fossilized into institutionalized religion with the exclusion of those that came later.

Each arena would remain impoverished without the valuable insights that are contained in this pioneering book. My research decodes the bible, uncovers the prophets' mediumistic testimonies and proves their spiritual legacy for humankind. These pages should help to stop the ignorant prejudice and hostility which is frequently directed towards spiritually sublime direct voice trance mediumship because it sets elevated spiritual mediumship in its rightful context, as a prerequisite for spiritual prophethood.

Superlative spiritual communications from the non-physical realms can thus be seen as an umbrella-like factor that can synthesize, harmonize and blend all of humankind's religious ideologies together, at the highest spiritual level. Significantly, it might be suggested that the birth of each religion represents the human response to, and limited interpretation of, that which was communicated by various celestial communicators. The communicators themselves appear to demonstrate a broad range of spiritual orientation. Hence various aspects of religious teachings reflect different degrees of spiritual maturity, the most spiritually mature, preach love and respect for all living creatures, committing no harm or murder!

Arguably, the most elevated spiritual truths are intrinsically 'one,' yet reflect the richness of diversity inherent in the human spontaneous physiological filtering and interpretation of the messages received. Each mediumistic experience is shown to be interpreted by the mediumistic individual, seer, sage or prophet according to their personal spiritual and intellectual level of understanding, their quality of clairaudience (hearing), clairvoyance (seeing) and in accordance with the spiritual maturity of their histoiric age.

If orthodox religion would open its firmly locked doors to the delivery of ongoing profound spiritual truths gained by spiritually orientated mediumship, a muchneeded spiritual rebirth could take place. Every person could aspire to reach their highest spiritual and creative potential. Through meditation which is the catalyst for inducing mediumistic inspiration and communication individuals would become aware that their thoughts and deeds attract to them positive and negative inspirations and influences from the nonphysical world affecting both their physical and post death existence.

They would become aware that their thoughts and deeds are responsible for the manifestation of positive and negative events in this life and the next. The hidden mysteries of these fascinating secrets are discussed in the following pages. From the earliest times to present day spiritual mediumistic prophets and teachers have cumulatively gained spiritual insights based on their mediumistic experiences.

We can all seek to cultivate such inspirational mediumistic

experiences, accessing elevated spiritual knowledge for ourselves. As a result of transformative spiritual experiences that have spanned the ages and the globe, testimonies are corroborated. They tell us of the existence of a Creator God beyond all comprehension and of the transition of the soul or consciousness at death to an immortal, non-physical state of existence. Death is a transition of consciousness, a rite of passage for all animals, human and non-human.

We can also learn for ourselves that all flora and fauna are inter-connected – This includes all living creatures all animals, human and non-human, birds, marine life and vegetation. Many people are ignorant of the fact that humanity's four-legged human ancestors originated in the sea and that all living creatures including humankind are related – or else they choose to forget this fact. We are told that if we hurt any other creature through action or neglect it will have reciprocal harmful effects on ourselves both during the physical life and in the non-ordinary reality of amplified space and time experienced after death.

We are taught that our thoughts and actions shape our 'soul,' which can alternatively be described as our 'surviving consciousness. This is housed in our non-physical, immortal, auric energy body which survives death. The composition of the soul determines which post-death landscape is appropriate. There are many successive hierarchical, non-physical, celestial, infernal and purgatorial landscapes which await all creatures after physical death. In these thought responsive, fluid, energy dimensions which are discussed in the following pages, a perfect justice awaits all, as predominant positive and negative aspects of personality are exter-nalized in the sense that they draw to the individual the appropriate landscape.

This is why a particular religious tradition cannot call itself a genuinely spiritual path if it does not preach peace and love for all creatures and condemn those who do harm to the smallest creature. All feel pain and most fellow animals are sentient, they feel stress and possess emotions. A civilization can surely be judged by the way it values and treats its animals as this reflects the value that is placed on 'life' itself and further reveals the yardstick by which civilizations treat each other.

The gaining of spiritual truths through transformative spiritual mediumistic experiences is shown to be a dynamic, on-going, progressively spiritualizing personal process, offering spiritual illumination which over time becomes disseminated thoughout civilizations.

Elevated spiritual revelations communicated to mediums throughout the ages are substantiated by the reports of near-death experiencers, who describe their consciousness, soul or spirit, floating out of their physical body. Typically, they observe and hear doctors announcing them clinically dead, watch their body taken to the hospital morgue, meet relatives and pets who had passed to spirit during their own illness or years earlier and experience 'life reviews.'

Life reviews logically determine which of the countless non-physical landscapes a person will initially inhabit after physical death. During a life review, near-death experiencers feel the pains their thoughts and deeds inflicted on all those creatures they had contact with during their physical lives. An individual's predominant thoughts and deeds shape the malleable, fluid, non-physical, after-death environments of vast eternity, creating realms of various degrees of enchantment, or conversely, deserted, barren wasteland.

Jesus described the non-physical dimension visited by shamanic metaphysical soul-journey travelers and near-death experiencers when he said, 'There are many rooms/mansions in my Father's house.' Arguably, there are many ways of getting there, as death opens untold numbers of doors.

During the physical and post-death, non-physical life each individual animal soul, human and non-human, can strive to make contact with the highest and best spirit and angelic communicators. They can request that they accompany them and mentor them, assisting them to live progressively spiritually elevated lives.

Spiritual mediums claim that they receive descriptions of the after-death realms of existence and elevated spiritual truths. Mediumship is a faculty that all creatures have to a greater or lesser extent; it is a tool that can be used for good or bad purposes in the same way as a surgeon and a murderer can both wield a knife yet produce very different outcomes. Similarly, spiritual mediumship can be and should be utilized to lead the medium and others forward spiritually.

Alternatively, mediumship can be used in selfish, egocentric ways for the purpose of self-aggrandizement. Much depends on the spiritual and intellectual quality of the communicator's messages and on the level of intelligence, quality of mediumship and spiritual maturity of the medium, who has to interpret the information conveyed to them (if it was not produced in the form of direct-voice trance mediumship). The accuracy of the information delivered by the medium to the recipient (the sitter) can be extremely evidential, clearly indicating the objective reality of a genuine, surviving non-physical communicator.

The contents of spiritual, spirit and angelic communications have to be evaluated, as the range and quality of information that mediums convey to others varies enormously in quality and quantity. Arguably this is the result of 'who' or 'what' the communicator is (this will be explained in the next chapter).

Evaluating communications is imperative as analysis can reveal the quality, clarity and the possible distortions and misinterpretations that have occurred during or after the transit of information. However, if communicators do not teach us to love and do no harm to all sentient creatures at all times, their message cannot be spiritually orientated and must be discarded.

The biblical New Testament tells us 'to test the spirit for their spiritual authenticity rather than to blindly follow their advice. This is because the New Testament writers were aware that there is a diverse range of potential non-physical communicators living in the oceans of eternity. These range from the spiritually inane to the most angelic who inhabit the countless, hierarchical, alternate, non-physical domains..

The enlightened research contained in this book cannot prove survival beyond physical death, nor the existence of non-physical inhabitants who dwell in domains beyond the physical, nor can this book seek to prove the existence of an immortal, Divine, creative energy, permeating all creatures and life-forms, namely God. These issues will inevitably remain perennial questions and defy any comprehensive explanation. However, this research offers convincing evidence that all creatures survive physical death and make a transition of consciousness to the non-physical planes of alternate reality, and that contact between the physical and non-physical dimensions regularly occurs.

*Chapter I*

# Mediumship: Definitions and Complexities

This chapter will tell you virtually all you need to know to understand mediumship. It reveals many of the fascinating complexities associated with this incredible phenomenon. The people who receive communications from the surviving recognizable personalities of people and animals who have traveled beyond physical death are known today as 'mediums' or 'channels.' 'Sitters' or 'recipients' are people who visit a medium for evidence of survival beyond physical death, in the hope of making contact with their deceased relatives, pets and spirit guides. The latter may have shared a life with them in a previous incarnation.

As a rule, most materialist parapsychologists have come from a background in psychology. Consequently, they have little, if any, knowledge of the wonderful wealth of historical and present-day psychical research into cases of mediumship. Many of these are remarkably evidential that the medium is actually in contact with recognizable, surviving, non-physical personalities, not a lifeless memory system.

Many materialist parapsychologists try to deny the reality of mediumship and seek alternative explanations to the reality of survival beyond death. Put simplistically they argue that the medium gains information for the sitter as a result of psychic person-to-person, telepathic communication. This suggests the medium 'reads the mind' of the sitter. Some materialist parapsychologists accept that telepathy is possible, yet they will not accept the explanation that the information is provided telepathically to the medium by those who have survived physical death!

Later we will explore some amazing features of mediumistic demonstrations, but to give one example here: mediums have accessed information that has later been found in rare documents locked away from the public. Evidence suggests that the information was given to them by the surviving 'dead' writer of those documents. It is very important to understand that when mediums work *psychically* they can telepathically access information from the minds of those people in the physical body who visit them.

However, this is markedly different from when they work *mediumistically*. Not all those who call themselves mediums can do this, but working mediumistically may access information that the sitter does not know; the sitter has to go away to verify it. The simplest explanation is that the information is given by one or more third-party communicators, those who at death have made their transitions to the non-physical state of existence.

Mediumship, unlike psychic work, is communicating with those no longer in the physical body. It is not reading the sitter's mind or auric energy.

If it is argued that mediums can telepathically access information from the minds of physical sitters, then, if survival after death is a fact, mediums of varying abilities would also be able telepathically to obtain communications of varying quality and quantity from surviving non-physical personalities. It is believed that all mediums are psychic but not all psychics are mediums.

I will be discussing 'false communicators' below and explaining the difference between contacting a surviving recognizable intelligence or personality – a spirit who communicates information to the medium – in contrast to the experience of making contact with psychic *systems*. The latter are also known as 'memory systems'. If they actually manifest, they are perceived as a ghostly apparition. I will provide definitions and descriptions of terms such as psychic, extrasensory perception, parapsychology, telepathy, mediumship, clairvoyance, clairaudience and altered states of consciousness. The latter are, known as varying depths of mediumistic trance states.

We will also examine the beliefs of the worldwide religious movement known as Spiritualism. Spiritualists believe that they obtain their teachings regarding the many levels of non-physical landscapes experienced life after physical death from spirit and angel communications made to mediums. By this means, Spiritualists are taught that each individual has a specific purpose for each physical lifetime on the earth and that each lifetime is an, an opportunity for spiritual advancement. They are taught that at the end of each lifetime all beings will have a life review during which their whole life passes before them, revealing all their interactions with other people and animals.

Mediums who give entranced talks have learned that in association with life reviews each of us will feel another animal's pains, human or non-human, as if they were our own. This makes every individual directly responsible for the consequences that their thoughts and actions have had on others. The landscape that we each find ourselves in after death will be directly determined by the type of life we led and the thoughts we had during our physical life on earth.

Spiritualists believe that their actions and thoughts during their physical life will be reflected in the quality of the colors in their auric energy, which can be understood as mirroring the individual's soul, spirit or consciousness. A verified law of physics states that energy cannot be destroyed it simply changes form. Spiritualists believe that the physical body disintegrates at death but the energy of the soul/spirit/consciousness continues in a non-physical dimension. Acting like a magnet, it attracts to it the same type of spirit people spirit animals and the particular non-physical landscape that suits the individual's level of spirituality.

As a result of trance mediumship, Spiritualists believe that there are a multitude of non-physical landscapes in the geo-psychic dimensions. The information gained through mediumistic communications has been corroborated by the most ancient shamanic experiences, which spanned the globe, to those recorded accounts of the 18th century genius and medium Emanuel Swedenborg and those of present day mediums and near death experiencers.

It is remarkable that the information about life after death obtained through mediumship and from millions of global near-death experiencers is identical. This suggests that Spiritualist beliefs are accurate. Some near-death experiencers find themselves in the hospital morgue awaiting burial hours or days after a death certificate was written for them by the doctor. When they return to physical life they talk of their life review, during which they felt the pains they caused in others as if they were their own.

During their death state they met other people and animals who had also made their transition after physical death to the non-physical world. This is a dimension they have entered temporarily. Many near death experiencers describe seeing vibrant colors and wonderful landscapesin these non-physical dimensions.

Others talk of frightening, hell-like infernal landscapes that they desperately want to forget, – of which they fear to speak. Significantly, when doctors ask them about these infernal realms a few days after they first spoke of them, their emotions have suppressed their memories; progressively they remember less and less.

This is not the case for many near-death experiencers who have a positive experience. Many of these have vivid memories and talk of meeting a 'Being of Light' or spirit relatives who tell them that they have not yet fulfilled their life's mission in the earth dimension. For this reason they are told that it is not yet time for them to remain in the co-existent alternate non-physical dimension.

Remarkably, some talk of the spirit people and animals they met when their consciousness left their body whilst they had been pronouncedclinically dead. Because they had been in intensive care themselves, no-one had told them of the demise of relatives and pets they met during their state of clinical death. Relatives had not informed them of the passing of these loved ones as they were fighting for their own life in hospital at the time.

Some of the most wonderful evidence for survival comes from adults and children who have been blind from birth and were

27

certified clinically dead. When they return to life they describe all that they *saw* when they were physically dead. Their descriptions of sights, sounds and events that occurred both in the hospital and in their homes many miles from the hospital are amazingly accurate. They saw all this when their lifeless physical body was lying inert in the hospital morgue awaiting their funeral. There are millions of documented cases such as these that give us fantastic evidence that the physical body and the consciousness (soul, spirit, auric energy) separate at physical death, with the consciousness, as energy, living on.

When near-death experiencers return to life a regular pattern emerges. Many admit to being materialistic people before their experience, with no interest in spirituality or the post-death realms, but family and friends now notice that their loved one is remarkably transformed from the person they were before. Many leave their well-paid jobs or rich partners if they feel there was a lack of love or spiritual purpose in their former lives.

They begin to live a more spiritually orientated life. Some near death experiencers become spiritual healers. Others help in charity centers for people or animals in need of assistance. Others write about their experiences in order to help others negate their fear of death and understand that every human and animal life has a divine purpose. Many near-death experiencers have their death certificate framed and hung on the wall in their homes.

Modern hospital technology is responsible for saving the lives of those who would otherwise have died and therefore not returned to describe what occurs when we make a the transition from the physical into non-physical life. Ironically, hospital technology, which is the by-product of materialist science, is inadvertently causing people to have spiritually transformative psychic experiences of the after-death dimension. Hospital technology is responsible for democratizing experiences of the after-death realms which were previously the preserve of those who died and did not return to the physical life. Much literature exists, revealing that historically, before this technology exited, people did have near-death experiences. Even in modern times people have had near-death experiences when they were beyond the reach of hospital technology and drugs, proving that their experiences were real and not artificially induced by medication or procedures.

Significantly, the accounts of global, historic and modern-day near-death experiencers confirm the information received by mediums. Some of the most superior information received by mediums is that which is channeled directly during the state of trance.

Entranced, third-party human and animal communicators provide detailed information regarding the after-death spheres. Both male and female voices emanate directly through the medium. This is pure and direct information in the sense that it is not polluted by the medium's interpretation as they are in an altered state of consciousness at the time.

## Definitions

The following section will provide a brief summary of definitions relevant to psychic phenomena and mediumship. These will help to underline the intermittent relationship between mediumship and other psychic faculties. Telepathy from mind to mind of those in the physical body has long been proven to be authentic. The sitter will formulate their own opinion as to whether mediums telepathically access the thoughts of surviving personalities.

## Psychic/Psyche

The term 'psychic' is derived from the Greek word *psyche*, which means soul or spirit.[1] Today, the term is used to describe non-physical phenomena that are apparently extrasensory; that is, they appear to lie beyond the range of the normal senses. As an umbrella term, the term psychic 'includes a whole range of phenomena associated with human behavior: behavior that cannot be explained by what we currently know scientifically.'[2]

The Oxford English Dictionary clarifies the related terms 'psyche' and 'psychic':

Psyche: breath, to breathe, hence life, the animating principle in man and other living beings, the source of all vital activities, rational or irrational, the soul or spirit, in distinction from its material vehicle, sometimes considered as persisting in a disembodied state after separation from the body at death ... The soul or spirit as distinguished from the body; the mind. Psychicism: The theory or study of psychical or ... spiritualistic phenomena... one who studies psychical research ...

Psychically: in a psychic or psychical manner with reference to the soul or mind, mentally ... The doctrine or theory of the existence of forces unexplainable by physical science in connection with spiritualistic phenomena.[3]

The term 'psychic' is a similar umbrella term to 'extrasensory perception,' which includes the use of faculties which lie beyond those of the known senses.

Extrasensory perception' (ESP) The umbrella usage of the term, extra-sensory perception is explained by the Encyclopaedia Britannica. It states that it is the result of

perception that occurs independently of the known sensory processes. Usually included in this phenomena are telepathy, or thought transference between persons; clairvoyance, or supernormal awareness of objects or events not necessarily known to others and precognition, or knowledge of the future. Scientific investigation of these and similar phenomena dates from the late nineteenth century.[4]

## Parapsychology

The Greek prefix 'para' denotes 'beyond.' Consequently, the term 'parapsychology' denotes the study of that which appears to lie beyond psychology.[5] The following two definitions clarify the meaning of parapsychology;

> Parapsychology in a restricted sense, is defined as the scientific, statistical, the experimental approach to extrasensory phenomena. Parapsychology is placed within the framework of science. Parapsychologists are scientists and use the scientific method in their research. They are hesitant to include matters of a religious or philosophic nature.[6]
>
> Regarding parapsychology Angoff states; The study of those forces within the mind or of human behavior which are beyond the scope of or cannot be explained by conventional psychology or other sciences.[7]

Transformative spiritual, psychic and mediumistic experiences and related religious experiences do not readily lend themselves to being investigated by scientific opponents in laboratory conditions.

## Telepathy/Telepath

These terms are usefully defined as follows: 'communication between mind and mind otherwise than through the known channels of the senses ... telepath one who practices telepathy.'[8]

## Medium

Two valuable definitions of a medium are provided below by Professor Archie E. Roy and the Encyclopaedia Britannica respectively:

> A medium is a person who has the ability to allow one or more ostensible communicators to manifest. Some mediums are clairvoyant and/or clairaudient, 'seeing' and/or 'hearing' ostensible communicators who provide information which is then relayed by the medium to the sitters.[9]
>
> ... a person reputedly able to make contact with the world of

spirits, especially while in a state of trance. A Spiritualist medium is the central figure during a séance and sometimes requires the assistance of a spirit go-between called the control. During a séance, disembodied voices are said to speak, either directly or through the medium. Materialization of a disembodied spirit or body can allegedly take shape from a mysterious, viscous substance called ectoplasm that exudes from the medium's body and subsequently disappears by returning to its original source.[10]

## Two Broad Categories of Mediumship: Mental and Physical

The mediumship that is regularly demonstrated by mediums for sitters and psychical researchers falls into two broad categories: 'mental mediumship' and 'physical mediumship.' Although there are many common patterns during demonstrations of mediumship, each medium develops slight variations in the way they work to access and make sense of spirit communications, and these become idiosyncratic to them. Mediums progressively develop their own personal system of working.

For example, a particular medium may discover that all barely audible voices heard (clairaudiently) on the left-hand side of their head may be taken to belong to a male spirit communicator, while those voices emanating from the right-hand side of their head may be taken as a female spirit communicator. Other mediums may hear voices so clearly that they know instantly the gender of the communicator.

Many mediums have noted that spirit communications possess some or all of the following features: they may be heard very speedily, or faintly, or in the form of many spirit voices calling messages or fragments of messages simultaneously.

## Mental mediumship

This can involve a range of mediumistic abilities such as:

Clairvoyance (clear seeing) – The medium sees the spirit in their mind similar to how we see people in our dreams. Alternatively, they may see them manifest externally.

*Clairaudience* (clear hearing) – The medium hears the spirit's voice in their head or calling in an external sense. Alternatively, information is heard in the medium's head in the sense of thoughts distinct from the medium's own thoughts.

*Clairsentience* (clear sensing) – The medium senses the height, gender and description of the spirit and the message they wish to convey. Surprisingly, amazingly detailed information can be given using this highly sensitive faculty.

*Precognition* – Knowledge of future events

*Retro-cognition* – Knowledge of past events

*Trance* – Communications are delivered while the medium is in altered states of consciousness known as 'trance.' Varying depths of trance can be achieved. Sometimes the medium remembers what they said and sometimes they do not.

*Telepathy* – Mind-to-mind transfer of information

*Psychometry* – Typically, this is when the medium or psychic holds an object and gives out information gained through the use of psychic abilities. The object is not usually seen by the medium or psychic and is often sealed in an envelope. Holding the envelope, these individuals receive pictorial images gained through the use of their psychic abilities. However, some mediums would also say that pictorial images and telepathic communications are also delivered to them by spirit communicators. The information received may relate to the first, second or later owner of the object. In the case of a historical artifact, the medium may learn psychically of its historical origins and events surrounding it. Working mediumistically, they may make contact with a surviving spirit person who may have had previous connections with the object.

*Automatic writing* – Typically, this involves the production of writing or drawings by the medium while he or she is in a deep or light altered state of consciousness. It is believed that the hand and/or mind is used as an instrument in order to deliver written messages. These vary enormously regarding the information that they contain and in their literary quality, detail, accuracy and length. Remarkably detailed historic epics were written at unbelievable speed when the early 20th-century American housewife Mrs Pearl Curran was entranced. She was observed over many decades by experts from all professional fields. Researchers accepted that Mrs Curran herself was not writing these books and that she was not educated in the books' subject matter. Yet she was observed writing them and answering questions simultaneously. The communicator was known as Patience Worth.

## Physical Phenomena

The second broad category of mediumship is described as physical mediumship. In this form of mediumship, observable physical phenomena are produced independently of the medium.

*Direct-voice trance mediumship* – Here the medium is directly used as an instrument through whom a voice different from their own is heard by observers; these can be male or female and may be of a different gender from the medium. In some cases the medium's mouth is covered and their hands are bound to the chair yet still the voices arrive. This was the case with the laboratory research conducted in the last century into the direct-voice trance mediumship of Leslie Flint. Alternatively, the voices may appear to manifest in close proximity to the medium, rather than exuding from the medium. The medium is usually in a deep state of altered consciousness when direct-voice phenomena occur.

*Materializations/Manifestations* – Apparent externalized physical manifestations of non-physical spirit people and spirit animals

*Levitations* – The lifting off the ground of, for example, the medium, a table or a chair

*Apports* – Objects such as gems, flowers or stones which appear from nowhere in the room of observers

## Further definitions of key terms

*Mediumship* – The following three statements further supplement our understanding of mediumship.

[The medium] differs from others in that he/she has supernormal faculties, due apparently to a condition of semi-freedom or detachment of his subconscious mind or spirit, which enables it, on occasion, to liberate itself from the close fetters of the material organism and obtain knowledge of external things otherwise than by the usual sense organs.[11]

It is true also that mediumistic powers are bestowed on persons without reference to intelligence or character; in this respect they are like other talents. Some mediums seem to be rather unintelligent and lacking in culture. However, there are striking exceptions. William Stainton Moses ... was a gentleman in the English sense of that word, a clergyman of the Church of England and a schoolmaster [from] Oxford.[12]

Ursula Roberts, a British medium who traveled extensively, writes:

"A really sensitive medium may be used in a variety of ways at different times, though it is usual for one faculty to be developed to a higher degree of responsiveness and occasionally this one faculty may become so strong that the other powers fall into abeyance. It is my opinion that good mediumship can manifest all the varied forms of phenomena. During the period of development a medium often passes from one phase to another.[13]

*Clairvoyance and Clairaudience* – The terms 'clairvoyance' and 'clairaudience' have been mentioned in connection with associated definitions but More specific definitions are given here. The Chambers Dictionary notes that the term clairvoyance is a French derivative which implies clear seeing and notes that the term refers to the 'alleged power of seeing things not present to the senses.'[14]

The Encyclopaedia Britannica describes clairvoyance and clairaudience as accessing knowledge or information not necessarily known to any other person, not obtained by ordinary channels of perceiving or reasoning; thus a form of extrasensory perception (ESP). Spiritualists also use the term to mean seeing (clairvoyance) or hearing (clairaudience) the spirits of the dead that are said to surround the living.[15]

*Trance* – Trance is an altered state of consciousness that some mediums are able to demonstrate and may be observed by psychical researchers and sitters alike. While some mediums can acquire this level of consciousness naturally and spontaneously, others can only do so after years of training in meditation and breathing techniques. Mediums obtain various depths of trance.

Mediums may remember some, all, or nothing of what was said by their own voice or spoken directly through them by a male or female spirit voice. Frequently, the medium feels as though they were asleep while all the apparent spirit communications took place. Various languages, including ancient Egyptian, that are personally unknown to the entranced mediums have been witnessed and carefully recorded by psychical researchers and observers.

Related terminology The following terms will enhance your understanding of the exciting realm of psychic and mediumistic phenomena.

*Possession* – The alleged 'supplanting of a personality by another with or without the former personality's permission'.[16]

*Obsession* – The apparent state 'where the personality, while still present, is influenced so strongly by another personality's knowledge, desires, skills and personality that the obsessed personality is forced to behave like the obsessor'.[17]

*Overshadowing* – The apparent state of a 'far milder degree of obsession akin to inspiration'.[18]

*Communicator* – Professor Archie Roy defines a communicator as "an entity that claims existence and can manifest either directly through a medium, utilizing the medium's voice or by writing using the medium's hand, or indirectly by conveying and receiving information via an intermediate entity called a control. The communicator may claim to be the surviving spirit of a recently deceased person ... or a spirit of profound spiritual maturity with a guiding and teaching mission, or an angel. Very few claim to be devils.[19]

*Control* – Roy defines a control as

an ostensible communicator who usually manifests through a particular medium, taking charge of or possessing the medium's body while the medium's normal personality is absent. The control acts as a master or mistress of ceremonies relaying information to and from communicators and sitters. The control may on occasion allow communicators to manifest directly, a bit like a radio presenter handing over the microphone to someone else.[20]

*Séance* – The Encyclopaedia Britannica offers the following definitions:

A séance is a meeting (usually small) around a medium to seek messages from the spirits. Telepathy is the communication of ideas through other than physical means. (At séances clairvoyance and clairaudience may be demonstrated.) Clairvoyance is the power of seeing though means other than the physical eye. Clairaudience is the power of hearing through means other than the physical ear.[21]

Further clarifications regarding Spiritualism and mediumship

*Materialism* – 'the doctrine that denies the independent existence of spirit and maintains that there is but one substance, matter ...

blindness to the spiritual'.[22]

*Spiritual/Spiritualist –*

[*spiritual*], the nature of [or] relating to ... spirits, the mind, the higher faculties, the soul, highly refined in thought and feeling ... naturally looking to things of the spirit, incorporeal, ecclesiastical, religious ...

*to spiritualise,* to make spiritual: to imbue with spirituality, to refine, to free from sensuality, to give a spiritual meaning to ...

*spiritualism,* a being spiritual ... the doctrine that spirit has a real existence apart from matter: the interpretation of a varied series of abnormal phenomena as for the most part caused by spiritual beings acting upon specially sensitive persons or mediums ...

*Spiritualist,* one who has a regard only to spiritual things ... one who holds the doctrine of spiritualism ...

*spirituality,* state of being spiritual[23]

[*Spiritualism*] in philosophy ... affirms the existence of immaterial reality imperceptible to the senses ... Most patently, it applies to any philosophy accepting the notion of an infinite, personal God, the immortality of the soul or the immateriality of the intellect and will. Less obviously, it includes belief in such ideas as infinite cosmic forces or a universal mind, provided that they transcend the limits of gross materialistic interpretation.[24]

*Spiritualists in ancient history –* Of the ancient nature of contemporary Spiritualist beliefs, the Encyclopaedia Britannica states:

In ancient Greece Pindar [who flourished in the 5th century BC] expounded in his odes the substance of a spiritualist Orphic mysticism by attributing a divine origin to the soul, which resides temporarily as a guest in the home of the body and then returns to its source for reward or punishment after death. Plato's view of the soul thus marks him as a Spiritualist and Aristotle was a

Spiritualist for distinguishing the active from the passive reason and for conceiving God as pure actuality (knowledge knowing itself).[25]

*Soul* – The soul, which might also be called the 'spirit', is:

an entity supposed to be present only in living things, corresponding to the Greek psyche and Latin anima. Since there seems to be no material difference between an organism in the last moments of its life and the organism's newly dead body, many philosophers since the time of Plato have claimed that the soul is an immaterial component of an organism. Because only material things are observed to be subject to dissolution, Plato took the soul's immateriality as grounds for its immortality.

Neither Plato nor Aristotle thought that only persons had souls. Aristotle ascribed souls to animals and plants since each exhibited living functions. Unlike Plato, Aristotle denied the transmigration of souls from one species to another or from one body to another after death; he was also more skeptical about the soul's capacity for disembodiment – roughly, survival and functioning without a body ... As the subject of thought, memory, emotion, desire, and action, the soul has been supposed to be an entity that makes self-consciousness possible.[26]

## A Contemporary Spiritualist

The Encyclopaedia Britannica clarifies what is meant by the term 'Spiritualist' today:

[a] person who believes that communication with those who have 'passed into the higher life' (died) is possible ... This article deals with the spiritualist religion, not with psychic research, which is a study on what are believed to be the scientific lines of communication with the dead, telepathy, precognition and kindred subjects. The important terms in spiritualism are defined

in the following ways. Spirit is the essential part of [living creatures]. After the death of the body the spirit lives on. The spirit world is the world of disembodied spirits. A medium is a person on earth who is sensitive to vibrations from the spirit world and is able to convey messages between that world and this one and to produce other Spiritualist phenomena. A control is a disembodied spirit who gives messages to a medium who in turn gives them to men and women on earth.[27]

Spiritualists would accept that throughout global human history, non-physical intelligences known as spirits and angels have communicated with humankind. Mediumistic people, including 'prophets,' have reported that they have been contacted by non-physical personalities. Inevitably, these experiences are spiritually transformative mediumistic experiences. Historically, non-physical messengers were thought to be so different from physical people – and many were clearly of a more advanced spiritual character than those observing them – that they were confused with gods or angels and deified.

Many historical spiritual teachers have reported their transformative, spiritual encounters with angels and spirits and these have cumulatively led to the birth of many of humankind's religious beliefs. These 'prophets' who could be called mediums or channels transferred the angelic or spirit communicators' moral teachings and teachings about life after physical death to others. Communications included information regarding the landscapes found in the different leels of the after death state and that all living creatures enter this dimension after physical death.

## The Founding and Organization of the Spiritualist Religion

It was in the 19th century that Spiritualism became organized into a religious movement. The catalyst for this was the remarkable events surrounding the lives of two girls known as Margaret and Kate Fox who lived in the small village of Hydesville, in western New York state. These two sisters believed that they were in regular receipt of communications from a non-physical, surviving spirit personality who informed them that he had been murdered and buried in the cellar of their house. The bones were later found and dug up, confirming the mediumistic communications the girls had received.

The Hydesville phenomena were a precursor to the establishment of the Spiritualist religion. The impact of the phenomena is yet another example of the ongoing legacy mediumistic communications have, regarding in the development of religious beliefs and the founding of religions (many other examples will be given in the following chapters).

Emanuel Swedenborg, and in later years Andrew Jackson Davis, are considered by Spiritualists to be the first prophets and forerunners of what became the newly established Spiritualist religious movement. I will discuss the mediumistic experiences of both prophets in more detail later, but will provide a brief introduction here.

The Swedish scientist, mystic, philosopher and theologian Emanuel Swedenborg was born in 1688 in Stockholm. He experienced communications from beings he believed to be spirits who had progressed to the status of guardian angels. He was also convinced that he experienced soul-journeys whereby he visited labyrinthine, non-material landscapes existing beyond ordinary three-dimensional time and space.

Spirits asked him to convey their messages to their families regarding their unfinished business, ., before they had made their transitions to this malleable to e thought-energy dimension. They wanted him to tell their loved ones that they were fine and that they had discovered that life continues after physical death.

Upon his return to the normal waking consciousness, Swedenborg convinced many people of his beliefs, supported by the spiritual content and predictive accuracy of the information he received from the surviving personalities he met.

Swedenborg was a highly respected figure who wrote extensively about his soul-journey explorations of the countless, hierarchical after-death landscapes. This body of spiritual knowledge, together with that received by the American medium Andrew Jackson Davis, gave impetus to the development of the Spiritualist religious movement. It was against the backdrop of the teachings of these two prominent spiritual, mediumistic figures that the Hydesville mediumistic phenomena were interpreted and given a greater spiritual context.

In the following years, after the extensive media coverage of the mediumistic transfer of information during and after the initial Hydesville phenomena, increasing numbers of people joined the fast growing Spiritualist movement. In the United States of America and the United Kingdom, in particular, the Spiritualist movement was organized into congregations which were led by regional and national bodies.

In America these became known as the National Spiritualist Association of Churches (NSAC), founded in 1893, the International General Assembly of Spiritualists, and the National Spiritualist Alliance of the USA. These groups have joined the English-based International Spiritualist Federation, which was founded in 1923. The Spiritualist National Union is based in Essex, England.

A number of organizations who belong to more traditional denominations that have some Spiritualist interests have developed. Two of these include the American Spiritual Frontiers Fellowship International[28] and the Churches' Fellowship for Psychical and Spiritual Studies (England).[29]

There are more than 1,000 Spiritualist centers in the United Kingdom, a large number can be found in Glasgow and Edinburgh. Here, every evening, people observe a wide variety of visiting mediums demonstrating communication with beloved spirit relations and animals.

The congregations sing and worship God, send their love, pray for people, animals and the planet, practice spiritual healing, raise money for charities, and learn spiritual philosophy. Visitors can also have one-to-one meetings, known as sittings, with many visiting mediums. There are large numbers of similar Spiritualist centers elsewhere in Europe, the USA, Canada and Australia.

## Psychical Research

Interest in mediumship and associated psychic phenomena took an alternative organized form with the founding of the Society for Psychical Research in London in 1882.[30] This organization is not interested in the spiritual aspects of mediumistic phenomena. It was founded with the objective of conducting investigative research into evidence for the authenticity of mediumistic phenomena and possible scientific explanations for it.

Many eminent professionals from diverse academic backgrounds have shared an interest in researching these phenomena and have joined the ranks of psychical researchers. Among the acclaimed British scholars,, public figures, writers and politicians who have pursued research into this enigmatic area of enquiry are Sir William Crookes, Sir Arthur Conan Doyle, Frederick H. Myers and Sir Oliver Lodge. Eminent professionals and scholars who are representative of some of the membership of the American Society for Psychical Research,[31] which was founded in 1885, include esteemed individuals such as William James, J.H. Hyslop and J.B. Rhine.

## Spiritualist Beliefs

A brief outline of some of the predominant beliefs of contemporary Spiritualists is given here. As stated earlier, the religion of Spiritualism was founded upon and continues to be nurtured by communications believed to be from ethically advanced spirits and angels.

Mediums are trained to communicate with surviving, non-physical personalities who demonstrate a high degree of spirituality. They are also able to see and hear relatives and friends connected with the sitter or the sitter's friends. Some higher-level mediumistic communications can be profoundly spiritual.

The Spiritualist movement in the United Kingdom states that members:

> have no fixed creed but the Spiritualist National Union has adopted the following Seven Principles [these are believed to have been given to them by communicating spirits or angels]: The fatherhood of God, the brotherhood of man, communion of spirits and the ministry of angels, the continuous existence of the human soul, personal responsibility, compensation and retribution hereafter for all the good and evil deeds done on earth and eternal progress open to every human soul.[32]

Some people visit a medium or Spiritualist center only in order to receive predictive information about their future, associated with a supportive communication from a loved one in spirit. It is unfortunate when they do not internalize the spiritual philosophy that comes from communications with angels or highly evolved spirits, since Spiritualist religious philosophy goes much deeper than offering predictive information.

Spiritualist teachings advocate that each individual's earthly life has a distinct purpose, whether they work behind the scenes or in the spotlight. Spiritualists are taught that as a matter of paramount importance that every individual life in every lifetime should be used in order to obtain spiritual progression. This point is substantiated by the spiritual truths gained by near-death experiencers who return with the belief that every creature's their life is vital and has a specific purpose.

Spiritualists are taught by mediums in trance that spiritual development continues after physical death. They believe that non-physical personalities – spirits – also continue to further their own spiritual progression in the spirit dimension of life. They believe that this might be achieved through guiding and supporting the productive and creative work pursued by those living in the physical body, They are also taught that spirits have the opportunity to evolve spiritually in the non-physical spheres when they work with animals or people who have died and woken up in this energy dimension.

Spiritualists believe that right thoughts and right action are of primary importance as these will attract positive events in this life and the next. They believe that there is a rich diversity of people who possess innumerable abilities, and each person should use these for the good of all other living creatures, which includes animals, birds, marine life and the earth herself. Increasing numbers of Spiritualists in the United Kingdom have become vegetarian in more recent years, as typically they feel that Spiritualist teachings have touched them on a deeply spiritual level.

Spiritualists often feel that they do not wish to condone by passive inaction or acceptance the inhumane, negligent and torturous treatment and murder of animals. They oppose animal experimentation as increasingly people have become aware that plants are valuable medicines, and research is better employed in this area. Pioneering medical research, including computer-modeling techniques, is producing more accurate medical research results confirming the enormous differences between the related physical bodies of all animals, human and non-human.

This underlines the waste of time and the immoral nature of carrying out useless barbaric experiments on animals as the results are of no use to us. Many Spiritualists also oppose the fact that living animals are taken on journeys that last days in cramped conditions to diverse countries. Here many types of murder are perpetrated on them to access their flesh and blood by people who must surely lack compassion, sensitivity and feeling.

Vegetarianism is easy to follow, even in the western world. In the west, low-fat soya proteins and other vegetable protein substitutes are abundantly available in the healthy-eating sections of most supermarkets. The vegetarian diet has been medically verified for its pronounced reduction of the development of heart disease, strokes, cancers and other animal flesh/fat induced diseases.

This underlines the fact that humans do not benefit from eating the flesh and body parts of our related animal brethren. Many Spiritualists, akin to other spiritual, religious philosophies also oppose needless, profit orientated experimentation on animals. These take on a myriad forms. Much of which can be alternatively carried our as stated, by the use of computer model experiments.

These are known to produce far more accurate results and are not barbaric and hostile to our animal brethren. These relatives share and beautify both this planet and the non-physical realms to which Spiritualists believe we are all collectively destined. Spirit communications inform us that animals, particularly domesticated animals who live with loving humans, significantly spiritually evolve during their lifetime. Many animals have none of the negative human traits in them at all, but are like vulnerable, innocent infants for the whole of their lives on earth.

Through the impetus of building relationships with humans, they progressively express their innate qualities of innocence, love, loyalty, selfless protection and devotion, all of which enhances their spiritual progression. There are many case histories of animals demonstrating supreme acts of self-sacrificial protection of total strangers.

This involves a whole range of animals including dogs, cows, horses and dolphins, This is not an exhaustive list. In the wild, too, animals can demonstrate the most superior forms of love and compassion. The highest medals are awarded to honor those rare people who likewise lay down their lives to save others.

To give only one example, female foxes are frequently seen running from the safety of their den in the ground. Instinct alone would make a terrified family huddle there and face death together. The female consciously acts as a decoy. Sacrificing her life, she has the fruitless hope that by allowing the relentless, merciless hunters to kill her, their killing appetites will be quenched, and her beloved infants' lives might therefore be saved.

Sadly, after her murder the hunters usually move on to those who are left defenseless in the den. Sometimes the infants run out to be with their squealing, pain-wracked mother, the only one who has shown them love. As she dies, ripped apart, they are murdered too.

Spiritualists are taught by mediums who obtain trance information that the soul does not enter the physical embryo until it is several months old. Hence stem-cell research on human embryos should be carried out as a replacement for the inaccurate, horrific, painful research conducted on animals.

Spiritualists learn that these experiments produce terrible karmic consequences on all those who perpetrate, and are associated with, inflicting such gruesome torture on animals. The negative energies are thought to affect them during both their physical and non-physical lives. they will also feel the pains they inflicted on the animals when they reach the non-physical, post-death dimension.

Spiritualists are also taught that if the soul of a living creature is destined for the earth plane, the purpose of which is to gain an opportunity for spiritual growth, and it is miscarried, it will try again until successful. The soul may be born to the sister or cousins of the original mother or may be forced to skip one or more generations.

The Encyclopaedia Britannica further describes beliefs shared by many Spiritualists:

Spiritualists believe that the human spirit exists eternally as a part of the universal Spirit and thus antedates the creation of the body and the soul ... that the soul enters the body ... a few months after conception. The soul, like the body, is said to be manufactured out of material elements, such as food, water and air, but these are more refined than the bodily elements. The soul is the duplicate of the body in structure. At death the soul and the spirit are believed to go to one of the seven spheres that surround the earth.

The lowest sphere is occupied by [people] who on earth were wicked ... and dominated by material desires. At the death of the body, most people go to the Third Sphere often called the Summerland ... Here they wear clothing, live in houses, and have animals for pets. Each spirit finds and marries his soul mate ... Beyond the seven earth spheres are higher and more universal spheres; they surround planets and suns, and even solar systems ... God [is] defined as Infinite Intelligence ... The souls of children who have died are believed to assume adulthood over a period of time. Persons in the lower spheres eventually attain higher spheres ... Thus Spiritualists are universalists; that is, they believe in salvation for all ... though persons who have lived essentially evil lives must suffer [such as through living in an infernal non-physical environment] before they can progress to the higher spheres. The law of progression ... [is an opportunity for success or failure for all].[33]

Spiritualists are taught by elevated spiritual communicators that all animals, human and non-human, indeed, all living creatures make a transition at death, as all are governed by the same God-given natural laws. Logically, if animals, birds and marine life did not make their transitions to the celestial levels, these dimensions would be frighteningly barren, deserted places, devoid of life.

There have been countless spirit communications received on this subject. Near-death experiences, mediumistic trance lectures and mediumistic soul-journeys to the non-physical dimensions regularly describe spirit animals and spirit people living in the celestial levels. It is a fact that a heavenly landscape would not be a heavenly place of beauty without the shared loving company and beauty of all animals, birds and marine life.

The celestial non-physical realms are described as being ideo-plastic planes of existence. This means that on arrival there, a creature may find that their initial thoughts, expectations and needs are met, as the first non-physical landscapes arrange themselves to be what the individual thinks, expects or needs them to look like. If an individual is depressed, angry or harboring vengeful thoughts, then likewise the more negative landscapes will arrange themselves accordingly.

Moving on, in this thought-responsive, malleable to thought, non-physical energy world – like begins to attract like. Consequently, the landscape and companions befitting the thoughts and actions of a creature's lifetime are drawn to that individual. Interestingly, many contemporary experiences of angels share this feature of ideo-plasticity, They too are fluid in nature with respect to their externalized manifestation and form.

Accounts of near-death experiencers and those regarding experiences of angels have a common feature, both frequently describe scenes and encounters which the experiencers were most comfortable with at the time. For example, there was a case where a child was prevented from walking onto a busy motorway by the arms of a child-like angel who, after helping her, immediately disappeared.

This event was supported by approximately 100 German witnesses. The child needed a child to stop her, had an unknown adult arrived, she would have become fearful and might have taken that fatal step onto the motorway. In another example, witnesses observed a woman who was about to fall to her death being grasped by a powerfully strong male angel who then disappeared. Again, this was what was needed at the time.[34]

Similarly, during one particular case of trance mediumship a spirit lady communicated through the entranced medium. She revealed that throughout her physical life her image of heaven had been a cottage in scenic countryside. After her physical death she found herself in an equivalent cottage in beautiful countryside in one of the many non-physical landscapes of heaven. She said she was contacted regularly by more spiritually elevated spirits who asked her what activities she would like to pursue in order to continue her spiritual progression.

Another interesting example of the non-physical world's malleablility to thoughts and emotions comes from a near-death experiencer. At the time this woman physically died of a heart attack, she was filled with hate for her husband. Sadly, he had left her for a younger woman after the best part of a lifetime together. This lady's near-death experience consisted of a lion trying to push her into a horrific pit of hellfire.

Inevitably, the manifestation of this hell-like near death experience was directly related to her anger, hate and desire for revenge. The rage of the lion was symbolic of her powerfully destructive emotions, despite there being some justification for her anger. This experience demonstrated that the woman's negative thoughts and emotions were not destroying her husband but herself in this non-physical energy world. It might be concluded that our predominant thought-patterns over a lifetime and angry emotions at death manifest into landscapes and events, drawing to us scenes in the non-physical dimensions.

Arguably, last-minute deathbed repentances would not necessarily undo the accumulated energy of a lifetime of negative thought-patterns and prevent their negative consequences in the labyrinthine realms of the after-life. In a sense the natural laws of the universe which we are now discovering have arranged themselves to carry out a form of justice. Historically, this was understood simplistically in the form of punishment meted out by a wrathful God.

Accounts such as those above corroborate the spiritual teachings from celestial communications with psychic sensitives which have been cumulatively gathered over the millennia.

There is a great deal of literature detailing accounts of near-death experiences and investigations into their legacy. Margot Grey, P.M.H. Atwater PhD (Hon) and George G. Ritchie MD have written and taught extensively about near-death experiences as have scores of other scientists, including doctors Elizabeth Kubler-Ross, Kenneth Ring PhD, Dr Peter and Elizabeth Fenwick, Michael Sabom, MD Melvin Morse M Dand Bruce Greyson.

Many Spiritualists believe that everyone has the potential to become a medium. However, they believe the mediumistic ability is stronger and more spontaneous in some people than others. There are enormous differences in the spiritual quality of information received through mediums. Some mediums live very spiritual lives, others do not. Some mediums are egocentric and their only motivation is money, yet they may still be a good messenger of the spiritual information which they largely ignore in their own lives. Mediums frequently receive descriptions of the non-physical landscapes.

These are recorded in books. Differing degrees of accuracy are demonstrated by mediums regarding descriptions of spirit communicators and their messages. Messages may contain discussions of the sitter's past and offer future predictions. Through meditation and the recognition of the importance of cultivating a spiritual life above materialistic and egocentric pursuits, many Spiritualists believe that they may achieve spiritual progress. It is possible that the more spiritually orientated the medium is, the more likely they are to attract increasingly elevated spiritual celestial communicators.

The gift of mediumship should not be perceived as being a reward for living a spiritually virtuous life as there are many non-virtuous mediums. Messages can originate from relatives and pets who have made a transition of consciousness at death, or from more spiritually advanced intelligences who inhabit the higher levels of the invisible realms.

Many Spiritualists believe that the inspirations, ideas and guidance that they receive through mediumship facilitated by their intuitive, heightened sensitive faculties and meditative training techniques, may benefit their siritually creative pursuits and allow them to help others, especially the bereaved. They also believe that some spirit communication may originate from compassionate spirit guardians who seek to teach and guide especially when asked, most particularly in times of personal anguish and trial.

It will be shown that not all communications are of a high spiritual content and not all communications originate from surviving personalities. Two brief summaries taken from the Encyclopaedia Britannica bring this discussion to a close.

> Mental phenomena include ... messages that come when a medium goes into trance. Through mediums in trance, prophecies have been made, books written, instructions given to surgeons on how to perform difficult operations, and intricate experiments proposed for proving the non-earthly source of the communications.[35]

> Spirit messages are not thought to be infallible ... in view of their origin and the complex nature of the line of communication that they follow to reach the [medium]. They originate with a spirit who of course is not infallible. Then in getting a message to earth, a spirit must contact a medium, or more probably a medium's control. Neither the control nor the medium is thought to be infallible.[36]

## Descriptions of the After-Life

In preparation for Chapter 2, which provides the salient features of a number of key explanations as to what occurs during mediumship, we shall now look at some interesting features of mediumistic phenomena and spirit teachings regarding the nature of the non-physical after-death landscapes. It is important to thoroughly understand mediumistic and survivalist phenomena and the experience-based beliefs they produce, as a prerequisite to ascertaining how well the explanations fit these enigmatic phenomena.

Many of humankind's religious beliefs claim that survival beyond physical death occurs. Religious survivalist beliefs include the belief that survival occurs after a 'Judgment Day.' This occurs either at the end of time or shortly after the individual's death or they are reincarnated in an animal body, human and non-human.

Spirit communications appear to demonstrate that the being who continues to survive after death, in the more immediate term at least, has the same intrinsic personality traits as they did before their transition to the non-material life. Sometimes negative and idiosyncratic characteristics are expressed as a means of helping the sitter to recognize who they are. Spirit communications have informed us that over time in the metaphysical realms, negative characteristics are refined as the soul continues its spiritual development.

Trance communications conveyed through Spiritualist mediums have often provided the most detailed descriptions of the countless meta-geographic landscapes experienced after physical death. Many Spiritualists believe that to a greater or lesser extent these ideoplastic realms are initially reflective of the person's energy field, known as the individual's psyche or soul.

Spirit communications inform us that every soul works through a myriad situations and emotions in order to progress spiritually in these malleable to thought, fluid landscapes. This is achieved as the soul experiences the pains and emotions of all creatures that their thoughts or actions wronged or neglected during the their earthly physical life. Spirit communications inform us that opportunities for spiritual growth are given to all discarnate souls. They may choose to influence, support and guide the thoughts and actions of others, particularly their loved ones, who still inhabit the material plane of existence.

They may offer support and companionship to those disorientated people and animals who find themselves newly arrived in their new mode of existence. A person may ask, are these the 'beings of light' near-death experiencers witness? They may assist those spirit beings who are ready to progress to higher spiritual planes to do further spiritual work.

Spirit communications inform us that in the discarnate realms a Divine Law of nature causes like to attract like. We are told that if a person has had more than one spouse, it is the soul mates who stay together. People find themselves with those that they have most affinity with and this includes the company of their beloved animals. Spirit communications tell us that the same types of people are drawn together.

We may meet all whom we met on the earth plane and many more if we wish. We are told that in the comparatively early days in their newlyfound existence, people continue to act as they have always done and receive the same back from their like-minded companions.

They are amongst those of like minds, for either a short or long time, until the fuel of hate, power or selfishness ceases to energize their activities. For example, two individuals who despise one another during their physical life, might find themselves fighting in the spirit dimension. Once they have killed one another, they would be seen to continue fighting. They do this continuously until an emotion of forgiveness stirs in them or they question why they are doing this. At that time, they and others move on to a different level which exhibits different landscapes and companions.

To summarize the alternate levels of existence:

A fairly good consensus exists throughout the channeling literature that there are levels, dimensions, or planes of reality, the physical plane being only one of them – and the lowest (or one of the lowest at that). Tracing the ascending, ever-finer levels away from the physical as we know it, the occult literature (for example, H.P. Blavatsky's Theosophical, Alice H. Bailey's Arcane, Rudolf Steiner's Anthroposophical, and Rosicrucian) and the channels associated with it contend that there is an etheric (or higher physical) subtle-energy plane that acts as a template for the organization of physical structures like our bodies.

There is an astral plane within which emotional reality is located. The mental plane is the arena for all forms of thought. The initiation of intentionality takes place on the causal plane ... And there are, depending on one's viewpoint, a number of ever-more spiritual planes beyond the causal, involving will, wisdom, power and love, approaching the source of All That Is. We are told that all of these planes operate and interact in a superimposed, coherent manner, with causal succession flowing from higher to lower spheres.[37]

## Mediumistic Phenomena

Many psychical researchers believe that many mediums genuinely communicate with surviving spirit personalities. This is in sharp contrast to those who merely demonstrate the operation of alternative psychic faculties. Prior to discussing several explanations regarding the phenomena it is useful to first draw attention to some interesting features found amongst mediumistic phenomena that any explanation of the phenomena would need to consider.

First of all, let us look at the types of information that can be received through mediumship:

> Psychical researchers of experience such as Lodge, Hodgson, James and Balfour know that there is a lot of trivia and waffling. But they also know that when conditions allow it, the ostensible communicator can show coherence, intelligence, knowledge, memory, debating and expository skills on as high a level as the person he or she claims to be ever demonstrated in life. Communicators such as George Pelham or Richard Hodgson (through Mrs Piper) or Drayton Thomas's father John and sister Etta (through Mrs Leonard) or the Myers, Gurney, Sidgwick group communicating through Mrs Willett are cases in point. Other cases of great interest are Myers and Mrs Willett herself ostensibly communicating by automatic writing through Geraldine Cummins.[38]

Over the decades, psychical researchers have held extremely meaningful conversations with the voices that emanate from entranced mediums. This indicates that such voices were surviving personalities, not mere memory systems. During these discussions the spirit communicators have explained their difficulties in communicating through the medium's body. For example, mediums who smoke are typically informed by fellow entranced mediums that smoking creates obstructive barriers, preventing genuine spirit communication.

Communicators often complain that when the medium is not in trance, the lengthy, detailed messages they seek to convey often result in mere fragmentary messages due to the medium's inadvertent distortion or lack of understanding. Messages from a spirit mind, telepathically transferred to the medium's mind, are obviously vulnerable to the quality of the mediumship. A picture received on the screen of the medium's mind or an audible phrase, in the case of clairaudience, can be misunderstood or partially received.

Some information received by the mind of the medium can be derived from the mind of the sitter. This is a point that has been noted by sitters, psychical researchers and mediums alike. This situation affects some mediums more than others and affects the quality and accuracy of the information that they relay to the sitter. However, it has also been found that a person can inadvertently think of someone and their thoughts attract that person to make contact through the medium.

To clarify these points, one day in 1894 Richard Hodgson, the famous psychical researcher, had by chance been reading information regarding the life and works of Sir Walter Scott. The following day he was due to have a sitting with the renowned medium known as Mrs Leonora Piper in order to further his psychical investigations into her work.

The next day at that sitting he received information from a spirit claiming to be Sir Walter Scott. Interestingly, the mischievous entity, when questioned, did not demonstrate with any accuracy the knowledge and personality of the real Sir Walter Scott.[39] A further example of the mind of the sitter influencing or creating communications received by the medium is highlighted in the following interesting case:

[In the] experiments carried out by the 'Philip' group in Canada ... [researchers] planned a fictitious person down to the last detail. The experimenters set him in England in the seventeenth century and deliberately included a few anachronistic mistakes in his life. In subsequent table-tilting sessions they found that they were able to contact Philip and converse with him in a convincing way.[40]

However, over time the psychical research group mentioned above realized that Philip had no independent life or identity separate from them. They discovered that 'Philip' was fueled and energized by the group. These facts came to light when they questioned 'Philip.' They asked him what he had been doing since the last group meeting and he had no answer whatsoever. It soon became apparent that when the group was not together Philip did not exist. These conversations were very different from those carried out with conclusively proven, recognizable surviving personalities.

Whilst it has been scientifically proven that mediums can obtain information telepathically from the minds of sitters, arguably, information can also be derived telepathically from surviving minds of spirits, many years after their physical death.

Ockham's Razor is the best principle for assessing the quality of an explanation. William of Ockham was a highly esteemed and influential 14th-century English philosopher. Ockham's principle states that the simplest and most straightforward explanation is superior to convoluted explanations which are faltering attempts to explain evidence. Telepathy between 'the medium and sitters' and between the 'the medium and disembodied surviving minds,' arguably offers the most direct explanation for evidential mediumship.

Parapsychologists often argue that mediums telepathically access the intense emotions of the deceased at the time of death and that they do not access surviving intelligences. However, mediums hold conversations with spirit communicators many years after their death when the intensity of their emotions at death would inevitably be greatly reduced.

Conversations are frequently lengthy on a wide variety of subjects and do not depend on the intensity of emotions at death. Their deaths are not usually discussed as they are very much alive as communicators. These facts discredit this materialist parapsychological explanation which does not explain mediumistic communications.

Many mediumistic demonstrations have included the medium transmitting family and other information that is not contained in the minds of the sitters. Sometimes no one alive knows the information given by mediums, but later on it may be uncovered in archives storing rare historic documents – archives which had not been physically visited by the mediums.[41]

Mediums frequently state that it is the 'love link' or unfinished business that helps to trigger the spirit communicator's contact with a responsive medium: 'At least some communicators can be called up or activated from the archives by the links, strong or weak, between the sitter and the deceased person the communicator claims to be.'[42]

With regard to the emotions, thoughts, or words which are the keys that instigate mediumistic communications, there are also further phenomena known as 'drop-in' communicators. These remain something of an enigma. These alleged spirit communicators communicate through the medium in order to have their unfinished business conveyed to a person who may not be at the sitting and may not even be known to either the medium or the sitter. Cases such as these indicate that it is not a great 'Common Unconscious' (i.e. a static 'Great Memory' store) that is accessed by the medium but actual surviving personalities.

These surviving spirit intelligences appear to still be motivated by their unfinished business, their love for someone still physically living, or other emotions. They passionately need to be heard by those in the earthly physical body before they can be content. Further accounts of psychical researchers' experiences of drop-in communicators can be found in Archie Roy's book *The Archives of the Mind*.[43]

Interesting mediumistic phenomena are demonstrated daily at

the Arthur Findlay College for mediumship in Essex, England. To give one example, a clairaudient medium named Mary Duffy from Edinburgh, Scotland, wished to demonstrate that she could access the same spirit communicator simultaneously accessed by the psychic artist from southern England named Coral Polge. This experiment showed that an objective link to the same spirit could be accessed by two mediums working simultaneously. Mediumship has much in common with a long-distance telephone call to a spirit who wishes to communicate with a member of the audience.

Polge, the psychic artist medium, began to draw the face that she could see either on the screen of her mind or externally. Duffy, the clairaudient medium, simultaneously began to hear accompanying information describing the spirit communicator, together with messages for the sitter. All was believed to be derived from the surviving spirit personality who was currently being sketched.

When these two mediums picked the person in the audience to whom the picture and information was to be given, the recipient stated that she had not said anything earlier despite the accuracy of the information and portrait, as she had never witnessed a mediumistic demonstration before. The results of this experiment were fascinating as the recipient said that the woman whose portrait had been drawn and the information given was very accurate yet the woman was not dead. The recipient explained that the woman had in fact been asleep in a coma for many years in a hospital bed.[44]

Arguably, we should ask two questions regarding this unexpected by-product of the demonstration. Firstly, at what stage do all living creatures enter the non-physical mind-world? Secondly, do we all access it every night in our sleep state?

## Chapter 2

# The Predominant Explanations and Debates

In this chapter I will provide a summary of some of the most commonly used explanations for mediumship; I will also discuss the surrounding debates and some further interesting features of mediumistic phenomena.

Explanations have to be dynamic rather than fixed in nature, as they are progressively forced to assimilate new research results and personal experiences. Professor Archie E. Roy observes in his book *Archives of the Mind* that it may prove to be impossible to ever develop a grand universal theory (GUT). He points out that new developments provide new data which inevitably contradict previous assumptions and theories.[1]

Roy states that:

it is not unknown in science to formulate a hypothesis and attempt to apply it to as wide a field of phenomena as possible, for there is little doubt that the wider the area it illuminates and makes sense of, the more confidence its author or authors can have that it is a useful and fruitful paradigm. Three outstanding examples of this are Newtonian dynamics, with its law of gravitation and three laws of motion, Einsteinian relativity and thirdly quantum mechanics. Nevertheless ... it is unlikely that we will ever have the ... Grand Universal Theory; it is to be expected that sooner or later the observer will encounter phenomena alien to his or her theory.[2]

Research and debates continue on many academic and experiential fronts regarding mediumship and other psychic phenomena. Some say that the medium is not telepathically contacting surviving intelligences (spirits) and that a remarkable degree of extrasensory perception is at work. ESP, as defined earlier, is an umbrella term for the use of a range of psychic faculties beyond the five senses (hearing, sight, smell, taste, touch).

Some people argue that the telepathic transfer of information can only be thought of in terms of mind-to-mind communication between physically living persons. Some mediums also demonstrate precognition, which is knowledge of future events, and retro-cognition, which is knowledge of past events. Debates center on questions such as: What is happening when a medium appears to demonstrate mediumistic contact with surviving spirits? The question is also asked, is it possible to use a range of other psychic abilities to access this information without really communicating with a spirit?

All conclusions relating to this enigmatic area of enquiry have to remain the responsibility of each individual. It is also a fact that when we deal with experiential phenomena, evidence that is considered to be conclusive by one person might not be accepted as conclusive by another. People's conclusions are often shaped by their deepest entrenched beliefs. For some, no amount of evidence is enough to change their hard and fast opinions.

It is a fact that if a group of people observed a horse race they would each remember different aspects of the event. However, they would all agree that the race took place. Unfortunately, people who watch psychical research experiments do not act in the same way. Their initial reactions and conclusions are usually shaped by deeply held personal convictions.

Their conclusions would be shaped by their beliefs regarding the purpose of life, belief or non-belief in the existence of God, their belief or disbelief in the soul's (spirit, consciousness, or auric energy) survival, eternal or otherwise, after physical death, and whether the soul houses the surviving recognizable personality of all living creatures.

A large and ever-increasing part of the world's population is brainwashed from birth by the western materialistic, reductionist understanding of the world. This affects our opinion on covert levels of which we are not aware, as we have no other way of under-standing our world. Newtonian physics, which was developed in the 17th century, cannot explain psychic phenomena and shapes many people's belief systems. However, the new physics of quantum theory is explaining the behavior of particles at diminished scales. Some of the observed quantum phenomena appear to be explaining the reality of observable psychic and mediumistic phenomena.

Roy notes that:

The normal theories assume that a human being is a complicated physico-chemico-electro-mechanism with but five senses to the outside real world, a mechanism bounded by birth, death and its skin. The so-called mind is the brain in action. These theories also assume that the real world, including living things accessible to those senses and technology's extensions to these senses, is all there is. In contrast, non-normal or paranormal theories have to assume that there is something else.[3]

Roy criticizes parapsychologists who deny the reality of mediumistic and psychic phenomena. They are ignorant of, or choose to ignore, the vast amount of experiential and research evidence that has been collected for more than a century and supports the existence of mediumistic and psychical phenomena. Such a limited, simplistic response by ignorant critics denies the integrity of human experience. Roy states that the 'way forward is not to ignore the phenomena, not to sweep them under the carpet of belief.'[4]

The quality and quantity of information that is transferred from the medium to the sitter can vary enormously during the same sitting. Other mediums receive the information in better quality and quantity on a regular basis. Either they have a better spirit commu-nicator or guide who helps them receive the information or they have a better ability to receive the information without distortion or loss. Some of the best evidence to suggest that the medium has made contact with a surviving 'deceased' person is when the medium gives information to the sitter of which the sitter has no knowledge. The sitter has to go away and verify the accuracy of the information they received. Cases such as these prove that the medium is not telepathically taking the information from the recipient's mind.

Proxy sitters have been used in experiments to replace the 'real sitters.' They receive messages from the medium intended for the 'real sitters.' Importantly, the proxysitters do not know the 'real sitters' or anything about them. When the 'real sitters' are given the information received by the medium and it is found to be accurate, such cases prove that the medium is not taking the information telepathically from the sitter. Parapsychologists do not have useful materialist, reductionist explanations regarding such mediumistic phenomena. They are defied by the weight of evidence that suggests that the information is obtained from a surviving spirit.

## Theory: Chance or Lucky Guesses

One non-paranormal explanation is that the medium demonstrates knowledge of information relevant to the sitter by pure chance or through lucky guesses. After more than a century of psychical research it is safe to say that the 'theory that the cases can be explained by coincidence may be dismissed as one totally contrary to the evidence.'[5]

## Theory: 'Research Fatally Flawed' Accusation

A second non-paranormal explanation given by some materialist critics of mediumship is directed at those who conduct psychical research investigations. The investigations concerned, often took many years and were researched and documented in detail. These were carried out by groups of psychical researchers who were academics in their own right.

The results of the research frequently concluded that communication with surviving spirit personalities had been evidenced.

Researchers were careful to identify how these cases differed from other instances when telepathic access was restricted to contact with mere husks of the personality, such as a memory or psychic system. The latter are clearly not surviving intelligences and are easily identifiable as such.[6]

Rather than agree that authentic mediumistic access to surviving spirit consciousnesses occurred, some critics simply attempt to discredit the academic background of the psychical researchers or their methods of investigation. Roy states that the theory that:

> The cases are fatally flawed because they have been studied by careless, incompetent, inexperienced, gullible people unaware of the frailties of human testimony is likewise untenable. Among the investigators are numbered Dr Richard Hodgson, Professor William James, Professor James Hyslop, Professor Sir Oliver Lodge, and the Rt. Hon. Gerald Balfour, Mrs Henry Sidgwick, Mr J.G. Piddington, Miss Alice Johnson, Professor Ian Stevenson, Dr Walter Franklin Prince and Dr Morton Prince, to name a representative few.
>
> Anyone putting forward the 'incompetent investigator' theory is revealing more about their own incompetence as a critic than anything else. Those people who know the abilities and experience of the investigators and who have studied their original reports will be aware of how inappropriate the 'incompetent investigator theory' is.[7]

## Theory: Fraud Accusation

A further non-paranormal, materialist explanation targeted at demonstrations of mediumship is that the medium must have used fraud to discover the accurate information. Some people may indeed be frauds. However, that is not the case for the scores of case studies that have been carried out for over a century by psychical researchers from diverse academic backgrounds.

Roy states that the:

Theory of fraud is frequently hazarded as an explanation of ostensible paranormal cases. To have any plausibility in the [most documented and researched] cases, it must be shown explicitly in each case who perpetrated the fraud, how it was done and what was the motive. Speculation of the 'Possibly it could have happened that ...' type is really worthless unless there is solid evidence backing it up. Critics must expect that their idle speculations justifiably produce a reaction similar to one such a critic would experience themselves if a psychical researcher indulged in such unscientific musings. It may also be remarked that even if one case should be dismissed as fraudulent, it does not demolish the others. It is up to the critic to provide convincing evidence that such a hypothesis is the correct one. I have not seen that done with respect to any of the cases [researched or evaluated by Roy in *The Archives of the Mind*].[8]

Roy continues: 'With so many different investigators scattered over a century and many countries, the cases stand or fall by their own internal evidence. Nevertheless family resemblances among them also form a sort of bonus of evidence supporting the theory that they are genuine.'[9]

Regarding the cases that Roy has investigated or evaluated, he notes with regard to the weight of the evidence that 'there is no evidence whatsoever that they are fraudulent. In the mediumistic cases a wealth of positive evidence exists that the mediums had genuine psychic gifts and that they took no steps to acquire in a normal way the vast amounts of information proffered by them.'[10]

Of the lengths that were frequently taken by psychical researchers, over the decades, during their investigations into alleged cases of mediumship, Roy notes that some mediums:

were followed by private detectives. Much of the information was of such an intimate nature that the most skilled detectives would have experienced great difficulty in finding it ... In addition the lives of mediums such as Mrs Piper or Mrs Leonard were so long that each had hundreds of sitters during their careers, many of high intelligence and long experience in assessing mediumistic utterances. It is not really plausible to suggest that the medium's reputations were built on the willingness of a proportion of their sitters to doctor these utterances.[11]

## Theory: Personation Plus Cryptomnesia

'Personation plus cryptomnesia' is the name given to a further materialist explanation that attempt to explain how mediums give amazingly accurate details about both the sitter's life and that of the spirit communicator. This theory suggests that the medium commits unconscious fraud by innocently or systematically gathering information regarding the lives of the sitter and their relatives. It is assumed this is done consciously or unconsciously through reading, listening to the radio and watching television programs.

It is then argued that the information gathered through the above means is forgotten by the medium's conscious mind and stored by the medium's subconscious mind. It is argued that the information stored by the medium's subconscious is given by the medium to the sitter, in the belief that he/she received it from a surviving spirit.

As a result of two and a half decades of observing and evaluating psychical and mediumistic phenomena, I would categorically state that the above theory cannot be correct in the vast majority of cases. Mediums frequently carry out ten half-hour readings a day, several days per week. These are given to sitters whom they do not know, have never met before, and who come from all parts of the globe. It would be impossible for mediums to conduct extensive research into the lives of all their sitters, including their families and deceased relatives, especially when they do not even know who will be visiting them, nor their names or addresses.

Roy also feels that this argument is a poor criticism of mediumship.[12] He states that:

Again it is noteworthy that the mediums' long careers involved hundreds of sitters ... in a high proportion of sittings the information given was highly specific and appropriate to the sitters. Many of the items were of such a private nature that they could not have been acquired by the mediums by casual listening and viewing or even by employing private detectives ... That the subconscious has remarkable powers to role-play is well known, especially in hypnosis, but that it could personate so skillfully in the cases remains unconvincing. We have only to think of the difficulty experienced by a police identifit artist in constructing a picture from even a detailed description by a witness to realize the difficulties.[13]

## Non-Normal Theories Regarding Mediumship

The following non-normal theories assume that there is something more to existence than is believed to be the case by many materialist parapsychologists who believe that nothing can operate outside the five senses. Theories with 'a religious background assume the existence of a spiritual realm and usually assume the existence of entities called spirits or angels or demons. Such theories may also variously hold that from this realm comes inspiration, guidance, the communion of saints, malevolent and mischievous influences and so on.'[14]

## The Game-Playing Demon Theory

Certain religious fundamentalists believe that all contacts received from the non-physical realms are made by demonic beings. They believe that through the use of deceit and disguise these demons fool the mediums, psychical researchers and sitters into believing they are who they claim to be. This view is much too naïve.

Infinite numbers of spirit messages are filled with love for the communicator's bereaved family and friends; in their loving concern the spirit seeks to assure them that he/she is still alive in the spirit realm. Messages frequently inform their loved ones that they should not grieve as all families, friends and pets will have the opportunity to be reunited again in the future.

Roy concludes that it is far too simplistic to say that all spirits are demons. He notes that 'some paranormal phenomena may be the work of malicious or mischievous entities ... but the theory that absolutely everything paranormal is caused by them is implausible in the extreme.'[15]

## The Super-ESP Debate

This argument can be amended to suit the sitter's particular experiential situation, hence it can be presented 'with' or 'without' personation. The following scenario gives a brief yet clear understanding of the 'super-ESP argument *with personation*:'

A person might unexpectedly find themselves at the brink of death. They become emotionally intense, terrified, as they face dangerous, life-threatening circumstances. It is both natural and inevitable for their mind to try to escape its present predicament, traveling to their loved ones elsewhere, with whom they long to be.

A member of the person's family some miles away might suddenly become aware that their loved one is being confronted by or has been confronted by a potentially tragic life-threatening situation. This family member may report their experience of a clairvoyant sighting or manifestation of their loved one. Some parapsychologists claim that when this occurs, as it regularly does, the family member has had nothing more than a simultaneous experience of telepathy with an accompanying hallucination of their loved one (i.e. 'super-ESP *with personation*').

This explanation is amended to describe what might be occurring during demonstrations of mediumship. This type of argument denies the authentic existence of a communicating, surviving spirit personality. It suggests that mediumistic demonstrations are nothing more than the result of telepathy with or without hallucinations of the deceased. Significantly, these would only occur at the time of the communicator's death, yet mediums demonstrate that they make contact years after a person's death.

Mediums frequently give information to sitters from surviving grandparents in spirit whom the sitter had never known. This information regularly has nothing to do with the emotions that the grandparent had at the time of their death, and these communications take place decades after their transition of consciousness into the spirit dimension. Significantly, their messages frequently give advice concerning current issues in the sitter's life, of which the grandparent is aware.

The materialist super-ESP hypothesis does not fit the great weight of mediumistic phenomena which offers survivalist evidence. Of the failure of this type of argument, Roy states:

In its strongest form, the super-ESP theory supposes that the medium's subconscious mind has access not only to the memories of every living human being on the planet but to every physical record in existence – book, newspaper, tombstone, registry office, and so on.

The claims of such a theory, however, go much further ... it may be that the sitter is sitting in a proxy capacity ... the medium uses her power presumably to find out which family, why it wishes to utilize the medium's services, which member or friend of that family has died and in what circumstances. In many cases even the members of the family will not have the relevant information in their minds.

The medium, possessed of all this marvelous telepathy and clairvoyant ability to tap all the stores of knowledge in existence – memories of living people, physical records in libraries, etc – must also have the ability to know where to find the correct information. The theory also supposes that the medium's mind possesses a data retrieval system of miraculous powers.

And having retrieved all the information *almost instantaneously*, the information must be dramatized convincingly to be presented from the point of view of the deceased person. In passing, it is surely fair to ask those who favor the telepathy explanation of mediums' genuinely paranormal abilities, but who believe that the mind is merely the brain in action, where this marvelous retrieval system software and hardware is situated in the human brain, this system that can delve into all other human brains at will?[16]

Psychical researchers around the world are faced with intense, ongoing debates. They seek to answer the question whether mediums have genuine access to surviving, recognizable spirit personalities or do they merely access memories and hallucinations of the deceased which have no surviving existence of their own? (The latter phenomenon is described as a 'memory system,' a 'husk' or a 'psychic system')?

These are not surviving, recognizable, living, spirit personalities. Not only is there the question whether survival of physical death occurs but also what is the nature of that survival? Does survival consist of being a surviving personality or does it take the form of a psychic or memory system?

The super-ESP theory suggests that telepathy can only make contact with the thoughts the deceased person had during their earthly life, not thoughts they have when in the spirit realm. The super-ESP theory does not accept that a person continues to survive in the spirit dimension. Similarly, this theory suggests that a person may only be observed as a hallucination, depicting what they were like when they were physically alive, not as they are now. This theory is a materialist reductionist theory.

This theory does not fit frequent statements from mediums claiming that the surviving person informs them that they passed to the higher life with a particular condition yet the medium can see that they are now restored to full health in their new non-material environment.

This is also the case when a medium describes accurately that a spirit had had an amputated limb when physically alive yet they can now 'see' the restored limb. The super-ESP argument denies that the medium can make contact with dynamically alive, surviving, non-physical, recognizable spirit personalities.

## The Cross-Correspondences

Psychcal researchers seek to ascertain whether the mediumistic communications that purport to originate with personalities surviving in the apparent invisible realms, prove that a dynamic, on-going, coherent, intelligence that retains the personality exhibited before death, actually survive death. One of the highest orders of mediumistic phenomena to shed light on the weaknesses of the super-ESP hypothesis are the cross-correspondences. These cases clearly demonstrate that after-death survival takes the form of recognizable personalities, not that of memory systems.

These incredible mediumistic phenomena began in 1906 and continued for three decades. They have provided psychical researchers with enormous evidence that survival of an intact personality does occur beyond physical death. These cases demonstrated continuity among a number of mediums who lived in different continents. Due to the fact that these communications demonstrated evidence of several vibrant communicative spirit personalities, the source of the communications became known as the 'Script Intelligences.'

The mediums involved had something in common. Each had the ability to write down the information they were given and draw the symbols they saw, despite having no knowledge or understanding of them. This is known as automatic writing; mediums who demonstrate this type of phenomenon are known as automatists.

The vast documentary evidence provided by both the mediums involved in the cross-correspondences and also the case investigators has convinced all who have studied the documents in depth that recognizable survival is a fact of nature. The complexity underlying the cross-correspondences has provided ample evidence that dynamic, on-going survival after physical death occurs.

Roy notes that:

> It is astonishing ... the majority of psychical researchers who
> have studied them have come to the conclusion that they have
> provided us with the strongest objective evidence so far that at
> least some people not only survive death, but also retain their
> intelligence and memories and their concern for those they have
> left behind ...
>
> As the investigators of the automatists' scripts proceeded
> painstakingly over the years in their studies, it became clear that
> the scripts did demonstrate ... purpose, intelligence and
> education far beyond anything that could be assigned to any one
> automatist ... The themes were represented in fragmentary refer-
> ences to classical subjects or in quotations from relevant poems or
> in short phrases or hinted at in symbols or names of figures in
> literature and legend, scattered among the automatists' scripts.
> Once the key to the puzzle was perceived, the themes suddenly
> made sense like the picture on a completed jigsaw puzzle.[17]

## The automatists

The consensus of opinion amongst the investigators of the automatists (mediums) involved in the cross-correspondences was that they
were sensitive, gifted and sincere individuals. 'Mrs Holland' was the
pseudonym for Mrs Fleming, who lived in India and was the sister
of the eminent British writer and poet Rudyard Kipling (1865–1936).
Dame Edith Lyttelton was the second medium who received communications. Mrs Margaret Verall, the third, was a lecturer in classics
and was married to a Cambridge scholar named Dr A.W. Verall.

The fourth medium was Miss Helen Verall, Margaret Verall's
daughter. The fifth medium involved in the case was Mrs Leonora
Piper, from Boston in the USA. Piper had been investigated by
psychical researchers for many years due to her remarkable mediumistic abilities. She would self-induce trance and then give detailed
communications from spirit personalities dwelling in the ideo-

plastic thought responsive realms of energy and mind. Eminent academics investigated Mrs Piper's mediumship. As a result of this, many of them became deeply involved in psychical research. Some of Piper's investigators included Professor William James, Professor Sir Oliver Lodge and Dr Richard Hodgson.

The sixth and possibly the principal medium who received automatic writing and other forms of communications was 'Mrs Willett.' Willett was a pseudonym for Mrs Charles Coombe-Tennant. Coombe Tennant was a professional person who was the first female Justice of the Peace. She was appointed in Glamorgan, in Wales in the United Kingdom. Coombe-Tennant was also the first female delegate, who in 1922, was appointedby the British Government to the Assembly of the League of Nations.

## The spirit communicators

The apparent non-corporeal communicators included a number of the major founding fathers of the Society for Psychical Research in London: Henry Sidgwick, Frederick Myers and Edmund Gurney. During their physical lifetimes they were deeply involved in evaluating the strengths and weaknesses of the evidence for post-mortem survival. However, in their day, survival in the form of recognizable, ongoing intelligences could not be proven beyond a shadow of a doubt.

Historic and present-day psychical researchers, after reviewing the cross-correspondence communications, conclude that after death these surviving men concocted an ingenious plan to create complex evidence to prove the reality of the dynamic nature of survival beyond physical death. Their evidence proves that survival does not take the illusory form known as memory, psychic systems or husks which possess no living personality.

Four other ostensible spirit communicators communicated through the use of automatic writing. These included a scientist named Francis Maitland Balfour who had been professor of animal morphology at Cambridge University. He had died prematurely in

1882 due to an accident at the age of 31. His two brothers included the first and second earls of Balfour, namely Gerald and James Balfour. Both became presidents of the Society for Psychical Research in London.

Other communicators called back from the grave, predominantly through the use of automatic writing. Communications were received from Annie Marshall, who had passed to spirit at a tragically young age. Frederick Myers was heartbroken as he had loved her deeply. After his death, Frederick Myers made extensive contact. Other communicators who joined their ranks included Laura Lyttelton. She had been the first wife of Arthur Lyttelton and passed to spirit during childbirth in 1886. Her sister Mary Catherine Lyttelton also became a communicator.

## The cross-correspondence researchers

There were five predominant cross-correspondence psychical researchers. These professional men were known for their integrity and were highly respected for their academic prowess. Significantly, the mediums who received the communications lived all over the globe. The information received by them was frequently in different languages. When it was fitted together like a jigsaw puzzle, it gave clear communications.

Sir Oliver Lodge was a member of the team of researchers. He was 'the eminent physicist and pioneer in radio who first became interested in psychical research because of his friendship with Edmund Gurney.'[18] Others included Gerald William, second Earl of Balfour who had 'a distinguished career in politics ... [including being] Chief Secretary for Ireland. He was President of the Board of Trade from 1900–1905. A strong classical scholar, he ... studied metaphysics, philosophy and ... his later life became devoted to psychical research.'[19]

Mrs Eleanor Sidgwick, the sister of the Balfours, was known for her 'formidable intelligence [and was] a brilliant mathematician.'[20] Mr J.G. Piddington was 'a business man of high intelligence.'[21] Ms

Alice Johnson pursued a 'distinguished career. She was the first Demonstrator in Animal Morphology in the Balfour Laboratory from 1884–1900.'[22]

Most researchers who have examined the 30 years of alleged spirit communications have concluded that they were not the result of telepathy or hallucinations. They accept that they offer extensive evidence proving that recognizable intelligences survive physical death. In conclusion, Roy states:

Does the case, with its thirty years of scripts filled by poetic references, symbols, drawings, allusions persuade one ... that the communicators were who they claimed to be? [Did the communicators] on the far side of death, create and transmit the monumental and labyrinthine structures of the cross-correspondences to show their continued existence? ... If however we are dealing with the result of telepathy and clairvoyance coupled with subliminal dramatization, then it is on a scale never demonstrated in any parapsychological laboratory. If we still dismiss that faculty as the cause, then we must take the survival hypothesis very seriously indeed.[23]

## The Holographic Analogy

Two useful 21st-century explanatory models represent attempts to offer an improved context for understanding mediumistic phenomena. The first model is called the holographic theory, metaphor or analogy; the second model is the universal archive theory, alternatively called the 'archives of the mind.'

Michael Talbot's book *The Holographic Universe*[24] explores this analogy, which is summarized here. For further information, readers are urged to consult *The Holographic Universe*.[25] Talbot's model provides an improved context into which mediumship and a range of other psychic phenomena can be fitted. It is being applied by pioneering scholars from diverse backgrounds to progressively formulate a fuller, cohesive explanatory picture.

This new and as yet controvercial model was born of the mechanical worldview and is being applied in part to possible features of consciousness. This valuable theory is still in its developmental, embryonic stages. It consists of a number of views and progressive evidence, all of which is cumulatively being intetgrated and synthesized within this model of understanding. It is attracting interest from scholars from diverse academic backgrounds.

The holographic model indicates that there is a unity, interrelatedness and interdependence underlying all of creation at a very deep level of existence. This is perceived as being beyond space and time and that 'mind' can interact with physical reality. This model is progressively providing a potentially unifying scientific, holistic understanding of psychic and mediumistic experiences.

This is a far superior intellectual approach, stretching our minds in order to understand these very real phenomena. This model is above the simplistic attempts by materialist parapsychologists to ignore the evidence that has been collected for more than a century from cases that have been researched in an exemplary manner.

The holographic explanation states that all matter, whether living or non-living, exists in an interconnected state of flux, between implicate order (unseen, implicit, enfolded) and explicate order (seen, explicit, unfolded), which can manifest according to the observer's perspective, at its most reductionist form as matter or alternatively as light, which is photonic energy.

The scientific findings which have resulted in this paradigm will radically transform our understanding of reality. It provides an understanding which conceptually integrates human testimonies of psychic experiences. Therefore it testifies to the integrity of the millions of reports of psychic and mediumistic phenomena that have been gathered across the globe since the earliest epochs of humankind's psycho-spiritual history.

People who have a materialist attitude ignore the accumulated evidence with regard to the psychic realm of the experiential simply because they cannot provide a meaningful context for understanding these phenomena. This is due to their academic prejudices and the limitations of their understanding and experience. They have told experiencers worldwide that throughout history human beings' profoundly transformative, spiritual, psychic or mediumistic experiences simply did not occur.

Materialistic explanations are reductionist. They leave people with an inadequate, fragmented understanding of the world into which psychic experiences cannot fit. Talbot's holographic analogy is the result of his goal to find a context into which paranormal experiences can, indeed fit. Talbot leads a superior approach which is in sharp contrast to dismissing outstanding evidence, gained by acclaimed academics, simply because it cannot be fitted into the materialist view of the world.

The following explains how the holographic theory was born. Among the ranks of the researchers was Karl Lashley, a neurosurgeon at Yerkes Laboratory of Primate Biology (Orange Park, Florida) and Karl Pribram, a neurophysiologist who worked at Stanford University. Another scientist was David Bohm, a physicist at London University known for his contributions in the field of quantum mechanics. While working at Princeton University in New Jersey, Bohm had the opportunity to have close dialogue regarding shared research interests in this area with an eminent fellow colleague, namely Albert Einstein.

Initial theories for the physiological mechanism of memory have hypothesized that the sequential record of consciousness (memory) is kept within specific memory sites within the brain, called engrams. Lashley's work refuted these findings when he found that extensive surgical resection of rat brains could not eradicate their memories of maze solutions. Pribram[26] suggested that memories are distributed throughout the whole brain and therefore exhibit non-local behavior. He explained this using the analogical concept of holography.

The concept of holography can be explained as follows. Laser light, which has extremely pure, coherent, electromagnetic wave structure, is split into two beams; one beam is bounced off an object, and the second beam, colliding with the reflected light of the first beam, produces an interference pattern. When this interference pattern is illuminated by a third laser beam or strong source of light, a three-dimensional image of that object is recreated on a holographic screen or plate. Significantly, each and every part of this three-dimensional image contains all the information of the whole original image.

Pribram[27] suggested that the brain possesses a wave-like phenomenon as its structure consists of dendritic interconnectivity (fingers or projections which interconnect different neurological cells called neurones). These produce three-dimensional ripples of electromagnetic activity. If the brain possesses this functional structure, it may record memories in a holographic manner, which explains how the distribution of memories appear to be found throughout the whole brain and not just in a certain area of the brain.

Convincing evidence that the brain functions like a hologram comes from the fact that many central neurosensory organs (such as taste, hearing, vision, etc.) function like frequency analyzers or transfer functions that conform to the mathematics of the Fourier transform (which enables the decomposition of any signal into a series of wave-functions).

If the brain functions like a hologram, the question arises: What is the true reality of the objects that generate the interference pattern? Is it the objects themselves or the interference pattern itself? Do the world and the universe consist of a domain of resonating frequencies which give the illusion of reality after it is holographically processed by our brains? These theories are compatible with the findings of the physicist Bohm which have led him to believe that the universe is a hologram.

Bohm[28] suggests that the subatomic phenomena described by the category of quanta that possess properties of wave-particle duality (that is, they can behave like a wave or a particle according to whether they are being observed or not – the very act of looking at them collapses them into one or other state) and interconnectedness (divided quanta seem to have both the properties of communicating and synchronicity with each other, no matter how distant they are from each other) can be understood by the existence of an all-pervasive sub-quantum level of laws which he called 'quantum potential.' If, on a reductionist level, the whole universe exists as quanta, it can be understood how the properties of interconnectedness which exist at this level will apply to every aspect of creation.

Bohm theorized that the influence of quantum potential, unlike other physical fields such as gravity or magnetism, did not vary with distance and that the behavior of all parts of the quantum potential field was organized by the whole. He suggested that the illusion of the duality of subatomic phenomena resulted from our observational perspective as matter which is 'enfolded' or 'unfolded' as part of the level of reality known as the 'implicate' and 'explicate' order, respectively.

The appearance of electrons and all other particles is sustained by a constant flux between the two 'implicate' and 'explicate' orders. According to Bohm, both aspects of a quantum are enfolded in a quantum ensemble, but the way an observer interacts with the ensemble determines which aspects unfold. This can be simplistically understood in terms of dropping a drop of ink into a revolving drum containing a glycerine substance and then observing the ink dot. When this drum is spun round quickly, the ink dot initially being seen (seen: unfolded, explicate, explicit in structure) becomes unseen (unseen: enfolded, implicate, implicit in structure).

If the spin is reversed to the same degree, the enfolded (unseen) structure of the ink drop returns to its unfolded (seen) state and can again be seen by the naked eye. This demonstrates that the ink drop was in fact, there, in existence, all the time, but was not always seen by the naked eye.

When the drop of ink in the glycerine is clearly seen it is described as being explicit (seen: unfolded, explicate) and when, after stirring, the ink spot becomes invisible to the eye, Bohm describes it as being in its implicit state of existence (unseen: enfolded, implicate) – in existence but not seen. Increasingly, when the glycerine is stirred,

the drop of ink can be described as being interwoven or interconnected with the glycerine, rather than being described in terms of a
space/time separation. The ink in this state exists, yet is unseen. It is
invisible as it is infused in the glycerine at a deeper level of reality.
The ink can be said to exist; however, it does so at an unseen, deeper
dimension of existence.

Bohm, therefore, has a deep understanding of the unseen characteristics of reality, or deeper dimensions of existence. He describes
reality in terms of dimensions of existence. This has close parallels
with spirit communications and those of Emanuel Swedenborg
which describe many extremely different landscapes, or dimensions
of existence. This can be simplistically understood in terms of the
degree to which something is explicit (*seen*) or implicit (*unseen*).
Simplistically speaking, each dimension or level of reality is akin to
the number of times the ink is stirred to cause its disappearance from
the naked eye.

Bohm saw the properties of holography in the two orders he
described (implicate unseen and explicate seen). The interference
patterns of the two split laser beams recorded on a holographic film
appear disordered to the naked eye. However, it has implicate order
that is (unseen) enfolded. It requires the addition of further electromagnetic interference or observational interference provided by the
wave-form functional structure of the brain to enable unfolding of
the holographic image into part of the explicate (seen) order.

Bohm refers to this as our level of existence. If the universe
behaves as a hologram, it too would have non-local properties. Just
as part of a hologram contains all the information possessed by the
whole, part of the universe contains all the information of the whole
universe. This, in turn, explains the phenomena of interconnectedness.

Because a physical hologram is static and does not convey the
dynamic nature of the universe, Bohm prefers to describe the
universe as a sequence of holograms, which he calls
'holomovement.'[29] Bohm believes that consciousness is a more

subtle form of matter and therefore, likewise, matter or plasma (the material contents of the universe) possesses some of the traits of living things. Therefore, consciousness can theoretically be present, like matter, in various degrees of enfoldment or unfoldment.

Arguably, this explains the nature of the apparently invisible, usually unseen, human and animal spirit manifestations because they might have become enfolded (*usually unseen: implicit, in implicate form*) within the universe. It may also explain why certain people (sensitives, mediumistic people, animals, dogs, cats, horses etc. with their heightened psychic sensitivities) have the ability to see or hear the holomovement interference patterns of spirits in their enfolded form (*usually unseen: implicit, in implicate form*).

In the same way, our brains mathematically construct objective realities by interpreting the interference pattern frequencies that are ultimately projections from other dimensions. One of these dimensions could contain an enfolded (*usually unseen: implicit, implicate*) order of the spirit world, accessible by a holographic functioning brain.

The relevance of the holographic analogy to consciousness is that a person might consider that during speech, the mind is working close to the 'seen' explicate order of existence (*seen, unfolded, explicit, explicate*), a conscious level of mind. Subliminal levels of mind are at the deepest 'unseen' implicate levels of existence (*unseen, enfolded, implicit, implicate*). Some academics, including psychical researchers, believe that it is possible to access the collective unconscious, as at these deepest levels all forms of life, humankind and all other creatures, are interconnected, interrelated and interwoven.

The 'collective unconsciousness' is sometimes called 'the world mind.' It is described in eastern terminology as the 'akashic records.' These terms represent earlier attempts at describing the concept of a storehouse of all that is and ever has been. This concept indicates a static store of memories rather than a dynamic, ongoing store of the non-physical, surviving personalities of all creatures.

This profoundly deep level of consciousness might be understood as the interconnectedness of a mind of an infinite number of parts. Some scholars, including psychical researchers, believe that all of creation can potentially access this level of mind. From this level of the implicit, the unseen (*usually unseen but in existence, enfolded: implicate*), each individual extracts and makes explicit, seen (*seen, unfolded: explicate*), the nature of their own reality and psychic experience, which is observing that which is usually invisible.

The above discussion is of particular significance in view of the earlier discussion of the ongoing shared pattern of transformative spiritual, mediumistic experiences. These include near-death experiences, and experiences of angels and spirit communicators – each category of experiencer corroborates the other. The evidence from each strongly indicates that the non-physical realms are a fluid, malleable, thought-responsive world. Either the predominant aspects of personality (the spiritual or non-spiritual thought-patterns) are externalized, or like attracts like, attracting to us the appropriate level of landscapes and companions in these geo-psychic realms.

Consequently, our predominant thoughts and emotions create our non-material reality. Arguably, that which a person expects and needs, or the positive or negative energy of the emotions that they are giving out, draws a parallel to it – like draws like. Non-physical spirit people, animals and landscapes experienced are a direct reflection of the spiritual level of the experiencer.

The above alternative scientific paradigm indicates that the realm of psychic experience is closely associated with the enfolded, usually unseen (*usually unseen: implicit, implicate*) levels of existence. At these deepest levels of the collective unconsciousness, there might be found the universally understood language of symbols and archetypes, which are interpreted by a person's individual psyche. This testifies to the hypothesis that the minds of all humans, animals and all other creatures are unified, interconnected and interlaced at the deepest levels of mind. To harm any other creature ultimately harms us, having dramatic consequences for ourselves.

The more a holographic image is fragmented or cut, the hazier the image becomes, though each hologram still retains the original whole picture. This suggests that minds might be perceived as holographic in nature; each mind works within a universe with holographic characteristics. Therefore, psychic and mediumistic experiences might be thought in terms of those experiences that occur when the veil between the seen, unfolded (*seen: explicit, explicate*) and usually unseen, enfolded (*usually unseen: implicit, implicate*) becomes less clouded, producing a clearer image.

Significantly, there are salient parallels between pioneering 21st-century scientific concepts and ancient mystical beliefs. It is fascinating that both cutting-edge scientists and ancient shamans have discovered and experienced that all life-forms are interrelated. As a consequence of learning about the nature of the unseen levels of existence and the nature of the after-life, profound respect and compassion for all other creatures and the earth itself should be generated. If we harm by thought or deed another person, animal or creature, the negativity associated with it harms ourselves in the enfolded (unseen) ideo-plastic, after-death realms.

There are many accounts of hell-like near-death experiences. Looking into the background of near-death experiencers, if they had negative emotions, particularly at the time of their death, or led a predominantly unspiritual life, they tended to experience hell-like landscapes and entities. The opposite is true of those who experienced spiritual entities and celestial landscapes.

Interestingly, Hindus, Buddhists, Jews, Christians and Spiritualists teach that it is essential to demonstrate right action as well as right thought. They teach that the totality of existence – all creatures – is meaningfully interwoven at deeper levels of existence and that compensation and retribution for thoughts and deeds carried out during the physical life occurs later in some form. This may be indicated by the reincarnated physical existence in some way or in the non-physical landscapes experienced in the enfolded, unseen after-death dimension.

In this picture, if you harm another sentient life-form, at a deeper level you harm yourself, and though many souls experience a shared reality, we each draw from the deepest levels of mind and create our appropriate non-physical after death reality. These are described in broadly similar terms with individual variations by Spiritualists (who accept spirit descriptions) and near death experiencers alike. As a consequence, if a person spiritualizes their life and lives in harmony with all creatures, then they would potentially create improved physical and non-physical repercussions ranging from the deepest, unseen levels of existence.

Buddhist teachings have much in common with the spiritual philosophy received by Spiritualists from historic spiritual-mediumistic prophets, later spiritually entranced mediums and the near-death experiencers descriptions of the nature of the post-death levels of existence. Religious terminology, such as 'spirit' or 'soul,' can be translated into scientific concepts such as the 'unseen energy' (consciousness) which exists and is described by scientists as implicate, implicit and enfolded.

It is a scientific fact that energy can transmute in form but cannot be destroyed and is therefore eternal. Consequently, all life-forms, including human, animal, marine, bird, reptile, are energy – spirits who are made manifest as matter in the form of physical bodies.

Arguably, the concept of interrelatedness can be understood to have repercussions on a person's understanding of synchronicities. This concept argues that coincidences are not meaningless but the result of the creative flow of the life force, which is the catalyst for growth, with respect to spiritual and physical maturation and evolution.

The holographic analogy is currently building an improved, alternative model for understanding the features and nature of the deepest levels of authentic reality. It explaining and evidencing that there are many levels to the non-physical dimension that lies beyond mundane time and space. This alternative scientific construct of reality can accommodate the whole range of humankind's psychic and mediumistic testimonies.

Previously, materialists felt forced to deny the authenticity of these experiences despite the evidence to the contrary, as they lay outside the boundaries of earlier materialistic, reductionist science. The holographic analogy is born of an improved scientific approach and understanding. It is progressively helping to push forward the frontiers of our understanding of the true, complex, holistic nature of the unseen dimensions of reality.

Talbot underlines the value of the holographic model of understanding:

> ... it suddenly made sense of a wide range of phenomena so elusive they generally have been categorized outside the province of scientific understanding. These include telepathy, precognition, mystical feelings of oneness with the universe and even psychokinesis or the ability of the mind to move physical objects without anyone touching them. Indeed, it quickly became apparent to the ever growing number of scientists who came to embrace the holographic model that it helped explain virtually all paranormal and mystical experiences.[30]

## The Interface Brain and the Archive Interface: Universal Archives

The universal archive theory is described by Professor Archie E. Roy, who kindly wrote the Foreword for this book, giving its message his full support. The model suggested by Roy is the result of his research into astrodynamics, celestial mechanics, archaeo-astronomy, psychical research and neural networks.

Roy presents this theory using the analogy of a computer (further explained below) in which all information is actively stored over the millennia by the 'modem,' despite the actual destruction over the years of successive computers. Roy argues that his model has marked differences from Carl Gustav Jung's concept of the collective unconsciousness.[31]

Jung's concept can be thought of in terms of a psychic repository which has some similarities with the eastern concept of the akashic records,[32] in which all memories or the totality of experiences are stored. The 'archives of the mind' model is different in that it is described as a turbulent, dynamic, ongoing ocean, rather than Jung's passive reservoir, devoid of the continuous existence of life. The active, ongoing nature of the archives of the mind is described as possibly being accessed through a data retrieval or activation system. This may be analogous with the highly charged, emotive love link or that of important unfinished business which intermittently connects surviving discarnate spirit minds with the minds of physically alive mediums.

Roy's theory is survivalist in nature. The concept of the collective unconscious, in terms of Jung's writings, implies that a medium's mind gains telepathic access to mere psychic systems, memories, husks, rather than to surviving personalities. Consequently, there is a profound difference between Jung's collective unconsciousness model and the archives of the mind model.

The universal archive theory is set out in Roy's book *The Archives of the Mind*.[33] His theory is a development of, rather than incompatible with, the eastern belief in the akashic records,[34] the belief in a cosmic reservoir or cosmic consciousness held by William James,[35] and the universal unconsciousness, or collective unconsciousness, developed by Carl Gustav Jung.[36] All of these theories have to some extent the shared concept that there exists a central, universal store of all thoughts and actions, to which those who have developed psychic senses can access.

Roy has presented his alternative yet related model in an attempt to explain how the universal experiences of all creatures, including all perceptions and knowledge, throughout all time, is centrally archived and how this knowledge is accessible to individuals. Through his model Roy hypothesizes an alternative explanatory context for understanding mediumship and other paranormal phenomena.

Roy describes the model as containing 'the totality of experiences, beliefs, fantasies and characteristics belonging to all human beings living or dead.'[37] He continues by contrasting his model with the cosmic reservoir model and states that:

Far from being simply a passive reservoir or repository of the deeds, thoughts and fantasies of mankind from which under suitable conditions excerpts can be made, it appears that the model makes a case on a number of levels for a form of survival … the model suggests that the archives of the mind is not just a cosmic-reservoir with its implications of stillness, of sleeping, of non-active depths; it is rather a cosmic ocean with powerful currents of activity within it.[38]

Roy's theory draws upon the analogy of a person who owns several computers, which over a number of years are repeatedly destroyed by house-fires. All the information contained by the computers would be expected to be utterly lost and inaccessible. However, the computer owner had cautiously always kept a modem, which acted as a central file, as it had repeatedly stored all the information that had also been stored in the lost series of computers.

Consequently, the loss of the physical material of the computers is of no importance to the man, as through the use of the modem he is able to reactivate and call up in totality all the information he has stored over many years.

Roy believes that this analogy helps people understand that we live in an information universe that has a central storage capacity to which everything is connected and is therefore retrievable. It is clearly analogous to the modem. Roy continues the analogy with reference to the human senses and the brain, which he calls the 'Interface Brain,' and its interaction or interface with the universal archives. He describes the interface brain as an area of the brain that converts the flow of electromagnetic vibrations into a range of colors. Roy explains that vibrations in the air are converted by the interface brain into sounds.

Roy used the analogy of a computer hard-drive memory to represent the simplistic brain consisting of conscious perceptions, memory and motor cortex. Analogous to the way electric impulses from neurosensory receptors interface with the brain to produce conscious perceptions and memory, is the input of code via the keyboard into the hard drive and memory of the computer. Similarly, the interchange of information between the memory centers and centers of consciousness give perceptions of world memory and body. There is an exchange of communication between the hard-drive software and the hard-drive memory. Roy has not become embroiled with the concepts of conscious awareness in his model as it is beyond the scope of that particular work.

The conscious perceptions are then interfaced with the subconscious archives of memory and can be represented by the interface of the hard-drive software and memory being interfaced with the local modem memory store. Again, there is an interchange of communication between both the center of conscious perception of memory and archival perceptions from the subconscious archived data store. Similarly, there is an exchange of communication between the local modem and hard drive.

Roy continues to explain how the personal subconscious archive data again is two-way communicated to a universal centrally archived data store from multiple sources throughout time (relating to every living creature). As stated, this theory has equivalences with the beliefs in the existence of the akashic records and the collective unconsciousness, though survival is in a dynamic, ongoing, rather than static memory form.

In Roy's computer analogy, the local modem communicates with a centrally networked archived data store. The central archive data store is accessible by the multiple subconscious archived data systems of all living creatures (human, animal, bird, marine, reptile etc). Similarly, the central archive computer data-store is networked and accessed by multiple modems and their corresponding terminals.

Roy explains mediumship as the gift of certain individuals to access the central archival system of the universal unconsciousness (the collective unconsciousness), through the medium's subconscious archival interface. He explains that this is the reason why many mediums appear to be in an altered state of consciousness or trance when communicating with spirits. A sitter inputs certain keywords or thoughts into the medium's brain. This in turn triggers, through a system of perceptions, a linking or cross-referencing of information held within the central system of the universal archives with the archival system of the medium's subconscious.

In this analogy a medium is like a computer terminal which has an upgraded local modem interface (mediumistic super-sensitivity) which interfaces with the networked central archive data-store, and when certain key thoughts or words are input into the medium's terminal, in-depth cross-referencing is facilitated by networking with the central archive data-store.

Figure 1 (see Appendix) shows the corresponding components of the interfacings between brain, subconscious archive and central archive with the analogous interfacings between terminal modem and networked central data-storage system.

The computer terminal consists of the hard-drive software and the hard-drive memory. This is equivalent to the human brain. The modem has a local memory storage capacity and interfaces with the computer terminal. This is equivalent to the subconscious archive of memory. The internet or worldwide web is networked with multiple hard drives through multiple modems and has equivalences with a dynamic, ongoing form of akashic records or universal unconsciousness. This is better known as the universal archives, which are accessed by the subconscious of all living creatures which represents their archival interfaces.

Roy suggests that:

The archives' fundamental property is to record faithfully. In that sense it is a source of comfort and promise to all. We have seen that those who return or are returned are ordinary people, even very young children, implying that even the briefest, most tragic life of the most insignificant (in worldly terms) human being is automatically and faithfully recorded in a totality utterly beyond our most capable electronic information storage and retrieval systems. No-one is forgotten, the record of their life is not wiped out with the death of their body. In that respect it makes perfect sense of Jesus of Nazareth's assurances to his disciples.

'Are not five sparrows sold for two farthings? Yet not one of these falls to the ground without your heavenly Father noting it.'

Constellations would form based on mutual interests ... just as they do in the normal living world ... Something like the visionary Swedenborg's 'heaven' and 'hell' might evolve, peopled respectively by those who had been loving, selfless and self-sacrificing and those who had been hate-filled, selfish, brutal and corrupt. In some such way, perhaps, would like gravitate to like.[39]

Arguably, it should be equally possible for mediums to also access the consciousness of other physical and non-physical life-forms who exist in our vast universe. Roy is in agreement with this suggestion.

## Summing-Up

Some people deny the existence of the whole range of psychical and mediumistic phenomena despite accumulated evidence to the contrary. Unfortunately, when they cannot fit these phenomena into a meaningful context of understanding, they feel forced to deny their reality.

Partly responsible for this negative reaction is the fact that many people are unaware of the 21st-century explanations that successfully accommodate the phenomena. The two pioneering explanations summarized above help people to understand and integrate the existence of psychical phenomena into their worldview regarding the nature of life.

Perhaps all that is needed is that people accomplish the difficult task of looking at reality from deeper, fresh, more informed perspectives. As we are ever evolving with regard to physical, spiritual and intellectual maturity, knowledge of the grand universal theory (GUT, the theory that explains absolutely everything) may always be beyond our grasp. With physical evolution may come the mediumistic ability for all; most animals have not lost their insightful knowledge into herbs and foods that heal them, and many books have been written as a result of research into the psychic and mediumistic awareness of animals.

We should view human testimonies of transformative spiritual-mediumistic and psychic experiences with the respect they deserve. This should be the enlightened starting point for research into these enigmatic experiences. They have far-reaching implications for the nature of post-mortem survival and the physical lives we lead. Our continued search to formulate a grand universal theory should not detract from observing and respecting the rich variety of phenomena themselves.

However, as already alluded to, it is a fact that all information conveyed, from whatever source, is open to distortion and interpretation at many personal and cultural levels. Consequently, demonstrations of mediumship vary enormously regarding accuracy of information, level of detail, spirituality of content and information about the spirit communicator.

Significantly, the above scientific analogical explanations, Spiritualist and Buddhist views have equivalences with the beliefs of Plato, the eminent Greek philosopher. Plato firmly believed in the continued existence of the soul after physical death with regard to all animals, human and non-human, and all other living creatures.

Plato also believed that souls could transmigrate after death, from the human animal to the non-human animal and vice versa, depending on the lessons the soul wished to learn. It is a fact that some people are far less spiritual than many reported cases of loving, loyal, protective, self-sacrificing, devoted dogs and other animals.

Significantly, if a person chooses to believe in the concept of the static great memory store, the common unconscious, the universal unconscious, this would imply that mediums do not access surviving human and animal spirit personalities. This is markedly different from Roy's model of the surviving store of the minds of all living creatures. It would suggest that mediums access hallucinations with accompanying telepathic content such as their last emotions or thoughts before death, known as husks or psychic and memory systems. These would be associated with the dead but they would not display evidence that the person or animal had survived physical death because they would not hold telepathic conversations with the medium regarding present-day issues in the sitter's life as spirits regularly do.

This subject is different from any other subject as more than a century of psychical research evidence is usually ignored. Opinions on this and related perennial questions regarding the characteristics and purpose of existence are often deeply held and interwoven with a person's deepest psychology and worldviews. Unfortunately, these are shaped by our previously limited science which has given birth to the western materialist, reductionist worldview.

Psychic and mediumistic experiences have repeated themselves across the globe and from the earliest historic stages of human awareness to contemporary times. I will provide an encyclopedic overview of mediumship in the following pages , including an evaluation of its spiritual content and legacy. Mediumistic communications are arguably accessed from the universal archives, allegedly storing the unseen, enfolded, implicate, surviving, ongoing consciousness of all creatures (animal, human and non-human, bird, marine, reptile etc).

## Chapter 3

# Global Mediumship Throughout the Ages

### The Enduring Nature of Mediumship

A large part of this chapter is devoted to giving examples of mediumship, beginning with ancient times and including the four most populated continents. This proves that this enigmatic paranormal phenomenon, which is popular today, is as old as humankind itself. Mediumship (channeling), particularly in the contemporary western world, has a pervasive and historically resilient character. Evidence reveals that it has been variously incorporated into the beliefs and practices of humankind since the beginning of time.

This is demonstrated by the fact that since the dawn of history, all peoples across the world have terms for mediums who apparently receive spirit communications.

Klimo confirms that mediumship

can be found in all times and across all cultures … This universal, enduring and still enigmatic phenomenon has permeated history, providing the wellsprings for virtually every spiritual path. For thousands of years, channelling has tantalized people with the prospect that physical existence is by no means all there is and that the life of mind and spirit is vaster than most have led themselves to believe.

Throughout history and among varied peoples, channels have been named according to what they do. Besides the term *medium* and the more recent *channel*, other names have included shaman, witch doctor, healer and medicine man in native cultures. They have also been called fortune-tellers, oracles, seers, soothsayers, savants and visionaries. In religious contexts, they have been known as priests, gurus, prophets, saints, mystics and holy ones. And in the esoteric schools they are called light workers, initiates, teachers, adepts or masters. The majority of mainstream psychologists and psychiatrists would probably regard these channels as dissociated, delusional, suffering from multiple-personality disorder, schizophrenic or simply as persons with runaway imaginations, or even as downright frauds.[1]

In the following discussion I will clarify the parallels between the historic mediumship found in different cultures and more contemporary mediumship, both of which have provided spiritual insights.

In the ancient world, archaic shamanism was geographically extensive. These were preliterate primitive cultures. Regarding humankind's earlier, prehistoric ancestors, our knowledge of their beliefs and practices is limited.

However, archaeological evidence supports the view that archaic, shamanic cultures echo some of the features of the practices and beliefs of our earliest, prehistoric ancestors. These ancient practices indicate that both prehistoric and archaic shamanic cultures shared the belief that humans and animals make a transition of being at death.

Humankind's earliest beliefs accepted that all creatures continue to survive after death, inhabiting otherworldly realms and that these spirits can communicate with those who inhabit the physical level of existence.

The widespread ancient phenomenon of shamanism was found in particular in North America, Indonesia, Oceania and the expansive wastes of Siberia and Central Asia. Though there were many underlying shared beliefs and practices, regional variations existed. Shamanism is important because there are vast numbers of historical and modern-day reports by observers which describe shamanic paranormal phenomena.

Certainly, our shamanic ancestors probably represent one of the earliest expressions of human psycho-spiritual experiences. These include their apparent communications with humans and animals who have made their transitions at death. As seasoned travelers in the non-physical realms, shamans described their soul-journey exploits, out of the body, to non-physical realms beyond mundane time and space.

Shamans of antiquity developed arduous practices to enhance their ability to attain altered states of consciousness in order to communicate with ostensible, surviving spirit beings. They received knowledge and advice from them for the benefit of both the individual and the tribe. Typically, after an initial initiation process, which frequently involved various forms of life-threatening ordeals, shamans endured many further grueling years cultivating their abilities. Arguably, shamans would have been emotionally, physically and mentally strong with pronounced leadership abilities, self-discipline and passionate dedication.

As a result of their dangerous, daring and lengthy ordeals and years of training, it is believed that they sensitized their sensory perceptions to such levels that they reportedly developed amazing abilities. These included the capacity to access precognitive and retrospective information, gain knowledge of events occurring geographically distant from their physical body, diagnose and heal their patients, and receive advice from non-physical beings. It is reported that they were also proficient in conducting soul-journey visits to the diverse levels or landscapes implicit in the otherworldly realms.

The ancient experiences, beliefs and practices of archaic shamanic cultures have parallel features with mediumistic experiences that have been repeated and described over the centuries and echo present-day mediumship. Shamanic cultures still exist in the contemporary world although they are represented in far fewer numbers.

Shamans cultivated altered states of consciousness in order to communicate with the inhabitants of the non-physical realms. They were familiar with these non-material landscapes. Their spiritual philosophy and beliefs in the after-life were born of these mediumistic experiences. Reports of such shamanic psychic and mediumistic activities have been confirmed by more contemporary researchers into anthropology.

Shamans have been mentioned here in order to set them in their early historic context. Later chapters will discuss shamanic paranormal exploits in specific detail.

## Ancient Egyptian Examples of Mediumship

The following discussion gives examples of mediumship (channeling) in ancient Egypt. Robert Masters[2] is renowned for his research into ancient Egyptian paranormal and mystical phenomena. He and his partner Jean Houston are directors of The Foundation for Mind Research in Pomana, New York, and Jean Houston is also a psychologist and philosopher. Masters states that ancient Egypt 'is where, as far as we know, the use of trance in achieving mystical states and talking to the gods really began.'[3]

Masters believes that Sekhmet, who was believed by the ancient Egyptians to be a god, has repeatedly communicated through a number of his patients. His experiences of his patients' mediumship are remarkable and thought-provoking. It is incredible that both the faculty of mediumship and the same apparent ancient spirit communicator have spanned the millennia.

Masters believes that the character and content of these messages correlate with ancient reports of communications with this historic Egyptian spirit or archetype. Hypnosis was used as a means of helping the clients relax into an altered state of consciousness, symbolically opening the door of the mind to facilitate communication from alleged non-physical beings.

The resplendent pharaonic Egyptian empire endured for approximately 5,000 years dating from 5000 BC. This powerful and pervasive culture was deeply rooted in the conviction that life continues after the cessation of physical life. Many ancient Egyptian beliefs can be found in one of the Egyptian mortuary manuals known as The Egyptian Book of the Dead.[4]

> The early Egyptians saw *du* or breath, as the vital principle, which at death could separate from the body and become *ba* or spirit. *Du* was the embodied soul; *ba* was the disembodied spirit. They also believed in a third, weaker aspect, the *ka*, a kind of etheric subtle-energy version of the physical body.[5]

In common with other historical and geographically widespread examples of mediumship, the ancient Egyptians believed that communication with recognizable surviving spirit communicators could be accessed during the sleep state. The sleep state is recognized as an altered state of consciousness. The Classical Egyptian writings known as the Instructions from Merikare, dated at 2100 BC, prove the ancient Egyptian belief that diverse information, including knowledge of future events, can be delivered through dreams.[6]

Amenhotep IV, otherwise known as Akhenaten, apparently received spiritual illumination and philosophy from a non-physical communicator whom he deified. The receipt of these spiritually inspirational messages cumulatively fostered his monotheistic spiritual insights. In turn these gave rise to Akhenaten's revolutionary spiritual teachings regarding the compassionate nature and singularity of God. Incredibly, Akhenaten's descriptions of God are believed to have been copied and used in Psalm 104 in the Christian Bible.

It has tremendous significance that he chose the name Aten, meaning the Sun-god, to name his non-physical spirit communicator. The sun radiates out an intensely bright light not dissimilar to that observed by near-death experiencers. Perhaps Akhenaten, like near-death experiencers, witnessed a bright light when he communicated with his non-material spiritual teacher. The light of the sun is also associated with life, growth and healing, without which all would die. Akhenaten's apparent otherworldly receipt of revelations from a spirit communicator made him the first known person in history to teach humanity that there is only one God.

The following writings were discovered on a papyrus believed to have been written at the time of Jesus Christ of the Christian New Testament. They tell of a woman's sighting of a non-physical being whom she described as the god Imhotep-Asclepius. The woman was apparently the mother of a Greek who fell ill while they were together in Egypt:

'A divine and terrifying vision came to her. There was someone whose height was more than human, clothed in shining raiment and carrying in his left hand a book.'[7]

## Ancient Chinese Examples of Mediumship

The ancient Chinese also believed that life continued after physical death and that contact could be made between surviving spirit beings and those in the physical body. The exact nature of that existence, and the whereabouts of that non-physical domain, remained unclear in their thinking and terminology. They used the term *kuei* to describe the soul or spirit aspect of the constitution which they believed survived physical death.

Translated, the term *kuei* also meant 'to return' and was also thought of in terms of the breath, namely, *ch'i* or *p'o* and *ming*, which significantly means 'light.' Similarities between these ancient Chinese beliefs can be found in the ancient Egyptian beliefs reflected in their term *du*, which also meant 'breath.'

The ancient Chinese believed that during sleep the soul left the physical body. They used the term *wu* to describe shamanic individuals who could go into an altered state of consciousness and have non-physical spirits communicate through them. Due to the varying depths of trance experienced, the *wu* would only sometimes be aware of the information and conversations that were conveyed through them during their trance state.

Klimo confirms that: 'Early historical Chinese reports contain descriptions of channeling-like communication from such souls.'[8] This point is substantiated by the fact that the most ancient reference to the use of an instrument similar to the relatively modern day planchette is described by the Chinese of 4,000 years ago. Through thee movements of this piece of wood, this ancient planchette spelled out messages on materials or in the sand that were apparently communicated by surviving spirits to humankind. This instrument appears to be the forerunner of the modern-day divining rod, which points out directions and is commonly used to discover water.

It is likely that this ancient instrument of communication was also the ancestor of automatic writing or automatism. This is a process whereby a medium typically enters into an altered state of consciousness and allows their mind or hand to be used by alleged unseen spirit communicators to write or type messages in order to guide and speak to humankind. Different mediums work at various speeds and produce information of differing lengths and quality.

The writings of Wang Ch'ung in the 1st century AD prove that mediumship was practiced in China at this time. He said: 'Among men the dead speak through living persons whom they throw into a trance: and the wu, thrumming their black chords, call down the souls of the dead, which then speak through the mouths of the wu.'[9]

Fluency with mediumship is evident during the Han Dynasty.

[The] Emperor Wu was known to consult a female wu whose source was a princess no longer in the physical world: Her message was written down and thereafter became the law. In 825, the ruler Li-Hsiang was told by a female wu: 'I am a spectre-seer who can summon spirits by calling them hither ... [some] have a vital spirit which is so vigorous and healthy it enables them to speak with men from time to time ... [others are] so exhausted that they are obliged to employ me as their mouthpiece.'[10]

Mediumship and mediumistic trance phenomena, which are

observed and researched today in the 21st century, many millennia later, have been shown by the above examples to have been practiced in the ancient Egyptian and Chinese cultures.

## Ancient Japanese Examples of Mediumship

The earliest writings that can be found regarding trance mediumship in Japan date back to the 8th century AD. However, it is probable that it was practiced before this date.[11] Significantly, these writings discuss life in Japan at a time when it was believed that gods visited the Japanese. (Non-physical communicators, namely spirits, were often confused with gods, they were called gods due to their non-human nature).

In Japan's great national shrine of Ise there is a temple that was built to honor 'Rough August Soul.' This name refers to the Sun Goddess who again is significantly associated with the bright, intense light of the sun. Importantly, this goddess was perceived as having a certain fluidity of form. This was due to the conviction that this spirit communicator, known as an otherworldly goddess, temporarily took on the physical form of the entranced medium during communications with the people.

Japanese empresses, those affiliated to the emperor's court (the *kan-nagi*) and those found in the countryside (*kuchiyose*), are further early historic examples of people demonstrating mediumistic and trance communications with spirits. It was believed that these mediums became entranced, with their whole persona being overshadowed by a visiting spirit communicator, in order to convey messages through them to the people.

The esoteric order known as the Shingon Sect was established in Japan during the 8th century AD. This school was a branch of Shintoism. Its members were renowned for their use of mediumship in order to access spiritual philosophy and knowledge about the future from otherworldly, spiritually orientated spirit communicators.

Historically, apparent spirit communicators were often described as gods due to their otherworldly nature. This fact will be explored further in later chapters, with particular reference to ancient biblical descriptions of mediumistic practices associated with witnessed communications with and physical manifestations of Yahweh. Over the millennia, the names 'God' and 'Yahweh' have been used interchangeably due to suppression of the facts and later ignorance. Yahweh has thus become confused with the concept of God, who does not speak and manifest in this way in front of countless people.

The writings of the ancient Israelites report that, on a regular basis, Yahweh verbally communicated with members of his chosen people and manifested his presence. Similar to the biblical references to communications from the god Yahweh, the Japanese believed that the otherworldly being(s) who allegedly spoke through their entranced mediums were also gods (*Nakaza*).

It is significant that since ancient times our ancestors bequeathed the status of god upon otherworldly communicators who apparently utilized mediumistic practices in order to convey their messages. Those beings who communicated through the medium were deemed to be sufficiently different from physical mortals, supported by parnormal, mediumistic experiences of them, arguably fuelled the conviction that they had an otherworldly origin, habitat and nature.

Consequently, these non-physical communicators were afforded the honors and respect given to gods. If these communicators were people who had made their transition from the physical to non-physical spheres after death, then they were indeed human ancestors. Then, in a sense, it is fair to say that the reputed ancient Japanese religious beliefs associated with ancestor worship originated with spirit communications through ancient Japanese mediums.

## Ancient Indian Examples of Mediumship

The research contained in the book *Spiritism and the Cult of the Dead in Antiquity*[12] proves that from the earliest times the Indians practiced forms of trance mediumship. The beings with whom entranced Indian mediums consorted were many and varied. Depending on the personalities exhibited by these spirit communicators during these entranced communications, they were graded in terms of greater and lesser gods and otherworldly good and evil beings. The ancient Indians feared that evil spirit communicators possessed the power and desire to take long-term control over the medium's mind and body. Highly respected academics have investigated this phenomenon in modern times.

Importantly, some eastern spiritual beliefs regarding spiritual evolution and reincarnation were almost certainly received through mediumship. Notably, these beliefs echo Spiritualist spiritual philosophy, obtained through spiritually orientated mediumistic communications. Eastern spiritual beliefs indicate that the rightfully earned, future, reincarnated body, attained through the processes of the perfect justice of karmic law, would be found in the next incarnation or life span of every animal, human and non-human.

The reincarnated body is believed to be dependent upon the degree of spiritual evolution previously earned by each soul. A particular animal body, human or non-human, may be chosen before birth to become the vehicle from which an individual is destined to, or chooses to, experience life. Each physical body chosen, provides a unique vantage point, offering opportunities to enhance every creatures' spiritual growth or that of others they are destined to be associated with.

The medium known as Madame H.P. Blavatsky founded the Theosophical Society in 1875 in New York City after her extensive travel in India. The society was originally established in order to study eastern religions and science. Blavatsky advanced the belief in a number of successively rarefied levels of body and modes of being (otherworldly realms).

Each of these was successively further beyond the physical world of matter. Consequently, Theosophists believe that the constitution of all living creatures develops over time into increasingly rarefied, finer and more subtle bodies, ranging from the physical to the non-physical or etheric in nature. These teachings have much in common with Spiritualist beliefs and the teachings of Emanuel Swedenborg.

Blavatsky believed that she was in receipt of communications from spirits who confirmed to her that reincarnation is a reality and is one possible option for a creature's soul during its journey towards progressive of spiritual evolution. Many of Blavatsky's teachings can be found in her book *Isis Unveiled*[13] and in *Man and His Bodies* by Annie Besant.[14]

## Ancient Greek Examples of Mediumship

There was widespread use of mediums in ancient Greece, where it was common practice to visit a medium in order to receive spirit communications offering guidance and advice to individuals. A great deal of information about mediumship can be traced to the Greek Thracian Dionysian cults of the 6th century BC. Significantly, the ancient Greeks demonstrate the same pattern of behavior as other cultures in deifying their ethereal communicators.

They believed that spiritually elevated spirit communicators were gods or demi-gods who wished to nurture humankind's spiritual growth. Non-physical messengers were called *angelos* (angels) and similarly the term *daimon* (later 'daemon' and 'demon') was originally used to describe communicators who were perceived to be divine spirit beings.

Pythagoras, Plato, Plotinus and Heraclitus were among those esteemed philosophers and polymaths whose doctrines and practices supported the mediumistic Orphic, Dionysian and Eleusian schools of thought. Advocates of these schools of thought sought contact with otherworldly beings due to their experience-based belief that they would progressively gain spiritual knowledge from these spirit communicators.

Pythagoras, Plato, Plotinus and Heraclitus used communications received through mediumship in order to learn spiritual philosophy and contribute to humankind's spiritual progress and knowledge base. They believed that the more advanced spiritual philosophy humanity received, the more it would serve to emancipate all creatures from the endless wheel of rebirth. Spiritual knowledge would restore all creatures to their rightful and original home in the heavenly landscapes.

In the book *Theagetes*[15] Plato discussed the spiritual communications he believed were received from spirits. Plato also discussed Socrates' conviction that Socrates could hear clairaudiently; the guidance, he believed, came from the voice of a demi-god. Socrates claimed the spirit communicator offered him advice that he could choose to follow or not.

As a result of his research, D.C. Knight believes that the ancestor of the Ouija board, which is used today to make contact with spirits, was used in ancient Greece. The Ouija board is best described as an overturned glass which is placed on a board. Around the perimeter of the board sits every letter of the alphabet. People sit next to one another around the perimeter of the table and the board. Each person is asked to keep one single finger on the overturned moving glass. It is believed that spirit energy moves the glass to the relevant letters, spelling out spirit communications.

Knight has proven that Pythagoras and Philolaus in 540 BC used the ancestor of the Ouija board to make contact with spirit communicators. These geniuses learnt many things from these communications, including information concerning the nature of existence after death and spiritual philosophy. They used a 'mystic table, moving on wheels, which glided toward signs, which the philosopher and his pupil Philolaus interpreted to the audience as being revelations supposedly from the unseen world.'[16]

The esteemed ancient Greek philosophers claimed that they also obtained predictive knowledge about future events from spirit communicators. The name for 'prophecy' in Greece was *manteia*. Today, the terms 'akashic records,' the 'universal unconscious' or the 'universal mind' are used to describe the possible storehouse of all past, present and future knowledge.

Some people believe that this is what is accessed when mediums demonstrate accurate knowledge of past, present or future events; Their abilities are deemed authentic when it is known that they had no other way of knowing this information. Some individuals describe this fund of all knowledge as the Divine God. They believe God permeates all realms and all creatures (is omnipresent), omniscient (all-knowing) and omnipotent (all-powerful). Mediums believe that they make contact with spirits who give them information about a person's life or world events; Arguably, these spirits, being non-physical, are out of time and space, in a non-material realm and therefore able to access past and future information.

Many mediums conduct meditative training in order to heighten, sensitize and alter their state of consciousness. For other mediums these states occur spontaneously at will. Some mediums believe that knowledge about the past and future is given to them by spirits, for others, this information is gained psychically. The early Greeks visited mediums – this was considered to be both normal and popular. They believed that sincere spirit communicators, some of whom might have been 'deceased' relatives, guided them through difficulties and provided information about future events, all of which they were at liberty to accept or decline.

The Orphic School of thought gave rise to oracles, who were ancient mediums (alternatively known as seers, prophets and shamans). These mediumistic men and women frequently lived solitary lives in caves and were visited throughout each day by countless individuals who often traveled great distances to see them.

Oracles often gave information when they were in trance. Usually they were unaware of what was communicated through them as frequently spirit communicators spoke directly through them. This practice is a form of physical mediumship known today as 'direct-voice trance mediumship.'

The following historic example of mediumship has many parallels with the experiences of modern-day mediums and their observers, proving that this practice has changed little throughout the centuries.

> The pythia [female medium] at Delphi received her inspiration in historic times from Apollo ... [She] became ecstatic by inhaling a vapor that rose through a fissure in the earth ... the god penetrated her body and forced her to yield to his guidance ... the divine afflatus ... she succumbed and uttered words that were not her own but those of the one who controlled her.[17]

Finally, muses (spirit communicators) as depicted in Greek literature, were described as being otherworldly goddesses who inspired and enhanced the creative pursuits of mediumistic people. People sought to attune themselves to muses, resulting in the production of the finest of the creative arts, including poetry, painting, music and song. This is another example of the belief echoed throughout the ages that psychically sensitive mediumistic individuals can receive inspiration of the highest order through communication with those spirits who wish to share their abilities or gain spiritual advancement by enhancing those of others.

These apparent inspirers from otherworldly spheres may or may not have lived physical lives on earth. Notably, a number of famous musical composers such as Amadeus Mozart claimed they heard wonderful musical symphonies in their heads and they simply wrote it down as dictation. This would suggest that they were mediumistic, creative psychic sensitives, whose abilities were enhanced by those in the non-material spheres.

## Historic Middle-Eastern Examples of Mediumship

The ancient Babylonians and Assyrians[18] are further examples of nations whose people regularly visited mediums, believing that they received communications from those who had survived physical death. Their channels or mediums known as priestesses received spiritually enlightened information including guidance and knowledge of future events to help all those who visited them. Research proves that the practice of mediumship in these ancient times was widespread and that repeatedly throughout different cultures the spirit communicator was called a god.

The prophet known as Zoroaster was born between the 10th and 6th centuries BC and founded the religion known as Zoroastrianism. He was convinced that non-physical celestial, angelic or spirit communicators gave him the spiritual writings known as the Avesta Text. Significantly, the religion of Zoroastrianism was based upon these spiritually orientated communications. These spiritual chronicles describe life in the non-physical realms and offer spiritual guidance on how a person might live their physical earthly life according to more spiritual principles. This is a further demonstration of the on-going belief found throughout history, that spiritual knowledge and guidance can be received through spiritually orientated communications from otherworldly beings who inhabit an alternative, implicit, unseen realm of existence.

Similarly, during the 7th century AD the Saudi Arabian prophet Muhammad received a succession of spiritual revelations from an angelic figure he believed was named Gabriel. They commenced with the simple command to recite, and descriptions indicate that Muhammad recited spontaneously, while shaking in an entranced condition.

His words were later recorded in a number of religious texts, of which only one was permitted to remain, and that version was later compiled into the holy book named the Koran. Muhammad founded the revealed religion of Islam based upon these spiritual revelatory communications. He supplemented these communications with his own teachings which he formulated while living in the religious community which he established in Medina.

Due to the belief that it was an angel who delivered the Koran mediumistically to humankind, many Muslims believe that this beautiful, poetic literary work is the pure word of God – a belief reinforced by the fact that Muhammad was illiterate. Scholars the world over describe the Koran as a literary masterpiece.

Many Muslims around the world memorize and recite the whole or part of the Koran in Arabic, even though for many it is a foreign language, as they feel they are speaking the words of God. Significantly, in the early days there were a number of versions of the Koran which have been lost today.

Muhammad, the mediumistic prophet who founded Islam based on mediumistic communications had mediumship in common with other historic spiritual prophets. Akin to countless mediums today and those throughout the centuries, he also received spiritual guidance in the form of visionary and verbal communications during the sleep state, which is an altered state of consciousness. The Arabs used the term *jinn* to describe spirits who they believed communicated with physical beings on earth or attempted to manipulate them.

## 7th to 12th Century Examples of Mediumship

Many European paintings from the 7th century onwards provide colorful and graphic scenes publicizing the early belief in two spirits known as *incubi* and *succubi*. They were portrayed as being spiritually unevolved, malevolent personalities who inhabited the non-physical realms and preyed on emotionally vulnerable individuals. It was believed that these spirits could either manipulate or fully possess and control people.

By this time the Christian church had become a harsh, powerful institution. Under its authority, organized inquisitions tortured people who sought to maintain their own spiritual independence and freedom of thought and practice. Such people followed the centuries-old global tradition of using mediums to make direct contact with spiritually orientated spirit or angelic communicators. They did not want to blindly obey the fickle political and religious dogmas propagated by the institutionalized church.

Any individual suspected of practicing mediumship in order to gain information of future events or non-institutionalized spiritual philosophy, including knowledge of healing and herbal remedies, was branded an evil heretic. Mediumship gave great emotional strength to the public, guiding them through difficulties and giving them knowledge of the future. This enabled people to stand their ground and think for themselves. Consequently, mediums were seen as rival spiritual leaders and healers who challenged the authority of the people at the head of the institutionalized church. The public were taught to fear mediums, who were branded witches and wizards. Brainwashing campaigns were carried out to stop the general public consulting mediums. People were told that mediums worked for the devil when they contacted the dead. Yet visiting mediums has been a normal and popular practice since the dawn of humankind, evidenced by the global and historic examples already given.

Even among members of the institutionalized Christian church, accounts of nuns and monks exhibiting psychic and mediumistic abilities were not uncommon. Research has uncovered reports from these early times of mediumistic clergy who not only accessed knowledge of the future and spiritual philosophy but were also gifted with the ability to levitate.

To provide a 7th-century example, prophetic information was received through the mediumship of Odile of France. Significantly, this woman was made a saint for her mediumship rather than being condemned for it. Odile was not classed as a heretic as a result of her abilities to channel information from the non-physical world to this. This case underlines the unstable religio-political attitudes and vicissitudes of the leaders of institutionalized religion regarding mediumistic people, some of whom will be shown to be prophets who received spiritual philosophy and made a profound contribution to humankind.

The following is one of Saint Odile's predictions: 'The time is come when Germany shall be called the most bellicose upon the earth. The epoch is arrived when from her bosom shall arise the terrible man who shall make war on the world.'[19]

Two 12th-century examples of mediums who were convinced that they received communications from spirits or angels, including knowledge of future events, are the famous prophetic advisor to King Arthur known as Merlin,[20] and Saint Hildegarde of Bingen. Saint Hildegarde recorded for future generations everything that was communicated to her by what she believed was a spirit or angelic voice.

Significantly, the Pope of that time, Eugene II, believed the information she received was profoundly spiritual and declared these writings to be the authentic word of God rather than that of celestial beings. Here is another example of celestial communications being confused with the word of God, who is not known to speak face to face in this way.[21]

## 15th to 16th Century Examples of Mediumship

Five 15th and 16th century examples of mediumship follow. Joan of Arc[22] was a child when she first believed that she could hear spirit or angelic voices offering her guidance and instruction. She was finally asked by the voices to lead the French military against the English troops to prevent a possible English invasion of France.

Joan had an amazingly strong faith in the guidance the voices offered, as it was unheard of for a young, physically weak girl to request that she lead the French soldiers into battle. She had much in common with the young boy named David who fought the giant of a man named Goliath (accounts of this can be found in the Christian biblical Old Testament).

The soldiers who followed Joan, the young girl who believed she could protect France against her enemies, must have felt it strange to follow this frail woman into battle. Joan must therefore have generated great belief in her sincerity and leadership as directed by her voices. These communicating voices had apparently decided to protect the French against English incursions. Importantly, if the church leaders and military had had the slightest doubt in Joan's authenticity, they would have ridiculed her and would never have given her mission a second thought.

Over time, Joan lost favor with the institutionalized French and English church leaders. Perhaps both feared her growing reputation as a possible alternative leader who led armies and spoke with spirit communicators. Others, perhaps for political reasons, took the view that the spirit communicators must be evil yet they certainly did not oppose the bloodshed the forthcoming warfare would bring. Joan was asked to deny that she heard voices, which she bravely refused to do and was finally burned alive by the English after she was betrayed by some of her own countrymen. However, all recorded history knows Joan the medium as Saint Joan of Arc.

Mother Shipton is a second example of mediumship in the 15th century. This medium is of particular importance due to the accuracy of her poetic prophecies. Most of her predictions had actually occurred by the 21st century. Shipton predicted the advent of the motor vehicle, she described them and the accidents vehicles would cause. Shipton predicted the invention of iron boats that would float on water and of other vehicles that would fly. Amazingly, she also predicted that thoughts would travel across the globe. Telephones, faxes and computer email and internet prove the accuracy of this prophecy.[23]

The third and fourth examples of mediumship include two Spanish Christian mystics who lived in the 15th century. As mediums they believed that spirits or angels spoke to them. They are known as Saint Teresa of Avila and Saint John of the Cross. Saint Teresa states in her book *The Interior Castle*: 'I commend myself to the Holy Spirit and by Him from this point onward to speak for me.'[24]

The writings of Saint John of the Cross are characterized by his wish to please the institutionalized Christian church and at the same time to recognize the spiritual philosophy that was obtained through the widespread use of mediumship. To pacify the church he sought a compromise. He argued that the source of all otherworldly communications is ultimately communication from the Holy Spirit, a view that has shaped church attitudes to this day.

He explains: 'Although it is the spirit itself that works as an instrument, the Holy Spirit oftentimes aids it to produce and form those true reasonings, words and conceptions. And thus it utters them to itself as though to a third person.'[25]

The fifth example of mediumship from the same era is that of Michel de Nostradamus. Nostradamus believed that he received instructions from his spirit or angel guide, enabling him to provide accurate prophetic information to many European leaders of his day. Charles Ward's writings in 1555 talk of Nostradamus's conversation with his son, explaining his belief that his prophetic knowledge had its origins in the Divine: 'But the perfect knowledge of causes cannot be acquired without divine inspiration; since all prophetic inspiration derives its first motive principle from God the creator ... For the human understanding, being intellectually created, cannot penetrate occult causes.'[26]

Nostradamus's belief is similar to that found in the biblical Old and New Testaments. Here, all invisible communicators offering spiritual knowledge are called spirits, angels, the Lord and God. To ward off the dangerous wrath of the institutionalized church of his day, Nostradamus disguised or cloaked the predictions he received in his writings.

## 17th to 18th Century Examples of Mediumship

The Englishman George Fox began to hear an otherworldly spiritually elevated voice communicating with him around 1642. He can therefore be described as being a clairaudient medium. Fox took the personal view that the communications he heard were from God – or at least this is what he taught. He may have taken this approach to avoid the wrath of the church. Fox's beliefs may alternatively have been shaped by the 17th century institutionalized church which was the lone voice on such matters at that time.

Notably, Fox akin to Nostradamus, would have had to tread very carefully to avoid antagonizing the powerful church leaders as most free thinkers who opposed their dogmas and edicts had been silenced by that time. As has been shown, throughout history and the world, people describe spirit and angelic communicators as a god or God. This has been the case because either they have little or no knowledge about life continuing after death and that it is possible to see and hear surviving spirits and angels or as a means of self-protection from hostile religious authorities.

The spiritual guidance received from Fox's communicators gave birth to yet another religion, that known as the Quakers or the Friends. To firmly establish the divine origins of the voice heard, when conveying spiritual teachings, Fox generally used the phrase: 'The Lord opened unto me ...'.[27]

Just as Fox and others before him believed that the communicator who gave them spiritual philosophy was God or gods, so did the ancient Semite Hebrews who called their communicator 'Yahweh.' Future discussions will explore the accounts of biblical Old and New Testament prophets in the mediumistic context, suggesting that spirit or angelic communicators have frequently had the intention of guiding humankind spiritually forward.

The 18th century gave birth to several highly regarded mediums. Some were important sources of advice for the kings, queens and aristocracy of their day due to the accuracy of their mediumistic and precognitive guidance. Cagliostro and Cazotte of France believed that their knowledge of the future was received through their communications from spirits who advised them of the forthcoming French Revolution.[28] The Hungarian Prince Rakoczy, known as the Comte de Saint Germaine, is another historical example of mediumship.

## Emanuel Swedenborg

Emanuel Swedenborg was a highly respected 18th-century scientist and scholar. He had many interests and was a prolific writer of approximately 100 books, on physics, mineralogy, anatomy and psychology. Consequently, many religious authorities have great respect for Swedenborg's writings which describehis profound, spiritually transformative experiences of the many levels inherent in the non-physical realms and his communications with its non-physical inhabitants.

At the age of 56, Swedenborg began to undergo two types of mediumistic experience. He was taken in an out-of-body state to visit the many hierarchical levels of the after-death realms, where he met animal spirits, both human and animal. This type of experience has close parallels with the shamanic journeys known as soul-journeys and with astral traveling or out-of-the-body experiences. At other times, non-physical communicators, whom he called spirits and angels, spoke with him and taught him while he was in his physical, earthly surroundings.

There are close parallels between Swedenborg's spiritually orientated mediumistic experiences and those of ancient shamans, biblical prophets and contemporary mediums. Many prophets and mediums believe that they have received spiritual philosophy and knowledge about life after death. The writings of Paul in the Christian New Testament[29] show that he was familiar with mediumship. He describes the ability to receive communications from non-physical communicators as possessing the 'gifts of the spirit.'

Swedenborg's prolific visionary and clairaudient experiences gave him knowledge of the celestial and infernal landscapes that all creatures go to after physical death. He also learned that all creatures live physical lives so that they can evolve spiritually and that the type of actions and thoughts that are prevalent during our physical lives determine which non-physical landscape we will be drawn to after physical death.

The elevated spiritual philosophy which he believed he received from spirits and angels offers a further example of a religion being born of spirit communications. These communications gave birth to the religion of Spiritualism and to a church in Swedenborg's own name dedicated to the teachings he received.

For Spiritualists, Swedenborg became a further spiritual father much in the same way as the prophet Abraham is for the Jews (Spiritualists also accept Abraham as a spiritual father). Swedenborg's theological writings were first documented in 1760 and the first English translation of his work was published in 1778 in London. He believed that spirits and angels spoke to him regularly and that the conversations lasted for a considerable time. When reading his works, a person regularly finds statement such as: 'I have several times talked with angels about this matter ...'[30]

Swedenborg questioned his spirit and angel communicators regarding the Christian churches' teachings regarding the Trinity – which involves the Father, Son and Holy Ghost, were these articles of faith correct? Swedenborg received a reply, and wrote: 'They have constantly declared that in heaven they are unable to distinguish the Divine into three, because they know and perceive that the Divine is one and that it is one in the Lord.'[31]

When Swedenborg asked about the nature of heaven and its spirit inhabitants he was told:

> The angels taken collectively are called heaven, because they constitute heaven but yet it is the Divine proceeding from the Lord which inflows with the angels and is received by them that make heaven in general and in part. The Divine proceeding from the Lord is the good of love and the truth of faith. To the extent, therefore, that they receive good and truth from the Lord, in that measure they are angels and in that measure they are heaven.[32]

Swedenborg also learned that: 'They say that not only everything good and true is from the Lord but everything of life as well ... Similarly, all things continue in existence, for continuing in existence is a perpetual coming into existence...'[33]

As a result of his questions about the nature of heaven Swedenborg was told:

> As there are infinite varieties in heaven and no one society, nor

even any one angel is exactly like any other, there are in heaven general, specific and particular divisions. The general division is into two kingdoms, the specific into three heavens and the particular into innumerable societies ... They are termed kingdoms because heaven is called the kingdom of God.[34]

Because of this difference between the angels of the celestial kingdom and the angels of the spiritual kingdom they are not together nor do they associate with each other. They are able to communicate only through intermediate angelic societies which are called celestial-spiritual.[35]

Swedenborg painstakingly documented the spiritual knowledge he learned from his communicators. As a result of his soul-journey excursions to the many celestial and infernal after death landscapes he documents these realms to edify future generations. This information can be found in Swedenborg's books.

These include *Principles of Nature*,[36] *Death and After*,[37] *Heaven and Its Wonders and Hell* (the common English title is *Heaven and Hell*),[38] *Arcana Coelestia*[39] and *Divine Love and Wisdom*.[40] In his book *Emanuel Swedenborg: Essential Readings*[41] Michael Stanley summarizes Swedenborg's experience-based teachings.

Swedenborg learned that the institutionalized Christian church was wrong to break away from direct mediumistic communications with spiritually elevated spirits and angels whose constant role is to nurture and develop humankind's spiritual knowledge. Swedenborg learned that this was a tremendous loss for the organized church as it had set up barriers obstructing communications with celestial spiritually advanced teachers.

## 19th Century Examples of Mediumship

Joseph Smith and Miki Nakayama are 19th century mediums who founded religious movements based on the teachings they received from spiritually elevated spirits and angels.

## The medium Jopseph Smith founder of the Mormon Church

Joseph Smith (1805–1844) was an American medium who founded a religious movement based upon the spiritual information he believed he received from an angel named Moroni, in 1830 in New York state. As a result of these communications Smith[42] established the Church of Jesus Christ of the Latter-day Saints (also known as the Mormon Church).

The communications from the celestial messenger Maroni commenced in 1827 in New York and were initially observed by others. The Mormons believe that Smith, through celestial guidance, found and translated divinely inspired records regarding the early history and religion of America. This is known as the Book of Mormon, which, supplemented by Smith's writings and the Bible, forms the Mormon scriptures.

Smith wanted Mormon converts to live together in Ohio and Missouri, rebuilding Zion, the Promised Land, in the American west. However, persecution and hostilities between Mormons and non-Mormons broke out and Smith was murdered in 1844 by Illinois militiamen. In 1847 the Mormons established their headquarters in Salt Lake City, Utah, where their chief Temple is situated.

Members of this religious movement believe they are the chosen people; who together with the Native American Indians are the descendants of the tribes of Israel who migrated to North America before the birth of Christ. They believe that their religion was founded upon and continues to be fed by highly ethical spiritual philosophy received by their mediumistic leaders from spiritually advanced spirits and/or angels.

Church members are known for their discipline, orderliness, activism, enthusiastic proselytism and high moral standards. However, in the earlier years they allowed polygamy, which was abolished in 1890. They are also characterized by their exercise of political, secular and commercial control of the state of Utah.

This religion has a lay priesthood, which in turn is organized into local units known as 'stakes', consisting of 4,000–5,000 members, led by presidents who supervise religious practice, social activities and numerous welfare activities.

There are approximately 3 million members of the Mormon Church today, the majority of whom live in the United States of America. Many people today would be surprised to learn that so many religious movements have been founded as a result of a spiritual philosophy obtained through communications with spiritually elevated spirit and angelic communicators.

## The Japanese medium Miki Nakayama (Tenrikyo sect)

Miki Nakayama (1798–1887) was a young Japanese medium who became entranced for three days, during which she received spiritual philosophy that gave birth to a further religious movement. The Tenrikyo school of thought was a branch of an ancient Shingon movement which had, itself, earlier branched off from Shintoism.

The Tenrikyo and Shingon sects were both deeply involved in mediumistic practices due to their beliefs that communications from the non-physical world gave them profound spiritual guidance. The Tenrikyo sect, who worshipped a god named Tenri, claimed that Nakayama had been divinely inspired and had acted as a mouthpiece for this god.[43] It is significant that throughout the centuries and the world apparent communicator from the non-physical world are often described as a god. Significantly, akin to Nakayama, mediums from the earliest times including the shamanic epoch, have experienced trance communications.

## The medium Andrew Jackson Davis

Andrew Jackson Davis is another interesting spiritual mediumistic figure of the 19th century. Davis believed that he was in receipt of spiritually orientated communications from spirits and angels. This famous medium is recognized as a prophet in the religion known as Spiritualism. Davis is known as the father of the American Lyceum Movement, which is closely associated with Spiritualism. Due to the large amount of accurate predictive information he received, he is also known as the Poughkeepsie Seer. This fact could indicate that he was both a medium and a psychic.

Davis was born on 11 August 1826 at Blooming Grove, Orange County, in the state of New York. His alleged mediumistic abilities surfaced through the use of mesmerism, otherwise known as hypnotism. He believed that Swedenborg, who had died 50 years earlier, was one of the many spirits who communicated with him. Another notable communicator was Galen, an ancient Greek healer. Davis's five volumes of writing are known as *The Great Harmoni* and are summarized by W.H. Evans in his book *Twelve Lectures on the Harmonial Philosophy of A.J. Davis.*[44]

Stating the objectives of Davis's work, Evans wrote at Merthyr Tydfil in 1924: 'The mission ... of the Harmonial Philosophy is the destruction of all antagonism between science, philosophy and theology; and the harmonization of the elements and the attributes of the human soul and consequently to accomplish the millennial union of social interests.'[45]

Of Davis, Evans writes:

From his earliest days he was subject to visions and was at times conscious of the nearness of the unseen world ... [Some years later, in the] magnetic [hypnotized] condition Davis exhibited such remarkable powers of clairvoyance that all who attended the séance were astounded. For a long time he exercised his powers for healing purposes and was surprisingly successful.[46]

Of Davis's mediumship, it is reported that at intervals, during altered states of consciousness, he spoke in the ancient Hebrew language – a fact confirmed by a professor of linguistics.[47] The famous writer and psychical researcher known as Sir Arthur Conan Doyle wrote down for future generations Davis's prophecy that the religion of Spiritualism would be born:

It is a truth that spirits commune with one another while one is in the body and the other is in the higher spheres – and this, too, when the person in the body is unconscious of the influx and hence cannot be convinced of the fact; and this truth will ere long present itself in the form of a living demonstration. And the world will hail with delight the ushering-in of that era when the interiors of men will be opened and the spiritual communion will be established.[48]

Immediately prior to the commencement of the spirit communications which led to the foundation of Spiritualism in 1848, Davis stated that a voice told him: 'Brother, the good work has begun – behold, a living demonstration is born.'[49] It is believed that the spirit communicator was referring to the beginning of spirit communications to the mediumistic Fox sisters in Hydesville, New York. Thousands of people in America and the United Kingdom believed that spirit communicators were making contact and as increasing numbers joined their ranks, the Spiritualist religion was born. Its first public meeting was held in 1849 in Rochester, New York.

Before discussing the Hydesville phenomena, it is interesting to point out that in the USA in 1837 it was believed that American Indian spirits made contact with members of the religious movement named the Shakers. After seeking permission from the Shakers, these spirits used the physical voices of these mediumistic individuals as channels and communicated with each other in their native Indian language.

## The Hydesville phenomena

In the mid-19th century in New York state there was an occurrence of mediumistic phenomena that had profound and widespread repercussions and gave rise to the religion known as Spiritualism. Spiritualism is the ever-evolving spiritual philosophy that is believed to be communicated to humankind by highly evolved spirit and angelic communicators. To this day, Spiritualists commemorate these events with the publication of the *Hydesville Millennium Magazine*.[50]

As predicted by Davis, 'a living demonstration was born' in 1848 and gave birth to Spiritualism. The paranormal events surrounded the Fox family who lived in Hydesville, New York. John Fox, his wife and three daughters were disturbed by the noise of unexplained knocking and their furniture would move without anyone touching it. They feared they had a ghost living in the house. Finally, they asked the spirit to communicate with them by knocking; for example, one knock to say 'no' and two knocks to say 'yes.' In this way they learned that a peddler had been murdered and buried in the cellar and that he was making the noises in order to communicate with them.

As the communications continued, visitors came to the Fox farmhouse from all over the country to observe the phenomena. The spirit communicator was asked to knock in a particular way to indicate the letters of the alphabet, which were then written down. This method of communication was faster and gave more detailed answers. They learned that the spirit communicator was named Charles B. Rosma. Investigators began digging in the cellar and discovered human bones and possessions that would have been familiar to a peddler.

Other phenomena that occurred included extremely loud noises that were similar to the sound of artillery firing and the intermittent appearance of lights and other strange manifestations. Despite various house moves in future years, each of the Fox sisters continued to experience similar phenomena for many years to come.

Highly respected professionals from various countries, including judges, politicians, doctors and clergymen, investigated the phenomena and their findings were published in the press. Many investigators were angry that the phenomena appeared to clearly prove that all living creatures survive physical death. Others were hostile to the claim that communication between the physical and non-physical world could take place.

Indeed, the phenomena had brought in many highly prejudiced investigators who believed that the phenomena could not exist. The excessive media coverage, involving ongoing negative scrutiny, caused the Fox sisters to become depressed, and their health, personal lives and marriages were adversely affected.

The following excerpt testifies to the sincerity of the Fox sisters and is taken from the *New York Tribune*, whose editor was Horace Greeley:

It would be the barest cowardice not to say that we were convinced beyond doubt of their [the sisters'] integrity and good faith in the premises. Whatever may be the origin or cause of the 'rappings,' the ladies in whose presence they occur do not make them. We tested this thoroughly and to our entire satisfaction.[51]

Scientists from the University of Buffalo ridiculed the rappings, and much fierce debate raged between other eminent professionals who conducted investigations into the phenomena. It is widely known that the Fox sisters were treated with ignorance and intolerance by investigators. They were considerably abused throughout the entirety of these early psychical research investigations. The three women were each bound hand and foot, naked and perched on pillows in terrible distress, yet observers and investigators continued to hear loud knocking noises from an apparent spirit wishing to make its presence known.

These events were traumatic for the young Fox sisters whose lives had been totally taken over by events. Prejudiced mobs fighting against any evidence for life after death began to show violence towards them. The pressures of being hounded and having to constantly produce phenomena for hostile investigators exhausted the girls and contributed to the sad and chaotic lives they eventually led, involving divorce, alcoholism and, later, disputes with one another. At one point, they rejected the phenomena – of which they had little understanding – and became Catholics in order to gain social acceptance and peace of mind.

In later years they confessed that they had not genuinely rejected the phenomena, but had been pressurized and paid to do so by those fiercely opposed to the Spiritualist belief that life continues after physical death. They claimed that they were forced to make a public rejection because no one could find them guilty of fraud and the phenomena were found to be genuine by all investigators. One example of the inadequate explanations that were offered was that the Fox sisters' joints produced the loud knocking noises. Yet they suffered no broken bones or dislocations and the noises were extra-ordinarily loud.

The peddler can be compared to other apparent spirit communi-cators who have communicated through mediums over the years, stating that they are close to those they love who are still living physical lives. Frequently, they also state that they have unfinished business to conclude. Sometimes, understandably, this is simply getting a message to loved ones that they are all right and there is no death. Until they have done this, many cannot be content. Other, more highly evolved spirits state that they work towards enhancing humankind's spiritual evolution.

They seek to unite human beings with each other and with our related animal brethren, so that all creatures come together under one universal spiritual umbrella, despite humankind's differences in religion, race and creed.

Their objective is to empower humanity by explaining to them the relevance of compassionate spiritual philosophy to the life after death, warning all that here, like attracts like. They teach that all creatures survive physical death and that humans should show compassion to each other and all other creatures and care for our planet. We are warned that both negative thoughts and actions attract non-physical, barren, purgatorial landscapes after death.

The emphasis of many apparent spirit communications is that a perfect form of justice occurs after physical death. This justice takes account of our earthly acts and thoughts carried out towards any other living species and determines the otherworldly environments to which each of us go at death. A further recurring theme communicated when mediums are in trance is that the purpose of physical life is for us all to grow spiritually.

## Nettie Colburn, Abraham Lincoln's medium

The spiritual nature of the mediumistic work carried out by the medium Nettie Colburn in the second half of the 19th century proves the elevated spiritual purpose of many spirit communications. Colburn believed that spirit communicators asked her to contact President Abraham Lincoln. Lincoln consulted Colburn between the years 1861 and 1863, and was profoundly convinced of the authenticity of the spirit communicators with whom he conversed while Nettie was in trance. This highly esteemed president of the United States obeyed the spirit guidance communicated through Colburn on many occasions. The most significant of which was Lincoln's decision to abolish slavery which, was a direct result of spirit directives communicated through Colburn, the medium.

Mediumship was responsible for Lincoln taking the momentus and courageous decision, with its far reaching repercussions on the unity and economy of America, to emancipate the six million Negro slaves in America. So impressed was President Lincoln by the spirituality of the spirit communications he received through Colborn's mediumship that he said to her: 'My child, you possess a very singular gift; but that it is of God, I have no doubt. I think it more important than perhaps anyone present can understand.'[52]

## Allan Kardec, medium and psychical researcher

Allan Kardec (1804–1869) was both a researcher into psychic phenomena and a mediumistic automatic writer, who began writing in France around 1850. His books consist in the main of a diverse range of questions and answers. He believed the responses were from spirit communicators. These communications provide teaching on spiritual matters including the perfect justice found in life after physical death. His most popular book was originally published in 1866 and is called *The Gospel According to Spiritism.*[53]

## The medium Daniel D. Home

Born in Scotland in 1833, Daniel D. Home moved to America with his family when he was a boy. He toured Europe, including the United Kingdom, in 1855. He became famous for his demonstrations of direct-voice trance mediumship, clairaudience, (hearing), clairvoyance, (seeing), materializations, (facilitating spirits to appear), and levitations, (making objects lift off the ground) in full daylight to many of Europe's political leaders, royal families and respected psychical researchers. Some of those who watched Home's demonstrations included Napoleon III and Czar Alexander II. All those who observed this man's mediumship confirmed their belief in the authenticity of the spirit communications. Home never accepted money for his demonstrations.

## The medium Florence Cook

Some years later, around 1873, the contents of Florence Cook's mediumistic trance communications were publicized. Two highly esteemed psychical researchers, Sir Arthur Conan Doyle and Sir William Crookes, spent years investigating Cook. Both researchers concluded that she was sincere and truthful and that surviving spirits communicated through her. Cook's apparent non-physical communicator, known as Katie King, claimed that during her earthly physical life she had been Annie Owen de Morgan, the daughter of the pirate named Sir Henry Owen de Morgan.

It is interesting that some people become very emotional when faced with the possibility that as a result of a law of nature all living creatures survive physical death and that communication from spirits is possible. Trevor Hall, who was not a psychical researcher, wrote a book in which he claimed that Florence Cook was a fraud.

He also stated that the most notable psychical researcher in his day, Sir William Crookes, an eminent physicist, chemist and president of the Royal Society, must have compromised his reputation and fallen in love with Cook. Hall made this accusation because Crookes had confirmed the authenticity of Cook's mediumship, as did Sir Arthur Conan Doyle.[54]

## The medium Rev. W. Stainton Moses

The Reverend William Stainton Moses believed that he was inspired by his spirit communicators to write. One of this medium's most famous books is *Spirit Teachings and Higher Aspects of Spiritualism*.[55] Moses became widely known around 1872 for his mediumship and his automatic writings, which argue for compassion for all creatures and are sublimely spiritual in content.

## The medium John Ballou and the Kosman Bible

The voluminous writings communicated through the medium John Ballou Newbrough, a native of New York City, provide an important example of mediumship with a strong spiritual component. It is reported that Ballou was contacted by angels ten years before his automatic writing began, asking him to cleanse himself over the next decade in preparation for beginning his spiritual work. After a decade, these alleged luminous, celestial beings who had filled the room began writing through him each day, although he was asked not to read the 900-page volume until it was finished.

In 1882 his book was published. It was entitled *OAHSPE: A New Bible in the Words of Jehovih and his Angel Ambassadors: A Sacred History of the Dominions of the Higher and Lower Heavens on the Earth for the Past Twenty-Four Thousand Years*. These writings are known as the Kosman Bible by the religious group known as the Essenes of Kosman. Their religious movement is yet another example of a religion born of elevated spiritual philosophy apparently communicated by spirits or angels.[56]

## The medium Frederick S. Oliver

In 1886 the book *A Dweller on Two Planets*[57] was finalized by

Frederick Oliver. He believed that he heard communications from a spirit describing life in ancient Atlantis. The book's predictive information regarding technological inventions was vindicated in the latter part of the 20th century, long after Oliver's death. His predictions included the development of lasers and voice-recognition computers.

### The medium Leonora Piper

Leonora Piper, born in 1859 in New Hampshire in the United States, was a famous trance medium. It is believed that her spirit communicators utilized her voice box as an interface for the non-physical to communicate with the physical. Piper was described as a vehicle used by spirit beings for the purposes of communication. She also worked as an automatic writer, a process whereby the alleged communicators manipulated her thoughts and/or hand in order to convey their teachings.

William James of Harvard University is known for his scholarly contributions to the academic disciplines of psychology and philosophy. After investigating the phenomena communicated through Piper, he was convinced of the authenticity of their otherworldly origins. His conclusions, discussed in *The ESP Reader* and also in the biography of Mrs Piper, refer to her supernormal abilities. James said: 'My ... knowledge of her sittings and personal acquaintance with her has led me absolutely to ... believe that she had supernormal powers.'[58]

### The medium Madame Blavatsky

Madame Blavatsky founded the Theosophical Society. Her spiritually inspired mediumship is discussed in her book *Isis Unveiled*,[59] published in 1888. Blavatsky believed that her work was inspired by both discarnate beings (invisible, beyond the physical body) and incarnate beings (in the physical body) such as eastern Mahatmas of a highly spiritually evolved nature.

Blavatsky taught that individual spirit communicators are

attracted to individual mediumistic people because they have something in common with the spirit communicator, such as the medium's level of spiritual advancement, interests, attitudes or personality traits. Blavatsky taught that spirits inspire the thoughts and writings of sensitive people to a greater or lesser extent, this is dependent on their innate, possibly undiscovered level of mediumship. Spiritualists largely accept these teachings. Arguably, a spirit may utilize a medium because he or she is a good mediumistic channel rather than having something in common with the spirit.

## The medium Robert J. Lees

The following example of spiritually orientated mediumship found in the 19th century finalizes this broad ranging historical and global survey of mediumship. Robert James Lees was a British medium who wrote a book called *The Life Elysian*, containing what he believed were writings communicated to him by a spirit communicator named Aphraar.[60]

Lees believed that this spirit had been an English man who had recently found himself in the non-physical world and wished to communicate his findings to humankind. These apparent spirit communications describe the landscapes experienced after physical death. They teach us that the type of earthly life we lead determines which landsape we enter after death, in the countless hierarchical levels of the non-physical, geo-psychic regions.

## F.W.H. Myers, Famous Psychical Researcher

I draw this chapter to a close with the conclusions of F.W.H. Myers, the famous psychical researcher who left detailed records describing the mediumship he had observed over many years. He was born in Cumberland in England in 1843 and died in 1901. Myers was part of a group that founded the Society for Psychical Research (SPR) in London in 1882.

Amongst this group was the medium Reverend William Stainton Moses and the eminent British physicist and author Sir William

Barrett. The SPR was established to 'examine without prejudice or prepossession and in a scientific spirit those faculties of man, real or supposed, which appear to be inexplicable on any generally recognized hypothesis.'[61]

Myers' encyclopedic writings included his collection of people's experiences of deathbed visions, and his objective, thorough analysis of demonstrations of mediumship. The original 1903 version, *Human Personality and Its Survival of Bodily Death*,[62] filled two volumes. Myers' contributions to the fields of psychology and psychical research have been significant, and his work has significantly increased our understanding of the workings of the subliminal mind.

As a result of his many years of investigations into mediumship, Myers became convinced of the authenticity of many spirit communications. He was particularly moved when he received communications from a beloved young friend named Annie Marshall who had tragically passed away. Myers accepted the repeated message that was communicated through the mediums he investigated, namely that the purpose of the physical life is to obtain spiritual evolution for soul growth.

Myers believed that if telepathy occurs between people in the physical body then it is also possible, through the same process, for telepathy to occur between surviving spirit personalities and those physically alive. Telepathy between people physically alive has been conclusively proven. There has been much work by Professor Rupert Sheldrake, a highly respected academic researcher, which has proven that telepathy is genuine and common between human beings and their pets, especially pet dogs, cats and horses. This work, among other research, proves that communication from consciousness to consciousness certainly occurs.

Discussing the subliminal mind, Myers stated:

I propose to extend the meaning of the term, so as to make it cover all that takes place beneath the ordinary threshold ...

outside the ordinary margin of consciousness ... And I conceive also that no Self of which we can here have cognizance is in reality more than a fragment of a larger Self ... revealed in a fashion at once shifting and limited through an organism not so framed as to afford it full manifestation ... For we shall find that the subliminal uprushes ... the impulses or communications which reach our emergent from our submerged selves, are ... often characteristically different in quality from any element known to our ordinary supraliminal life ... We can, in that case, affect each other at a distance, telepathically; and if incarnate spirit can act thus in at least apparent independence of the fleshly body, the presumption is strong that other spirits may exist independently of the body, and may affect us in similar manner.[63]

This chapter has provided examples of mediumship from ancient to modern times, proving that it is a universal phenomenon that has spanned the centuries. My research has also provided many examples of the spiritual focus of many apparent spirit communications, which have often given birth to religious movements. Many modern-day mediums, particularly trance mediums, believe that they are providing a spiritual service to humankind.

In trance, they often convey compassionate spiritual philosophy for all creatures and teach that we are all responsible for the type of landscape we go to after physical death. They frequently emphasize the need to demonstrate love for all creatures in all our thoughts and actions. It should be noted that direct voice trance philosophy and spirit messages delivered through mediumship vary enormously, reflecting different degrees of spirituality, from the lower to the most sublime.

Many mediums throughout the centuries and around the world have in common the belief that a non-physical component of all creatures survives physical death. They believe that there is a hierarchy of spirit and angel communicators. They accept that spirit communicators can range from evil to highly spiritually evolved and that they populate many levels in the non-physical, otherworldly realm.

The practice of mediumship, whether cultivated or naturally occurring, has been shown to give birth to, and cultivate knowledge and belief that all physical creatures survive death and that communication between the physical and non-physical world has occurred since the dawn of time. Communications teach through mediums, that it is the extent and nature of the ethical manner in which all beings live their lives which determine the after death landscape which they are destined to inhabit.

This research is cumulatively proving that many of the more spiritally profound examples of these communications to mediums have inspired many of humankind's spiritual insights, giving birth to the world's revealed religions. Sadly, how many of the highest ethical teachings have been buried in the sand, destroyed, never recorded and lost for all time and how much has been distorted by humankind?

The following comments by Klimo demonstrate the contemporary interest in making contact with spirits in order to obtain information about the future, spiritual guidance, and knowledge about the landscapes involved in life after death:

... the human story is punctuated with both local and global periodic cycles of movement toward the physical realm as the primary reality, or toward inner or spiritual, super ordinate realities and truths. Spiritualism and our present wave of channeling activity would appear to be two of the most wide-scale moves in the latter direction.[64]

## Chapter 4

# The Ancient Shamanic Origins
# of Mediumship

In the next two chapters we will look at shamanism with five different objectives. The first objective will be to provide a detailed discussion of the ancient phenomenon known as archaic shamanism. This will provide a historical context for modern-day mediumship, which is predominantly demonstrated today in the religion of Spiritualism. The religion of Spiritualism was born in the same way as other revealed religions – as a result of communications from spiritually elevated spirits and angels. However, in contrast to the revealed world religions, Spiritualism is still nurtured by spiritual philosophy obtained through mediumship.

Fulfilling this first objective, I will discuss the following features of shamanism. These include the role and function of the shaman, the 'shamanic state of consciousness' (which enables the shaman to contact the inhabitants of the non-physical realms), how this altered state of consciousness is obtained, shamanic descriptions of the hierarchical levels in the non-material world, the closeness of their spirit helpers, themes of psychic dismemberment through suffering, later reintegration creating spiritual transformation, and how these states led them to communicate with spirits and to soul-journey to the geo-psychic spirit realms.

The second objective is to reveal that the out-of-body soul-journeys taken by the shamans of antiquity, to visit alternate, other-worldly, co-existent realms and receive mediumistic communications from spirits, possess many of the features of transformative spiritual, mediumistic and psychic experiences. This evidence will be supported by the writings of the eminent French scholar Mircea Eliade, who is a comparatist of religions and a religious historian.

Eliade explains that ancient shamanic experiences of flying through the air like a spirit and mediumistically communicating with the spirit inhabitants of meta-geographic realms, through the use of psycho-spiritual senses, possess all the features of spiritual experiences despite their ancient nature. Notably, these shamanic experiences have many parallels with many historic and contemporary mediumistic, out-of-body and near-death experiences.

These shamanic spiritually orientated mediumistic experiences gave birth to shamanic experience based spiritual beliefs in survival after physical death for all creatures. Shamans, like modern-day mediums and near-death experiencers, describe observing animals living in the non-physical realms. Shamans believed that their mediumistic encounters taught them about the importance of ethical behavior, respect and compassion for animals and the earth, and about the interconnectedness and interdependence of all of creation.

The mediumistic communications received by historic shamans, from the human and non-human inhabitants of the metaphysical realms inevitably gave rise to shamanic spiritual beliefs. These realms transcend time and space and represent the source of spiritual knowledge. Animals were eaten by humans in ancient times as there were no other protein substitutes. However, as an inevitable result of the spiritually sourced communications, shamans learned to hunt and kill no more animals than were needed to feed and clothe the tribe.

Respectfully, they wasted nothing. They prayed for the animal's speedy, painless transition to the ethereal realms. Indebted, shamans thanked the animal's spirit as they were acutely aware that they had tragically cut short the happy earthly life it was meant to lead.

The third objective will be to prove that many shamanic mediumistic experiences, and the beliefs they cultivated, are highly significant and influential. It will be shown that shamanic experience-based beliefs lie at the roots of much of the world's spiritual philosophy. This is a fact of which many people are unaware. Shamanic beliefs and practices are the ancestors of all cultures. They can be found in alchemy, yoga techniques, the Hermetic Tradition, the eastern traditions of Buddhism and Hinduism, the Wisdom Tradition or 'Perennial Philosophy' taught today by the Theosophical movement, Judeo-Christian traditions and the Spiritualist religion.

The writings of Shirley Nicholson and Larry Peters support the accumulated evidence presented in this book. Nicholson was a senior editor for the Theosophical Publishing House which co-ordinates Quest Books and is known for her many articles and books. These are of an esoteric-philosophical and theosophical nature and frequently discuss altered states of consciousness.

Larry G. Peters PhD is an American author known for his anthro-pological research into the psychological and sociological aspects of shamanism in Nepal. Peters worked as an assistant professor of psychology at the California Graduate Institute, Graduate School of Psychology, in Westwood, California and also as a psychotherapist in private practice.

Having carried out extensive research on shamanism both Peters' and Eliade's findings support the shamanic research set out in this book, which proves that ancient shamanic, psychic and mediumistic experiences are essentially spiritual in nature. They have been a significant influence giving birth to many of humankind's spiritual and esoteric traditions. These lie at the roots of many global religious beliefs.

The fourth objective is to reveal the similarities between the beliefs and practices of the highly respected ancient biblical prophets of the Judeo-Christian tradition and those of the ancient shamans. The ancient echoes of mediumship (shamanism) will be clearly revealed in accounts taken from the ancient Semite Hebrew sources. Many Old Testament accounts will be shown to be describing shamanic, mediumistic practices.

The research of the scholar Rabbi Yonassan Gershom supports the evidence that mediumship was used in biblical traditions. Gershom is a Jewish spiritual teacher and the spiritual director of the

Disciples of the Light, which is a Jewish fellowship in Minneapolis, Minnesota. Gershom's private practice in the USA was characterized by its shamanic features. It is most revealing that Gershom unearthed his shamanic practices and techniqes in historic Jewish mysticism. These have assisted him in counseling and psychological healing.

The fifth objective is to show that the psychic and mediumistic abilities of ancient shamans are regularly demonstrated today. Reference will be made to the writings on the paranormal by D. Scott Rogo, who worked at John F. Kennedy University in California before his death.

He wrote approximately 25 books on the paranormal and held research positions with the Psychical Research Foundation and with the Maimonides Medical Center's former Division of Parapsychology and Psychophysics in Brooklyn, New York. Rogo also worked as a member of the editorial staff at *Fate* magazine and was a columnist for *Human Behavior* magazine.

Altered states of consciousness were, and still are, entered into spontaneously, or are methodically cultivated, by shamans and present-day mediums. This is evidenced, in particular, during mediumistic trances sometimes used in settings known as séances. Séances are conducted for many purposes.

They can be used to: learn the correct medical diagnosis for a problem that can then be alleviated by psychic healing and conventional healing; to receive knowledge of events at vast geographic distances away; to receive precognitive or retro-cognitive information (i.e. regarding future or past events); to gain spiritual philosophy; and to learn the natural laws which govern the fathomless after-death realms.

Information such as the above is obtained today by mediums for their sitters as it was historically by shamans for their tribespeople. This information was sought after because it helped both the tribe and the individual. Incredibly, while studying shamanic tribes, a number of highly respected anthropologists and other researchers have clearly heard spirit voices during shamanic séances.

Their detailed evidential accounts have been documented for posterity. It was not the anthropologists' intention or expectation to witness spirit voices. These experiences came as an astonishing by-product of spending years living with shamanic tribes. These incidents, including other reported shamanic, psychic and mediumistic abilities will be revealed below.

During observed entranced states, the diverse voices of apparent spirit communicators utilized the voice box of the shaman. These experiential phenomena fostered many spiritually ethical beliefs among the shamans. Shamans who demonstrated more power, in terms of successful psychic healing, accurate telepathic or precognitive abilities, were taught that these enhanced gifts should be accompanied by their increased responsibility to help the tribe.

Any shaman who abused their power knew, as a result of the scenes witnessed in the after-death landscapes, that they would be punished. They knew that their misdemeanors would have direct repercussions for them in the type of non-material environment they would attract to themselves after death. They were also aware that punishment would occur during their physical, earthly life as their negative actions would draw to them negative events.

The most noticeable parallels between shamanic mediumistic practices and present-day mediumistic practices will be highlighted. Both shamans and mediums have experiences and receive communications which give birth to a spiritual worldview. Reported spirit communications continue to enrich the vast spiritual philosophy known today as Spiritualism. Both the shamanic and present-day medium share the belief that guidance can be obtained from a non-physical ancestor or other spiritually elevated guide who has passed to the higher spheres.

Chapters 4 and 5 have together, cumulatively demonstrated that ancient shamanic practices that cultivated mediumistic communications from spirits and soul journeys to invisible realms have spanned the centuries. In Chapter 10 a more contemporary example of mediumship, Emanuel Swedenborg, will be cross-referenced back to archaic shamans, further highlighting the parallels between shamans and mediums.

Modern-day mediumship will be shown to be better understood in the context that mediumistic experiences date back to humankind's earliest psycho-spiritual beliefs and practices. The research of Rogo and Eliade supports this book's claims that ancient shamans represent one of the earliest human expressions of psycho-spiritual experiences.

## Important Features of Archaic Shamanism

Shamanism was enormously geographically widespread in the days of antiquity and inevitably possessed regional variations. Shamanism could be found in North America, Indonesia, Oceania and the vast areas known as Siberia and Central Asia. There is an encyclopedic wealth of material on this subject gathered by religious historians, anthropologists, psychologists, sociologists, ethnologists and psychical researchers. However, uncorrupted shamanic cultures are rare to non-existent in the modern world.

Shamans of antiquity and those of today are viewed as being extraordinary individuals who always occupied a central role and function within the tribe. It is believed that they were either born with their exceptional mediumistic abilities or gained them after a life-threatening accident or illness known as an 'initiatory illness.' Shamans received their calling to carry out their future vocation in different ways.

They may have been called to become a shaman in a vision during their sleep state, through a waking visionary encounter of a human or animal spirit, or by the sighting of a deceased relative or a semi-divine being. They may have begun to shamanize after an experience of the diverse after-death landscapes, perhaps induced by a life-threatening accident or illness like that of a near-death experiencer.

After receiving their calling, the shaman's dedication and mental, emotional, spiritual and physical strength had to be proved, as they committed themselves to many arduous and exhausting years of further training. During this training the shaman was expected to master life-threatening quests that other people would not dare to attempt.

It is believed that the neophyte (trainee) shaman cumulatively learned how his or her consciousness could transcend mundane time and space. Shamans did this by sending their spirit or consciousness, in an out-of-body state, to the invisible realms to communicate with previously invisible inhabitants.

This provided the tribe with guidance no-one other than a shaman could access. These abilities are believed to be of paranormal significance. The role of the shaman included those abilities which are known today as mediumship or channeling. It was believed that through accessing the invisible realms the shaman obtained valuable spirit guidance.

Shamans received information regarding past and future events. They learned when their enemies intended to attack them and gained knowledge of geographically distant events, including knowledge of areas where the tribe could find food. Historic shamans believed that they progressively received spiritual insights into the purpose and nature of creation, little-known post-death laws of nature, the interrelatedness of all life-forms, and that the quality of a person's life determines their after-death landscape.

Consequently, shamans were highly respected individuals. They believed that they gained the ability to diagnose and cure illness as a result of abilities and knowledge gained during their soul-journey excursion to the co-existent, invisible, alternate realms. In order to cure a patient, sometimes it was believed that the shaman had to travel in an out-of-body state to find the patient's lost soul. In many ways, this was fruitful, symbolic activity both for the shaman and the patient.

Shamans are known as 'psychopomps.' Psychopomps are beings thought to escort the souls of the newly dead through a labyrinth of unfamiliar sights, sounds and scenes en route to the soul's rightful after-death landscape. Escorting the soul after death was not considered to be a symbolic activity. Here, in their correct non-material environment the soul was believed to be reunited with people and animals with whom they had lived and loved during their physical life.

These soul excursions took place after the shaman had become adept at entering into a state of trance known as the 'shamanic state of consciousness.' It was in these trance states that the shaman soul journeyed to the sub-divisions of the upper, middle and lower regions of this alternate, immaterial reality. Here, they became familiar with the now visible landscapes and inhabitants. It was in these geo-psychic realms, accessed through the endurance of many years of rigorous training, which finely tuned their psycho-spiritual senses, enabling them to become seasoned travelers in this multi-faceted realm of non-linear time and space.

Eliade notes:

Shamanism is ... one of the archaic techniques of ecstasy – at once mysticism, magic and 'religion' in the broadest sense of the term ... When it becomes a matter of entering so vast and varied a mental universe as that of shamanism ... we are dealing with a whole spiritual world.[1]

Less seasoned shamans were trained by and worked with older, experienced shamans. However, they believed that other spirits, including spirit relatives and spirit animals, also became their guides and helped to train them. Other spirit beings were believed to visit the shaman. Many of whom were described as gods due to their non-physical nature, knowledge of the after-death realms and elevated spiritual wisdom.

They offered the shaman the benefit of their guidance to empower the shaman to help others. Common amongst historic peoples is the recurring pattern of deifying spirit communicators.

Spirits and angels are repeatedly described as gods and often confused with God, namely the Divine.

Due to the geographically extensive nature of ancient, nomadic shamanism, regional variations existed with regard to their names, training and the methods used to help them attain an altered or shamanic state of consciousness. These men and women were variously known as healers, priests, priestesses, magicians, counselors or seers. However, a common shared feature was for the shamanic medium and healer to work towards obtaining sensory overload. Shamans needed strong mental, emotional and physical health in order to endure the hours and rigors that it typically took to cultivate sensory overload. Once achieved, these states facilitated their soul-journey or astral excursions, trance and healing feats.

In order to act as the intermediary or medium between the invisible world of spirit and the world of physical matter, shamans deprived themselves of one or more of the following: sleep, water, food and/or endured weeks of isolation and darkness. Other methods to facilitate channeling activity involved enduring excessive temperatures of heat or cold.

Shamans used hours of rhythmic and monotonous drumming, beating of other percussion instruments, chanting, singing, dancing and hyperventilation. To access the desired states of consciousness, some smoked herbs or ingested psychoactive plants such as *datura* (jimson weed), peyote and psilocybin mushrooms. However, the use of psychedelic drugs made the experience far harder for the shaman to control.

The concept of the shamanic *axis mundi* is associated with the physical use of climbing up and down steps, a ladder, a tree, a mountain or a tent pole. These props symbolically interconnected the various after-death spheres.

Shamans did this to demonstrate that through these tools, they could ascend to the highest regions or descend to the lowest realms during their soul excursions. When the shaman's consciousness gained its liberty to explore the many levels of the meta-geographic realms beyond the threshold of ordinary circadian time and space, they left their lifeless, entranced, inert physical body behind, sometimes for days at a time.

Eliade elaborates on how male and female shamans became familiar with the otherworldly topographies:

> Through his (her) initiation, the shaman learns what he (she) must do when his soul abandons the body – and first of all, how to orient himself in the unknown regions that he enters during his ecstasy. He learns how to explore the new planes of existence disclosed by his ecstatic experiences. He knows the road to the centre of the world; the hole in the sky through which he can fly up to ... heaven or the aperture in the earth through which he can descend to the underworld. In short, he knows the paths that lead to Heaven and Hell.
>
> All this he has learned during his training in solitude or under the guidance of the master shamans. Because of his ability to leave his body with impunity, the shaman can, if he so wishes, act in the manner of a spirit; he flies through the air, he becomes invisible, he perceives things at great distances; he mounts to heaven or descends to Hell, sees the souls of the dead and can capture them and is impervious to fire.[2]

The various initiatory experiences took the shaman to the very boundaries of physical life, returning him/her back again to the physical world of matter. Notably, a fundamental shared feature of archaic shamanism was the theme of death and rebirth. This was represented by actual or symbolic experiences of physical and/or mental fragmentation and reassembly. Shamans commonly speak of discovering themselves reduced to skeletal proportions emotionally or physically and then experiencing reintegration as they return to mundane waking life.

Upon return, they now possess heightened paranormal abilities. These life-threatening initiatory experiences resulted in shamanic soul flights in an out-of-body state to the hierarchical non-physical world. Ostensibly these are facilitated through the gateway of the mind. These shamanic experiences have many close parallels with near-death experiences.

One example of a shaman's adventures with consciousness, while his physical body lay lifeless in his tent, is taken from the writings of the distinguished scholar Mircea Eliade:

> Stricken with smallpox, the future shaman remained unconscious for three days, so nearly dead that on the third day he was almost buried. He saw himself go down to Hell and after many adventures he was carried to an island, in the middle of which stood a young birch tree, which reached up to Heaven ... During his adventures in the other world, the future shaman met several semi-divine personages, in human and animal form, each of which instructed him in the secrets of the healing art. When he awoke, in his yurt, among his relatives, he was initiated and could begin to shamanize.[3]

Arguably, these protracted experiences of intense suffering break down the existing conditioning of the shaman's mind, a process which is thought to extinguish the rigid ego structures of the personality once the episode is healed. This is comparable to a psychotic experience. The new malleability created after the extremities of the experience might contribute to the reshaping, integrating, spiritual and psychic transformation reported after the experience.

Similarly, the shaman has thus undergone a spiritually, transformative psychic or mediumistic experience. After experiencing intense personal suffering, a heightening of the shaman's empathy and compassion for all other life-forms appears to have occurred, which is indicative of the spiritually transformative psychic or mediumistic experience they have undergone.

Historically, shamans demonstrated a profound respect for the human and related animal kingdom and the natural world. They knew to take only the bare essentials for survival from animals and the planet. They were taught not to exploit their psychic and mediumistic abilities for personal gain as this would inevitably incur punishment during the physical and non-physical life.

Holger Kalweit, author of *Dreamtime and Inner Space*, makes the following perceptive comment regarding the compassion of the shamans: 'Psychic dismemberment results in a clear mind, enhanced perception, greater capacity for compassion and true gentleness toward our fellow beings. It would seem that only self-borne suffering will stimulate true tolerance and genuine compassion.'[4]

## The Mental Health of Shamans

Shamans inevitably possessed strong mental, physical, emotional and spiritual health in order to endure the original initiatory near-death type of experience. This was followed by years of arduous training. This again was followed by exhausting ceremonies in order to attune their psycho-spiritual senses to the geo-psychic realms. Arguably, members of the tribe would not have trusted their health, their family's health and the eternal fate of their souls to a shamanic person they thought to be unbalanced or untrustworthy.

It is important to emphasize that the state of the historic shaman's mental health was no different from that of people in modern societies who have transformative, spiritual, psychic experiences. These experiences frequently change the person's worldview, causing them to rearrange their life so that they can follow a more meaningful, creative and spiritual vocation.

Eliade points out that psychologists merely explain the mechanical workings of that which occurs in the psyche when a person has a spiritually transformative psychic or mediumistic experience.

Eliade notes:

The writer who approaches shamanism as a psychologist will be led to regard it as primarily the manifestation of a psyche in crisis ... he will not fail to compare it with certain aberrant psychic behaviour patterns or to class it among mental diseases ... we consider it unacceptable to assimilate shamanism to any kind of mental disease.

But one point remains to which the psychologist will always be justified in drawing attention: like any other religious vocation, the shamanic vocation is manifested by a crisis, a temporary derangement of the future shaman's spiritual equilibrium. They show us, in actual process as it were, the repercussions, within the psyche, of what we have called the 'dialectic of hierophanies' – the radical separation between profane and sacred.[5]

Many researchers into shamanic phenomena, including Eliade,[6] Ackerknecht[7] and Silverman,[8] share the same conclusions that the shamanic initiation process may have begun with a perilous, lengthy initiatory feat, sickness or a life-threatening accident, but that the shaman is not sick when they begin their vocation as a shaman. Of the legendary respect accorded to the exhausting paranormal feats believed to be accomplished by the shaman, Jean Houston writes:

The way of the shaman calls for initial steps of radical disintegration and dissociation, as well as procedures for consciously entering into chaos. Living at his edges, standing outside and beyond himself, the shaman experiences ecstasy as a condition of his mastery, although the ordeals and voyages into shadow worlds bring with it a harrowing of the soul that few but the shaman could endure. In the shamanic journey, psyche and cosmos gain access to each other; the shaman becoming the channel for creatures and spirits, for the animates of nature and the designates of gods. The art and discipline needed for so special a relationship are enormous and do much to explain the reverence in which the shaman has been held for millennia.[9]

## Shamans and Trance Mediumship

The shaman's years as an apprentice taught him/her to become adept at mastering altered states of consciousness. These include differing depths of trance, which he/she would learn to enter into spontaneously or to methodically cultivate, control and exit at will.

Shirokogoroff,[10] among others, believes that a core feature of being a shaman was their 'mastery of spirits.' Firth[11] noted that the shamanic trance involved the shaman using his body as a 'placing' into which spirits enter and communicate and from which the evil spirits can be cast out. In modern-day language, mediums often describe their bodies as being used as a 'vehicle' for spirit communication and trance.

The research carried out by Peters and Price-Williams discovered that in 81% of the 42 contemporary examples of shamanic cultures that they studied, the shaman, during altered states of consciousness, remained aware and in communication with both the audience and patient.[12] Peters states: 'The Tamang shaman ... remains in full rapport with the audience, describing what he sees or diagnosing the illness in the voice of the spirit and answering questions put to him by spectators.'[13]

## The Spirituality of the Shamanic Experience

To fulfill the second objective we will now look at evidence for the religiosity of the experiences of the shamans of antiquity. Shamans are frequent travelers in durative, amplified, sacred time and space. Those realms are believed to be beyond the threshold of ordinary, circadian mundane, three-dimensional time and space.

As a result of their soul journey excursions to the invisible realms, shamans held mediumistic communications with a animal spirits, human and non-human. These psychic and mediumistic experiences will be shown to possess the features required to categorize them as spiritual experiences. They are, in fact, spiritually orientated psychic and mediumistic experiences.

Eliade evidences his respect for the ancient shamanic cultures.

He states that from the 'Overwhelming "grey mass" of cultural data stemming from the so-called "ahistorical" peoples ... we begin to distinguish "history" where we were in the habit of finding only ... primitives.'[14] Eliade's academic research into the encyclopedic subject of shamanism is considered to be a classic among scholarly writings on the subject.

Eliade makes abundantly clear that spiritual experiences date back to the beginning of life itself. Spiritual experiences are not merely the result of one culture influencing and transferring techniques of ecstasy to another. Eliade supports the tenets of this book, confirming that experiences of the non-physical world and its angelic and spirit inhabitants occurred simultaneously throughout the world and did so from the dawn of human history. Consequently, Eliade's writings concur with the belief that transformative spiritual-ecstatic experiences have occurred throughout the length of known time, throughout the breadth of humanity, and mark the volume of the profundity and credibility of their spiritual nature.

Eliade notes:

The Altaic shaman ritually climbs a birch tree ... the birch symbolizes the World Tree, the steps representing the various heavens through which the shaman must pass on his ecstatic journey to the highest heaven; and it is extremely probable that the cosmological schema implied in this [particular] ritual is of Oriental origin ... But ... the history of a religious phenomenon cannot reveal all [about] this phenomenon ... similar ideologies and rituals appear all over the world ... [it] appears to be a primordial phenomenon, that ... belongs to man ... not to man as a historical being.[15]

Arguably, spiritual experiences of ineffable manifestations of celestial beings and spirit messengers, frequently thought of as gods, are interpreted both at the level of spiritual maturity of the person having the experience and that of the historical age. An individual's psyche has also to make sense of the experience as the non-physical messenger is made of malleable, fluid, thought-responsive energy.

The experiencer has to interpret the experience of the non-physical as something physically meaningful. On some level, their consciousness may even unconsciously filter out aspects of their profound experience which often defies mundane description. As in the case of manifestations of angels, the energy form may manifest into something recognizable to the shamanic medium.

Spiritual experiences of a broad spectrum of spiritually orientated spirits and angels have occurred globally since the beginning of time; evidencing the universality of mediumistic experiences. Eliade emphasizes that religious historians, being the best equipped to judge the spirituality of an experience, should not be obstructed by parapsychologists and those from other academic disciplines:

All these dreams, myths and nostalgias with a central theme of ascent or flight cannot be exhausted by a psychological explanation ... This work of deciphering the deep meaning of religious phenomena rightfully falls to the historian of religions ... But it is the historian of religions who will make the greatest number of valid statements on a religious phenomenon as a *religious phenomenon* – and not as a psychological, social, ethnic, philosophical or even theological phenomenon.[16]

Eliade confirms that religio-ecstatic experiences possess a spiritual nature that transcends the centuries:

The historian of religions makes use of all the historical manifestations of a religious phenomenon in order to discover what such a phenomenon 'has to say'... The history of religions is not always necessarily the historiography of religions ... [it is to] study religious facts ... on their specific plane of manifestation. [They are] ... *historical*, concrete, existential, even if the historical facts manifested are not always reducible to history.[17]

Eliade has spent decades (as I have) carrying out historical, comparative research into the religions of humankind. He has noted (as I
have) the repeated features of transformative spiritual experiences
and agrees that they are echoed in shamanic psychic and mediumistic phenomena. Eliade's scholarly conclusions are of great value
for present-day researchers who try to evaluate the spirituality of
ancient and modern mediumistic and psychic experiences. This is
because many present-day psychologists, parapsychologists and
philosophers strive endlessly to explain away humankind's religious
experiences as meaningless. Today, they also claim that transformative spiritual, psychic and mediumistic experiences, past and
present, do not have a spiritual impact on a person's life.
Descriptions of shamanic experiences have much in common with
near-death experiencers' accounts. It is an accepted fact that after a
near-death experience, experiencers become dramatically changed
spiritually transformed individuals. The most advanced method of
research for evaluating comparative and religious history involves
exploring the meaningfulness of the experience for the person
involved. Eliade's research concurs with this.

Eliade concludes that ancient shamanic experiences are religious
experiences. Since mediumistic experiences globally throughout the
centuries have many parallels with shamanic experiences, it appears
that authentic mediums continue the role of the shaman; indeed
mediumship is a modern term for shamanism. Both the shamanic
and modern-day medium's spirit communications have a profound
effect on the beliefs and worldviews of the tribal member and sitter
alike.

> The manifestation of the sacred in some stone or tree ... to the
> most complex (the 'vision' of a new 'divine form' by a prophet or
> the founder of a religion) ... everything is in some sort condi-
> tioned by history. Yet in the humblest (society) there is an 'eternal
> new beginning ...' ... A historian of religions cannot ignore them
> ... his eye will have learned to decipher the properly religious

meaning of one or another fact...the very dialectic of the sacred tends indefinitely to repeat a series of archetypes, so that a [society] realized at a certain 'historical moment' is structurally equivalent to a [society] a thousand years earlier or later.[18]

Regarding the interpretation of the spiritual experience by an individual's consciousness, despite the historic cultural epoch in which that experience is found, Eliade offers his pertinent insights:

But (societies) have the peculiarity of seeking to reveal the sacred in its totality, even if the human beings in whose consciousness the sacred 'shows itself' fasten upon only one aspect or one small part of it. In the most elementary [society] *everything is declared.* The manifestation of the sacred in a stone or a tree is neither less mysterious nor less noble than its manifestation in a 'god.' The process of sacralizing reality is the same; *the forms* taken by the process in man's religious consciousness differ.[19]

Of the many levels of spiritual experiences Eliade states:

Not only can a community – consciously or unconsciously – practice many religions, but the same individual can have an infinite variety of religious experiences, from the 'highest' to the most undeveloped ... any cultural moment whatever can provide the fullest revelation of the sacred ... which the human condition is capable of [experiencing]. Despite the immense historical differences involved, the experiences of the monotheistic prophets can be repeated in the most 'backward' of primitive tribes.[20]

Eliade's conclusions are in close harmony with mine in that he is emphatic that spiritual experiences have occurred throughout history and share common features. Notably, these experiences have a transformative spiritual effect on the experiencers' beliefs, often changing the way they live their lives. However, all experiences are interpreted at the level of understanding of the individual and the society in which they occur.

Eliade states that

mystical experiences are possible at … every degree of civilization and of religious situation … for certain religious consciousnesses in crisis, there is always the possibility of a historical leap that enables them to attain otherwise inaccessible spiritual positions. Certainly, 'history' – the religious tradition of the tribe in question – finally intervenes to subject the ecstatic experiences of certain privileged persons to its own canons. But it is no less true that these experiences often have the same precision and nobility as the experiences of the great mystics of East and West.[21]

Shamanic,' mediumistic and trance experiences occurred as a result of their psychic and mediumistic sensitivities which were further sensitized through years of training. Eliade confirms that shamanic spiritual-ecstatic experiences have much in common with the religiosity of the experiences of the respected, historic, spiritual 'prophets.' The following pages will reveal that shamanic spiritual beliefs lay at the roots of worldwide religious philosophies. The historic prophets, continuing the shamanic mediumistic legacy of their ancestors, built upon the shamanic tradition and world religions were born.

Shamanic "…ecstatic experiences have exercised and still exercise, a powerful influence on … religious ideology, on mythology, on ritualism. But neither the ideology nor the mythology and rites of the Arctic, Siberian and Asian peoples are the creation of their shamans. All these elements are earlier than shamanism, or at least are parallel to it, in the sense that they are the product of the general religious experience … [shamans are] separated from the rest of the community by the intensity of their own religious experience ... [we] find shamanism within a considerable number of religions ... and [it] represents ... the mysticism of the particular religion. A comparison [can be made with] that of monks, mystics and saints within Christian churches ... This small mystical elite ... directs the community's religious life [and] ... guards its 'soul.' The shaman is the great specialist in the human soul; he alone 'sees it' [and] knows its 'form' and its destiny.[22]

One significant shared feature found among the diverse tribal groupings of archaic shamanic cultures is the spiritual belief in an almighty creator, a supreme God on high. Descriptions of God are expressed in different shamanic languages yet they share the same belief in God's fundamental spiritual characteristics. The following descriptions range from shamans in the Arctic to Siberia to Central Asia.

The Yakut called God, the supreme being, the Lord, Father and Chief of the World. The Turki-Tatars described God as Chief, Lord, Master and Father. The Koryak spoke of God as the One on High. Shamanism was distributed across a large part of the ancient world, yet due to their spiritual psychic and mediumistic experiences, all tribes universally believed in God as a supreme creator.

Eliade states that:

Despite their ethnic and linguistic differences, in general their religions coincide ... [they] know and revere a celestial Great God, an all-powerful Creator ... Sometimes the Great God's name even means 'Sky' or 'Heaven.' ... Even when the concrete name of the 'sky' is lacking, we find ... its most characteristic attributes – 'high,' 'lofty,' 'luminous,' ... shining, light.[23]

The following highlights the religiosity of the shamanic experience-based beliefs. Countless, historic, shamanic tribes believed, as a result of their shamans' spiritually transformative mediumistic experiences, that a supreme God inhabited the highest region of the highest celestial realm. There were minor variations in their beliefs regarding the number of God's messengers, and sometimes these messengers were described as God's children or servants.

Another shared feature among the many shamanic cultures was the belief in the existence of lesser spirits who had a semi-divine nature and inhabited lower heavens. These lesser beings were thought to watch over and guide humankind. Further shared features found among widespread ancient shamanic beliefs, was their experience-based belief in the continued existence of the spirits of ancestors and animals who had passed away. These are undoubtedly religious beliefs, generated by spiritually transformative mediumistic experiences.

These beliefs have much in common with Spiritualists' religious beliefs, which are composed of accumulated and ongoing spirit teachings. Shamans believed that they could communicate with all such spirits, as do modern-day mediums, many of whom are Spiritualists.

Contemporary mediums likewise do not fear those who have physically died. Instead, like shamans, they believe that they communicate telepathically with spirit people and spirit animals, who convey love and guidance for a person's life, and receive spiritual philosophy and information about the non-physical realms.

It has already been noted that communications transmitted from the medium to the sitter vary enormously in quality, accuracy and length. Many Spiritualists ask the medium, in one-to-one sittings, to seek information regarding a person's specific spiritual life-purpose. They ask the medium to find out what they should do during their earthly life in order to enhance their spiritual growth and what innate potential abilities they could work on and develop.

This information, with its more spiritual focus, differs from that of simply acquiring knowledge about the future or observing repetitive evidence of post-death survival. This underlines the ongoing spirituality inherent in present-day shamanism, known as mediumship.

Significantly, the findings of Larry G. Peters and Eliade support the research that has generated this book. Notably, spiritually transformative shamanic psychic and mediumistic experiences are religious experiences. They demonstrate many of the features of religious experiences. Peters carried out anthropological research into the psychological and sociological aspects of shamanism in Nepal. One of the shamans he studied was named Bhirendra.

Questioned by Peters, Bhirendra described his vision of the non-physical, etheric world, including one of its spirit inhabitants. It is known that this experience caused a great spiritual transformation in Bhirendra's life, setting him on the path of training to become a shaman. Bhirendra's 'vision' demonstrated an experience of the after-death domains evidencing survival beyond death, as he spoke with a benevolent being in white. This description has much in common with modern-day spiritually transformative psychic and mediumistic experiences and those of near-death experiencers. The following is an excerpt from the personal testimony of Bhirendra, who is a contemporary shaman.

I walked into a beautiful garden with flowers of many different colours. There was also a pond and golden glimmery trees. Next to the pond was a very tall building, which reached up into the sky. It had a golden staircase of nine steps leading to the top. I climbed the nine steps and saw Ghesar Gyalpo at the top sitting on his white throne, which was covered with soul flowers. He was dressed in white and his face was all white. He had long hair and a white crown. He gave me milk to drink and told me that I could attain much shakti to be used for the good of my people.[24]

Peters concludes that the experience of this modern-day shaman

has many of the qualities reported in numerous mystical or

religious experiences. For example, the vision of the saving light is one element ... as is the initiatory structure of suffering the 'dark night of the soul' that precedes divine grace. Bhirendra's religious experience occurred within the cultural context of shamanism; through it he found meaning in his life and as a result of the training embarked upon after the experience, became a shaman.[25]

Shamans, mediums, near-death experiencers all have in common, despite the passage of the millennia, the shared experience-based beliefs that all creatures continue to live after physical death in non-physical realms. They each believe that natural laws create forms of judgment that evaluate the ethical quality of a person's earthly life. These are undoubtedly religious beliefs conferred on the experiencer, generated by spiritually transformative psychic and mediumistic experiences.

## Chapter 5

# Shamanic Mediums as Ancestors of Cultures

This chapter will explore shamanism with respect to the further three objectives. The third objective is to provide proof that shamanism, the ancestor of spiritual mediumship, had a profound and continuing influence on the spiritual life of humankind. Evidence will confirm the extent to which the ancient spiritually orientated psychic and mediumistic practices of shamans have given birth to ethical teachings.

In turn, shamanic experience-based beliefs have become embraced and incorporated into the world's spiritual philosophies and religions. Spiritualist mediums today practice a modern-day form of shamanism. Nicholson, a highly respected researcher and author on esoteric philosophy and shamanic states of consciousness, explains:

The world view of shamanism coincides with that of the Perennial Philosophy or the Wisdom Tradition ... and in fact probably forms a strand in that many-textured perspective. Hinduism, Buddhism, yoga philosophy, alchemy and other Western forms of esoteric knowledge, along with shamanism, hold in common a mystical and holistic view in which all things are interconnected and all inhere in a numinous background Source. Many other parallels with formerly secret esoteric and spiritual traditions are now evident ... The inner experiences associated with ... mystical journeys and rites of passage have commonalities across cultures ... Absorption states described in Buddhist scriptures have counterparts in shamanism.

The notions of change and impermanence are also prominent

in both traditions, as are the concepts of a spiritual path and the cultivation of such qualities as generosity. Also, the idea of human kinship with animals, trees, rocks, etc can be found in eastern religions as in shamanism. [Shamanism may be thought of as] an earth philosophy, which focuses on instinctual energies ... traditions such as Buddhism are sky philosophies that emphasize the mind.[1]

As a result of the shamans transformative spiritual psychic and mediumistic experiences, they built up a catalogue of spiritual beliefs. Many of which were born and nurtured through their exceptional ability to soul-journey out of their body into the non-physical world. These teachings, born of their accounts, have become incorporated into many of humankind's religious beliefs. The following are four examples of shamanic experience-based beliefs that have become religious teachings:

1. The existence of non-physical realms
2. The presence of all life-forms in the non-physical realms Transformative spiritual psychic and mediumistic experiences gave them conclusive mutually corroborated observational evidence that all life forms continue to exist after physical death.
3. The necessity of showing compassion and respect for all animals and for the earth itself
4. The interconnectedness of all aspects of creation, so that if a person harms another creature this action will inevitably cause direct harm to that person

These beliefs have close parallels with those later adopted by the ancient eastern traditions, particularly associated with the concepts of *ahimsa* and *karma*. These doctrines teach that a person should do no harm and if they do commit harm or neglect to any other creature it will have repercussions upon that individual.

Eliade explains that shamans visited the supernatural worlds ... to see the superhuman beings (gods, demons, spirits of the dead, etc) ... the shaman has been able to contribute decisively to the knowledge of death. In all probability many features of funerary geography, as well as some themes of the mythology of death, are the result of the ecstatic experiences of shamans. The lands that the shaman sees and the personages that he meets during his ecstatic journeys in the beyond are minutely described by the shaman himself, during or after his trance. The unknown and terrifying world of death assumes form and is organized ... [it] becomes familiar and acceptable ... the supernatural inhabitants of the world of death become visible ... display a personality, even a biography ... the world of the dead becomes knowable and death itself is ... a rite of passage to a spiritual mode of being.[2]

The Australian Aboriginals share many common features of belief and practice with other shamanic cultures, historic and contemporary. The Aboriginals talk of traveling in the 'dreamtime.' In this out-of-body state they allow their spirit to fly like a bird to the implicit (unseen) co-existent, metaphysical spheres. Here, through contact with non-physical beings, they acquire spiritual powers. These etheric beings can be described as spirits and angels.

The Aboriginals believe that mountains are places where interaction between the two worlds can best occur. They believe that their spirit can ascend to the higher realms and that the messengers, frequently perceived as gods, can also descend to them. They are aware that the divine, multifaceted, geo-psychic realm is interconnected with the material, earthly realm and can be accessed by training a person's psycho-spiritual senses.

In common with the eastern traditions the Aboriginal shamans past and present describe their psychic and mediumistic experiences as the result of an expansion of their consciousness rather than as possession by spirits. Significantly, shamanic beliefs predate the ancient eastern religions and have had considerable influence on those traditions.

The Aboriginal shamans pursue techniques of sky-gazing in order to cultivate trance states which facilitate their access to the non-physical realms. Here, as experience has taught them, they can acquire infinite knowledge. These practices reveal the Aboriginal shamans' spiritual beliefs. These shamanic practices have much in common with the meditative practices cultivated by Buddhists and Hindus when seeking entry into mystical states. The shamanic ancestry of the ancient religions of Hinduism and Buddhism becomes apparent, shamanism being even more ancient.

Also, the eastern traditions which place emphasis on discovering infinity inside oneself have parallels and probable origins in shamanic beliefs. The Perennial Philosophy, alternatively known as the Wisdom Tradition, on which the modern Theosophical movement is based, also echoes shamanic beliefs. These include the belief in life after death and the encouragement to spend the latter stage of a person's life dedicated to spiritual pursuits.

Ancient shamanism influenced the beliefs found in alchemy and yoga. Each of these spiritual philosophies has common shamanic themes among its techniques for transformation. In their psycho-spiritual training, these include, the use of breathing techniques and exercises, visual imagery and music.

Further evidence of ancient shamanic influence can be found in the Hermetic Tradition and in alchemy; significantly, both continue to use the shamanic symbol of the tree of life. Shamans made both real and symbolic reference to spirit animals as guides and protectors. They believed that they were literally helped by different spirit animals who each brought their own individual characteristics and strengths to help in any given situation.

For example, a lion would bring physical strength and courage, a gazelle would bring speed, and a dog would bring devotion, loyalty and protection. Shamans also made symbolic references to animals, parallels can be found in the hierarchical characteristics of the different energy centers known as *chakras*. The fact that the shamanic concept known as chakras occurs both in the spiritual philosophies of yoga and alchemy provides further ample evidence of their ancient shamanic origins.

Shamanic metaphors such as the 'shamanic spiritual journey,' 'dismemberment' and later 'reintegration and reassembly' are concepts that can be found in both the spiritual philosophies of the later Hermetic Tradition and in alchemy. Again, this proves that shamanism is the ancestor of worldwide cultures. Shamanic themes of reconciling dualities are expressed in terms of the Sky Father and Earth Mother. The influence of shamanism can be seen in the practices of many later yoga adepts as they similarly strive to synthesize the solar and lunar energies believed to be found in the spine.

The spiritual philosophy known as the Ancient Wisdom is taught today by the Theosophical movement. These teachings are evidently influenced by even more ancient spiritual shamanic beliefs. Shamans believed that all of creation, including the universe itself is

permeated by spirit and matter and seemingly miraculous feats depend on little known natural forces within this context. Theosophy, like yoga philosophy, depicts alternate realities as interpenetrating one another in a series of increasingly subtle and spiritual spheres of existence, which helps explain some of the feats of shamans ... who can function at various levels of [their] super physical continuum. Life after death and even reincarnation, prominent ideas in theosophy, are implicit in the notion of the shaman as ... guide after death ... an ancient spiritual way involving initiations and mastering alternate realities is central to both shamanism and theosophy.[3]

Regarding the historic shamanic influence on Hindu and Buddhist yoga practices, Peters explains that there are:

Historical connections between shamanism and Hindu-Buddhist

yoga practices ... the Siberian Tungus term saman (shaman) derives from the south ... meaning 'ascetic' or 'one who practices austerities.' The religious practices of such holy men are thought to have stimulated and influenced the development of the more ancient northern Asiatic shamanism ... The experience of arousing the kundalini to the crown centre is described by yogis as something very similar to an out-of-the-body experience ... To a large extent yoga has [used] the symbolism ... of shamanism.

The axis mundi ... the ladder reaching through the numerous levels of heaven, corresponds in Tantric yoga to the spinal column and the chakras ... traversed ... to attain the final initiatory experience. The Tamang shaman's activation of the three souls ... undertaken at different levels of initiation, culminates in the ritual ascent to heaven during gufa and parallels the ascent of the kundalini in Tantric yoga.[4]

Peters' research confirms the shamanic origins of Tantric yoga and reveals the striking similarities of Krishna's spiritual experience with the shamanic ecstatic experiences of his predecessors:

Both Tantric yoga and shamanism also involve the 'embodiment' of gods. The shaman [is] possessed by spirits which he masters; the master yogi 'identifies' with gods representative of universal forces to the extent of becoming one with them and thereby coming to utilize these forces ... the initiatory experiences of shamans have many parallels in the experiences undergone by yogis in the process of awakening and raising the kundalini.

For example Krishna describes himself as being terror stricken, fearing his own death: 'Shivering as if stricken with ague,' before being saved by a 'glowing radiance.' All of this is strikingly similar to what is described in shamanic 'ecstasy.' ... it is possible for shamans to have meditative-type trances ... and for yogis to have ecstatic experiences ... at the higher initiatory levels, imagery becomes mastered in both Tantric yoga and shamanism.[5]

Muhammad, the prophet of Islam, was presumably a meditative soul as he often sat alone in the countryside.

He is described as shaking uncontrollably when he was commanded by a celestial being, similar to the 'glowing radiance' above, to 'recite' and the original Koranic verses poured forth. Those who did not understand, criticized Muhammad, claiming this literary masterpiece was the result of epileptic seizures. This criticism indicates the intensity of Muhammad's spiritual experiences.

It has been shown that shamanic experience-based beliefs are ancestors of cultures and as such provided the major tenets of the world's spiritual philosophies. The shamanic research of Professor Robert Ellwood can be taken as evidence that shamanic beliefs lie at the roots of humankind's later spiritual beliefs, shaping people's beliefs about life after death and developing spiritual philosophies.

Ellwood confirms that the shamans endured years of arduous training in order to learn how to perform healing, how to protect and guide their tribe, and that this demanded dedication and compassion. His findings are in harmony with the argument that shamanic ecstatic experiences have many features in common with those of other respected historical, spiritual teachers frequently known as prophets.

Ellwood describes the transformation in personality and abilities after shamanic experiences:

It is seen as a remaking of the man of power, in a way which recreates him so that he is able to see and to travel between two worlds. The process can be compared to the agony and illumination associated with classic mystical experience, as in the enlightenment of the Buddha and with the descriptions of initiations in ... theosophical sources.[6]

The Tibetan Book of the Dead, alternatively known as the *Bardo Thodol*, is a Buddhist funerary text.[7] It is customary for the Buddhist priest to read the text to a dying or newly dead person. This information offers guidance to the soul as it has just left or prepares to leave the body and make its journey to the alternate immaterial reality. Importantly, this text provides guidance regarding the non-physical roads a person's soul should take when it enters the bewildering multifaceted scenarios and levels in the non-physical landscapes.

Significantly, the ancient shaman, as psychopomp, was believed to actually accompany the souls of the deceased. During the shamans' soul-journeys they escorted souls in the labyrinthine alternate realities. Acting as companion navigators, they ensured that the newly arrived souls found their correct future homes in these non-physical realms.

The Tibetan Book of the Dead clearly has shamanic origins and features. Shamanic and Buddhist spiritual philosophies share further features including the belief that sickness is often considered to be caused by the loss of the soul. Notably, both the ancient shaman and contemporary Buddhist priest recite incantations to the sick person to call the soul back.

To provide further evidence for the third objective, notably that shamanism had a profound and continuing influence on the spiritual life of humankind; the following facts evidence the shamanic origins and ongoing shamanic features of contemporary Lamaism. Lamas still today believe that they use magic in order to fight with one another. Significantly, this belief echoes its shamanic forbears, particularly those of the Siberian shamans. Lamas are also believed to have the power to change the atmosphere, to fly, and to utilize ecstatic dance to facilitate their psycho-spiritual practices.

Notably, the shamanic precursors of present-day lamas similarly used ecstatic dance to access the shamanic state of consciousness. The lamas' forefathers equally flew in an out-of-body state of consciousness. Whilst in that state of astral travel, their shamanic predecessors carried out their soul-journey exploits. Ancient shamans, like contemporary lamas, were equally known for their feats of changing the atmosphere and weather.[8] Tibetan tantrism also utilizes a secret language.

The shamans of north Asia, Malaya and Indonesia are also known for their special 'spirit' languages. These are born as a result of their ecstatic psycho-spiritual practices. The on-going influence of ancient shamanism has been clearly evidenced here with special reference to its impact on Lamaism in Tibet. Shamanic feats past and present have been evaluated clearly proving the shamanic origins of present day spiritual beliefs and practices. Due to the fact that these experiences continue today, there is a definite continuum of related experiences.

The shamanic concept of spirit languages has significant parallels with the Christian concept of spiritual gifts and talking in tongues. This clearly evidences the fact that shamanic concepts lie at the roots of early Christianity. Notably, the matriarchs and patriarchs, the originators of Christianity were spiritually orientated, mediumistically gifted shamans. The spiritual teacher Paul, who is recorded in the New Testament, is familiar with different individuals receiving a selection of mediumistic and psychic gifts. He discusses the varying levels of these gifts in 1 Corinthians 12:1–11 and 1 Corinthians 14:5–6, 18:

Now about spiritual gifts ... (to one) the message of wisdom ... (to another) the message of knowledge ... (to others) gifts of healing ... to another speaking in tongues ... to another the interpretation of tongues ... I would like every one of you to talk in tongues, but I would rather have you prophesy. He who prophesies is greater than one who speaks in tongues, unless he interprets, so that the church may be edified ...

Thank God that I speak in tongues more than all of you.[9]

Reports state that shamans have exhibited imperviousness to

extremes of temperature. They have been observed displaying the ability to stand with ease in icy water or to calmly walk on fire. Shamans have even spent days in icy water, before tribal members eventually retrieved them and were astonished to find them to be still alive. In such cases, the severity of the conditions would surely have caused the shaman to have undergone a near-death experience. Mastering extremes of temperature frequently played a significant role in the rigors of shamanic training and later initiation ceremonies.

Significantly, similar shamanic features can be observed in Yoga and Indo-Tibetan tantrism. Vedic texts describe mystical or psychic heat and it plays a significant role in Yogic-tantric techniques. Breathing techniques, including holding the breath, and visualization of sexual energy being converted into heat are employed in Indo-Tibetan initiation ceremonies. Wet sheets are dried rapidly on the novice's heated body.[10] Significantly, ancient shamanic beliefs and practices have given birth to Yogic-tantric techniques and these shamanic practices have survived the millennia.

Some contemporary near-death experiencers share parallel experiences with the ancient shamans. Near-death experiencers, like their shamanic predecessors, believe that they visit and return from the non-physical world. Akin to their shamanic progenitors, they too witness human and non-human animals in these realms. After their recovery, some near-death experiencers report that they have had accidents with heat and have not been harmed.

For example, near-death experiencers' accounts refer to one or more incidents when they have inadvertently put their hand into boiling water. Initially, they had not noticed that they had done so, because they did not feel the heat throughout the whole duration of the burning water episodes.

They later noted that they were not harmed by the heat and no physical blistering occurred. Following in the footsteps of their ancient shamanic forebears, akin to the ancient shamanic experience, some near-death experiencers find they have developed imperviousness to heat as a result of returning from the after-death realms.

The shamanic source and on-going influence of further archaic shamanic beliefs will be evidenced. Shamanic ancestors of cultures believed that they sought knowledge and guidance from the spirits who live in the typically indiscernible non-ordinary realms. Echoing their distant relatives, the yogi, likewise seek enlightenment, which is a form of knowledge. The yogi's objective, which echoes those from the distant past, is to also seek detachment from the world. This is anaologous with the goals of their shamanic ancestors. These ahistoric shamanic mediums equally employed detachment or solitude as a means to facilitate entrance into trance states. Whilst in this state of being, they were able to access knowledge regarding the many benevolent characteristics and ethical demands of the Source of all knowledge. They knew this being as the supreme God.

They were also able to communicate with many levels of beings, some of whom were perceived as messengers and were frequently thought of as demi-gods. The shaman's objectives were externalized as he/she acted as a channel between the spirit or angelic communicators and the members of the tribe.

As a result of their soul-journeys to the metaphysical realms, the shamans gained the belief in the interrelated nature of all of creation. Contemporary humanity has learned this comparatively recently from the many supporting facts of evolution. These have been successively corroborated by many academic disciplines. Ancient shamans were tutored in healing and in acquiring means of building up power in order to enhance their psychic and mediumistic gifts.

They believed in the pervasiveness of a creative essence that connected all creatures together, including all components of the natural world. Consequently, they viewed the whole of creation as being interrelated and interdependent. The shaman, therefore, believed that if they harmed any other creature it would ultimately be the same as harming themselves. The most elevated spiritual philosopy is evidenced in these shamanic beliefs.

It is important to be aware of these ancient shamanic spiritual beliefs because they reveal the spirituality and influential nature of the shamanic experience-based worldview which is echoed today in many spiritual traditions. This holistic shamanic belief system extended to their beliefs regarding the interdependence of mind, body and spirit, each of which are vital. They believed that by healing one of these, it would facilitate healing to the whole animal, human or non-human. The shamanic concept regarding the interrelated nature of creation is further evidenced by their belief that their soul-journeys did not cause them to leave the physical reality to go to the non-physical reality. They perceived each of these realities to be an integral part of one single, whole reality.

For our shamanic forebears, God was seen as a mysterious, powerful, creative essence, who, after fulfilling the act of creation, continued to nurture creation. The supreme God was understood to be the Source inherent in all of creation, including everything inanimate and animate. God also represented the source of the power that shamans believed they accessed in order to accomplish their healing, psychic and mediumistic work.

Arguably, further shamanic features can be found in humankind's religions, as they too, teach people to seek a relationship with the supreme power, namely God. Likewise they teach that an aspect of God dwells in all creatures and that God facilitates spiritual gifts such as the ability to perform spiritual healing.

The concept of accessing 'the power' is an important feature of both archaic and modern-day shamanism. It is described by Hawaiian shamans as *mana*. They express this belief in terms that the universe is made up of four core components of *mana* – physical, mental, emotional and spiritual. Mana is symbolically represented in their art as a lightning bolt. The commonalities and slight differences between shamanic beliefs in power and those of other spiritual philosophies are indicated by Serge King. King explains that power is perceived by Hawaiian shamans as being:

Inner or divine power and energy ... In spite of numerous references in modern literature which equate mana with the Chinese chi, the Japanese ki, the Hindu prana and Reich's orgone, the fact is that mana is not identical to any of these. It is not just energy in the physical or bioenergetic sense ... it is more. The word power is a better rendering, in the sense of effective energy. Everything has mana, but some things have more mana than others, either naturally or because it has been imparted to them... during their... interactions with spirits, nature and other human beings.[11]

When the shaman healed a patient, they told them that their illness was the result of an evil spirit that needed to be driven off. This symbolism gave the patient something to visualize. The patient's thoughts and emotions would have supported the shaman's work as the patient visualized their illness being driven off. Shamans also believed that illness was the result of the patient's negative conditioning, which had led to negative patterns of thought; this then caused disharmony in the emotional, mental or spiritual self.

As these aspects of self each overlap, one with the other, over time the physical self would become adversely affected, making the patient's immune system vulnerable to disease. According to shamanic reasoning, if several people came into contact with a disease it would be the negative person who would fall victim to it, unlike the positive person who would not be vulnerable and would stay free of disease.

Shamans had a holistic and integrated view regarding the workings of health, believing that healing took place in the patient at a fundamentally deep, spiritual level. They believed that disease, though introduced by external bacteria, had its real origins in the receptive vulnerabilities of individual patients.

It is true that several people can come into contact with a disease, yet only those who are vulnerable on some level would get the disease. The wisdom and insightfulness of shamanic beliefs is being substantiated in the 21st century by the findings of quantum physics which prove the unity and holistic nature of mind, body and spirit.

Shamans used a variety of methods to initiate the healing process within the patient, including visualization techniques such as the use of guided imagery, ceremony and ritual. Significantly, this shamanic practice has been resurrected today in order to prompt a positive response in the subconscious of the patient. The shaman was inevitably working with the patient at a deeper level than the analytical mind which can obstruct the healing process.

Jean Achterberg is known for her work as a clinical professor of psychology and physical medicine at the University of Texas Health Science Center in the USA.. Achterberg offers her insights into the shamanic methods of healing:

> The function of any society's health system is ultimately tied to the philosophical convictions that the members hold regarding the purpose for life itself. For the shamanic cultures, the purpose is spiritual development. Health is harmony with the worldview. Health is the intuitive perception that the universe and all its inhabitants [are interconnected] ... Health is maintaining communication among the animals and plants and minerals and the stars. It is knowing death and life and seeing no difference.[12]

Contemporary doctors are increasingly seeing the wisdom in using meditative visualization techniques to enhance their medical treatments, particularly with regard to cancer treatments. However, the majority of these present day doctors are unaware that they are copying ancient shamanic practices. Achterberg's research investigated pre-verbal imagery and transpersonal methods of healing.

As a result of which, she believes that at the mundane level, the shamans utilized the patient's imagination to rally the most minuscule components of the body, including cells, tissues and organs, to fight off disease.

Ralph Metzner has made significant contributions as a psychopharmacologist, a psychotherapist and as a professor of east-west psychology in San Francisco. Metzner explains the shamanic healing process with regards to the physical and non-physical worlds. He believes it is the

> disciplined approach to ... the non-ordinary reality, the sacred, the mystery, the supernatural, the inner world(s) or the other world. Psychologically speaking ... these expressions refer to realms of consciousness that lie outside the boundaries of our ... ordinary perception.
>
> The depth psychologies derived from psychoanalysis refer to such normally inaccessible realms as the unconscious or the collective unconscious. This would ... be too limiting a definition for shamanism if unconscious is taken to refer to something within the individual i.e. intrapsychic. Shamanic practice involves the exploration not only of unknown aspects of our psyche, but also the unknown aspects of the world around us, the external as well as the internal mysteries.[13]

This discussion has provided insights both into the spiritual worldview of the shamans and the pervasive influence which ancient shamanic beliefs and practices have had on the development of humankind's religious beliefs and spiritual philosophies.

## Shamanic Features in the Judeo-Christian Traditions

At this point we turn to the accomplishment of the fourth objective. Penetrating research which uncovers the shamanic features demonstrated during the lives of the biblical prophets from the Judeo-Christian tradition will be given. Supportive evidence from the scholarly research of Rabbi Gershom will be drawn upon to corroborate the prophets' shamanic origins and influences.

There are innumerable sacred, historic Jewish writings, only a fragment of which are stored in the Christian 'Old Testament.' Gershom discovered 'a vast wealth of material'[14] which proves that shamanic beliefs and practices were demonstrated throughout the lives of many prophets from the Judaeo-Christian traditions.

The prophets Jeremiah and Isaiah are remembered for their passionate sermons frequently delivered in the marketplace. The prophets Elijah and Elisha are remembered for their miraculous acts, some of which were carried out to prove the existence of God. Their extraordinary abilities were many and varied. Their supernormal abilities included feats of healing, raising people from the dead, making a metallic axe-head float, making bitter water sweet to taste, and increasing the volume of food.[15] These paranormal feats echo those of their more ancient shamanic forebears.

Similarly, the sermonizing prophet Ezekiel is also famous for his accomplishment of miraculous feats. The biblical passages report that Ezekiel received messages from spirit beings, both in the form of visions and during the sleep state. Clearly, these narratives inform us of Ezekiel's psychic and mediumistic experiences.

Some of the descriptions have much in common with experiences known today as out-of-body experiences.[16] This prophet's extraordinary psychic and mediumistic accomplishements have close parallels with the fascinating feats reported of his shamanic ancestors. The biblical writer's obvious fluency with and belief in out-of-body, psychic and mediumistic experiences clearly reveals the writer's familiarity with paranormal shamanic phenomena. Significantly, these preliminary examples prove that historic, biblical spiritual, prophetic teachers possessed core shamanic abilities. They demonstrated characteristics typical of archaic shamanism.

It is important to remember that in the early days the Jews were a nomadic tribal people, originally divided into twelve clans. Having carried out research into the early Jewish sacred records, that modern day society should be made aware that the actions reported of Abraham evidence that he was a shamanic vision quester. A vision quest is a shamanic feature, particularly prevalent among the North American shamans.

Gershom's research supports the evidence that Abraham's

purpose in building an altar and his willingness to sacrifice a sheep – an event described in the Bible – represented his belief that his actions would attract a non-physical communicator to make contact. Abraham heard communications from the voice of a non-physical being. Typically, – he interpreted it as being the voice of a god or God.[17]

It is being repeatedly shown that there is a recurring pattern from these earliest times onwards to deify non-physical communicators. This event is described in the bible and displays all the characteristics of a shamanic vision quest. Mediums and others today know that Abraham's willingness to sacrifice a sheep was totally unnecessary and unethical and would have karmic implications on the perpetrator during their physical and non-physical existence.

The life of the prophet Moses also evidenced features of shamanic behavior. Over time, Moses communicated in the form of copious dialogue with a celestial messenger named YHVH (the Hebrew letters denote the name 'Yahweh'). At their first meeting, when the voice initially instigated communication with Moses, the celestial messenger used a burning bush as a physical interface to help draw Moses' attention. It is important to reiterate, in the present context, that talking with non-physical spirits and angels has close parallels with the beliefs and practices of historically earlier shamans.

It is also very significant that a number of Moses' shamanic, psycho-spiritual experiences occurred at the top of a mountain and have much in common with the experiences of his ancient shamanic predecessors. Shamans frequently performed feats on mountain tops. Likewise, they used physical steps and trees, each of which were knows as *axis mundi*.

These symbolic tools demonstrated the interconnection of the physical with the various non-physical spheres. These features were both physical and symbolic representations of ascension, descension and transition from the mundane, human condition to the invisible, sacred, celestial realms. They were utilized by the shaman in order to seek communication with otherworldly messengers.

Further familiar shamanic features can be evidenced with regard to this famous spiritually orientated, biblical prophet. Moses communicated with a celestial messenger – an angel or spirit. He received a powerful magical staff and was given a difficult vision quest. Moses was commanded to liberate the Hebrews and lead them out of Egyptian bondage. He was instructed to take them to a named safe haven, referred to as the 'Promised Land,' the 'land of milk and honey,' alternatively known as Canaan.

The exploits of the biblical prophet Jacob reported in Genesis 30:25 – 31:13 also exhibit many interesting shamanic features.[18]

Jacob's wrestling with an angel (malach) and receiving a blessing is part of a shamanic journey. Alone in the desert, on his way to meet his hostile brother Esau, Jacob was troubled. Would there be war or peace? Then comes the malach, a word which can mean either a spirit being (angel) or a physical messenger. Jacob wrestles with the malach and is wounded in the leg, but wins the battle and is blessed with a new name, as is the shaman. No longer would he be called Yaakov, 'the Heel;' now he has become Yisrael, the 'Godwrestler.' [See Genesis 32:23–33[19]] If, as some Jewish accounts suggest, the mysterious messenger was Esau's guardian angel come to kill Jacob, then the episode is even more shamanic, because the power to subdue evil spirits is associated with medicine people the world over ... the change within Jacob has its effect on Esau and the two brothers embrace in peace. [See Genesis 33[20]]

It is of interest, at this point, to look into the meaning of the most frequently used Hebrew term for 'a prophet.' This word is *nah-vee*. Translated, this means 'to flow' or 'to gush forth.' This is most significant as it echoes the entranced shamanic outpourings of knowledge regarding the spiritual realms. It clearly describes an awareness of the altered states of consciousness of the historic prophets, including Muhammad, the Prophet of Islam and that of spiritual mediums today.

Another commonly used Hebrew term is *nah-vuv*, meaning 'a hollow,' indicating that the shamanic/mediumistic person who received otherworldly communications was an empty, receptive vessel. They act as a hollow receptor or channel, transmitting the otherworldly communications for others to hear. Otherworldly contact or 'divine blessing,' *shay-fah*, is frequently described as being 'poured out' like water.

Samuel was described as a *ro-eh*, literally 'one who sees.' The Bible indicates that the term 'one who sees' is an earlier term for a mediumistic 'prophet.' The biblical prophet is therefore a medium, in the same sense as the ancient shamans. The above translations evidence the direct mediumistic parallels between shamanism and the biblical prophets.

The Old Testament biblical narrative regarding Samuel found in 1 Samuel 9:1–15[21] tells us that Samuel is accustomed to receiving predictive information from non-physical communicators. He is referred to as 'the prophet,' 'the man of God' and 'the seer.' Samuel's knowledge of future events is demonstrated when he was told by an unseen communicator to expect a meeting the following day with a man named Saul who would become the next king of Israel.

The accuracy of Samuel's precognitive knowledge and his important reputation is revealed in the narrative which explains how Saul met Samuel. Whilst searching for his lost donkeys, Saul encountered Samuel, Saul asked Samuel to predict where they might be found. This event clearly indicates that knowledge of Samuel's psychic and mediumistic abilities must have been widespread.

Saul had heard that the prophet, Samuel, could be found at the 'high place.' As we have seen, communicating with non-physical beings and offering psychic and mediumistic services from mountainous locations are two specific and important shamanic features. Evidently, Samuel's life displayed many shamanic features. Today, Samuel would be described as a spiritual medium or channel.

The following biblical account makes clear that the terms 'the man of God, 'the seer' and 'the prophet' refer to one and the same person. Supernormal knowledge was expected of such people. 1 Samuel 9:9,[22] informs us that the term 'the seer' originated in earlier times, presumably archaic shamanic times, and that later the same person would be called 'a prophet:' 'Formerly in Israel, if a man went to enquire of God, he would say 'Come, let us go to the seer,' because the prophet of today used to be called a seer.'

At this historic meeting, Samuel gave Saul further accurate predictions of future events that would occur when Saul was en route home. As predicted, Saul met a group of singing, dancing, chanting prophets who used musical instruments. These prophets were clearly conducting shamanic practices in order to communicate with immaterial spirits with the goal of receiving predictive information and guidance. Their singing and dancing was conducted to evoke the ecstatic 'trance state of consciousness' believed necessary to contact spirit or angelic messengers.

It becomes clear that both the lesser known and more famous biblical prophets commonly demonstrated shamanic psychic and mediumistic behavior. No one was shocked by these practices; instead, all were familiar with them, and in fact mediumistic and psychic abilities were the expected norm. Inevitably, many biblical prophets were fully acquainted with shamanic experience-based beliefs.

The above biblical account regarding the prophets Samuel and Saul, exemplifies their typical shamanic behavior, which was used to cultivate mediumistic/shamanic states of consciousness. Singing and dancing were commonly used by shamans as a catalyst for communication with an array of non-physical messengers. 1 Samuel 10[23] explains that Saul joined in with the singing and dancing prophets and became caught up by 'the spirit of the lord' and also began to prophesy.

Saul evidently entered into a quasi trance state. Accounts such as these prove that famous historic biblical prophets including those in Samuel's day deliberately accessed shamanic altered states of consciousness. They were adept at cultivating such mediumistic states with the use of an assortment of music, rhythmic dancing, singing and chanting. A broad range of non-physical communicators made contact, some of whom were referred to as the 'spirit of the lord,' alternatively described as 'Yahweh' (in Hebrew: 'YHVH').

Gershom supports the view that the biblical accounts of Joseph's life also demonstrate many shamanic features. These include Joseph's abilities to provide predictive information and to interpret hidden or symbolic meanings in a person's dreams. Gershom's research has revealed that the biblical descriptions of Joseph's special, colorful cloak was in fact referring to a fine gossamer priestly garment, a cloak used by shamanic prophets. The thin material may have made the cloak look effeminate and therefore drew attention to it.

This biblical account appears to indicate a further biblical shamanic feature. Gershom notes that many shamans were androgynous and it was not uncommon for shamans to put on the clothes of the opposite sex during ritual activity. Gershom points out that Joseph's brother, Gad, is described in markedly masculine terms,[24] possibly to clearly differentiate him from Joseph.

Gershom suggests that the real reason for the brothers' opposition to Joseph was not simple jealousy of the cloak but because it was a shamanic garment indicating that he was quite different from them. Joseph clearly possessed prophetic, predictive abilities and may also have been gifted with mediumship.

Joseph had much in common with his archaic shamanic predecessors who were also adept at dream interpretation. They too, looked for predictive dream symbols and keys in order to help a person gain predictive knowledge and a deeper understanding of their emotions and events in their life. Joseph is famously remembered for his accurate interpretation of the Egyptian pharaoh's dreams.

After hearing pharaoh's troublesome dream, Joseph predicted the forthcoming onset of several years of plenty followed by several years of famine. Likewise, Joseph's male shamanic ancestors often wore effeminate clothing while performing rituals that were used to alter their state of consciousness in order to access mediumistic dialogues. Clearly, the biblical accounts regarding Joseph are describing a shaman.

Dream interpretation, an ancient shamanic practice, has continued to be popular within the Jewish religious tradition, proving the ongoing influence of shamanism on yet another contemporary world religion. Shamanism is synonymous with psychic and mediumistic gifts. Significantly, Sigmund Freud, the famous Jewish psychiatrist and psychologist, examined the hidden depths and meanings inherent in dreams. Gershom draws attention to a Jewish rainmaker named Honi, who lived during the Talmudic Roman period. The people called him whenever they needed adequate rain to make the crops grow, too much rain was as destructive as a drought.[25]

In Talmudic times, many prophets with exceptional, magical shamanic abilities are described, some of whom had abilities that parallel those of Jesus. In 70 AD the Romans destroyed the Second Temple of the Jews. After this event, 1,900 years of exile followed for the Jewish people. Gershom notes that after the fall of the Second Temple:

The focus of Judaism began to switch from the magical to the intellectual. When Moses Maimonides wrote his famous Guide to the Perplexed in the twelfth century, he was attempting to reconcile Judaism with Aristotelian philosophy. In the end the rationalist [intellectual] school seemed to win out, but mystical practices continued secretly.[26]

A feature of the late Middle Ages is the rise of a group of people known as the *baalei shem*, a Jewish Hassidic sect whose title means 'Masters of the Name.'

> The Name was known as the Tetragrammaton, the secret, unpronounceable Name of God, written with the four Hebrew letters, Y-H-V-H ... A baal shem ... was someone who knew the pronunciation of the Name and could vibrate it silently within an altered state of consciousness known as the 'Great Voice.' ... Often the spirit messenger sent to initiate the seeker was Elijah the prophet, who, because he was taken up alive into heaven [see 2 Kings chapter 2[27]] was believed to live eternally.

The beliefs and practices of the medieval religious group known as the baalei shem had many shamanic features. They revered the historic prophet named Elijah because he was an adept at performing supernormal feats similar to other shamans.[28] They believed that various combinations of Hebrew letters had great power, as the Divine was thought to have used primal sounds when speaking Creation into existence.

Also shamanic in origin is the attempt at accessing the Source for power along with strict moral guidelines preventing abuse of that power. These features demonstrate further parallels with ancient shamanism. The *baalei shem* represented significant continuity with both the earlier Jewish mystical schools and those of the later medieval era. Each school clearly continued to demonstrate their shamanic origins and ongoing shamanic beliefs and practices.

> Careful observance of Jewish laws ... was essential, the greater one's power, the greater one's responsibility to live a saintly and moral life ... for a baal shem to 'call upon the Name of the Lord (YHVH)' was not merely to pray the words, but to invoke the power of the Creator to help heal the people and defend them against evil. God was the baal shem's 'helping spirit,' so to speak ... Israel Baal Shem Tov, the eighteenth century founder of

Hassidism [is portrayed] in exactly this mode ... a letter attributed to him describes how he first met his spirit teacher while immersing in the mikveh (ritual purification pool) at the age of eighteen. He was then instructed to go to a local cave between two mountains, where this angelic messenger taught him from a secret book.[29]

It was revealed that Israel Baal Shem Tov's spirit teacher was Ahijah the Shilonite who had been the spirit teacher of the prophet named Elijah. Israel Baal Shem Tov reported that he ascended to heaven during the sleep state to be taught by spirits who were honored for their wisdom and spirituality. It is also believed that he could travel vast geographic distances in one night, heal the sick and speak to angels whenever he chose. This account has many features in common with those of the shamans of antiquity. It was believed that they were similarly taught by wise spirit ancestors during their sleep and trance states and frequently accessed this guidance when alone in isolated caves and mountaintops. This account has much in common with the out-of-body journeys made by the genius and seer Emanuel Swedenborg in the 18th century and will be discussed in detail later.

The name 'Baal Shem' became synonymous with Israel Baal Shem Tov, as he was the epitome of their movement. Increasingly, no other person could be called a *baal shem*. The magical, kabbalistic teachings which mirrored many earlier shamanic beliefs and practices became increasingly overshadowed by rationalistic, intellectual thinking. In more contemporary times, the leader of a Hassidic sect is known as a Rebbe and the term *baal shem* is not used.

In early times, Hassidism selected its leaders in one of two ways. They were chosen either because of their moral piety and integrity or through the intervention of a spirit or angelic messenger who selected them in a vision or dream. The act of angelic intervention took priority over any candidate's intellectual accomplishments. By the late 1800s things had changed, and the position of Rebbe was simply passed down from one generation to the next, from father to son. Hereditary succession replaced the previous desire for either humanly observed moral piety or celestial selection.

Jewish narratives, however, have shown a remarkable continuity regarding the role of the Rebbe. Even today, some Rebbes are reported to have spiritual powers such as healing and the ability to defend the soul after death in judgment scenes. Clearly, the strong shamanic origins and ongoing shamanic features are inherent in these narratives. Gershom believes he is one of a growing number of Neo-Hassidic Jews who work to synthesize the New Age consciousness with historic mystical Hassidic teachings. These include practicing Jewish forms of spiritual healing and other human-potential disciplines. The shamans of antiquity mastered these abilities, which are continued today.

Clearly, many original shamanic beliefs and practices are being continued today within the Jewish religious tradition, proving the link between the psychic and mediumistic abilities and religions today. This discussion has proven that ancient shamanic mediumistic and psychic beliefs and practices have dominated the Judeo-Christian tradition.

It has shown that these beliefs and practices have continued throughout the millennia through the lives of many significant, historial, spiritual figures. Many people today are unaware of this fact. Regarding the shamanic features in Judaism, Gershom notes:

Shamanic practices have probably never been considered mainstream within Judaism; nevertheless, there is a persistent and continuous thread of teachings which weaves itself in and out of the Jewish tradition. From Abraham to Moses to the prophets to the baalai shem to the Hassidic Rebbes, these teachings have been transmitted from teacher to student for over 5000 years.[30]

## Shamanism, Psychic Abilities and Mediumship

In order to fulfill the fifth and final objective regarding shamanism, it will be shown that shamanic phenomena are indeed psychic and mediumistic phenomena. The wealth of shamanic, mediumistic and psychic abilities should not be viewed in isolation from related modern-day spiritually transformative psychic and mediumistic experiences and the paranormal abilities demonstrated by near-death experiencers.

These exceptional human abilities are being studied today by individuals from a range of academic fields, including psychology, parapsychology, medicine and psychical research. Shamanic experiences possibly represent the most ancient human expression of psycho-spiritual encounters with the inhabited, non-physical realms of existence. In order to make a significant contribution to our contemporary understanding of mediumistic experiences of spirit or angelic communicators, it is important to demonstrate that shamanic mediumistic experiences are related to modern day mediumistic experiences. This will then clarify the correct historical context for understanding many shamanic experiences.

This in turn, will reveal that shamanic mediumistic experiences are ancient in origin and that the broad range of inhabitants in the invisible world have never stopped breaking through the boundaries separating the physical and non-physical realms. As shown, mediumistic experiences have occurred throughout the world and the millennia and are still frequent today. The following research offers a historical context in which to fit more contemporary mediumship.

D. Scott Rogo has written extensively on psychical research. He notes that many traditional academic researchers have never 'grappled directly with the issue of whether shamanism developed as a practice because, in all cultures and religions, certain people have sought and developed powerful psychic abilities and have institutionalized their practices over the ages.'[31]

A brief summary of shamanic abilities follows, noting the contemporary significance of each with regard to psychical research.

One of the most important roles of the shaman was to communicate with those spirits who experienced a transition of consciousness at physical death. These included relatives, friends and animals. As noted, some spirit or angel communicators who were accessed in the realms of durative, amplified, sacred space and time were described as gods due to their otherworldly nature.

Adverse health and welfare conditions of members of the tribe were believed to be the work of enemies' magical spells and could be counteracted by the special abilities of the shaman. Usually working with the guidance of their spirit helper, shamans believed that they could cast out illness from their patients and could change a person's luck. Since they believed that the onset of illness was often due to the patient losing their soul, shamans could restore health by traveling on soul-journeys and returning with lost souls.

The shaman was also trusted to be able to send his or her own soul to the non-physical world to guide members of the tribe at death to the level or landscape they had earned during their physical life.

Rogo states:

By tradition the shaman is supposedly endowed with several specific supernatural (or psi) powers. The same phenomena are mentioned over and over within widely separated cultures. These include the power to heal, to diagnose and 'read' people clairvoyantly, to control the weather, to levitate, to become immune to fire and to project the soul from the body.[32]

The range of shamanic abilities might be described today as the utilization of their 'psi,' psychic and mediumistic abilities. Parallel experiences and abilities can be noted between shamans and mediumistic prophetic individuals. A number of these were discussed earlier including the more contemporary example of Swedenborg.

I will now provide five examples of regularly repeated shamanic abilities, taken from widely diverse contemporary shamanic cultures. It will become clear that these same phenomena can befound today in western cultures – with significant implications for modern-day psychical research.

## The Araucanian shamans of South America

The first example is drawn from the Araucanian shamans. A central feature of Araucanian shamanism is to send out prayers to the invisible alternate landscapes. These shamans request clairvoyant and healing abilities to enable them to 'see' the illness in their patient's bodies and to heal them. They believe that they utilize a 'power' in order to carry out such healing. This practice is carried out today by spiritual healers who believe that they also channel a healing power into their patient. This practice is called spiritual or psychic healing. Remarkable results have been achieved both by historic and contemporary shamans and by historic and contemporary spiritual or psychic healers, many of whom can be found in the modern-day western world.

## The Carib shamans of Venezuela and Central America

Of the second example of shamanic abilities Rogo states that the Caribs

> traditionally possess the ability to know psychically the innermost secrets of their tribesmen, including knowledge about the fate of the dead ... these abilities are very similar to the religious traditions of the Roman Catholic Church, whose mystics and saints were (and are) known to discern psychically the nature of unconfessed sins and the disposition of a deceased individual's soul. Such shamanistic practices may be cross-cultural and inherent in the development of mystical gifts and powers within a wide range of religious traditions.[33]

As a psychical researcher, I have observed entranced mediums pouring out elevated spiritual philosophy, which in turn becomes absorbed into the spiritual philosophy of the religion of Spiritualism. This is just one of the many examples of religions born as a result of mediumship, but, unlike many other religions today, Spiritualism has not cut itself off from the mediumistic source of elevated spiritual philosophy and descriptions of the natural laws which govern the after-death realms.

Rogo's research supports the view argued by this book that shamanic experience-based beliefs and practices have shaped and lie at the source of many of the world's religious traditions. These influenced their ethical beliefs and those concerning the continuation of life after physical death.

Of the third example Rogo notes that the accepted paranormal characteristics of the American Indian shamans include 'the ability to control the weather, to become immune to fire, to discern clairvoyantly who has perpetuated certain crimes and to see into the future.'[34] Similarly, imperviousness to fire, knowledge of future events and those occurring at vast geographic distances away, and guidance from relatives and friends who have passed to the higher spheres are among the paranormal abilities included in the personal testimonies of near-death experiencers and many mediums today.

## The Malayan and Kamba shamans (East Africa)

The following highlights the fourth and fifth examples of enigmatic paranormal phenomena. Discussing the psychic abilities of the Malayan shamans, Rogo draws attention to the 'special initiates [who] allegedly possess the power to see into the future and to discover the whereabouts of lost objects.'[35]

Of the psychic abilities reported of the Kamba shamans of East Africa Rogo notes:

As in so many other African cultures, the Kamba ... practice voluntary spirit possession and trance. The Kamba have high expectations of their shamans. If a shaman 'brings through' a spirit from another locale or tribe, he is expected to speak in the language or dialect of the spirit's tribe – even if he has never learned or studied it.[36]

Rogo endorses the fact that scores of anthropologists in the field have confirmed that psychic and mediumistic phenomena are core features of shamanism.[37] Many books have been written at supernormal speeds by mediums in trance in recent centuries. This phenomenon has been observed by psychical researchers and other academics who have shown that these mediums had no previous knowledge of the information in the books they wrote. Mediums have also been observed writing or speaking in dead languages. Each of these phenomena has direct parallels with the mediumistic abilities of historic shamans.

Joan Halifax[38] is known for her work as a medical anthropologist at the New School for Social Research in New York, USA. She has traveled extensively in order to observe modern-day shamanic paranormal phenomena. A further contemporary western anthropologist is Marlene Dobkin de Rios[39] from California, who carried out an extensive study concerning a number of Peruvian shamans. Both modern-day anthropologists have unwittingly stumbled on present day shamans' psychic and mediumistic phenomena.

They are among a growing number of researchers who have documented their observations. It is highly significant and evidential that the psychic and mediumistic phenomena claimed of ancient shamans are being verified by the reports of modern-day researchers.

The following information is taken from two early 20th-century reports which document observable shamanic psychic and mediumistic abilities.

The first was written by a Russian ethnologist named Vladimir Bogoras[40] who evaluated a number of shamans from the Chukchee Eskimos of Siberia and the St Lawrence Islands. Bogoras' final report was published in 1904 by the American Museum of Natural History. He reported that he observed psychic surgery and shamanic mediumistic séances. During the latter, contact was made with diverse spirit voices who spoke through the entranced shaman. Borgoras' research documents tell us that he also observed a walrus skin become animated while it hung over a shaman's shoulders; it took on a life of its own and moved around.

Bogoras was unable to explain any of the shamans' psychic and mediumistic phenomena despite acting as a witness to it. For example, he observed a deep incision made by a shaman, without using physical tools, into a young boy's chest and found the experience incredibly fascinating yet unfathomable. The shaman in this case carried out a procedure currently known as psychic surgery which is conducted today by other comparable psychics and mediums.

The writings of the anthropologist David Barker, who worked for the University of Virginia, USA, provide another early 20th-century example of observed shamanic phenomena. Barker carried out ethnological and anthropological research and reported that he witnessed innumerable psychical and mediumistic events. For example, his records reveal that he was present when shamans predicted future events which after a short time were verified as accurate.

He also heard spirit voices manifesting through shamans and observed psychokinetic events facilitated by shamans.[41] Evidently, the commonality of shamanic beliefs and practices has continued globally throughout the millennia. Documentary evidence inherent in reports such as these, have many parallel features with those seen today in the 21st century.

Diamond Jenness, born in Canada, carried out extensive research on the Copper Eskimos, a shamanic tribe that lived in the northwest Arctic region of Canada. They placed particular emphasis on their shamanic ability to access predictive information and spirit communication during the altered state of consciousness which naturally occurs during the sleep state.

Jenness' records authenticate predictive information that he personally received from a shaman. The prediction given to Jenness by a shaman foretold of a forthcoming natural accident. The shaman predicted a large fall of snow and ice which would directly affect Jenness' homebound vessel. Jenness emphasized that it would have been impossible for anyone to have had future knowledge about this particular incident by use of normal means. The event occurred exactly as it had been prophesied.[42]

Further anthropological accounts of observations of shamanic psychic and mediumistic phenomena occurring up to the mid 1970s can be found in the writings of Adrian Boshier[43] and Irving Hallowell.[44] Boshier lived among the African shamanic tribes most of his life. Hallowell studied, in particular, the shamanic people known as the Salteaux who lived on the shores of the Beress River in Manitoba, Canada. The phenomena these researchers witnessed echo those mediumistic accounts given earlier and have distinct parallels with those described in the following chapters.

## Shamans and Direct-Voice Trance Mediumship

Further examples of mediumship in shamanic cultures include the phenomenon of voices emanating from entranced shamans. Significantly, the voices heard are distinctly different from those of the shamans involved and includes voices of a different gender to the shamanic medium. Today, this phenomenon is known as 'direct-voice trance mediumship.'

Similarly, the direct voice trance phenomena of more contemporary mediums have been observed by modern-day psychical researchers in the western world. The following example of direct-voice trance mediumship, taken from Rogo's work, is typical of the large number of anthropologists' accounts of more contemporary shamanic direct voice trance phenomena.

In trance the [shaman] began to speak in an old man's husky voice, definitely not the voice of the woman [shaman] ... The presenting spirit identified himself as a chief under Mzilikazi, the great Matabele king and said that he had died after the Europeans took Matabeleland ... [A researcher] checked all this [information] out and found it to be correct ... [and] in trance this witchdoctor who knew nothing about the African [man] with cancer confirmed everything that the hospital had told him.[45]

Rogo's observations support this book's argument that shamans were mediums or channels both in ancient and contemporary times: 'Accounts of ESP in shamans parallel observations by parapsychologists on clairvoyance (or distant seeing) and on precognition (or knowledge of future events) in psychic subjects.'[46] The psychic and mediumistic abilities of historic and contemporary shamans have been shown to have much in common with present day psychic and mediumistic phenomena.

Such abilities are commonly found in all cultures including that of the western world. Notably, shamanic practices and experience-based beliefs, born of their supersensitive abilities are paralleled in all cultures of the world. Shamanic gifts are known as psychic and mediumistic gifts today.

## The Reality of the Invisible World
This book cannot prove that the invisible, hierarchical levels or realms are a reality. Its focus is on proving that transformative spiritual, psychic and mediumistic experiences are directly related to, and feed into, the evolving nature of world religions and related spiritual philosophies. Such phenomena furnish experience-based beliefs regarding the continued existence after physical death, many of which are a result of apparent spirit or angelic communications.

The eminent scholars Mircea Eliade, Henri Corbin and Michael Harner support the argument of this book that these non-physical, alternate realms are a reality and that they have objective externalized form. They help substantiate the claims of people, past and present, who believe that they have experienced the fluid, non-physical energy realms and its human and non-human spirit inhabitants.

Despite the objectivity and reality of the experiences, the energy realm is malleable to thought, alternatively known as 'ideo-plastic in nature. ' It would appear that, after death, at first we see what we expect or need to see, alternatively we draw to ourselves landscapes and inhabitants that match our emotional state or our predominant thought patterns. As individuals progress they each become acquainted with the full nature of these invisible hierarchical landscapes.

Shamans believed that plans for historic, earthly cities were first obtained from observations of their celestial prototypes in the metaphysical spheres. Shamans believed that the invisible or celestial form preceded the physical earthly form. With reference to the Iranian cosmology of the Zarvanitic tradition, Eliade states: 'Every terrestrial phenomenon, whether abstract or concrete, corresponds to a celestial, transcendent invisible term, to an "idea" in the Platonic sense.'[47]

The writings of the eminent Islamic scholar Henri Corbin make a distinction between fantasy or imagination and genuine experiences of the reality of the invisible world and its inhabitants. Corbin conducted extensive research into Arabic and Persian Islamic texts dating back to the 12th century. These early texts gave descriptions which aimed to prove the objectivity and reality of the metaphysical landscapes.

These texts described experiences of an objective, though non-physical, world. Spirit inhabitants can be found living in and among cities, valleys, deserts and mountains. In this world, the writers of the texts, like archaic and contemporary shamans and Emanuel Swedenborg, found that earthly thoughts and desires had, in effect, taken on form.[48]

Michael Harner has worked as a professor and former chairman of the anthropology department of the Graduate Faculty at the New School for Social Research in New York. He was also the founder of the Center for Shamanic Studies in Connecticut, USA. After carrying out extensive research into shamanic states of consciousness and their experience-based beliefs, Harner is emphatic that the non-physical spheres accessed through altered states of consciousness should not be thought of in terms of imagination.

Harner, like scholars before him, believes that the metaphysical world has as much ontological substance as that of the empirical world of the mundane senses. Related, spiritually illuminating experiences of the non-physical, etheric realms and their spirit inhabitants have been reported by mystics from many cultures. These include Gnostics and Islamic Sufis and many other historic, spiritual figures from the Judeo-Christian tradition. Arguably, these realms are accessed through the gateway of the mind, through altered states of consciousness which permit out-of-body soul-journeys to their non-physical shores.

Many people in contemporary western society may have difficulty in understanding the shamanic model of the universe, including shamanic beliefs in the integrated mind-body-spirit continuum. This is because vast areas of the planet are increasingly being overwhelmed and brainwashed by the pervasive, inadequate modern day, western, materialistic, reductionist understanding of the nature of life. There is a distinct difference between the shamanic, holistic worldview that accepts and integrates all psychic and mediumistic experiences into its frameworks of thought and that of contemporary western, materialist society. Unlike the shamans, the latter is unable to fit psychic and mediumistic experiences into its frameworks of thought.

This is due to the narrow limitations of the contemporary reductionist way of understanding the world. It typically forces its supporters to reject global human transformative spiritual, psychic and mediumistic experiences. This is a sad fact when such remarkable spiritually transformative experiences, with their invaluable legacy and implications, have spanned the planet and the millennia.

Experiencers are forced to adopt an unsatisfactory fragmented,

separatist, segregating approach. Unlike the shamanic understanding of the world, this limited, materialist reasoning does not
provide a context into which such authentic, valuable and global
experiences can be fitted.

Ralph Metzner states:

> Rather these traditional systems operated from an integrated
> world view in which physical healing, psychological problem
> solving and conscious exploration of spiritual or sacred realms of
> being are all considered as aspects of the way, or work or practice
> ... The split in Western 'civilized' consciousness between body,
> mind and spirit is reflected in a rigid separation of roles between
> the physician, the therapist and the priest.[49]

These pages have verified that accounts of shamanic experiences
have direct parallels with phenomena known today as psychic and
mediumistic phenomena. Frequently, this phenomena has spiritually
transformative consequences on the experiencer. This research has
cumulatively shown the profound influence shamanic, psychic and
mediumistic experiences have had on the birth and development of
the world's religions and spiritual philosophies. It has shown their
ongoing influence on the religion of Spiritualism as psychic and
mediumistic experiences continue to this day.

Religions are indeed born of ancient, global, shamanic, psycho-
spiritual philosophies furnished by shamanic experience-based
beliefs. Indeed, shamans have been shown to be the ancestors of
cultures. However, it has also been noted that the otherworldly
communicators display a lower to higher level of spirituality as do
the mediumistic individuals who interpret these communications.
This inevitably results in lower to higher spiritual philosophies.
Psychic and mediumistic experiences have been shown to have
existed since the dawn of animal life on this planet and will
inevitably continue hand in hand with all life forms. Indeed, as
human physical evolution can be traced back to our four-legged

animal ancestors and beyond, it would appear from research that psychic sensitivities are also a trait exhibited by all animals, human and non-human.

Clearly, most animals have superior, heightened senses and sensitivities compared to those of their human brethren. It is highly likely, therefore, that they have related heightened paranormal senses also. .

## Chapter 6

# Archaeology Supports Biblical Accounts

Many biblical prophets were mediums or 'channels.' This is a fact that the following chapters will substantiate. They will provide the results of examinations of the correct translations of biblical narratives, revealing the underlying accurate texts. These texts describe the lives and mediumistic practices of many eminent spiritual, prophetic leaders.

The prophets, who are proven to have had mediumistic abilities and practices are sampled from a number of generations, spanning a period of approximately 1,000 years. It will be shown that they channeled spiritual truths from the alternate invisible realms to this material realm.

Before we discuss the mediumistic abilities and practices of such highly revered biblical figures, it is important to prove that these individuals did in fact exist. The purpose of this preliminary chapter is to show the results of historical and archaeological research, proving the accuracy and historicity of biblical accounts. Such accounts describe in detail the events surrounding the lives of globally famous prophets.

This research brings these influential individuals to life, enriching our understanding of their historic epochs and the context in which they lived their lives. However, it is important to be aware of the fact that the authors of the books which were later chosen and consolidated together as the bible, did not necessarily record historical dates in the same vein as we do in modern day history books.

We are finding that the oral traditions regarding family, clan and tribal history which were passed cumulatively, from one generation to the next and finally recorded for posterity was painstakingly carried out. The accuracy of these biblical records are successively being confirmed by archaeological excavations. Significantly, archaeological excavations have not disproved biblical records rather thay have confirmed them. They resurrect the individuals, buildings, towns, cities and civilizations that are recorded in the ancient texts.

After looking at the archaeological evidence which supports biblical accounts, we will look briefly at how the Bible came into being, noting its many authors and several languages. The Bible is still today a perennial world bestseller despite the fact that religious orthodoxy is aware that it contains many confirmed mistranslations based on many misinterpreted concepts which as a consequence produce mistranslations.

In addition, all too often, for religio-political purposes much ancient authentic spiritual literature was quashed or excluded from the Bible. Some known mistranslations are introduced in this chapter as a preliminary to later chapters which decode and reveal mistranslated and suppressed texts. At this juncture, it is suggested that the reader refers to the historical timeline (see Figure 2 in Appendix), which clarifies the wide time span in which the numerous mediumistic prophets lived.

## Archaeology Corroborates the Bible

Archaeology can be used as a tool to substantiate the accurate historicity of biblical accounts. It helps prove that the mediumistic prophets did in fact live. It is impossible to discuss here all the archaeological evidence to confirm the existence of the prophets and the historicity of all biblical records.

Event after event as described in the biblical Hebrew record appear to be proven historically accurate as a result of excavations. Archaeology has given us a method of externally confirming the reliability of biblical accounts. It has confirmed countless biblical records as historical fact. The evidence from archaeological excava-tions has in fact re-established biblical authority particularly in connection with areas of the Old Testament that were criticized as myth by skeptical scholars.

One of the most highly esteemed biblical archaeologists, Nelson Gleuck, is famously known in archaeological circles to have said that 'no archaeological discovery has ever controverted a Biblical reference.' On the contrary, archaeology has given us invaluable information about the lives of ancient people and cultures as described in the Old and New Testaments. Biblical archaeology has resurrected ancient peoples and rediscovered nations and empires. Successive discoveries have shown the accuracy of biblical records, showing that they can be regarded as an historical source.

There are many examples of archaeological excavations which have proved some skeptical biblical historians wrong. To give some examples, for many years there was a total lack of any archaeological evidence for the Hittite empire of the second millennium BC as described in the Bible. Skeptical biblical historians were adamant that the biblical accounts were false. Their case was buoyed up by the fact that no remains had ever been found of a single Hittite village or town. This seemed incredible in view of the descriptions of the considerable size of this empire. Skeptics argued that the existence of the Hittite empire was a biblical legend or myth rather than fact. Finally, the ruins of the Hittite empire were excavated in the first part of the 20th century in central Turkey. This momentous discovery proved skeptical biblical historians to be totally wrong. They had lacked faith in the honesty of the biblical accounts.

A second example relates to Sargon the Great, who is described in the ancient biblical records as a powerful Assyrian king. (E.g.Old Testament: Isaiah 20:1) Some biblical historians denied the existence of this king and the accuracy of the biblical texts but were proved wrong when archaeologists excavated King Sargon's palace in modern-day Iraq.

Now, thousands of years after events described in the Bible, when we cannot presently trace all biblical locations and events we should be patient and learn from experience. We should not dismiss the accuracy of historic biblical events out of hand as successively new archaeological data is bringing to life once questioned biblical accounts.

## Archaeology Proves Moses Existed

Moses is held in high esteem today as a prophet who was a great religious leader by followers of numerous world religions. He is revered as a prophet by the Jews, Christians, Muslims, Baha'is, Mormons, Rastafarians and members of the Raelian Church. The fact that the archaeological evidence corroborates the biblical accounts of the events surrounding Moses' life therefore has great relevance for billions of people today.

It proves beyond doubt that Moses and the Hebrew slaves did exist, that he lived in Egypt and Midian (Saudi Arabia), and that his liberation of the Hebrew slaves from Egypt actually occurred. This event is known as the Exodus.

Moses was the architect of the famous law code contained in the Hebrew Torah, including his mediumistic receipt of the Ten Commandments at Mount Sinai. The Ten Commandments, represented morally superior ethical codes of conduct. For these reasons, Moses is highly respected in both Jewish and Christian canonical and non-canonical literature. Jews know the prophet Moses as 'Mosheh.' Traditionalists accept that Moses wrote the Jewish Torah, which is the same as the first five books of the Christian Bible.

Likewise, Muslims have a high regard for the prophet Moses, whom they know as 'Musa' (Koran 20:9). Interestingly, Moses spent many years of his life in ancient Midian, which is the western part of today's Saudi Arabia. Significantly, many sites in Arabia and Saudi Arabia have ancient names associated with events in Moses' life. Moses is described in the Koran, the holy Islamic scriptures, as a man who spoke with angels.

Musa also possesses the Arabic title of *kalim Allah*, which means 'the speaker with God.' Musa's many years of witnessed conversations with a non-physical entity will be clarified in the next chapters.

The Koran tells us that it was the angel Gabriel who materialized in front of the prophet Musa in the valley of Tua and told him to return to Egypt to free the Hebrew slaves.

Musa's life and events are discussed in the Koran 136 times. He is discussed considerably more than any other prophet. Both Musa and the holy Islamic prophet Muhammad are described as having seen and spoken with the angel Gabriel, a non-physical entity, however, references to Musa's countless conversations and negotiations with the angel are more profuse. Sometimes the non-physical communicator is called an angel and at other times the communicator is called God. This perpetuates the pattern already shown in earlier times, in which a non-physical communicator was thought of as a god.

Archaeological evidence is provided to substantiate the existence of Moses and events in his life as a preliminary to evidence which proves that Moses is, arguably, the Old Testament's greatest mediumistic figure. He will be shown to have been one of the world's most powerful channels. Accounts tell us that the Hebrew tribal peoples observed Moses speaking daily with the materialized presence of Yahweh, his angelic spirit guide.

## Archaeology Corroborates Moses' Life During the 13th Century BC

Moses is the most imposing figure in the Old Testament (Exodus chapters 2 to 14). The 'signs and wonders' found in Exodus 7:3 were predicted by Yahweh and conveyed by the medium Moses to the Egyptian pharaoh, to the Egyptians and to the Hebrew people. Moses transmitted Yahweh's accurate predictions of ten successive plagues that would fall upon the Egyptian overlords, with chaotic and tragic outcomes. As a result of the accurate predictions and the plagues themselves, Pharaoh finally freed the Hebrew slaves, setting them on their path to eventually becoming the Jewish nation.

Scholars offer two possible dates for the historical life of Moses and the exodus-conquest period, i.e. the period when the Hebrew slaves were liberated and resettled in towns in the area of Canaan.

The earlier date offered is the 15th century BC (1440 BC) and the later date is the 13th century BC (1290 BC). Many respected archaeologists, linguists and historians believe that the best evidence dates Moses to the 13th century BC, as the earlier date is based on an inferior literal interpretation of symbolic 'numbers' found in several disjointed biblical texts. These are sometimes used in an attempt to indicate that Moses lived 2 centuries earlier, in the 15th century BC. Passion and closed-mindedness can create unsound biased judgment. In order to accurately date Moses' exodus from Egypt, it is best to rely upon the hard facts unearthed by archaeological excavations.

It is impossible here to review all the historical, archaeological and linguistic evidence to support biblical records. However, even a brief review of the evidence for the Bible exodus will reveal that the biblical narratives do in fact describe the lives of mediumistic prophets, people, locations and historical events with great accuracy.

## 19th Century Excavations

Dennis Bratcher points out in his article 'The Date of the Exodus: The Historical Study of Scripture:'

> Fixing the date of the exodus has proven to be one of those contentious areas of biblical study that has produced two opposing views. As with many biblical historical issues, the two views are more a clash of how people view the Scripture and differing methods of study based on those views than they are a result of conflicting interpretation of the historical evidence.[1]

The 19th century brought in a new field of biblical research. This new historical method of enquiry involves both the historical-critical investigation of ancient documents and the examination of artifacts found in ancient ruins. Bratcher notes that: 'In terms of the Bible, prior to the 19th century, Scripture was basically accepted for what it appeared to say without careful examination of the details of *how* things were said, or how the biblical recounting of history related to historical sources outside the Bible.'[2]

During the 19th century scholars gained access to ancient source documents, inscriptions, artifacts and ruins. Bratcher states that: 'For the first time, there was available a great deal of information that could be used by historians to verify and cross-check the biblical accounts.'[3]

Regarding the two possible dates applied to the life of Moses, Bratcher informs us that:

The early date relies on two specific bible passages understood literally, while the late date relies on a more general view of the nature of Scripture combined with archaeological evidence.' 1 Kings 6:1 tells us: 'In the four hundred eightieth year after the Israelites came out of the land of Egypt, in the fourth year of Solomon's reign over Israel ... he began to build the house of the Lord.'[4]

Bratcher explains that the 15th century BC date, namely 1440 BC, for the exodus, is derived from a literal understanding of dates found in 1 Kings 6:1:

This verse gives a time period of 480 years between the exodus and the beginning of Solomon's work on the Jerusalem Temple. From John Bright's chronology, Solomon ascended the throne around 961 BC, which would make the fourth year of his reign and the beginning of temple construction about 959–957 BC. If we assume that the number '480' is to be taken as a precise number of years, much as we would count years on a calendar today, working backward from this date we arrive at a date around 1440 BC for the exodus.[5]

It is important to be aware of the fact that the Bible authors, like people in other traditional cultures, used numbers in a symbolic way rather than using them to convey a precise calendar date or exact number of years. Bratcher clarifies that:

> A great many numbers in both Testaments are used symbolically, are stylized for other purposes than simple counting, or are approximate numbers based on different cultural ways of reckoning time than just counting years ... the number three (often used ... to mark the passage of a short period of time or extent without intending specifics; Jon 3:3, 1:7), seven (symbolizing completion; Gen 2:2, Gen 29, Matt 15:35), twelve (symbolizing wholeness and community; Gen 35:22, Jud 19:29) and forty (a schematized number used for a generation or simply an unspecified long period of time; Gen 7:4, Ex 16:35). Some of these numbers are then used in multiples for much the same purpose, such as 70 or 77 (Gen 4:24, Matt 18:22), 120, 144, and 144,000 (10x12 and 12x12, Gen 6:3, Deut 34:7, Rev. 14:1), and multiples of 40 (400, Gen 15:13; 4,000, 1 Sam 4:2; 40,000, Josh 4:13, 1 Kng 4:26; 400,000, Josh 20:2).[6]

In Hebrew culture, which was later known as Israelite culture, the passing of time was delineated in terms of the number of generations who had been born. Consequently, the '480 years' mentioned earlier, is most probably meant to simply indicate the passage of time. This is in keeping with Israelite cultural modes of reckoning rather than referring to a specific number of years.

Further literal support for the 15th century BC exodus from Egyptian bondage is found in Judges 11:26. This account tells us that 'a judge' named Jephthah asked the king of the Ammonites to stop trying to recapture land that had been taken 300 years before by Moses.

'Judge' was the term used to describe a psychic or medium. In earlier times, judges were called seers, and as always, they guided the people using their mediumistic gifts. The period of the Judges as dated by John Bright is 1200–1120 BC (13th to 12th century BC). It is accepted that Jephthah lived in approximately 1100 BC (13th century BC).

Many scholars believe that precise calendar dating of events was not the primary concern of the author of this account. They claim that the author was simply denoting a passage of time and for this reason this number cannot be relied upon to date Moses' life and the exodus.

After the exodus from Egypt, the Hebrews spent a period of time in the wilderness as nomads. Slaves making their escape from bondage and traveling through the wilderness are not in the habit of erecting monuments to date their plight and commemorate their chaotic nomadic sojourn. Likewise, Egyptian pharaohs were not in the habit of erecting stone or clay tablets known as stelae to commemorate their failures, such as the loss of their slave workforce. After some years in the desert this disparate rabble of Hebrew slaves bonded together as a people.

At this juncture they captured a number of towns and created permanent settlements in their new lands. Archaeologists have excavated the towns named in the biblical records which describe their capture and re-settlement by the Hebrews (Israelites). A large number of excavations have taken place including those in the ancient towns of Jericho, Hazor, Edom, Moab, Lachish, Debir and Bethel. After evaluating the levels of occupation by successive peoples over the centuries and the remains of pottery, the material evidence corroborates the 13th century BC date for Moses and the exodus-conquest period.

Regarding the town of Hazor, which was captured by the Hebrews according to the biblical accounts, Bratcher adds:

> Much more extensive excavations by Y. Yadin in the 1950s revealed that a major destruction of the city had occurred in the 13th century BC ... According to Yadin's interpretation, the archaeological evidence ... could fit within the broad outlines of

the Bible narratives, with the city destroyed by the invading Israelites, rebuilt and fortified by Solomon, destroyed by the Assyrians and then rebuilt under Assyrian control.[7]

There is a convergence of opinion of highly respected scholars who accept the 13th century BC date as a result of historic information and archaeological excavations including those in Edom and Moab. Bratcher adds:

Archaeology surveys and excavations on the eastern side of the Jordan river (Transjordan), pioneered by N. Gleuck, reveal that there was no settled civilisation in the Edomite and Moabite areas of southern Transjordan until about the 14th or early 13th century BC. Also, the earliest record referring to the Edomites is an Egyptian letter dating to the 13th century BC. There is scarcely any evidence of these settlements in the 15th century BC. Since we know from the traditions that Israel encountered settled people in this area (e.g. Num 20:14), it seems that a 13th century date for the exodus is more likely and less problematic than a 15th century date. Also the Moabite city of Heshbon was the first city taken by the Israelites in the Transjordan area, becoming a part of the tribal territory of Reuben (Num 21:21–24, 32:37).[8]

Excavations at three cities conquered by Joshua, Moses' successor, which were specifically documented in the Bible accounts, have also revealed destructive evidence that can be dated to the 13th century BC. These ancient cities were Lachish (Joshua 10:31–32), Debir (Joshua 10:38–39) and Bethel (Judges 1:23–25). The later 13th century date appears to be positively proven by archaeological evidence.

Archaeological excavations of the towns conquered in the exodus period offer some of the most accurate evidence for the correct dating of these famous biblical events. The 15th century BC evidence relies on a literal understanding of the biblical narratives, despite the fact that numbers were frequently used in writing in a symbolic, metaphorical way. Numbers were not used in the same way by the Hebrews as they are in today's technological societies. The idiosyncratic use of numbers peculiar to particular cultures has been found to be paralleled historically in other traditional tribal cultures.

The biblical accounts tell us that Moses spent 40 years in Egypt, 40 years in Midian (present-day Saudi Arabia), returned to Egypt and led the slave exodus out of Egypt and spent 40 years traveling in the wilderness with these newly liberated nomadic Hebrew tribes. The number '40' is symbolic and represents a long period of time. It is indicative of the life and death of a generation of people. If this number was taken literally, Moses would have been over 120 years old when he passed away.

The biblical account tells us that Moses was told by Yahweh that he should return to Egypt and free the slaves. He was informed in this conversation that many of those in Egypt who wanted him punished were now dead themselves. (Prior to this event, Moses had himself originally fled Egypt as a result of accidentally killing an Egyptian guard. This was the reason for his exile.)

Due to the considerable length of time that Moses was in exile from Egypt, living in Midian for '40 years,' a number that represents the passing of a generation, it is accepted that the pharaoh concerned had an unusually long reign. Consequently, it is thought that either Thutmose III or more likely Rameses II was the pharaoh at the time of the exodus, since both are known to have had long reigns.

It is interesting that the son of Rameses II, named Merneptah, commemorated on a stele his successful military conquests of Syria and Canaan in the 13th century BC. This stele represents the first Egyptian reference to the Hebrew/Israelite peoples as a nation. However, this 13th century stele does not necessarily indicate a 15th century BC date for the exodus, giving the Hebrews two centuries to become and be described as a nation.

Bratcher notes that 'even if we take the ... 1290 BC [date] ... and allowing for the 40 years in the wilderness, they would still have been in the land around 50 years by the time of Merneptah's campaign ... sufficient ... time for the Israelites to emerge as a nation.'[9]

The revolutionary pharaoh named Akhetaten (Akhenaten, Akhnaten, Ikhnaton) created a new capital in the south of Egypt (Upper Egypt) called Akhetaten, which lasted from 1400 to 1350 BC (14th century BC). This ancient capital is known in present-day Egypt as Amarna. The pharaoh's name, Akhetaten means the 'Effective Spirit of Aten.' Formerly, he was known as Amenhotep IV and Amenophis IV. This 14th century BC pharaoh is the first recorded monotheistic person on earth to worship a single, invisible god whom he named Aten. Aten is pictorially represented as the sun disk. Akhenaten and the cult of Aten failed to win over the traditional priests in northern Egypt (Lower Egypt) who continued to worship many gods.

Akhenaten's Egyptian spiritual revolution of 1350 BC (14th century BC), which was the result of his transformative mediumistic, spiritual experiences, was eventually suppressed. However, his practices and experience-based beliefs inevitably influenced the 13th century BC Moses (1290 BC). Significantly, Moses is the second recorded mediumistic monotheist. Living in the 13th century BC, Moses lived approximately less than 60 years after Akhenaten.

The following information further supports the deduction that Moses' spiritual beliefs were influenced by Akhenaten. Despite the suppression of Akhenaten's unique revolutionary monotheistic spiritual revolution and his god Aten, objects associated with Akhenaten's revolutionary Amarna period have been found in the tomb of Akhenaten's successor. This discovery provides evidence of the continuing influence of Akhenaten's monotheistic beliefs after his death.

Akhenaten was succeeded by Tutankhamun who was buried in the Valley of the Kings with these monotheistic artifacts. Tutankhamun is widely believed to have been Akhenaten's son, though a few suggest he was his brother. Tutankhamun was succeeded by Ay. Significantly, Ay, the second to succeed Akhenaten, was also buried in the western area of the Valley of the Kings with a 'Hymn to Aten' inscribed on his sarcophagus.

This undoubtedly proves that monotheism had not been wiped out. It is very significant that such a monotheistic hymn should have been inscribed on a royal sarcophagus and even more significant that the monotheistic influence should still be felt so many years later. Interestingly, this hymn has remarkable similarities to Psalm 104 in the Bible which commences with:

Praise the LORD, O my soul

... you are clothed with splendour and majesty.

He wraps himself in light as with a garment. (NIV)

Clay tablets, known as the Amarna Tablets, were excavated in the ancient revolutionary capital. In these letters Akhenaten (14th century BC) is asked to help the satellite states, including Canaan, to defend themselves against the 'Apiru' (Hapiru, Khapiru). Formerly, some scholars believed that the name 'Hebrew' was a derivative of *apiru* and that these clay tablets presented evidence that dated Moses and the exodus period to the 15th century BC.

Bratcher informs us that

scholars concluded that the term is actually Sumerian ((the area of later Babylon (modern-day Iraq)) in origin and dates much earlier than the Hebrews. The term was used throughout the Middle East to refer to groups who lived on the margins of civilised society, outcasts ... mercenaries. While the term is not linguistically related to the term Hebrew, it is possible that it could have been applied to the Israelites [Hebrews] ... there is absolutely no evidence that the references in the Amarna letters can be identified specifically with the Israelites ... that eliminates any use of the Amarna letters in trying to date the exodus.[10]

Most biblical scholars cannot accept a 15th-century BC date for Moses' leadership of the exodus out of Egypt as most historical and archaeological evidence supports the 13th century date. Further evaluation of evidence to support the 13<sup>th</sup> century BC date follows. It is believed that an ancient nomadic Hyksos people from the Fertile Crescent conquered and ruled Egypt from 1667 to 1546 BC (17th to 16th century BC) or 1720 to 1580 BC (18th to 16th century BC). We learn that the Egyptians later resumed control of power and exiled or enslaved the Hyksos people.

Some scholars argue that the Hyksos period is approximately the same time as that of the Patriarchs (*Avot* in Hebrew). According to the Judeo-Christian Old Testament, the prophets known as Abraham, his son Isaac, and his grandson Jacob were the three early patriarchs. Joseph, the oldest son of Jacob, is also described as a patriarch. He was the psychic and possibly mediumistic prophet who interpreted the pharaoh's dreams commencing with those predicting famine and drought.

As a result of his guidance Joseph became highly influential in ancient Egypt. These scholars argue that the Hebrews were the Hyksos peoples. However, there is no biblical or other reasonable evidence or historical dating evidence to suggest that the Hebrews were historically known as the Hyksos peoples. The Hyksos people were a Semitic, Asiatic people. Consequently, dating the exodus from the movements of these people is considered to be unsound.

Many scholars use the biblical accounts regarding the Egyptian treasury cities called Pithom and Rameses (Exodus 1:11) to date Moses and the exodus period to the 13th century BC, as these accounts tell us that the Hebrew slaves built these cities. Such academics argue that these cities were built to commemorate a pharaoh named Rameses. Rameses I reigned for only two years from 1293 to 1291 BC (or 1314 to 1312 BC). Rameses II is believed to have reigned in the 13th century BC for over 60 years from 1279 to 1212 (or 1290 to 1224 BC).

As Rameses II has a historically accurate reputation for being a pharaoh who commissioned great building works, they argue that he is the pharaoh responsible for having at least the city of Rameses built to commemorate his name. This argument is used to provide yet further strong evidence that Moses' exodus occurred in the 13th century BC.

However, Bratcher speculates that the Israelites may not have built the city for Rameses and it should not necessarily be used as a means of dating the exodus:

> It is not necessary that the city of Rameses built by the Israelites was constructed by a pharaoh. The name Rameses was in use before the 13th century, and could have been associated with someone else. The name means 'Ra is born,' referring to the sun-god Ra and could have been associated with a temple complex.[11]

Offering further support for the 13th century BC exodus rather than a 15th century date, Bratcher adds:

> If the Israelites were already well established in the land, as the 1440 BC date of the exodus would suggest, they would have been continually battered by the incursions of these two pharaohs (Seti 1305–1290 BC and Rameses II 1290–1224) as they marched north [back and forth through Palestine where the Hebrews settled] to engage the Hittites in Syria and Eastern Asia Minor.[12]

The Bible records make no mention that the post-exodus, newly settled Hebrews were adversely affected by the Egyptian warfare of the 15th and 14th centuries BC. Egypt's conflict was against the neighboring powerful enemies in the north, with the goal of consolidating its territories. This warfare would have been conducted through the Hebrews' newly settled territory of Palestine (Canaan/Israel), causing opposing militia to trek back and forth through that land.

Inevitably, the Hebrews would have been catastrophically

affected and this conflict would have been mentioned in the biblical accounts. Significantly, there is no biblical complaint about such warfare – a fact that appears to offer strong proof that the Hebrews were not settled in this area during the 15th and 14th centuries BC. It seems more reasonable to assume that they settled there in the later 13th century BC.

Opponents of this argument claim that the Egyptian aggrandizement by Sethos I and Rameses II (in the early part of Rameses' otherwise peaceful reign) involved no quarrel with the Hebrews in Canaan. They claim that the Egyptians were only concerned with suppressing powerful empires, including the Canaanites and the Hittites. However, it may be reasonably presumed that the Hebrews would have recorded these chaotic years of turmoil and warfare had it occurred around them if they had been settled in the area at that time. The biblical silence may provide further evidence to strongly indicate a 13th century BC date for the exodus and post-exodus settled period in the area of Canaan.

Bratcher adds:

It is entirely possible that the periods of 'rest' mentioned in the book of Judges (3:11, 30; 5:31 etc) were times of increased Egyptian control of the area that would restrict raids from surrounding Canaanites. When the Egyptians withdrew or were forced back, the Canaanites surrounding the Israelites [Hebrews] were freer to raid the Israelite settlements.[13]

Biblical accounts inform us that the Hebrews were attacked by the Canaanites. These events seem to have occurred in the 13th century BC, a date which is historically the most plausible. Prior to this, the Canaanites were involved in warfare with the powerful Egyptians. It is reasonable and logical to assume that the Canaanites would have regrouped at intervals, gaining much needed respite from Egyptian attacks.

The earlier date would indicate that the Canaanites raided the

Hebrews when they should have been taking much needed rest from Egyptian attacks, a scenario which is most unlikely. It is highly unlikely that the Canaanites would fight both nations simultaneously. This information offers further confirmation that the exodus and settlement of the Hebrews took place in the 13th century BC. The Canaanite conflict would have occurred during the Hebrew settlement in these lands.

At that time the area was governed by the Hebrew/Israelite 'Judges' who offered psychic and mediumistic guidance to the people. The 13th century BC date for the exodus-conquest period was originally advocated by William F. Albright based on Palestinian archaeological evidence. This hypothesis has been successively vindicated over the years by respected archaeologists and historians.

## The Ancient Egyptian Context for Moses' Exodus

Although we may never be able to place an exact historical date on the exodus, we can be sure that the exodus narratives do have a historical Egyptian context. Bratcher adds, 'from a sociological perspective the biblical traditions bear a clear memory of Egyptian ancestry. The tradition remembered that Moses had an Egyptian name, in spite of the fact that the traditions try to give it a Hebrew meaning (Exod 2:10).'[14]

Biblical scholars, including James K. Hoffmeier, the author of *Israel in Egypt: The Evidence for the Authenticity of the Exodus Tradition*, agree that the root of Moses' name is *msi*, which can be found in pharaonic Egypt at the time of the New Kingdom.[15] As further confirmation of Moses' Egyptian heritage, the Egyptian *msi* root for the name of this mediumistic Hebrew prophet, can also be found in the names of the following Egyptian pharaohs: Amenmose, Thutmose, Ahmosis, Ptahmose, Ramose and Rameses. Moses' Egyptian name would have been transliterated into the Semitic language Hebrew, finally producing the name 'Moses' which we have today.

It is an interesting fact that during the rule of Thutmose III

(1457–1425 BC) the sons of subject kings from the region of western Asia were brought to the Egyptian court for education and training in the Egyptian way of life. When their fathers passed away, they were returned to their neighboring kingdoms and became kings themselves. Here they would propagate the Egyptian culture in their territories, which in turn, belonged to the Egyptian empire.

This Egyptian practice set a precedent for the later Egyptian education and training received by Moses the Hebrew (Israelite) in the royal court. We also know that tremendous building projects were accomplished, including the building of amazing monuments to commemorate the ancient Egyptian culture. The use of Egyptian and slave laborers would have been imperative to complete these amazing projects. These facts together appear to prove the historical reality of the man Moses. Evidence for Moses' mediumship will follow in the next chapters.

## The Exodus Routes

Biblical scholars, archaeologists, historians and geologists have successively tried to reproduce the route taken by the exodus slaves from ancient Egypt to the lands known today as Israel. Unfortunately, a number of the places in the biblical record cannot be identified with total certainty today. This is due to the loss over the millennia of the ancient city names and uncertainty regarding some of the landmarks described in the biblical records (Exodus chapters 13 to 15). However, the biblical scribes provide us with a variety of landmarks which we use to guide the way. These have led to much scholarly debate.

The exodus route commenced with the crossing of the waters of the *yam suph*. It is thought that the Hebrews continued their journey through approximately 40 locations en route to Canaan (essentially modern-day Israel) from Egypt. Momentous spiritual events occurred in some of these locations – known as 'stations' – including the receipt of the Ten Commandments and the accompanying Mosaic Law.

Three cities known as Ramases, Pithom and Succoth, named and described at the beginning of the Hebrews' sojourn in the wilderness, have been accurately identified. Many other landmarks passed through, in the second half of their nomadic journey, have also been relatively easy to locate. One example is the identification of the ancient site of Kadesh-Barnea.

The Hebrews passed through this location at a later stage in their journey. Many locations visited earlier by the Hebrews are either completely unknown today or the subject of contention. There followed many nomadic years in the wilderness during which the disparate tribal rabble of slaves bonded together as a people. Increasingly, they became ready to return to and recapture the lands they believed had belonged to their ancestors.

The Jewish Torah tells us that the Hebrews' ancestors had historically lived in Canaan and had resettled in ancient Egypt before becoming enslaved. This resettlement occurred at the time when Joseph – regarded as a patriarch, one of the founding fathers of the Hebrew nation – had been appointed to the powerful position of vizier of Egypt.

According to the ancient records, the Hebrews lived there in Egypt in peace for 400 years before they were forced to carry out slave labor. After 30 years of slavery, however, Moses emancipated the slaves and led their departure, known as the Exodus. The importance of the exodus event is commemorated by the Jews today in a religious holiday known as the Passover.

## Crossing the Red Sea or Reed Sea

After finally being granted their freedom to leave Egypt, the slaves, led by Moses, commenced their departure, or exodus. However, shortly after, the pharaoh changed his mind and sent his forces, in chariots, to bring his slaves back. As the chariots encroached upon the Hebrews, who were mostly on foot, we are told that the slaves made a successful crossing of water and the Egyptian chariots became bogged down and embedded in the soft sand below. This event had tragic consequences for the Egyptians who failed to recapture the slaves. A number of areas have been suggested for the Hebrews' successful crossing of the waters: the Pelusic branch of the Nile, various locations along the network of Bitter Lakes and canals, the Gulf of Suez southeast of the city of Succoth and the Gulf of Aqaba south of Ezion-Geber.

Significantly, the term which has been translated as the 'Red Sea' or 'Sea of Reeds' – *Yam Suf* or *Suph* – has also been used in the Bible to refer to the Gulf of Aqaba, the Gulf of Suez and also to what is known as an Egyptian papyrus marsh, namely the Sea of Reeds. Bratcher writes in an article called 'The Yam Suph: "Red Sea" or "Sea of Reeds"':

> ... nowhere in the entire Old Testament Hebrew text is the body of water associated with the exodus ever called the 'Red Sea.' Instead in the Hebrew text the reference is to the yam suph. The word yam in Hebrew is the ordinary word for 'sea,' although in Hebrew it is used for any large body of water whether fresh or salt. The word suph is the word for 'reeds' or 'rushes,' the word used in Ex 2:3, 5 to describe where Moses' basket was placed in the Nile. So the biblical reference throughout the Old Testament is to the 'Sea of Reeds' (e.g., Num 14:25, Deut 1:40, Josh 4:23, Psa 106:7).[16]

Bratcher continues: 'The translation "Red Sea" is simply a traditional translation introduced into English by the King James Version through the 2nd century BC Greek Septuagint and the later Latin Vulgate. It then became a traditional translation of the Hebrew terms.'[17]

We are told that the Hebrews passed through cities known as Rameses and Pithom (Exodus 1:11). A consensus of archaeological opinion places these two cities in the eastern Nile delta. Excavations led by Manfred Bietak have been conducted at the store city of Rameses. Some scholars accept that the Hebrews fled south from this city to the marshy area of Bitter Lakes, which is north of the Gulf of Suez, and argue that is was here that they crossed what has erroneously been called the Red Sea.

Regarding the rest of their journey, biblical historians have suggested three possible routes. Some scholars suggest that the Hebrews traveled north during their remaining nomadic period in the desert. Others suggest they travelled south. The route to the north would have taken them across the northern Sinai Peninsula. Some supporters of this route claim that the authentic, biblical Mount Sinai is today known as Jebel Helal, located approximately 30 miles west of the Kadesh-Barnea oasis. Bratcher informs us about the contentious possible southern route:

> The southern route assumes a turn directly south after crossing the sea travelling along the eastern shores of the Gulf of Suez into the depths of the southern Sinai Peninsula. In this route Mount Sinai is identified with the traditional Jebel Musa [Moses' Mountain]. The problem of the routes is compounded by the fact that we do not know certainly of the landmarks mentioned, including the location of Mount Sinai.[18]

The third suggestion is a totally northern route, which took the fleeing Hebrews along the coast of the Mediterranean; *yam suph* would therefore refer to an area of coastal shallows called Lake Sirbonis. However, Bratcher points out that this theory is flawed:

> since that would lead directly through Philistine territory ... [-(Exodus 13:17) When pharaoh let the people go, God did not lead them by way of the land of the Philistines, although that was nearer; for God thought, 'If the people face war, they may ... return to Egypt.' (Exodus 13:18) So God led the people by the roundabout way of the wilderness.'[19]

## The Real Mount Sinai

The Bible accounts (Exodus 19) tell us that Mount Sinai is the mountain on which Moses received the Ten Commandments on the third month after the exodus. However, some passages tell us that this occurred on Mount Horeb. Significantly, these two names may refer to the same mountain, but this cannot be proven.

Many archaeologists and explorers have used the ancient records in order to determine the location of the authentic Mount Sinai as described in the Christian Bible, Jewish Torah and Muslim Koran. We are told that the early prophet Elijah traveled to Mount Horeb, which indicates that the mountain's precise location was historically, accurately known for a number of centuries after the exodus (1 Kings 19:8).

At the time Moses received the Ten Commandments (Exodus 20:2–17 and Deuteronomy 5:6–21), the biblical record describes the mountain scene as being engulfed in a cloud; the ground quaked, smoke filled the air and fire burned at the mountain summit (Exodus 19:16–18; 24:17). Some scholars have interpreted this description as indicative that Mount Sinai was in fact a volcano, while others believe the text describes a storm.

Many Christians believe that the Sinai Peninsula in modern-day Egypt is the true location of Mount Sinai. The early historian Josephus tells us that Mount Sinai was the highest of all mountains. If it is accepted that Mount Sinai is located in the Sinai Peninsula then Mount Catherine, the highest mountain in this area, would fit this description. To commemorate this belief, in the 6th century AD St Catherine's monastery was built at its foot.

Many Muslims accept the ancient Bedouin oral tradition that Mount Sinai is actually an adjacent mountain called Jabal Musa (meaning the Mountain of Moses or Moses' Mountain). In the 16th century AD a church was built at the top of the Mountain of Moses and in the 20th century a Greek orthodox chapel replaced it. Consequently, historic and present day pilgrims and travelers visit the Mountain of Moses, believing it to be the famous location at which Moses received the Ten Commandments.

Interpreting biblical directions, other scholars have looked for Mount Sinai in more central and northern parts of the Sinai Peninsula. A number of mountains have been proposed, including a specific mountain on the northeast of the peninsula named Hashem el-Tarif. Hashem el-Tarif fulfills other features described in the Bible.

A cleft looks down upon a natural area similar to an amphitheater where the Hebrews could have listened to Moses' speech after he received the Ten Commandments. If this interpretation is correct, the thousands of newly liberated slaves would also have been able to camp on a nearby plateau which had vegetation for their flocks to eat (a fact proven by the excavation of an ancient nearby spring).

Mount Sinai is referred to as Mount Seir in a most ancient biblical passage known as 'The Song of Deborah' which indicates that Mount Sinai is situated east of the Gulf of Aqaba. This ancient song would indicate that the real Mount Sinai was located in the ancient land of Edom. Petra is an ancient Edomite city located in present-day Jordan, just north of Saudi Arabia. Significantly, besides Petra is a valley named Wadi Musa, meaning 'Moses' Valley,' which houses the 'Spring of Moses.' (A small village has grown up in this wadi at the entrance to the ancient city of Petra). Consequently, Mount Sinai might be more accurately located near this Arabian valley, at a place known in Arabic today as Jebel al-Madhbah. Again it is most significant that this Arabic term means 'the Mountain of the Altar.'

The biblical account informs us that when camped at Mount Sinai, the twelve Hebrew tribes heard a loud trumpet sound. It is fascinating to reveal that a natural phenomenon occurs at the Mountain of the Altar due to the wind funneling down an area known as the Siq. Amazingly, since ancient times, the Bedouin have called this phenomenon on the mountain, 'the trumpet of God.' Indeed Bedouin oral traditions, which are passed from generation to generation are known for their ancient ancestry and accuracy.

Significantly, the ancient Bedouin oral tradition tell us that at Petra in ancient Edom can be found Moses' Valley, Moses' Spring, the

Mountain of the Altar and a wind phenomenon named 'the Trumpet of God!' Furthermore, the biblical description of fire on the summit would also fit with the many documented observations of plasma phenomena at Jebel al-Madhbah, associated with storm conditions. This location fits well with the biblical account that tells us that the Hebrews heard thunder and saw lightning flashes among the thick cloud cover when the Ten Commandments were delivered to Moses.

Alternatively, if the 'fire' which is described on the summit of the mountain is depicting a volcano, then the genuine Mount Sinai might be located in northwestern Saudi Arabia, where volcanoes are found. Another Mount Sinai candidate is Jabal al-Nour ('Mountain of Light'), a volcano situated at the northern end of the Gulf of Aqaba. Jebel Ertowa and Hala-'l Badr are the names of two other mountains proposed as the historic Mount Sinai. In the first half of the 20th century Alois Musil claimed that he had identified Mount Sinai near a valley known as Wadi al-Hrob in northwestern Saudi Arabia. Musil believed that the biblical alternative name for Mount Sinai, namely Mount Horeb, had been derived from the name of this wadi. This mountain is known today as Al-Manifa.

Excavations on a mountain called Jabal Ideid, which is located equidistant from the Kadesh-Barnea oasis and the ancient city of Petra, have unearthed shrines, altars, stone circles, pillars and approximately 40,000 rock engravings. Jabal Ideid has been found to be a major Palaeolithic cult center (the Palaeolithic period was 2350–2000 BC, i.e. 24th to 21st century BC).

Scholars have concluded that Jabal Ideid is not a candidate for being the real Mount Sinai, mainly because the material remains of religio-cult activity found at the site are dated much earlier than the 13th century BC Moses. ( The importance of mountains to ancient shamanic mediumistic practices used to channel spiritual and other information from communicators in the non-physical realms have been highlighted previously).

Some archaeologists believe that when Moses fled from the Egyptian authorities after accidentally killing the Egyptian guard, he left the area of the Sinai Peninsula. Their belief is based on the fact that the pharaoh owned copper and turquoise mines in this area which were heavily guarded by a strong military presence which, as a wanted man, he would have been anxious to avoid.

They argue that in search of safety away from the Egyptian authorities, Moses traveled to Midian, in present-day Saudi Arabia. Consequently, these scholars believe that Moses returned to this familiar route for safety later in his life during the exodus. From these deductions it is suggested that the historic Mount Sinai is located in Saudi Arabia.

The company named Exploration Films sent an expedition to follow what they interpreted to be the exodus route. They claim to have found substantial evidence that the Hebrew slaves crossed the waters at Aqaba and that Jabal al-Lawz is the authentic Mount Sinai. The Wyatt archaeological team with its museum in Tennessee, USA, make the same claims. They believe that the volcano known as Jabal al-Lawz fits the biblical description of Mount Sinai. The results of these expeditions, however, are found to be contentious by many highly trained scholars. Due to tensions between Israel, Jordan and Saudi Arabia, less information has been gathered in this area than from other ancient areas of archaeological significance.

The following information summary may provide evidence to support the claims of the above two teams of explorers. Paul's comments in the Bible, found in Galatians 4:25a, tell us: 'Now Hagar stands for Mount Sinai in Arabia.' Exodus 3:1 also tells us that Mount Sinai is in the land of Midian (present-day Saudi Arabia). The term 'Arabia' throughout the centuries has always been used for a location east and south of Palestine. The Bible tells us that after Moses fled to Midian, after committing murder, he became a shepherd tending the flocks of his father-in-law Jethro, who was a priest of Midian. Moses then went to Horeb, 'the mountain of God.'

At the mountain, Moses was informed by Yahweh in the land of Midian, (Exodus 4:19) that the men in Egypt who had wanted him dead had now died themselves. Moses was told to return to free the

Hebrew slaves. We learn on a number of occasions from these ancient records that Moses returned to Egypt from the land of Midian. According to the teams, these records confirm the authenticity of the claim that the genuine Mount Sinai is in the vicinity of modern Saudi Arabia.

They also believe that the Gulf of Aqaba is where Moses led the fleeing slaves across the water, as this area better fits the description of the event found in Exodus 15:10, in which the Egyptians 'sank like lead in the mighty waters.' They claim to have discovered a natural land bridge beneath the waters of the Red Sea at the tip of the Sinai Peninsula, at the waters of the Gulf of Aqaba.

These excavators also believe that they have found the remains of other key features described in the Bible accounts associated with events in Moses' life. This list includes the twelve springs of Elim, the 70 palm trees (described in Exodus 15:27), evidence of the rocks Moses used to cordon off Mount Sinai (Exodus 19:23b), the remains of the altar which Moses built for Yahweh, evidence of the twelve pillars which Moses erected to commemorate each of the twelve Hebrew tribes (Exodus 24:4b), and the split in the rock from which Moses gave water to the thirsty tribes (Exodus 17:6). All of these discoveries have allegedly been found near Jabal al-Lawz or en route to this mountain. Significantly, some of these excavators were informed that Saudi Arabian archaeologists believe they have discovered the remains of ancient Hebrew graffiti on rocks and in caves.

In their Tennessee museum the Wyatt archaeological expedition display photographs of countless artifacts which they claim their teams unearthed. These include apparent recognizable remains of ancient chariot wheels and other chariot parts. They claim that their photographs of these ancient artifacts were taken on the seabed in the Gulf of Aqaba. It would be fascinating if these teams have indeed discovered the remains of the heavy, ancient Egyptian chariots described as having sunk into the seabed. In such conditions, the slaves on foot, would have been more suited to making their escape and the heavy chariots would have been greatly disadvantaged.

The following fact may lend some weight to the above expedition's arguments. It is an interesting fact that while some scholars have reinterpreted *yam suph* to mean 'Sea of Reeds' rather than the 'Red Sea', the same Hebrew phrase was used to describe the locations of towns which we know were situated besides the Red Sea.

This underlines the fact that the phrase *yam suph* may have been used to describe the Red Sea itself or an area around the Red Sea. This phrase is found in 1 Kings 9:26: 'And king Solomon made a navy of ships in Ezion-Geber, which is beside Eloth, on the shore of the Red sea, in the land of Edom' (KJV). Significantly, Eloth (Elath) was the name of a seaport located on the northern shore of the Red sea in the Gulf of Aqaba.

While some of these theories and the results of excavations associated with Moses' life are still passionately contended, they are fascinating to review as scholars seek to identify ancient spiritual sites. These famous sites are particularly relevant to Jews, Christians and Muslims. Proving the historicity of Moses, the sites he visited and events in his life prepares us for the remarkable findings revealed in the following chapters.

## 17th Century BC Volcano Hypothesis

A stele that was erected in Karnak in ancient Egypt describes the onset of cataclysmic storms, which the ancient Egyptians believed occurred as the result of the gods' activity. Many respected scholars believe that these storms occurred in 1623 BC (17th century BC). Others have tried to re-date this geological event to 1538 BC (16th century BC), claiming that it occurred during the reign of the pharaoh Ahmosis I (Ahmose).

However, many scholars consider the evidence for this re-dating to be weak. Geological evidence indicates that a volcanic eruption occurred on the ancient Aegean island of Thera (the modern Greek island of Santorini) and that this tremendous geological event would have had some repercussions in the ancient Egyptian delta.

A 2006/2009 television documentary by Simcha Jacobovici attempted to re-date this geological event to 1500 BC (16th century BC). The program claimed that the Hebrews fled Egypt through a northern marshy area which would have been flooded and drained by tsunamis created by the caldera collapse caused by the volcanic event in ancient Santorini. The dating of this geological event is highly suspect and the suggested exodus route to the north is considered by many to be misguided.

Advocates of this argument suggest that this geological event may have had some influence on the weather conditions experienced in ancient Egypt and may have been the root cause of some of the plagues Yahweh predicted and communicated to Moses. However, the accurate dating of the event is considered by respected scholars to have taken place several centuries earlier than the life of Moses and the exodus.

The general consensus of opinion among eminent historians and archaeologists is that the most probable dating of the exodus is the 13th century BC. Moses therefore lived three to four centuries after the much earlier 17th to 16th century BC volcanic eruption on the ancient Greek island of Santorini.

The program promoting the erroneously dated geological event argues that the Hebrews saw a cloud from the volcanic blast and called it 'Yahweh'. However, this does not account for the daily appearance of Yahweh as a cloud which rose every morning to lead the way to Canaan. The nomadic Hebrews followed this cloud to the 'land of milk and honey' (i.e. Canaan, which is modern-day Israel). Tribal members regularly heard and observed Moses and Yahweh having long, daily conversations.

During these observable negotiations, Moses received protective guidance and accurate predictive information from this celestial materialization named Yahweh. Many biblical accounts will be explained in later chapters which tell us that Yahweh materialized, upon request, as a substance whose composition was equated with that of a cloud, and that he spoke for all to hear. One biblical example is when Yahweh said to Moses: 'I am now coming to you in a thick cloud, so that I may speak to you in the hearing of the people, and so their faith in you may never fail' (Exodus 19:9, Revised English Bible).

A further example is: 'And the angel of God, which went before the camp of Israel, removed and went behind them; and the pillar of the cloud went before their face and stood behind them' (Exodus 14:19, KJV).

Jacobovici's program does not account for the fact that the people followed this communicating, materializing, guiding, protective, ectoplasmic cloud, which clearly demonstrated personality, throughout their many nomadic years in the wilderness. A volcanic cloud would not have lingered for all these years! Whenever the people heard and observed Moses speak face to face with this materialized presence, which significantly appeared upon request, they discovered that Moses' face was radiant for some time after-wards. It will be shown that in today's language, the people observed and described evidence of an auric glow around Moses, a phenomenon which is in the domain of psychical research.

We learn of Moses' first conversations with Yahweh after he had fled Egypt. He had unintentionally killed an Egyptian guard while defending a Hebrew slave who was being beaten, and found refuge from Egyptian punishment as a shepherd looking after his future father-in-law's flocks. This meditative, solitary, benevolent occupation was inevitably conducive to strengthening Moses' mediumistic ability to see and hear Yahweh. We are told that in the desert Yahweh turned Moses' shepherd's crook into a serpent and then back to a rod again. At the same time Yahweh pointed out the significance of the rod Moses carried.

Despite the great majesty and spectacle of the ancient Egyptian pharaohs, the symbol of their power throughout pharaonic history is the unassuming shepherd's crook. This universal symbol denoted Egyptian royalty in the same way as a king or queen's scepter. Moses was encouraged during this conversation with Yahweh that even as a mere shepherd, living in exile, he held the symbol of Egyptian power in his hands.

This information clarifies the ancient Egyptian context for the prophetic mediumistic leadership of Moses. The magnitude of Yahweh's materialized presence and communications, prompted Moses to audaciously return to a land where he was wanted for murder and demand that an incredulous pharaoh liberate his Hebrew slave workforce. The ruler's position would have been completely undermined by the successive onslaught of ten plagues and by the fact that Yahweh had accurately predicted each one through Moses, because Pharaoh was expected to demonstrate ultimate and universal power and control.

In Pharaoh's presence, Moses' psychic abilities, together with his demonstration of mediumistic physical phenomena overshadowed the psychic and mediumistic abilities of the Egyptian priests, priestesses and magicians in attendance. In the following chapters we will see that Moses was a great physical phenomena medium who had been tutored by psychic and mediumistic priests and priestesses in Pharaoh's ancient royal court.

## The Writing of Moses: 13th century BC

Some skeptical theologians have argued that Moses could have had no hand in writing the first five books of the Bible known as the Christian Pentateuch and the Jewish Torah. These ancient spiritual accounts record significant events in Moses' life and his prophetic leadership of the Hebrews. Skeptics claim that these biblical records were not written until the 10th or 9th centuries BC, approximately three to four centuries after Moses' death.

The art of writing, they argue, was unknown in Palestine during the 13th century BC, the Mosaic period and therefore a group of editors who lived after Moses wrote the Pentateuch/Torah and credited Moses with writing them. This argument is known as the 'Documentary Hypothesis.' Modernizing of old works may indeed have taken place. However, if and when that occurs, it does not necessarily compromise the historical contents of the literary works of the first five biblical books or others.

Examples of ancient writing have been found, proving that writing developed independently in at least three places in the world, including Mesopotamia (Iraq), Harappa (Pakistan) and Egypt between 3500 BC (36th century BC) and 3100 BC (32nd century BC). The following brief introduction to some of the findings of archaeological excavations proves that the art of writing pre-dated the 13th century BC, clearly indicating that Moses would have known how to write. Despite the fact that many significant archaeological excavations have proven that writing pre-dated Moses by over 2,000 years, the outdated Documentary Hypothesis is still influential today!

## The Hammurabi Code: Mesopotamia/Iraq 2000 BC

In 1901–02 a black stele was excavated by French archaeologists in Susa in modern-day Iraq. This was the ancient land of Elam in the ancient Mesopotamian empire. Large, sculptured, wedge-shaped characters were displayed on the 2.4 meter-high diorite rock detailing the laws of Hammurabi, known as the Hammurabi Code. Words composed of wedge shape characters had been inscribed into wet clay. This ancient script or writing is called Akkadian cuneiform script. The spoken language in Babylon was Akkadian. The Babylonian scribes wrote in columns from the left to the right on the clay tablets, then the tablet was turned over from the bottom of the tablet, not from the side, and the scribes wrote in reverse from the right to the left.

Hammurabi the Amorite, was a great lawgiver, as demonstrated by the 282 laws inscribed in the Law Code stele. The Amorites were a Semitic people who settled in ancient Mesopotamia (modern Iraq) in approximately 2000 BC (21st century BC). This area is known today as the Fertile Crescent due to the fertility of the soils that lie between the rivers Tigris and Euphrates which flow from the Persian Gulf. Mesopotamia is a Greek word meaning 'between two rivers.'

Hammurabi was the sixth king and chief priest of the first dynasty of the Old Babylonian (Amorite) Dynasty.

It is believed that Hammurabi ruled the ancient Mesopotamian civilization at approximately the same time that the patriarch Abraham left the ancient Mesopotamian (Iraqi) city of Ur (Ur Kasdim or Ur, City of the Chaldeans) for Canaan (present-day Israel). Ur was the capital of Sumer. It was located in the southern region of Mesopotamia in approximately 2000 BC, which was the time of both Abraham and Hammurabi. Therefore this black sculptured stone tablet was inscribed around the same time as Abraham lived in 2000 BC.

Hammurabi is credited with unifying the independent city-states around the Tigris-Euphrates. Progressively he created the Old Babylonian Empire, which is modern day Iraq. Ancient Babylon was located approximately 55 miles from present-day Baghdad and was a larger development than the city of Ur by approximately 1750 BC. From the discovery of the stele it has been deduced that writing and law codes were in existence long before those delivered through Moses. Consequently, we have two famous Middle Eastern law codes: the Hebrew Torah of which Moses was the architect and the even more ancient Code of Hammurabi.

## The Ebla Tablets: Syria 2300 BC

The 17,000 Ebla Tablets found in Tell Mardikh in northern Syria in the 1960s also testify to the fact that writing and law codes pre-dated Moses. This evidence makes it quite reasonable to believe that Moses 'could write down' the law code he most famously received. These tablets, which, like the Hammurabi Code, record laws, customs and events, were excavated by two professors from the University of Rome in the 1960s and 1970s. Dr Paolo Matthiaewas, the team archaeologist and Dr Giovanni Petinato, was the team epigrapher.

The Ebla kingdom flourished in approximately 2300 BC (24th century BC). As we have seen, a great body of opinion dates Moses to the 13th century BC. Moses therefore lived 1000 years after the Ebla Tablets were inscribed. Significantly, apart from pre-dating Moses, both the Hammurabi Code and the ancient Ebla Tablets were found in the same part of the world as Moses, proving that writing existed in the ancient civilizations in that area.

It is highly significant that the Ebla Tablets corroborate the ancient record found in the Torah and in the bible in Genesis 14 which describes the five 'Cities of the Plain,' namely 'Sodom, Gomorrah, Admah, Zeboiim and Zoar,' proving the historicity of the biblical account.

## The Nuzi Tablets: Mesopotamia/Iraq 1500–1400 BC

Four thousand 4000 cuneiform tablets were excavated in a city called Nuzi in modern-day Iraq. Inscribed in the Akkadian language, they have been dated from 1500 to 1400 BC (16th to 15th century BC) two to three centuries earlier than Moses, around the time of the later patriarchs. Again this indicates that there is no reason to believe that Moses could not write.

Nuzi was an ancient Mesopotamian city besides the Tigris River, located southwest of the modern town of Kirkuk in the north of Iraq. In Akkadian times, 2334 BC – 2154 BC, Nuzi was called Gasur. The Hurrians occupied the city in 1500 BC, renaming it Nuzi and making it an administrative center (at a later date it was absorbed into the ancient Assyrian empire). The Hurrians, who made these scripts, are mentioned in the Old Testament, where they are known as the Horites, the Hivites and the Jebusites.

The Nuzi Tablets record countless practices including matters of adoption, marriage, inheritance and property rights which have close parallels with those in the Torah and biblical Genesis chapters 12 to 32. These tablets prove that family, clan and tribal records were passed down from one generation to the next, for up to six generations. Importantly, they corroborate and enrich our understanding of Genesis and other Old Testament books and they provide early versions of the biblical accounts of Laban and Jacob.

## Writing in Pakistan: 3500–2600 BC

An archaeological dig in Harappa in Pakistan unearthed jars inscribed with writing from at least 4,600 years ago, i.e. approximately the 27th century BC. The site was located in the area where the Indus (Harappan) civilization thrived. Harappa was a small settlement dating back to 3500 BC, but by 2600 BC (27th century BC) it was a major urban society.

The writing has strong resemblances to the later Indus script and was apparently carved on the jars before and after firing in ovens. Experts have suggested that the script either described the contents of the jars or indicated the names of deities. Dr Richard Meadow of Harvard University, who directed this research, suggested that these ancient writings could pre-date all other known writing. This gives further evidence that writing was in existence before the life of Moses and therefore it is plausible to believe that Moses could write.

## Ancient Egyptian Writing: 3300–3200 BC

Early Egyptian writing has been found at the tomb of King Scorpion in Abydos in southern Egypt (250 miles south of Cairo) by Gunter Dreyer, director of the German Archaeological Institute in Egypt. King Scorpion, also known as Scorpion II, is the name of the second of two kings of Upper Egypt (southern Egypt) during the Protodynastic period. Dreyer's findings were published in 1999.

Since 1985, Dreyer's team have also unearthed several hundred extremely small clay tablets on which symbols related to hieroglyphs were inscribed. Inscriptions on clay jars also reveal the documentary records of linen and oil deliveries to King Scorpion. These were paid as taxes more than 5,000 years ago. Recorded on the jars are also the names of kings and institutions. Significantly, the results of carbon dating tests prove that these ancient Egyptian scripts date back to 3300–3200 BC. Again, this evidence proves that the Egyptians could write, long before the time of Moses, indicating that Moses, who was educated in Egypt 2000 years later could also write.

This discovery has revealed that Egyptian society in 3300 BC was far more advanced than previously thought. The writing dealt with economics, and recorded trade and taxation transactions with the Egyptian rulers who controlled different localities. Although the scripts are composed of symbols, they are classified as writing because each symbol represents a consonant and together they make up syllables. (The invention of writing is classed as the great divide between prehistory and history.)

3300 BC is an obscure period in Egyptian history. Shortly after this, possibly around 3100 BC, the land was unified and then ruled by the powerful Egyptian dynastic pharaohs. There is controversy whether King Scorpion or another early king known as Narmer unified Upper Egypt and then later united Upper Egypt with Lower (northern) Egypt.

A large slate palette commemorating the unification of the county has been excavated in the ruins of ancient Hierakonopolis. Known as the Narmer Palette, it may be the earliest written Egyptian document. It was found in the 19th century and has been dated to 3100 BC (32nd century BC).

In 1995 Egyptologists Dr John Darnell of Yale and his wife Dr Deborah Darnell made a discovery in the limestone cliff known as Gebel Tjauti, situated 250 miles south of Cairo. Carved in the rock was a 20-inch tableau describing events surrounding a triumphant Egyptian ruler. They believed that they had found the earliest known historical document, pre-dating even the Narmer Palette. They speculated that the writing – it is classed as writing as it consists of proto-hieroglyphs and describes an actual event – might be associated with King Scorpion, and so they named it the Scorpion Tableau.

It describes a successful military operation to take control over an Egyptian region of small warring kingdoms. It remains contentious whether the rulers described at Abydos (King Scorpion) and Gebel Tjauti were in fact the same person. King Scorpion and Narmer may have lived at the same time, shortly before the great dynastic pharaonic period. Again, we see that the ancient Egyptians had a long history of writing before the birth of Moses.

## The Sumerians

The Sumerians were believed to be the first people to write. However, the above Egyptian findings suggest that the Egyptians may have invented writing before the Sumerians. As the Sumerians traded with Egypt it is possible that they began to learn the benefits of recording information in a similar way to the Egyptian scripts.

Around 4000 BC the Sumerians moved into southern Mesopotamia (present-day Iraq). Over two centuries they supplanted the Ubaidians and Semites who had previously lived in this southern area. The Sumerians developed one of the earliest urban societies in the world, building cities such as Ur, Uruk and Kish. It is also possible that the Sumerians learned the rudiments of writing and basic numerical calculation from the Ubaidians. The Sumerians'progressively developed written records as their trade activity increased.

· They calculated their arithmetic based on units of ten and they divided a circle into 60 parts. Present-day methods of calculation of numbers, seconds and minutes have been greatly influenced by the Sumerian calculations. Picture representations in clay tablets developed over the centuries. Pictorial representations became symbols known as ideograms. Added to these were other symbols to represent spoken sounds, phonetic letters, which became known as cuneiform script.

By 2800 BC (29th century BC) the Sumerian writing system began to exhibit phonetic elements. Contemporaneous Mesopotamian people such as the Akkadians and Babylonians adopted and modified cuneiform scripts. Later Mesopotamian peoples such as later Babylonians, Assyrians and Persians also adopted and modified the cuneiform scripts. Although Sumerian as a spoken language died out around the 18th century BC, people continued to use the written language (as modern people learn to write Latin) up until the 1st century AD, making it one of the most long-lived writing systems.

From the above discussion, we see that writing predated Moses and the Hebrews for some considerable time and that there is no reason to suppose that Moses, who was educated in the royal Egyptian household, could not write and record events in his life.

## Early Hebrew Writing (Jerusalem 10th Century BC)

I include here the results of a 2005 excavation in the hill country south of Jerusalem as they appear to include the oldest Hebrew writing that western archaeologists have found and officially know about. According to several Harvard University experts in biblical archaeology and early Hebrew inscriptions, the carved letters that had been unearthed are the proto-Hebrew alphabet (early Hebrew). They dated the find to the 10th century BC.

The excavation team was led by Ron Tappy, an archaeologist from the Pittsburgh Theological Seminary in Pennsylvania. The excavations brought to light the Tel Zayit stone, a lime stone boulder into which a scribe had carved the alphabet. Inscribing the alphabet into a stone and embedding it into a wall was believed to ward off evil. This form of writing may have been democratized as cumulatively people learned to write in order to trade. Importantly, this discovery does not suggest that writing was not carried out by Hebrews in earlier centuries.

## Birth of a Nation and Moses' Death

There is a consensus of opinion among scholars that a nation would not fabricate it slowly beginnings as slaves fleeing from the Egyptian empire unless it was true. This fact is even more pertinent when set against the background of these ancient times. These were days when stelae (stone tablets) were erected to commemorate and grossly exaggerate a nation's victorious triumphs in order to satisfy the egos of the various rulers.

Deuteronomy 34:1–7 movingly records Moses' dying moments

and tells us that he was laid to rest on Mount Nebo, opposite Jericho. We are told that Moses was taken by his followers from the plains of Moab to the top of this mountain. From this vantage point Moses finally saw the Promised Land of Canaan before his death. His people would soon enter this land without him and make it their home. Time had run out for their leader. It was a kindness to him that Moses was able to see the land he and his followers had spent so many years traveling to and preparing for.

Mount Nebo is a peak in the Mount Pisgah range, located in modern-day Jordan. Moab was the biblical name for this mountainous area parallel to the eastern shore of the Dead Sea. The capital of this ancient kingdom of Moab is the present day Jordanian town of Kerak. Near to the present day Jordanian village of Faysaliyah, stands Mount Nebo, rising up from the Transjordanian plateau. This is approximately 10 kilometers west of the ancient Roman Byzantine town of Madaba.

From the highest point on Mount Nebo at an altitude of 800 meters, an almost aerial view can be gained, as nature has created a natural balcony. This would have been an ideal site for Moses to survey the land during the last moments of his life. As a person looks in different directions from this vantage point they can see many important places. These include Jerusalem, Bethlehem, other landmarks in present-day Israel, Qumran where the Dead Sea Scrolls were found, the oasis of Jericho, the Dead Sea, the desert of Judah, the Valley of Jordan, the mountains of Judea and Samaria, and the hills around Amman, Jordan's capital.

The late Pope John Paul II made a pilgrimage to Mount Nebo, to the site where Moses was buried, one of Jordan's most sacred ancient archaeological sites. Pilgrims from the earliest times have left records of their journeys to this revered ancient site. This information has helped archaeologists to identify the area where Moses was laid to rest. Possibly the earliest church built to commemorate the grave of Moses was constructed in the 4th century AD, followed by successive churches and a monastery.

Six later tombs have also been discovered here, as well as mosaic floors. This further archaeological information substantiates the very personal biblical account describing Moses looking across to the Promised Land from this location before passing into spirit. Moses had chosen a most suitable and befitting location for his bones to be finally laid to rest. He was undoubtedly an authentic, historical figure.

Archaeological excavations have corroborated biblical records regarding the existence of innumerable individuals and nations. These are too numerous to list here, however, they include evidence of the Hittites, King Sargon II (722–705 BC) and cuneiform stelae which refer to King Balshazzar. This king was named and described in the biblical book of Daniel.

Archaeological excavations have also proven that writing existed in the Canaanite-speaking cultures before the life of Moses. The authenticity of many biblical reports of individuals and events have been criticized as biblical fiction. However, thanks to archaeological excavations, claims of biblical historical inaccuracy inferring later misguided biblical authors – have successively been proven wrong.

Importantly, it has been shown that the Bible records regarding the authentic life of a man named Moses are being progressively corroborated by historical and archaeological evidence. These include artifacts unearthed in the ancient ruins of the settlements he captured. It is not necessary to provide any further historical and archaeological evidence to support the authentic historicity of accounts found in the Bible and Torah, particularly those relating to Moses.

## Chapter 7

# Ancient Spiritual Prophets Were Mediums

Chapters 7 to 10 will successively review Old and New Testament biblical primary sources, clarifying the biblical terminology used to clearly describe communications with a non-physical communicator. I will discuss the attitudes towards mediumship held by contemporary biblical commentators and also expose the fact that present-day Bibles still contain mistranslations which wrongly condemn mediumship.

These mistranslations originated in the 15th and 16th centuries. These mistranslations were placed in bibles at a time when the church accused countless innocent people of being witches and burnt them at the stake. Many people remain unaware that present day Bibles contain these mistranslations which wrongly condemn mediumship.

This chapter also begins the process of revealing suppressed biblical information regarding the mediumistic practices of a number of Old Testament prophets. These dominate and dictate each of the prophet's spiritual ministries. This research will demonstrate that significant details in these accounts can only make sense, if they are understood in the uncorrupted mediumistic context which the original biblical authors intended.

The religious narratives are clearly describing mediumistic communications which provided pivotal spiritual knowledge. These experiences are shown to be transformative spiritual-mediumistic experiences which lay at the source of later institutionalized religion. Latterly, this chapter will evaluate a number of biblical accounts including those in the books known as Genesis, Exodus, Leviticus and Numbers.[1]

It will be shown that the implications of mediumistic experiences have been and still are enormous. This research, like any other, may not conclusively prove survival after physical death, however, it goes a long way towards demonstrating the existence of a very real non-physical dimension whose inhabitants can and do communicate with our material dimension. Of course, beliefs are a personal matter, and it is left to readers to draw their own conclusions after absorbing the fascinating implications of this subject matter.

Contributing to the overall theme of this research the following chapters help bridge the gap between psychical research into the phenomenon of mediumship and the realm of humankind's spiritual beliefs. It is shown that the mediumistic receipt of spiritual communications gave birth to many aspects of world religions. It will become clear that if a person negates and discards mediumship as irrelevant he or she is largely negating and discarding the origins of much of humankind's rich spiritual heritage.

Through mediumship religious beliefs have cumulatively been born, such is the long suppressed interrelationship between psychic and mediumistic experiences and religion. These pages reveal that the domains of parapsychology and that of religion will remain impoverished if both areas of thought remain detached from one another.

I will provide proof showing that spiritually transformative mediumistic experiences, which is the realm of psychical research and parapsychology, have furnished spiritual experienced-based beliefs, which is the realm of religion. Evidence which is cumulatively provided throughout this book serves to improve the context for understanding mediumistic phenomena.

These pages prove that mediumship and its earlier related counterpart, shamanism, are part of a cross-cultural, historic and on-going continuum of spiritual experiences that have impacted humankind's evolving spiritual quest. Progressively it is being proven that spiritually transformative mediumistic experiences are clearly related to the realm of the spiritual.

It is important to reduce the perceived materialistic chasm

between the realm of the experiential and that of materialist parapsychology. Parapsychologists often draw simplistic conclusions regarding mediumship, condemning it as the product of mere imaginings. My research should result in future evaluations of mediumship being conducted in an improved context of understanding. It will lead to people having a better understanding of mediumship and its immense experiential contribution to the birth of many profoundly elevated global spiritual philosophies.

The following Old and New Testament narratives describe the lives, beliefs, practices and events surrounding historic spiritual figures of the Judeo-Christian tradition. The evaluation of the experiential testimonies of generations of 'historicprophets' proves these narratives to be a continuum of mediumistic accounts. These testimonies reveal the prophets' confirmed belief in mediumistic contact with celestial messengers and/or God Him/Herself. They believed these communicators to be from an authentic, co-existent, etheric realm. It becomes evident that the scribes who recorded the prophets' mediumship were totally fluent in their understanding of psychic and mediumistic categories of paranormal experience.

The following exploration evidences that mediumistic experiences belong to a cross-cultural, on-going continuum of spiritually orientated experiences.

The forthcoming discussion of a series of historic spiritual leader's experiences of conversations, presumably with, the surviving consciousnesses of spirits or angels, echoes those of the mediumistic exploits of the more ancient shamans.

With regard to their cross-cultural or global and ongoing nature, examples of mediumship have already been evidenced as ranging throughout the centuries and the globe. To show that mediumistic experiences still flourish today, many millennia later, I will provide a more detailed example of relatively contemporary mediumship in concluding chapters.

Many present-day international societies, such as the Society for Psychical Research in London and the USA, evaluate contemporary accounts by mediumistic individuals. These mediums believe that they receive communications from otherworldly sources. This evidence is progressively proving that mediumistic experiences are a global, ancient and ongoing related continuum of experiences. Evidence will be provided to indicate that many of these reports of otherworldly communications encourage human beings to exercise increasingly mature spiritual behavior. This proves the ongoing religious focus of many spiritually orientated mediumistic experiences. Due to their occurrance in the days of antiquity they inevitably lie at the source of humankind's evolving spiritual history.

The following represent a number of examples of the religious teachings believed to be gained from communications with non-physical beings. Due to the constraints of time and space a full list is not possible here:

- Inhabited otherworldly landscapes exist
- All creatures as a fact of nature inevitably make their transition to these non-material realms after physical death
- Forms of judgment occur after the transition from the physical to the non-physical life
- Contact can be made during the material life with non-physical communicators
- Some angels and/or spirits can provide spiritual and other guidance
- God exists
- God has a Divine Plan for all of creation,
- An aspect of God dwells in all life-forms who are in effect God's family
- All of creation is interrelated

Many of humankind's most enlightened spiritual beliefs and philosophies have been claimed to be the result of communications and manifestations of non-physical beings known as spirits or angels. However, the overpowering force of the prevailing materialist ethos forces many people to negate these profound experiences together with the rich spiritual beliefs they have fostered. Mediumistic experiences are perceived by many materialists as nothing more than brain chemical aberrations or illusions. Such is the gulf between contemporary materialist, reductionist paradigms of thought and those who encounter the enigmatic and profound world of the experiential. The contemporary materialistic paradigm of thought is quite unable to make any sense of historic and present-day mediumistic experiences.

The lack of understanding that occurs when we are confronted with enigmatic biblical narratives is inevitable, given the materialist, reductionist times in which we live. I will show that these narratives are clear accounts of mediumship. The fact that some present-day materialists cannot find a context in which to understand mediumistic experiences results in dichotomy and fragmentation. This is reflected in the fact that experiencers often suffer from the discrediting of their transformative spiritual-mediumistic testimonies.

This approach appears to reveal the materialists' fear of the realm of the experiential. Such is the power and pervasive nature of materialism that many people react to the subject of death in a contradictory manner. For example, many modern-day religious leaders avoid any discussion of topics such as 'existence after physical death' and 'communications with spirits and angels.' Ironically, the same people claim to believe in God and the after-death existence.

The following discussion offers an alternative context for viewing mediumistic phenomena and the role these have played throughout history. This is done by accepting the biblical accounts of conversations between historical spiritual figures and spirits or angels at face value. Due to the fact that many prophets received difficult tasks to perform from the non-physical communicators, it should be noted that spiritual belief should not be seen simplistically as an emotional crutch. Significantly, in many instances it is the non-physical communicators who initiate their incursions into the material world, not the reverse.

Consequently, the belief in life after death may have been inspired by human beings who fearlessly confronted death and by beings on both sides crossing its illusory borders. Various forms of manifestation and communication presumably facilitated by the prophets' receptive psychically sensitive abilities have been faithfully recorded by the early scribes, prior to later biblical distortions and mistranslations.

Narratives regarding dialogues with non-physical beings can be found amongst the foundations of many of the world's religious traditions. Otherworldly communications and manifestations reported by historic spiritual teachers appear to indicate that they share with contemporary mediums a psychically sensitive faculty. The experiences of ancient prophets represent historic precedents of modern mediumship.

It should be pointed out that some individuals have reported experiences they believe to be of the Divine or pure consciousness, the physical correlate of which, manifests itself in a sense of pure, overwhelming light. However, ineffable experiences of an unclouded blaze of living light, without the experience of a communicative personality, telepathic or otherwise, are markedly different to the pattern of experiences of communication and negotiation with a spirit or angelic being.

It is the latter which we are exploring here. It is being shown that there is an age old and long established tradition of reports of experiences of communication between the inhabitants of the material world and those who have made their transitions to a co-existent, populated, invisible reality.

I have been inspired to interpret biblical references in a mediumistic context by my contact with a number of organizations. To name but a few in the UK, these include the Churches' Fellowship for Psychical and Spiritual Studies, the Society for Psychical Research, the Arthur Findlay College (the property was left in trust by the psychical researcher and author Arthur Findlay, to become a college at which mediumship would be developed, demonstrated and evaluated);[2] and 100's of Spiritualist churches located throughout the length and breadth of the United Kingdom.

Before conducting a chronological evaluation of biblical narratives we must first evaluate the early translations of the Bible. The prejudicial attitudes and ignorance of historic translators regarding original accounts of mediumship have profoundly clouded and adversely misshaped present-day biblical accounts.

## Biblical Commentators

There are several predominant versions of the Bible in contemporary usage. These differ, subtle and otherwise, from various earlier translations. Bible commentaries are found in the different versions of the Bible. These instruct the reader to observe, each versions particular intepretations, these reflect each versions religious conclusions.

Traditionalist Bible commentators demand that readers believe the Bible's accounts of miraculous events, purely because they are recorded in the Bible's sacred pages. However, the miraculous or paranormal is not understood in any meaningful context in our materialist age, due to the commentators' lack of knowledge regarding psychical research and mediumship.

Ironically, many traditionalist Bible commentators do not believe that the same mediumistic experiences exist today. If they believe in mediumistic experiences at all, they argue that they are an extinct historical phenomenon. This leaves many modern-day people confused. They try to believe the historic accounts, which they do not understand, simply because they appear in the Holy Bible. Yet the accounts appear to be meaningless, especially when the same practices are condemned by many theologians today.

Some modernist Bible commentators cause even further obscurity. They teach the public that many biblical narratives are symbolic or meaningless fairytales. Such commentators know nothing of modern-day mediumship. Consequently, inevitably, many people today are perplexed and ill-informed of the facts. They have no framework of knowledge into which they can fit the biblical accounts of non-physical communicators.

Ironically, when Bible commentators, through ignorance of mediumship, attempt to explain away the Bible's record of non-physical communications, they simultaneously explain away religion – which often has its origins in the mediumistic faculty.

Eliade observed that religious experiences are more accurately and meaningfully understood within the context of religion, the area of life in which they are manifested. Hence, transformative spiritual experiences such as spiritually orientated mediumship are most meaningfully interpreted within the religious context. A religious interpretation is superior to that of materialist analytical, reductionist sociologists and parapsychologists who, often in a most emotionally damaging sense, claim that a person's experiences are illusory.

Arguably, some individuals who became known as 'prophets' were not necessarily selected to be spiritual teachers because of their own spirituality. Arguably, they were chosen because they were able to hear and/or see non-physical communicators. These angels or spirits typically led these individuals to their own spiritual unfoldment, which in turn encouraged others to progress spiritually. Biblical writers, familiar with mediumship, expected future readers to be equally familiar with mediumship, otherwise their accounts would be meaningless. Sadly, this is the current state of affairs.

It is not the exact historicity of the reported events that is important but rather the fact that the accounts provide lengthy and detailed descriptions of mediumship. Significantly, both biblical historians and archaeologists would confirm that many biblical narratives are historically and geographically accurate.

## Biblical Terminology

Biblical writers' descriptions of mediumship have been translated over the centuries in the following ways:

- 'God spoke'
- 'the Lord spoke'
- 'God appeared'
- 'the Lord appeared'
- 'the Angel spoke'
- 'the Angel appeared'
- 'the Angel of the Lord appeared'
- 'the Angel of the Lord was upon him'

Such related biblical expressions can only be meaningfully understood in the context of mediumistic conversations with non-physical beings, presumably spirits or angels as the following evidence confirms. These communicators were perceived to be sufficiently different from physical people hence they were frequently confused with gods or perceived as angelic messengers. Non-physical communicators frequently demanded that people should live by a higher spiritual code of conduct. The evidence in the following pages will prove that mediumistic experiences had an increasingly clear spiritual focus in historic times.

Examples of esteemed, historic, spiritual figures who laid spiritual foundation stones were inspired by the receipt of mediumistic communications. The most insightful umbrella term for understanding our ancestors' experiences of conversations with non-physical communicators is 'mediumship.' These biblical records represent ancient precedents of modern day mediumship. Once this is understood modern day people will understand these experiences in the same light as the biblical writers intended.

## Mediumistic Experiences

The following observations by biblical scholars represent their understanding of biblical accounts. A few biblical scholars have knowledge of present-day mediumship and can make sense of the biblical narratives. Others are less familiar with psychical research and believe the Bible talks of extinct miraculous events. Harold

Knight in *The Hebrew Prophetic Consciousness* states:

> It is surely a mistake to seek to eliminate the visionary element
> from the consciousness of the great prophets themselves ...
> (many phrases) ... denote some kind of supernormal ...
> experience. Once the prophet has received the call to prophesy,
> there breaks forth upon his consciousness the vision of an unseen
> and glorious world interpenetrating and transfiguring the
> prosaic world of every day. He is equipped with the psychical
> gifts befitting his office.[3]

Angus Haddow accepts that the biblical accounts describe
paranormal phenomena in his book *The Paranormal in the Synoptic
Gospels*. He states:

> Extra-sensory perception (ESP) is the acquisition of information
> about the world otherwise than through the known sensory
> channels. Under this general heading are telepathy (the commu-
> nication of ideas from one mind to another without the use of the
> recognised channels of sense), clairvoyance (a similar perception
> of objects or objective events), clairaudience (hearing by
> paranormal means), psychokinesis (the movement or influencing
> of an object by 'mental or spiritual force' – known as PK) and
> precognition (the sensing, seeing, or knowing something which
> will occur in the future). The dividing line between these aspects
> of ESP is blurred as they can overlap with each other.[4]

G. Ernest Wright, in *Isaiah: Layman's Bible Commentary*, suggests that:
'In Hebrew the visionary and auditory terms have simply become a
technical language for direct revelation. Even when "vision" is used,
the content is nearly always a word spoken or heard.'[5] Significantly,
the terms 'seer' and 'prophet' were used interchangeably in the
biblical accounts, indicating that the prophet was clairvoyant or
clairaudient or both. These faculties are understood today as

mediumship or channeling. T.H. Robinson writes in *Decline and Fall of the Hebrew Kingdoms*:

Both classes were men of peculiar and abnormal powers of behaviour. The seer, as his name implies, was a man gifted with the power of second sight, able to enter a world different from that which ordinary men inhabit and to become conscious of sights and sounds which were beyond the range of others.[6]

H. Wheeler Robinson writes in *Religious Ideas of the Old Testament*: 'Certain features of prophetic writings do seem to point to an identity of psychical experience.'[7]

R.C. Johnson in *Teach Yourself Psychical Research* claims there are:

Other states in which consciousness is withdrawn from the normal waking level – which collectively we may call trance states ... A medium or 'sensitive' can pass voluntarily to an interior level of the self and can at the same time maintain a 'communication line' – by writing and speaking to those around.[8]

J.G.S. Thomson in *The New Bible Dictionary* states: 'The border line between vision and dream or trance is difficult if not impossible to determine.'[9] When prophets received communications they were often described as entering into a trance – an altered state of consciousness – during which they received guidance, hidden truths and insights. These dialogues with angels or spirits were frequently perceived solely by the prophet, who, acting as a messenger, delivered these communications to others.

D.J. Bretherton states:

Similar physical sensations, often of an almost unbearable kind, which also included feelings of extreme heat and cold, have been a feature of the experiences of mystics and saints throughout the centuries. They were particularly apparent in conditions of ecstatic trance, with the accompaniment of physical pain and even visible marks on the body ... such visionaries, as Scripture indicates, were frequently misunderstood, abused, scorned, persecuted and even put to death. Yet there have been times when they have been chosen as special vehicles of revelation, the tested channels of truth and judgement and the media whom God has made his will and purpose known to others.[10]

Bretherton's comments describe mystical experiences of the Divine. These, though miraculous, are markedly different from the lengthy negotiations carried out by many prophets which are much more in keeping with discussions with angels or spirits. The condemnation some of these prophets experienced is akin to that experienced by mediums throughout the ages and today.

## 15th and 16th Century Biblical Mistranslations Prohibit Mediumship

Ironically, some biblical mistranslations have included the erroneous prohibition of spiritual mediumship. Yet many accounts clearly describe mediumship as the practice of many revered biblical mediums including the biblical judges, Samuel, Moses and Jesus. shortly. These mistranslations occurred during the 15th and 16th centuries. They have left people today, several hundred years later, with the belief that the Bible prohibits mediumship. Evidence for these statements will be discussed in the following pages. The Churches' Fellowship for Psychical and Spiritual Studies in the United Kingdom notes in their mission statement entitled 'Psychical Studies and the Bible:'

Some Christians mistakenly condemn psychic studies as evil and to be avoided at all costs, basing their authority on the Deuteronomic prohibitions (*Deuteronomy 18:8–14.*) These prohibitions must be seen in their context as an attempt to tell the people of Israel what they must on no account do if God is to lead and protect them in the new land of Canaan. Apart from the first reference to the Canaanite custom of child sacrifice (cp. *Leviticus 18:21; 2nd Kings 23:10; Jeremiah 32:35*) the others refer to specialists in three type categories. There are the three types of diviner (*auger, soothsayer, diviner*) [and] the two types of specialist spiritists ('those who traffic with ghosts and spirits' and 'necromancers'). Due to difficulties over language there have been inaccurate translations of these Hebrew words, e.g. *'mediums' (Revised Standard Version)* for *'One who makes enquiry of ghosts/spirits'* ... *A medium (in the proper sense of the word)* does not call up the dead, but claims that the dead come to or through him or her. It is the use of the psychic realm by using magic ritual to try to manipulate God for selfish ends, rather than to find the true will of God, which lies at the heart of these prohibitions.

God's will is paramount and any attempt to alter it is a sin against the Most High Himself. There are psychic elements in the Old Testament which are not forbidden, because they are used to seek God's will and to further His purpose ... Many spirit forces in the Bible are opposed to the will of God and that is why *St. John* says *'Test the spirits ...'* (1 John 4:1–3). To include all psychic power as evil is to be simplistic and prejudiced. Psychic gifts are to be used as all God's gifts are to be used, for the well-being of our neighbours in the context of ... love and for the ... guiding principle, *'Not our will but God's will be done.'*[11]

To highlight the present-day dilemma, Bretherton notes in *The Holy Scripture and the Trance-State, Part 1*:

In traditional church circles there are certain loaded words which are regarded with suspicion and ... antagonism [such as] *witch, familiar, spiritualist, medium, trance* ... [These] are heavily weighted by prejudice and misunderstanding and conjure up in some minds ideas of black magic, sorcery, devil-worship and communication with demons and evil spirits ...

Modern translations of the relevant passages of Scripture have given added support to views which, several hundred years ago, led to persecution, torture and murder of many innocent people ... accused of witchcraft ... Contemporary translators have unfortunately and mistakenly inserted the word 'medium' where the original passages actually refer to necromantic practices involving the resuscitation of dead bodies. In no sense can such abhorrent activities be equated with most present day mediumship as practised and recognised in spiritualist circles.[12]

It is a sad fact that all modern bibles contain many mistranslations which falsely indicate that the Bible condemns 'mediumship.' Instead, the Bible condemns 'necromancy.' Necromancy has been wrongly translated to mean mediumship. This is a glaring mistranslation of the original Hebrew that has resulted in misguidedhistoric and present day theological condemnation of mediumship. Ironically, it is these same psychic gifts that have given birth to a large part of the contents of the Bible. Further details regarding biblical mistranslations can be found in *Life, Death and Psychical Research.*[13]

All versions of the bible in present day usage display the mistranslated prohibitions against mediumship. Many modern biblical scholars of the institutionalized church are aware that the versions in current usage display the mistranslated prohibitions against mediumship. It appears that no thought is given to them or their implications for present-day attitudes.

These mistranslations have resulted in enormous confusion and opposition towards all mediumistic experiences. These grossly flawed attitudes leave the public ignorant of the enormous spiritual legacy given to spiritual teachers through mediumistic experiences. Tragically, many people are left unaware of the opportunity today to gain spiritually enriching mediumistic experiences through meditative spiritual practices.

## The Mistranslations of Endor (1 Samuel 28)

The following discussion clarifies mistranslations that appear to condemn mediumship. There is a contemporary need for this clarification as the ignorance and fear it directs towards spiritually orientated mediumship continues to this day. The mistranslations of the biblical narrative found in 1 Samuel chapter 28 have generated much historic and present-day intolerance which has been directed towards the practice of spiritually orientated mediumship.[14] The following discussion draws upon scholarly clarifications to reveal the correct translation of this account. The use of the Hebrew term 'ob holds the key to the correct interpretation of the true and intended meaning of this narrative.

1 Samuel 28 describes a historic event. King Saul asked a foreign woman from the neighboring idolatrous culture to contact the prophet Samuel. Samuel, the mediumistic prophet had passed to spirit some time before. During Samuel's life, working as a prophet, Samuel assisted Saul, providing Saul with predictive and mediumistic guidance. The reason for King Saul's desire for mediumistic communication with Samuel was Saul's fear of the forthcoming battle with Israel's enemies. Consequently, he asked for Samuel's advice from beyond the grave.

This idolatrous woman belonged to a different culture from that of Israel. She practiced perverse, barbaric, corrupted forms of divination and mediumship. The woman believed she needed to use a sacrifice to facilitate her spiritually inferior psychic and mediumistic abilities. This was her custom. The practices she employed involved murder, after which, she would examine entrails from animal corpses, both human and non-human.

From these she made her predictions and contacted spirits. The account states that Samuel's spirit appeared and predicted that King Saul would die the next day. The combination of both Samuel's tragically accurate prediction regarding Saul's impending fate and the later biblical mistranslations, has forcefully caused people to wrongly interpret Saul's impending death as a punishment for practicing mediumship.

It is important to examine the narrative, the background to it and the mistranslations. During his lifetime, Samuel the prophet, namely a medium, regularly practiced divination and contacted Yahweh for guidance and predictive information. Samuel then conveyed this information to assist King Saul and others. Samuel saw and heard the non-physical communicator and had lengthy negotiations with this celestial being, evidently, Samuel had clairvoyant and clairaudient mediumistic abilities. These accounts describe Yahweh as an otherworldly being, a celestial messenger, notably, 'the angel of the lord.' Importantly, Yahweh was perceived as a *messenger*. Mistranslations have confused Yahweh with God. We have seen in previous chapters the recurring pattern throughout the centuries of describing a non-physical communicator as a god or as the messenger of God.

The narrative in 1 Samuel 28 refers to the predictive divination stones named Urim and Thummim. Regularly, these stones were used to determine future events. Questions were asked of the stones; they would answer, and it was believed that in so doing they conveyed Yahweh's wishes. We are told that since Samuel's death they no longer used the predictive stones.

Obviously in his lifetime Samuel's psychic and mediumistic abilities had facilitated the accurate use of the stones.

Continuing the practices of his predecessors, Samuel had frequently utilized the Urim and Thummin. Samuel's provision of this psychic and mediumistic service, which answered Saul's questions, powerfully assisted King Saul's rulership. Bereft of Samuel and Samuel's use of the divination stones, King Saul had sought refuge with this foreign medium whose spiritually inferior level of mediumship was corrupted with perverse practices.

To give something of the background to this account, prior to Samuel's death Samuel was enraged with Saul. Their relationship had totally broken down. Samuel had admonished Saul and told him that Yahweh despaired of Saul's persistent disobedience and his rejection of Yahweh's guidance, which was requested and then not followed. As a result, Samuel told Saul that Yahweh would no longer guide the king through the use of the nation's prophets and the divination stones. Yahweh and Samuel had deserted Saul as Saul had demonstrated a lack of trust in Yahweh.

The account demonstrates that Samuel, who now spoke from beyond the grave, was further outraged with Saul when he realized that Saul had brought him back through this idolatrous, pagan mediumistic necromancer. By going to this foreign woman, Saul had shown further disloyalty to Yahweh who was already angry with him.

She used condemned, perverse ritualistic practices involving corpses to accompany her non-spiritual brand of mediumship and divination. It was necromancy, as practiced by such a woman, that was condemned, not mediumship. Saul had sought mediumistic and divination assistance from this idolatrous necromancer because Yahweh had abandoned him. Yahweh had told Saul through the medium Samuel, that he would receive no further guidance from living prophets from his own culture. Lesser prophets than Samuel, from Saul's own nation, would have obeyed Yahweh's command not to guide Saul.

Many people have been wrongly influenced by the various versions of the modern day Bible which each contain the same 15th-century mistranslations, misinterpretations and corruptions of these events. Bibles today wrongly claim or infer that Saul is to die in battle the next day because he consulted with a 'medium.' In fact, Saul consulted with a necromancer, a 'witch,' whose practice of murder and the use of entrails was condemned. The term 'witch' has been wrongly translated as 'medium.'

If this woman did genuinely make contact with non-physical communicators she (and her kind) would inevitably draw to them grossly spiritually inferior spirits in keeping with the natural laws of like attracting like. This profound principle is certainly a further reason why mediumistic psychics and necromancers were condemned.

The organized church in the 15th century was a very powerful, rich and feared institution. The church leaders at that time resented mediumship as it challenged their sole human, religious authority. They fiercely opposed those people who sought their own answers to spiritual questions. Such people would not blindly follow the church's leaders' commands and religious dogmas. At this time the organized church committed mass murder, condemning thousands of innocent people to death. Those murdered were typically psychically sensitive mediumistic individuals, with a further healing gift, who wished to seek spiritual truth not dogma and think for themselves. The church leaders branded them as witches in order to justify their horrendous executions. Unfortunately, something of this ignorant legacy continues today as many people have wrongly applied these historic mistranslations and condemnations to spiritually orientated mediumship.

The Israelite tribes were repeatedly chastised by their non-physical communicator Yahweh for worshipping idols and for their infidelity to him. The scholarly writings of Rev. Bretherton confirm that it was the foreign woman's necromancy, her use of corpses and use of idolatrous objects which was, in fact, condemned.

> Against arguments that the woman of En-dor (1 Samuel 28) was a medium and not a necromancer ... I consider overwhelming evidence that she was engaged in necromantic practices ... She is described in 1 Samuel 28:7 as 'a woman who possesses an 'ob' or a 'woman who is mistress of an 'ob' or the 'woman who is the controller of an 'ob.' Almost every serious commentator gives one of these alternative renderings.[15]

Saul was yet further condemned for his infidelity to Yahweh and God by going to an idolatrous woman. It was not mediumship that was condemned, as Samuel had been the mediumistic prophet who had guided King Saul before his death.

Bretherton's research confirms that it was idolatry and necromancy that was condemned, not mediumship. He states:

> In 1 Samuel 28:3 and 9, with reference to the action of King Saul in outlawing necromancy, it states that he 'cut off' (28:9) the 'oboth (plural for 'ob) and yiddeonim out of the land, with no direct reference to the operators themselves. It is the fetish-objects which are mentioned and 'cut off.' The word for 'cut off' (karath) is used of the 'hewing down' of idols, images and other idolatrous objects. Moreover the people are told that they must not possess such objects (Lev. 20:27), nor are they to resort to them (Lev. 19:31). The 'ob is also described as a manufactured object. In 2 Kings 21:6, we are told that Manasseh 'made an 'ob and yiddeonim' (*we 'asah 'ob we yiddeonim*) ... The Hebrew term 'asah is used of making idols.[16]

Drawing on the writings of the biblical scholar Dr Edward Langton, who states in *Good and Evil Spirits* that: 'Here the Hebrew expression which is translated, *"dealt with them that had familiar spirits"* ... means literally, *"and made an 'ob."'* Langton also claims that the general consensus of opinion regarding an *'ob* is that it was an external object and that it applied to something that could be made.[17] Significantly, this confirms that an *'ob* was a manufactured idol used by the foreign idolotrous necromancer who was also responsible for murder.

Bretherton continues: 'The 'ob is the instrument for raising up Samuel. When Saul asked the woman of Endor to conjure up Samuel, he said, "ba 'ob," i.e. "by means of [an 'ob]," or "with the help of [an 'ob]" (1 Samuel 28:8).'[18] Osterley, writing in *Immortality and the Unseen World*, also notes that the 'ob is a manufactured object and is external to the user: 'In the passages so far examined it is clear that there is a distinction between the 'ob and the person who uses it.'[19] Osterley confirms that scholars are agreed that when the Hebrew is accurately translated it proves that an *'ob* is an object. In

*Hebrew Religions*, Osterley writes: 'An 'ob can conceivably be regarded as an external object.'[20]

H.P. Smith confirms that: 'In the majority of cases an 'ob is classed not with persons but with things – objects of idolatrous and superstitious practices ... the most natural explanation makes them some sort of idol.'[21]

Bretherton adds:

So in 2 Kings 23:24, a description of the reforming zeal of King Josiah, we read that, 'Josiah put away the 'oboth [plural of 'ob] and the yiddeonim and the teraphim and the idols and all the filthy images ...' To resort to the 'oboth is like resorting to idols and so becoming unclean (defiled). The 'oboth are also classed with teraphim (household gods or images) in 2 Kings 23:24. To resort to the 'ob was adultery, equivalent to whoring after idols, which was also adultery, the penalty being death (Lev 20:6, 27). As such, the 'ob was also an abomination, as were idols. Saul was condemned for resorting to these [idolatrous] objects [not to necromancers as such]. He requested an 'ob in order to inquire ...'[22]

In this context it is vital to remember that Samuel, when physically alive, was King Saul's psychic and medium. Samuel gave Saul predictive information through the divination stones. These were believed to have their origins in Yahweh as Yahweh was perceived as working through all events and creatures, no matter how minor. Samuel also provided Saul with Yahweh's advice in a more mediumistic sense.

Bretherton states:

It is clear that the En-dor saga is a fragment of a much older tradition which has been inserted [in the wrong place] ... It is, however, legitimate to interpret the En-dor episode quite differently today and in terms of knowledge secured through the study of the paranormal and our understanding of the methods of modern mediums ... The 'ob was a ... bone, skull and so on ... [used] after some kind of blood-ritual ...

In this sense it would fulfil the task of a 'familiar' ... every reference to the 'ob (and yiddeoni) reflects views about a practice which was extremely old and primitive and derived from surrounding peoples as well as from Canaanite traditions. It persisted despite every attempt to eliminate it from the life of the nation. It was seen as a rival to the pre-eminence of Yahweh and linked with idolatrous rites of heathen nations. This despite the fact, as we know, that seers, prophets and others exercised extraordinary gifts of 'sensitivity' which were generally accepted and utilised.

In the struggle to cleanse the nation of dangerous magical practices there were times when they were all lumped together as 'abominations' and the innocent suffered with the guilty. The condemnation of necromancy did not apply to seership, genuine prophecy, or the higher forms of mediumship and this point should be made absolutely clear, particularly as modern translations of the Bible wrongly and dangerously interpret 'ob and yiddeoni as 'medium' and 'spiritist.' It is, therefore, of great importance, when using or quoting Scripture in relation to our modern understanding of parapsychology, to make sure that we do not create new problems of interpretation which would make it more difficult for our fellow Christians to accept our findings.[23]

It is clear that Saul was criticized for disobeying the religious laws by going to an idolatrous foreign mediumistic necromancer. It was this that was passionately condemned, as the 'ob is most certainly an idol and not a spirit. Bretherton states: 'If the 'ob is an object, a kind of fetish, an ancestral relic or a manufactured necromantic instrument, then it is not, as such, a ghost, a spirit, familiar or control.'[24]

The following comments in a paper by Bretherton entitled 'Psychical Research and Biblical Prohibitions' in *Life, Death and Psychical Research* further clarify the confusions and errors:

> The Deuteronomic 'Prohibition' (Deut. 18:9 to 12) has long been used by the prejudiced, the ignorant and the fearful as a reason for opposing genuine psychical research by Christian people. In the past, innocent folk have been denounced as sorcerers and witches or of being possessed by evil spirits. Others, who have exercised powers believed to come under the sacred ban, have been tortured or cruelly put to death. Such attitudes still persist. Those who seek to exercise psychical gifts are often warned of the dangers of Divine condemnation.
>
> Christians who encourage paranormal investigation are reminded that they are going against the teachings of the Bible ... The awful fate of Saul is sometimes quoted: for he enquired of one who had a familiar spirit [mistranslation] and not of the Lord and 'therefore he slew him.' These indignant protests would be understandable and ... justified, if this was the real meaning and intention of the Deuteronomic 'prohibition.' However, it is not a condemnation of the exercise of psychical gifts ... it is the condemnation of the Cult of the Dead and other associated practices. The terms 'medium' (R.S.V.) or 'consulter with familiar spirits' (A.V. and R.V.) are faulty translations which have persisted for centuries.[25]

Rev. L. Argyll in *Nothing to Hide*[26] argues that unfortunately, historical prejudice and ignorance have had a detrimental influence which has led to mistranslations, which were then perpetuated by misleading terminology. Consequently, it is a fact that these errors have adversely conditioned people's attitudes towards mediumship throughout the centuries. This state of affairs is tragic when the study of mediumship can lead to proof that life continues beyond physical death and that an individual's level of spirituality will determine their after death landscape.

This disaster is compounded by the fact that mediumship, as this book is revealing, has had and continues to have a profound spiritual legacy for the ongoing evolution and progress of humankind's spiritual beliefs.

The paper 'Psychical Research and Biblical Prohibitions in Life, Death and Psychical Research'[27] clarifies the extent to which these mistranslations have adversely affected people's understanding of mediumship. Since the 15th century, Christians and others have remained unaware that they are being misguided by historic mistranslations and distortions of the original Hebrew. Ill-informed-misguided loyalty to the biblical authors has led Christians and others to victimize psychically sensitive individuals known as mediums. Tragically, many loyal adherents of religion are also unaware that these mistranslations often occurred as the result of corrupt *political* intentions. This knowledge may now convince them that such loyalty is misplaced.

Further confusion has arisen as a result of the term 'familiar spirit.' This term has been wrongly placed into many biblical translations of narratives, particularly those that describe mediumship. Again, this error was deliberately carried out by employees of the church to satisfy church desire to condemn, for all time, psychically sensitive mediumistic individuals. Church victimization, outlawing and the conviction of mediumistic individuals was sealed in the pages of the Bible forever. It is possible that some people did murder animals, human and non-human in order to utilize their entrails, practices which are obviously evil and abhorrent. This cruelty went hand in hand with the worship of idols and sorcery. For those reprehensible individuals the church had also voiced its powerful opposition.

However, any person with psychic and mediumistic gifts was wrongly lumped together with murderous necromancers, historically and for all time though the biblical mistranslations. As a result of these prohibitative mistranslations which were wrongly applied to mediumship in this era, untold numbers of innocent people suffered excruciatingly painful torture then burnt to death.

The above paper explains:

The dread of witchcraft ... the late fifteenth century mind believed ... witches [could do] a terrifying list of things for which today's science for the most part is able to give natural explanations and its horrific associations has influenced the translation of the Deuteronomic formula in the Geneva Bible which in turn influenced subsequent versions, including the Bishop's Bible, the Authorised Version (AV) of King James, the Revised Version (RV) and modern renderings.[28]

This paper points out that the biblical book of Deuteronomy gives three addresses delivered by the prophet Moses. The first is what God has done (chapter 1 to 4:43), the second is what God requires (4:44 to 28:68) and the third is what God proposes (chapter 29 to 30:20).[29] The Deuteronomic Prohibition of 18:10–12 is part of the second address.

The practices mentioned are described as 'abomination.' It is most important to note that three statements about abominations enclose the whole passage. The reference is to all those rites which accompany the worship of idols, including pagan forms of divination. Four words are generally used in Hebrew to express the term 'abomination' and they are always used, directly or indirectly, with reference to idolatry in one form or another. The abominable is the idolatrous. Even when 'abomination' is used in an ethical sense it can be shown that there is a hidden reference to perverse and lying attitudes identified with the idolatrous people of other nations who worship and serve false gods.

Such associations are clearly distinguishable in the Deuteronomic 'Prohibition.' In the attempt to establish the unique righteousness and moral demands of Yahweh ... it was essential that all forms of idolatry and the practices associated with them should be condemned. The slightest taint of idolatry rendered certain customs and creatures 'unclean' to Yahweh. They were 'abominable' to Him. The people had passed through the lands of other nations seeing 'their abominations and their idols' and they must not follow after their ways nor adopt their gods.[30]

This point is reinforced by other scholars including Rollo Ahmed. In the book *Black Art*, Ahmed writes that it was a 'custom of Hebrew necromancers to use mummified bodies for divinatory purposes.'[31] The following observations further clarify the situation.

Just as the Ob was a mummy or sacred relic used to obtain oracles, so also the cult of the Yiddeoni (Yiddoa is a bird) was probably divination by means of the mummified corpse or bones of a bird or some other creature.

This would explain why the Oboth and the Yiddeonim were constantly mentioned together ... Moreover, totemism was linked with the cult of the dead. It was the representation in some form of a creature whose life was mystically bound up with that of the well-being of the tribe ... As an ancestor-creator it could be a semi-divine animal or bird ... Therefore, it is reasonable to suggest that the Yiddeonim were the mummified forms of semi-deified bird-creatures used much as the Oboth were used to obtain information.

This would include ventriloquism and fabricated messages from the dead. Thus we come to the last of the prohibited practices translated by the word necromancer in the A.V., R.V., N.E.B and R.S.V. [bibles]. However, the Hebrew says: 'doresh el hammethim:' 'they that seek unto the dead.' It was not basically contact with a familiar spirit: *it was prophecy by means of a dead body*. This at times included examining the entrails of a person who had died or who had been killed for the purpose ... the

255

practitioner of the art sought to revive the dead corpse in such a way that the spirit returned and he was able to converse with it. This crude and primitive belief in the association of the life or spirit of the dead with his mortal remains persisted for centuries. Abominable and horrifying rites were performed in order to 'raise the dead' to obtain information.[32]

In Babylon, some priests performed similar terrible rituals. This particular type of priesthood was known as the 'conjurors of the dead' or those who 'bring up the dead' or the 'questioners of the dead.'[33]

[All the practices] which come under the sacred ban in Deuteronomy 18:9–12 are illicit because they are idolatrous and involve:

A. The recognition and service of false gods.

B. Evil pagan rites.

C. Occult forms of divination practised by the heathen.

D. Animal worship.

E. Ancestor worship.

F. False prophecy and cheating.

G. Turning to false gods for guidance rather than to [Yahweh].

H. The cult of the dead.

... they are an abomination ... and an offence to His holy name. They represent primitive orgiastic attempts through false deities and magic formulae and the use of dead bodies to obtain information ... All this stands in vivid contrast to the recognised seers and prophets of Israel whose psychical and spiritual gifts of sensitivity and insight were dedicated to the work and service of Yahweh.[34]

Those psychically sensitive individuals who possessed spiritual gifts who lived during and after the 15th-century mistranslations which condemned mediumship were ironically following the same spiritually orientated mediumistic practices as those of the famous prophets. These blighted individuals helped their communities by practicing mediumship, precognition and healing.

## Psychic and Spiritual Studies

In the most ancient Hebrew beliefs there was no concept of those beyond the grave possessing a soul or being a spirit. At this time the Hebrews had undeveloped levels of understanding. These ancients believed in an after-life in which 'shades' of the dead lived on in a place called Sheol, with no personality, no body and no soul. When they reported communications from non-physical personalities, they originally believed the messages were delivered by gods. The communicator was perceived as a god or messenger of a god because these ancients had no concept of a person surviving death and keeping their personality intact.

Throughout the Old Testament, in particular, there are many accounts that tell us that the prophets of the tribes of Israel regularly sought Yahweh's guidance. We are informed that the prophets had long, passionate negotiations with Yahweh. The biblical accounts describe these conversations in the same vein as one person talking to another person, though that communicator was non-physical.

As previously referenced, a second method employed to divine Yahweh's will and to gain knowledge of the future was the use of the divination stones named Urim and Thummim. It was believed that Yahweh knew the future and could influence the smallest to largest events; Yahweh influenced the way these stones fell and the way the stones fell supplied the people with answers to their questions. Consequently, they believed that Yahweh was the source of the answers that the stones gave them.

The Old Testament accounts frequently inform us that 'the spirit of the lord came upon [an individual] and then he prophesied.' This is seen as a natural occurrence. Repeatedly, these accounts describe prophets 'talking in tongues.' Using today's terminology we would describe them as receiving 'mediumistic trance communications.'

In the early stages of this form of mediumship, messages usually do sound garbled and unclear, but as the medium's skill advances, the communications tend to slow down or speed up and clarify. Biblical accounts frequently refer to a range of abilities known as 'the gifts of the spirit.' These include receiving information about the future, receiving spiritual guidance, and channeling spiritual healing to the patient.

When a person develops the ability to receive mediumistic communications, it becomes evident that different qualities of information is received. It is imperative to evaluate the level of spirituality and accuracy of these messages. Information has to be assessed to evaluate whether it originates from a false communicator or lifeless psychic system, as discussed in earlier chapters.

Tragically, the fountain of spiritual guidance and information about life after physical death has been officially closed off by the church. This fact is illustrated by the ignorant and more often corrupt mistranslations and editing, resulting in distortions, omissions and the suppression of the entire original accounts. This has left many people who have had spiritually orientated mediumistic experiences which have enhanced their spiritual maturity feeling victimized and alienated. The church's legacy of condemnation has stretched its arm across the centuries, conditioning attitudes even today.

The mistranslations have been in part a product of the loss of highly significant detail, which is always a casualty of excessive brevity.

Breathing life into the historic biblical accounts in the light of psychical research and an informed awareness about spiritually orientated mediumship is both imperative and invaluable. This clearer understanding has enormous implications for people today.

Arguably, they should seek to demonstrate the living, active faith of our ancestors who, from the beginning of time, opened themselves as mediumistic channels. If people act as mediums today, they should be discerning, as advised in the Bible. They should ask for the most elevated spiritual sources to communicate and they should evaluate the ethical level of the information received. Obviously the communications are only of value if they teach a person to do no harm and to demonstrate love and compassion to all creatures.

A more informed understanding of mediumistic experiences is long overdue and needs to be widely popularized in order to expel present-day prejudice fear and confusion. To redress this problem, the Churches' Fellowship for Psychical and Spiritual Studies, founded in 1953 in the United Kingdom, states that it exists:

To promote the study of psychical and religious experience ... it continues to serve the churches and its individual members who come from many and varied backgrounds. Some have sought help from the Fellowship's extensive knowledge, at significant points in life where there may have been spontaneous gifts of the Spirit ... or simply a vocation to a spiritual life through a psychic encounter. Many bring a wisdom and depth of vision to enrich the understanding of others.

The Fellowship takes a positive view of psychic sensitivity which many people experience quite naturally in their lives, perhaps through an unsought telepathic communication. Some seem to have a greater awareness of this dimension than others and in some it is more refined. There is a gentle call on members to relate this to a fuller (Spiritual) life in which the psychic may find consecration.

Without this approach there may be a tendency to extol the psychic dimension for its apparent allurement alone which can lead to an emptiness of purpose or even open to the darker aspects of the paranormal. The psychic is the means by which there is real accord, soul to soul. It is what is given and received on this level that needs a discernment, which comes from the Holy Spirit ... Jesus himself showed the ease of the psychic in his relationships with others and with the Father as recorded in John 2 where it is said that he: 'Had no need of evidence from others about anyone, for he himself could tell what was in people.'[35]

## Old Testament Mediums

Many people today are unaware that historic spiritual prophets demonstrated ancient precedents of mediumship. This clearly combines psychical phenomena with religion. Many Bible readers today dismiss as fairytales the abundant biblical narratives which tell us of discussions with non-physical communicators. No sensible person can think in terms of God, the Divine, manifesting and having long conversations with humans in an anthropomorphic manner. Arguably, observations of modern-day mediumship hold the key to making sense of such biblical accounts, seeing them not as subjective pictorial images but as objective experiences of mediumistic communications. The religion of Spiritualism assimilates spiritually elevated philosophy conveyed through mediums from otherworldly communicators. Similarly I suggest that similar historic mediumistic communications have great spiritual importance and have played their role in religious history. The most reasonable way to make sense of biblical accounts is to understand them in the context of historic mediumship.

## Yahweh the Spirit Guide

We learn from the Bible that Yahweh had lengthy discussions with the biblical prophets. These conversations are reported to have occurred over many centuries and involved many generations of prophets. The earlier prophets, also known as the Patriarchs arguably had the mediumistic ability to receive communications from non-physical messengers. It is possible that throughout these centuries the same name of 'Yahweh' was applied to different non-physical communicators.

Yahweh was believed to be an elevated being, a non-physical communicator, a god, or a messenger of God. Yahweh guided the Hebrew people and gave them information about future events. Yahweh might be described as a spiritually elevated spirit or angel whose objective was to teach the importance of higher ethical standards and loyalty to those he guided.

In the most ancient of times, people thought of Yahweh as God as they had little concept of survival beyond physical death or of the existence of a non-physical world. Their spiritual code of conduct was immature and undeveloped. In these days of antiquity, the Hebrews and their descendants were repeatedly criticized by their prophets for returning to the worship of idols and sacrificing to them. Yahweh as a spirit guide might have alleviated the need for an anthropomorphic deity in these spiritually immature times.

As the centuries passed, the Hebrews learned from successive spiritual teachers who fostered their increasing spiritual maturity that the Divine was invisible and otherworldly and permeated both the visible physical and invisible non-physical realms. Akin to the Spiritualist religion today, which advocates that its spiritual philosophy is dynamically supplemented by the frequent incursions of invisible teachers, the historic biblical accounts also emphasize the value of dreams and sleep-state communications.

As an altered state of consciousness it is believed that through this method both an individual's soul and celestial messengers communicate. Further shared similarities of belief between contemporary Spiritualists and the ancients is the belief in the innate ability of most living creatures to hear non-physical communicators clairaudiently, or see them clairvoyantly.

Spiritualists also claim to have recognized the spiritual leadership of additional, more contemporary prophets, who were exemplary seers or mediums. Many of whom have demonstrated the ability to enter into altered states of consciousness known as trance states. In this direct voice trance state the information transmitted is less susceptible to human distortion and misrepresentation.

Many mediums perform automatic writing, whereby the hand, mind or spirit/soul of the medium appears to be utilized by non-physical communicators. Typically, they write down information of which they had no prior knowledge. Mediums today also practice spiritual healing, during which they believe energy is channeled through their body or their spirit to heal the patient. Some mediums also demonstrate levitation, manifestations and de-manifestations.

The important issue here is not that of providing conclusive explanations regarding these observable phenomena, though notably the field of quantum physics is progressively providing us with scientific explanations for the authenticity of such phenomena. What *is* important, is that arguably Spiritualist mediums hear information and observe materializations in the same way as the historic prophets described. However, it is a fact that the information conveyed through present-day mediums varies enormously in spiritual and predictive quality.

This could be the fault of the apparent communicator or alternatively the medium is not adept at receiving or interpreting the information correctly. Nevertheless, it could be argued that Spiritualism is the religion that is most faithful in following the traditions of historic spiritual teachers, as its mediums continue the ancient practices of these highly regarded figures.

## Adam and Eve

The following biblical evaluation will begin by exploring the biblical narratives which tell us of the lives of the first man and woman, the father and mother of humankind. The ancient scribe calls them Adam and Eve. Adam is a plural Hebrew word, meaning 'Humankind,' and Eve, in Hebrew, means 'Life.' Arguably, the symbolic message in the account of Adam and Eve is that 'life,' personified as the woman Eve, tempts 'humankind' to do harm.

It is irrelevant whether Adam and Eve actually lived. The important message clearly conveyed by these ancient recorded accounts is the scribes' total conviction that this couple were in constant communication with an anthropomorphic, yet non-physical communicator.

It is of enormous parapsychological significance that they were being taught to be loyal to his guidance and to demonstrate improved spiritual qualities. His first command to Adam and Eve, the parental role-model for humanity, was that they do no harm to the animals and live vegetarian lives. This communicator is perceived as being 'God.'

To better understand these biblical testimonies, we can utilize our knowledge of contemporary paranormal claims regarding hearing spiritual guidance and predictive information from non-physical sources. It would appear that the ancient authors expected the reader to be familiar with these same mediumistic practices otherwise their accounts would be meaningless.

Related mediumistic experiences of non-physical communicators evaluated today are described as clairaudience (hearing) and clair-voyance (seeing). The narrative only makes sense if it understood in the mediumistic context in which these early scribes were immersed and fluent.

## Abram the Medium

Genesis chapter 12[36] describes Abram's first call to become a spiritual leader. Notably, the contact was initiated by a non-physical communicator who gave his name as Yahweh. Yahweh repeatedly visited Abram and progressively commanded him to obey him and to travel to new lands. Yahweh informed Abram that he would become the founder of a great nation who would likewise be guided and protected by this otherworldly spirit or angel.

When Yahweh communicates, the event is referred to inter-changeably by phrases such as 'the lord appeared' or 'the lord spoke' or as "Yahweh appeared and spoke." Due to the combination of the historic deification of spirit and angel communicators and later translators' prejudicial attitudes and ignorance of psychical phenomena, translators, over time, began to refer to Yahweh as God, the Divine.

The biblical author is emphatic that Abram spoke with a non-physical communicator: 'The LORD had said to Abram ... Abram travelled ... [to] the great tree of Moreh ... The LORD appeared to Abram and said ... There he built an altar to the LORD and called on the name of the LORD.'[37]

Such descriptions echo and share many parallels with ongoing reports of observable mediumship which demonstrate clairvoyance and clairaudience. Viewed within this context, the account is clearly telling us that Abram received communications from an other-worldly being. This was a celestial messenger or discarnate spirit, alternatively known as a dynamically alive, surviving consciousness rather than a psychic system.

The biblical account tells us that Abram traveled to 'the great tree of Moreh.' The Hebrew term *moreh* means 'soothsayer,' therefore Abram visited 'the great tree of the soothsayer.' Continuing the tradition of the more ancient shamans, this soothsayer dispensed his/her mediumistic guidance while sitting beneath a tree. We learn that a 'prophet,' 'oracle' or in today's language a 'medium,' lived or still lived at the 'great tree of Moreh.'

Both in ancient shamanism and the Old Testament narratives a grand tree was often designated as a holy place. In the long established shamanic tradition, clearly continued in Old Testament accounts, people would visit such places daily, in order to speak with prophets, alternatively known as oracles, seers judges or priestesses. This was considered to be a popular, normal and accepted practice. They requested that these mediums contact non-physical communicators to obtain predictive information and guidance.[38]

Altars were built for the purposes of contact, worship and seeking the favor of the non-physical communicators, who were frequently thought of as gods. It was believed that the non-physical communicator lived temporarily at such designated places of contact and would reveal their presence there, either by speaking or materializing.

Equally, the more ancient shamans viewed trees, mountains and hills as symbolic symbols which enhanced access to the inhabitants of the invisible world. Certainly, the practice carried out in Abram's day possessed all the features of those ancient mediums, the shamans.

We are informed that Abram built a number of altars, to which he frequently returned, particularly when times were difficult and he needed celestial assistance. Indeed, Abram, the medium visited the altars in order to enhance contact with non-physical communicators. Evidently, Abram believed that such otherworldly contact was particularly conducive at these revered locations.

Building altars in order to gain access to Yahweh's spiritual and predictive guidance reveals that religious practice and mediumistic communications were 'one.' We learn that Abram had a strong faith, evidently due to the personal evidence he gained as a result of his mediumistic experiences.

These conversationsis are described in detail in the biblical texts. However, when Yahweh told Abram that he would inherit the land of Canaan, Abram asked Yahweh to provide evidential signs to support this prediction. Asking for proof reveals that Abram did not have a blind unquestioning faith, instead Abram conversed and negotiated with this otherworldly, living communicator. Yahweh was a demonstrable reality for Abram, not a matter of faith or dogma.

In the early 20th century the institutionalized church was critical of people who did not accept the Catholic faith as officially stated by church politico-religious elders in the Athanasian Creed. At this time, powerful church leaders warned that people who questioned the church's articles of faith would not receive eternal life in heaven.

The Reverend Maurice Elliott suggests that the institutionalized church's attitude was the result of its reliance upon a distorted interpretation of the prophet Habakkuk's guidance regarding the issue of faith. Elliott clarifies Habakkuk's intentions. The prophet did not ask people to have an unquestioning faith, but rather:

The correct translation of what that great medium – the prophet Habakkuk – wrote is this: 'The good man shall live by his faithfulness,' which means, 'the man who is faithful in all the relations of life and is sincere and upright in heart and purpose, has in his character a principle of permanence.' Habakkuk, the Spiritualist, wrote what Spiritualists are teaching and writing today.[39]

## Hagar the Medium

The biblical authors described people's experience of an angelic or spirit communicator in various ways, but always emphasized that the experience had an otherworldly quality. Equally, there is something otherworldly when a medium makes contact today with an apparent spirit or angelic communicator. The account of Hagar is found in Genesis chapter 16.[40] In chapter 21[41] we read that Hagar was the Egyptian servant of Abram and his wife Sarai.

Hagar later bore Abram a child, but due to the marital disputes that followed, she and her child were expelled from the household. Genesis 16:7–9 tells us most clearly that Hagar had regular conversations with a non-physical communicator. This angel or spirit communicator has been referred to in later translations as 'the angel' or 'the angel of the lord:' 'The angel of the LORD found Hagar ... And he said ... Then the angel of the LORD told her ... The angel added ...'[42]

Hagar was told by her spirit or angel communicator to call her child Ishmael. This name describes Hagar's conversations with the non-physical communicator, meaning 'God Heard' and equally 'Angel-Heard.'

Furthermore, it reveals the ongoing interchangeable nature of 'God and angel/spirit messenger' this is a result of translaters confused interpretions. The name was given to commemorate Hagar's experience of the angel's compassion. This communication took place as a result of Hagar's plight as she found herself and her unborn child to be homeless.

Hagar's immediate personal response was to name this otherworldly communicator Lahai Roi which means 'God-Seen' and equally 'Angel-Seen.' The name applied to the non-physical communicator reveals that not only did Hagar clairaudiently hear the communicator's instructions but also saw a manifestations of this celestial messenger as a result of her obvious clairvoyance. Hagar conversed with this communicator and heard the replies, and both she and the communicator could clearly see each other.

As noted previously, when the Bible was translated into different languages many centuries ago, the term 'Yahweh' or 'angel of the lord' was typically translated as 'God.' This error has been sealed within the pages of the Bible. An example of this can be seen in Hagar's reply: '"You are the [angel] God who sees me," for she said, "I have now seen the [angel] One who sees me." That is why the well was called Beer Lahai Roi [Well of God Seen/Well of Angel-Seen].'[43] People do not have sightings of God observing them or conversations with God in the manner which is described in these accounts.

We are told in Genesis 21:17–19 that a few years later Hagar and her child were alone in the wilderness and were both overcome with thirst, hunger and heat exhaustion. Death was imminent. The scene is described in which Hagar cannot bear to see her young son die before her. Then she hears the consoling voice of a spirit or angel. Soon after this, the translators call this same communicator 'God': 'God heard the boy crying, and the angel of God called to Hagar from heaven and said to her … Then God opened her eyes and she saw a well of water.'[44]

Either Hagar was given a psychic vision of the well where she would find water or was told where the well would be by the non-physical communicator. As a result of this experience Hagar was encouraged to use her last remaining energy to find water, with the result that she and Ishmael survived.

Genesis 17:17 tells us that Yahweh told Abram to change his name to Abraham and to change his wife's name from Sarai to Sarah. Similarly, bibles use the names God and Yahweh interchangeably with the goal of depicting one and the same communicator.

Yahweh told Abram to name his son Isaac – which means 'Laughter.' This name was given to remind Abraham of his initial spontaneous disbelief when he heard Yahweh's prediction that he and Sarai would have a son within the year despite their old age.[45] This account gives us a close insight into Abraham's relationship with the angel or spirit. His communicator demonstrates an anthropomorphic (human) personality and sense of humor and we see that Abraham did not always agree with Yahweh. Such accounts echo contemporary mediums' dialogues with communicators.

## Yahweh's Intervention

At this point in history animal sacrifice was practiced, both human and non-human. This atrocity was also carried out by many neighboring cultures. Abraham, like all individuals, was a product of his time, shaped by the culture in which he lived. Abraham either misinterpreted the angelic communicator's wishes or alternatively, he mistakenly believed in order to please this messenger he was expected to kill his son as a sacrifice.

A number of other historic biblical characters also believed they were required to offer a child as a sacrifice. These include the king of Moab who offered his son, the king of Israel named Jepthah who offered his daughter, and a king of Judah who also offered his son.[46] Abraham mistakenly believed that this act would demonstrate his loyalty and ensure continued communications from the invisible world. Mercifully, an angelic or spirit voice stopped him and therefore condemned sacrificial murder.

This non-physical communicator is described 'as a voice from heaven.' Biblical translators here refer to Yahweh not as God but as 'the angel of the lord,' in effect, an otherworldly messenger.' Genesis 22:11–12 states: 'But the angel of the LORD called out to him from heaven ... "Do not lay a hand on the boy."'[47]

The intervention of this separate, externalized, objective voice changed Abraham's previously set course of action. Yahweh taught him that murderous sacrifices were not required. This account provides evidence that it was a mediumistic experience which advanced Abraham's level of spirituality. Interventions such as these, from non-physical communicators, progressively elevated the religious practices of Israel above the lower spiritual level of its neighbors.

Such mediumistic events historically provided the Israelites with opportunities to progressively achieve a more elevated spiritual code of conduct. Historically, hand in hand with 'received' spiritual guidance, the Israelites were commanded to strive to become a moral example for other nations to follow.

For example, in later centuries, the prophets came to understand that sacrificial murder of animals was considered to be an abomination in the eyes of the ever merciful, compassionate, parent God! However, as a result of human intervention, distortion and interpretation, such obviously compassionate, spiritually elevated commands have not always been obeyed.

Elliott argues that: 'Revelation always depends on one's capacity to receive it and that capacity is psychical. Religion is revelation and were there no such thing as psychic faculty there would be no such thing as revelation or religion.'[48]

## Abraham's Mediumistic Servant

The continuum of spiritual mediumship, hearing and seeing, spirits or angels, can be regularly uncovered throughout the Old Testament accounts, evidence of this will continue to be demonstrated. These narratives record for posterity, the personal testimonies of mediumistic individuals who later became known as prophets. The ongoing common theme demonstrates repeated descriptions of mediumistic experiences.

Communications with spirits or angels guided the spiritual unfoldment of the various prophets, who, in turn, schooled their people. Repeatedly the biblical writers demonstrate their familiarity with mediumistic experiences. Using the lens of mediumship as the key to breaking the Bible code, these countless accounts can be understood literally, in terms of mediumship, just as the biblical authors intended.

A further example of experiences of a spirit or angelic communicator is provided in Genesis chapter 24.[49] This account is of particular significance as it describes the experience of a poor servant – not a central figure – who came to experience the same spirit communicator as his aged master Abraham. The servant had been sent to find a wife for Isaac, Abraham's son, from among their own people. He had been instructed not to find a wife from the Canaanite people among whom they were living.

Genesis 24:12 explains that the servant decided to test for the existence of Yahweh, the celestial spirit guide of his master, of whom he had previously heard reports. The servant petitioned Yahweh to prove that he existed, by helping him find the correct wife for Isaac. The servant asked: 'O LORD, God of my master Abraham, give me success today ...'[50] The servant devised a plan to enable him to choose the correct bride for Isaac. He suggested that the correct woman would unwittingly identify herself to him, by her use of words he had previously suggested to Yahweh.

Soon after, a young woman uttered the words that the servant had earlier arranged with Yahweh. The servant explained this to the woman, who was called Rebekah, and later to her family. They were so convinced by this form of divination or predictive guidance, which they believed was due to Yahweh working through events, that they agreed that Rebekah should marry Isaac. Remarkably, the servant later discovered that Yahweh had led him not simply to the correct wife but to a woman who was a distant relative of Isaac – the preferred option in those days. The servant stated: 'As for me, the LORD has led me on the journey to the house of my master's relatives.'[51]

## Isaac's Wife Spoke to the Spirit Yahweh

Some time later, Rebekah, who was now Isaac's wife, became worried by the unusual movement of the fetus during her pregnancy and asked Yahweh for guidance. Genesis 25:22 translates 'Yahweh' as 'the LORD,' implying that Yahweh is God: 'She went to enquire of the LORD.'[52] Arguably, the biblical term translated as 'to enquire of the lord' actually meant to visit a medium who would communicate with Yahweh on the visitor's behalf.

This term clearly suggests that Rebekah consulted with an oracle/seer/a mediumistic prophet, or in today's terminology, a spiritual medium or channel. This woman was in need of support and guidance and knew she would find the information she needed from a medium. The reply Rebekah received, recorded in Genesis 25:23 was:

Two nations are in your womb
and two peoples from within you will be separated;
one people will be stronger than the other,
and the older will serve the younger.[53]

Typically, echoing the practice of earlier shamans, the medium would have been found at a designated holy sanctuary, where it was believed Yahweh's presence could be accessed more effectively. The prophet would have provided this service on a daily basis to all who asked for assistance.

Clearly, to "enquire of the lord" (Yahweh) meant that an individual would request spirit communication facilitated by the medium, and predictive information and/or wise guidance would be dispensed. Yahweh, replied through the medium, giving his prediction to Rebekah. Yahweh informed her that she would give birth safely to twins who would lead two future nations and that, contrary to the traditional Hebrew practice, the younger child would lead the older.

### Jacob the Shaman/Medium

The predictive information Rebekah received through the medium proved to be accurate (she of course believed that Yahweh was the source of this information). Rebekah named her twin sons Esau and Jacob. Jacob, the younger brother, grew up to be deceitful, cheating Esau out of the inheritance that was traditionally his birthright as the elder of the two. This account can be found in Genesis chapters 27 to 28.[54]

Having fled from his brother's threatened revenge, Jacob spent the night on the hill of Bethel. Sculptured by nature, this hill markedly resembled a flight of stairs. During the sleep state, Jacob had a vision of angels ascending and descending and concluded that this hill was the door to heaven.

Jacob's belief is distinctly shamanic. Earlier mediumistic shamans also believed that access to and communication with the non-physical realms was more easily facilitated at hills, mountains and trees. The shamans revered such places as symbolic doors to the non-physical world.

Ideally, a psychically sensitive mediumistic individual is chosen in accordance with his or her exceptionally spiritual nature, as a person who would wish to do no harm to any living creature. However, Jacob's deceitful nature demonstrates that his future selection as a prophet, a spiritual leader, was not due to his original moral caliber. Arguably, Jacob was chosen because he had the mediumistic capacity to receive spirit communications. Progressively, these mediumistic communications elevate Jacob's level of spirituality.

Elliott notes that Jacob awoke afraid:

He had fled from the wrath of Esau into the presence of his ever-watchful guide. His alarms were transmuted into religious awe and he marked the sanctity of the spot by setting up ... a sacred pillar ... promising to give a tenth of all he possessed towards the maintenance of this sanctuary which he called Beth-el which means 'God's dwelling.'[55]

Due to translation errors, the name of this sanctuary can equally be understood as 'Yahweh's dwelling.'

After arguing with his uncle Laban, Jacob ran off with two of Laban's daughters, whom he intended to marry. Jacob also took some of his uncle's flocks, other possessions and most significantly, his uncle's divining instruments. Clearly, both Laban and Jacob were fluent with divination practices in order to determine future events and mediumistic communications. These instruments were named teraphim.[56] Jacob was saved from his uncle's revenge when Laban believed he heard the voice of Yahweh telling him to let Jacob go free, and he obeyed this instruction.

Clearly, Laban demonstrated the mediumistic faculty of clairaudience. Laban's previously planned course of action was radically altered as a result of hearing the commands of the externalized voice of a non-physical communicator. Arguably, as a result of Jacob's was gift of natural mediumship his life was being used for a spiritual purpose. Jacob could hear the guidance of a non-physical communicator whom he termed 'Yahweh' and was able to act upon that guidance. Consequently, Jacob became a mediumistic instrument through which Yahweh could guide the people.

## Joseph the Shaman/Medium

In future years Jacob fathered a son and named him Joseph. Genesis chapters 37 to 44[57] tells us about the life and mediumistic abilities of Joseph. The biblical scribes inform us that Joseph had prophetic dreams from an early age. These predictive dreams provided Joseph with information concerning future events. In this way Joseph learned that he would one day occupy an earthly position of power. Rejected by his jealous brothers, they sold him into Egyptian slavery.

In Egypt we learn that the slave Joseph became renowned for his mediumistic abilities and that a non-physical communicator worked with him. This angelic or spirit presence was again given the name Yahweh. Joseph's reputation spread, as he informed his fellow prisoners (and later the pharaoh) that Yahweh interpreted people's dreams for him so that he could help others. It is known that Joseph also used a silver divining cup which facilitated his ability to give people information about the future. In Genesis 44:5 Joseph's servant says: 'Isn't this the cup my master drinks from and also uses for divination?'[58]

Those contemporary mediums and psychics who look into crystal balls, presumably alter their state of consciousness and glean predictive and retro-cognitive information. They can achieve the same results by using a cup of water. This practice, which is still used today, clearly echoes Joseph's use of a divining cup and implies that Joseph is yet another historic example of a 'prophet' who was a medium.

The account of Joseph's mediumistic and psychic work carried out during his slavery in Egypt reveals his belief that even the unhappy episodes in his life were vital parts of Yahweh's long-term plan for him. Yahweh was using Joseph as a mediumistic messenger. These events culminated in Joseph being in the right place at the right time with the ability to interpret the dream of an anxious pharaoh.

Joseph informed the pharaoh that his dream predicted several years of good harvests, followed by several years of famine. Joseph advised the pharaoh to stockpile food to prevent future widespread starvation and death. Acting on Joseph's predictions, the pharaoh alleviated this impending calamity.

As a contemporary psychical researcher, who has investigated clairvoyant and clairaudient demonstrations of mediumship, I have discovered that mediumistic and psychic abilities appear to run in families and can be traced from one generation to the next. Significantly, these biblical accounts also reveal that the gift of mediumship has a family lineage. The mediumistic abilities of the parent appear to be repeatedly inherited by members of succeeding generations.

As a result of the tremendous impact of approximately six centuries of biblical mistranslations which wrongly condemn mediumship, many people today believe at best that if spirit communicators do exist, they should remain unsolicited and unheard. In direct contrast to this inaccurate belief, the biblical prophets demonstrated two-way conversations with one or more non-physical communicators.

Significantly, in most instances the first contact was frequently initiated not by the mediumistic figure but by the non-physical communicator. Many Christians think that they are following the beliefs and practices of many biblical prophets, yet in contrast to them, they condemn the mediumistic practices of these same prophets.

Moses, one of the most famous examples of highly esteemed biblical prophets with clairaudient and clairvoyant abilities, is the subject of the next chapter. As a result of his transformative spiritual-mediumistic experiences, Moses' life was transformed. The non-physical communicator, again called Yahweh initiated contact with him by calling out to him, and they held lengthy conversations. Moses asked Yahweh to give him both knowledge about future events and also spiritual guidance in order to support his leadership of many disparate tribes made up of unruly people.

## Chapter 8

# Moses and His Spirit Guide Yahweh

The following exploration of Moses' life will provide evidence of his profound mediumistic abilities. It further reveals that the paranormal phenomenon of mediumship belongs to a continuum of transformative spiritual experiences and that the relationship between the realm of the psychic and that of religion is irrevocably intertwined.

The detailed biography of Moses begins in Exodus chapter 1.[1] We are told that Moses' parents were from the tribe of Levi and, most significantly, that Yahweh had also been his father's guide. Clearly, therefore, this account tells us that Moses' father was also a medium. As a medium, he would have regularly requested spiritual guidance and information about future events from Yahweh. In addition we learn that Moses' father carried out divinatory practices in order to predict future events.

Growing up in the Egyptian pharaoh's household, Moses received a beneficial start in life, including the advantages of an Egyptian education. In later years, he accidentally murdered an Egyptian guard; his compassion had caused him to lash out spontaneously in an attempt to protect a Hebrew slave from the guard's brutality. Branded a murderer, Moses fled Egypt and became a shepherd.

After some time, a non-physical communicator spoke to Moses from the vicinity of a burning bush at the sacred high place on the mountain of Horeb. As previously alluded to, ancient shamans similarly utilized mountains (including steps, trees, ladders or tent poles) to enhance their communication with non-physical beings. Evidently, following the age-old shamanic tradition, Moses likewise demonstrated mediumistic practices.

276

The Bible translators inform us yet again that the non-physical communicator's name was Yahweh. Moses lived many centuries later than Abraham, yet their guides are equally known as Yahweh.

When Yahweh spoke, Moses removed his shoes. This act demonstrated his respect for the communicator's presence and guidance. At this time Moses was still a wanted man, sought by the Egyptian authority for murder, yet he was persuaded by this angelic or spirit presence to return to Egypt. He received the command to complete an amazing task, a shamanic vision quest: he was instructed to ask the astonished Egyptian pharaoh to liberate a large part of his workforce, made up of people from disparate Hebrew tribes.

Moses was to lead them out of Egypt. This otherworldly intervention is a strong testimony to Moses' personal heightened level of mediumship. This transformative spiritual-mediumistic experience of otherworldly intervention changed the course of Moses' life and that of the people he was to lead.

We are informed in Exodus 3:14–15[2] that Moses held a lengthy conversation with Yahweh. This was because he was in great need of Yahweh's reassurance before attempting the shamanic vision quest set before him. Yahweh reassured Moses that he had worked with many spiritual-mediumistic prophetic leaders before him. Yahweh, proved this by listing the names of a number of prophets with whom he had previously conversed and worked with.

Clearly, the names provided by Yahweh revealed that this non-physical messenger had guided many generations of prophets over a considerable time span. These included Abraham, Isaac, Jacob and Moses' own father. Now Yahweh sought to work with Moses to accomplish the spiritual task of liberating and guiding the enslaved, downtrodden Hebrews.

Yahweh told Moses to inform the pharaoh that 'I am that I am' had sent him. Elliott clarifies the translation of this term:

*I am that I am.* This is a descriptive name. It means 'I am (always) that which I am (now and always have been).' It also means 'I will be that I will be,' that is, 'I can become that which I choose to become; I am Lord of my own destiny.'[3]

Yahweh's name and description of himself is of immeasurable significance: 'I can become that which I choose to become' had sent Moses to speak to Pharaoh. Arguably, Yahweh was describing his fluid and malleable form; he appears to be describing the way his nature interacts with and manifests in accordance with a person's deepest psyche.

As a psychical researcher, I am aware of many personal experiences of angels. Each experiencer describes the form of the angel in terms that are meaningful to them. There have been a number of studies regarding people's experiences of angels. Interestingly, each account was witnessed by at least one further observer, independent of the direct experiencer. The common feature in these accounts is that the angel observed and witnessed, fulfilled the direct experiencer's expectations or needs during the emergency.

Features of this mediumistic phenomenon have been clarified previously. These eventualities are best epitomized by the angel who manifested its form as a small child in order to save a frightened child from running onto a motorway. Further examples include angels who manifest as strong men to fulfill the given need in a particular crisis situation.

These angelic manifestations are by no means the only examples available. The important point about the angelic nature is its apparent malleability and fluidity of form. This appears to be the very nature of Yahweh, which Yahweh was describing to Moses in his explanatory statement above.

Conclusions can be drawn from the accounts of both entranced mediums and near-death experiencers. The after-death landscapes they experience appear to be similarly malleable, manifesting in a responsive manner and bearing a direct relationship to the predominant thoughts and emotions experienced by an individual during his or her physical lifetime.

As previously stated, those contemporary materialist parapsy-chologists who do not accept that many biblical accounts are describing the prophets' spiritual mediumship, negate much religious history born of spiritual mediumship. It seems reasonable to accept that the thousands of biblical accounts which describe mediumistic experiences are genuine. This is evidenced by the fact that many of the prophets' lives were radically transformed by them. These mediumistic accounts involving successive generations of prophets demonstrate that contact from the non-physical world has occurred frequently from the earliest times.

These incursions of celestial messengers appear to progressively take humankind forward on a spiritual path. The historic narratives which describe the lives and spiritually transformative mediumistic experiences of the biblical prophets become total nonsense if they are not understood in the context of mediumship. Arguably, the only meaningful way in which to view these historic accounts is as a continuum of spiritually orientated mediumistic experiences.

Contemporary spiritually orientated mediums across the globe accept that contact continues to be made between the typically invisible, co-existent, non-physical world and the material world. They believe that spiritual and prophetic guidance can be gained from this practice. Trance lectures delivered by modern-day mediums in altered states of consciousness, observed by psychical researchers and others, provide evidence that this phenomenon, born in ancient times, continues to this day.

As is typically the case with most mediums, contact with Moses was initiated by the spirit voice, not the reverse. Moses, like Jacob and others, was a historic prophet who demonstrated moral failings. Moses also lacked faith in his ability to carry out the quest set him by Yahweh. This suggests that Moses was selected primarily because he possessed profound innate mediumistic abilities. Inevitably, Yahweh would also have been aware of Moses' latent leadership abilities and strength of character which would come to the fore under his guidance. Each of these gifts and qualities together would have created a powerfully charismatic leader.

The accounts of Moses' life demonstrate many inherent archaic shamanic features, the first of which was the vision quest set him by Yahweh, i.e. the task of freeing the Hebrew slaves. Likewise, historically earlier shamans were typically set a vision quest as part of their induction and initiation into shamanism. They received their vision quest when they first began to communicate with the inhabitants of the non-physical world, just as Moses received his vision quest when Yahweh first began to communicate with him. At that time, Moses appears to have come into a full realization of his innate mediumistic gifts.

It was through the operation of their psycho-spiritual senses that Moses and other prophets heard voices from the non-physical world. Significantly, these voices frequently contravened the future prophets' own personal opinions, as was the case with Moses, who was filled with fears and doubts.

Apparently Moses himself, with his biographers, wrote the biblical accounts of his life. It is evident that these accounts offer pertinent insights into the pronounced mediumistic culture of Moses' day. They demonstrate obvious familiarity with the experience-based belief in receiving communications from non-physical beings, especially those from the spirit or angel named Yahweh.

Due to the fact that we are told that successive generations of patriarchs and prophets spoke with non-physical communicators, it is possible that it was not the same Yahweh with whom each of them spoke. The term 'Yahweh' may have been the designated term used by the Hebrew forefathers for mediumistic communications with angelic and/or spirit beings. The communicator *may* have been the same Yahweh, as a non-physical communicator would not age in the mortal sense.

However, when contemporary mediums access the non-physical world it is noticeable that, many communicators spontaneously and simultaneously seek to convey their messages to their loved ones.

Due to the fact that many centuries of spiritually orientated mediumship is recorded for future generations in the Bible's pages, it is highly possible that a number of successive communicators were given the name Yahweh.

Certainly, different characteristics were shown throughout the long duration of these communications. Alternatively, as humans reached a higher level of spirituality they better interpreted the true underlying guidance they were given, rather than human misinterpretations of it. Notably, over the many centuries of mediumship recorded in the Bible's pages, the level of spiritual guidance given by the communicator or communicators appears to have fluctuated, suggesting that more than one non-physical being was involved.

From Moses' first meeting with Yahweh, the two had frequent lengthy conversations. Initially Yahweh was angry with Moses for rejecting the vision quest he had been set. Moses' spontaneous reaction had been to refuse to return to an all-powerful Egyptian pharaoh who would no doubt be incredulous when asked to liberate his large unpaid enslaved workforce.

After some deliberations Yahweh agreed that Moses' brother Aaron should both accompany Moses and speak to Pharaoh on Moses' behalf. Moses spoke on behalf of Yahweh and, in turn, Aaron spoke on behalf of Moses. Yahweh told Moses that Moses 'would be as a god to Aaron,' as Moses told his brother Aaron what to say. This compares with Yahweh, translated as 'the god,' telling Moses what to say. 'He will speak to the people for you, and it will be as if he were your mouth and as if you were God to him.'[4] The present biblical translation uses the word 'God.' However, the original authentic meaning is likely to have been 'angel' or 'messenger of the lord.'

The above description vividly illustrates the mediumistic communications that were occurring. Significantly, the mediumistic process described of Moses echoes the contemporary mediumistic process. Mediums today, claim to attune their senses to an external non-physical communicator in order to be mentally fed information from them.

Moses, like all other genuine mediums, had no prior knowledge of the information he received mediumistically. This account confirms that Moses' role was to mediumistically receive communications from Yahweh then transfer the information to his brother. Presumably, Aaron employed a degree of interpretation and used his practical skills in eloquent persuasion to convince Pharaoh of the need to free the slaves. Aaron was described as a priest, a role that was clearly differentiated from the role of medium carried out by Moses.

In contrast, Moses as medium, received regular physical proofs from Yahweh, which acted as signs to help him convince Aaron and the people of the reality of the non-physical communicator who wished to guide them. Many thought of this non-physical communicator as a god as they had little or no concept of angels or surviving personalities who could communicate with humankind. Likewise the materialist translators who translated the term Yahweh as another name for God had little or no concept of angelic or spirit communicators.

Interestingly, when the slaves finally escaped from Egyptian bondage, they took the bones of Joseph with them. Joseph the patriarch had passed away centuries before, but clearly much hope had centered on his remains during the Hebrews' 400 years in slavery. This fact illustrates their ongoing need for physical signs on which to fix their hopes.

The religious climate of antiquity was one in which people were familiar with psycho-spiritual practices. Religion and the paranormal were closely bonded. Common practices included the use of (predictive) divination stones and mediumship in order to seek advice and precognitive information from Yahweh. Typically, these quite different practices were translated as "enquiring of the lord."

During the time when Moses and Aaron labored to persuade Pharaoh to liberate the slaves, Yahweh provided Moses with foreknowledge of a number of future climatic events. Importantly, these events did not defy the laws of nature. It was the perfect timing of a succession or unexpected natural events that were each predicted in advance as a response to pharaoh's obstinacy that appeared to be miraculous.

We have already seen one example of Yahweh's use of nature when the slaves were finally freed but were fleeing the Egyptian army. It is believed that the slaves, who were on foot, crossed a body of water that was shallow enough to walk through – an event described in terms of the waters appearing to 'part' for them. When the heavy Egyptian chariots followed, they became stuck in the silt, and many soldiers drowned. It seemed that the unjust Egyptian attack had been sabotaged by Yahweh who directed the slaves' escape route.

Some time later, these disparate, chaotic, newly liberated tribes began to starve as their meager food supplies had run out.Daily, they walked through the wilderness, guided by Yahweh's messages to Moses, when another natural event occurred which also appeared to be a miraculous answer to the people's needs. When they finally became desperate for food, manna, a natural food, appeared to be blown towards them or to fall from the skies. The manna's timely arrival appeared to be Yahweh's miraculous answer to their need as this food alleviated their hunger.

Yahweh appeared to have knowledge of future events and the timely ability to utilize 'future' natural events to assist the tribes. Whenever the people requested help, they were told to trust in Yahweh and that he would solve their problems. Due to the fact that the anxious Hebrews were told to expect positive solutions and to trust in Yahweh, they seemed almost to attract positive outcomes to them, this is in harmony with the principle of 'like attracting like.'

Returning to the period before the liberation of the slaves, Yahweh had predicted a series of events that would frighten Pharaoh into submission. A succession of dire events ensued. These were the exact calamities that had been foretold to Pharaoh. As a result of the events and the clear evidence of Yahweh's predictive accuracy, the anxious ruler finally agreed to free the slaves.

Yahweh's foreknowledge of these events made it seem as if he had caused each of them. For example, Yahweh had predicted that the River Nile would turn blood-red. It is believed that due to natural occurrences the red marl mountains of Abyssinia caused the River Nile to look red with blood, as a result of timely flood water erosion.

After successive accurate predictions, the tribes came to believe that Yahweh worked through larger natural world events just as he did on a smaller scale through the divination stones, when he would answer 'yes' and 'no' to questions. Arguably, Yahweh operated from the deeper, implicit, non-physical realm, beyond ordinary, three dimensional time and space. This non-physical communicator appears to have had the ability to interpenetrate the physical realm and cause the divination stones to land in a fashion that gave predictive answers to questions.

Yahweh's predictive ability and his conversations with Moses convinced the rabble of Semitic tribes that he could and would protect them. The close relationship they had with this anthropomorphic yet ethereal communicator is reflected in their reports that Yahweh led them by day and also throughout the dark night. Many biblical descriptions state that this spirit or angel manifested daily from within a thick cloud for all to see and follow.

They followed this animated, cloud-like manifestation, which seemed to appear on request to support the needs of the tribes as it led them through the wilderness to the Promised Land. Importantly, this cloud-like manifestation has the features of a substance known today as ectoplasm. Ectoplasm has been produced by physical-phenomena mediums and in contemporary times it has been analyzed in laboratories. It has been observed to pour from mediums' noses, ears and navels and to mold itself into the shapes of apparent spirit people.

As previously stated, this non-physical entity was interchangeably described as 'the angel of God,' 'an angel,' 'Yahweh,' 'the glory of the lord' and 'the lord.' The fact that "the angel Yahweh" is frequently reported as being both observable and audible for all the people to see and hear strongly suggests that physical mediumistic phenomena regularly took place. This would involve manifestationsand audible voices, clearly seen and heard by members of the tribes. Erroneous biblical translations have misled readers by using the term 'God' instead of the above more accurate names.

The following biblical passages describe how these physical phenomena manifested for all to see and hear. They were separate from Moses' personal clairvoyant and clairaudient encounters.

- Exodus 13:21: 'By day the LORD went ahead of them in a pillar of cloud to guide them on their way and by night in a pillar of fire to give them light.'[5]
- Exodus 14:19–20: 'Then the angel of God, who had been travelling in front of Israel's army, withdrew and went behind them. The pillar of cloud also moved from in front and stood behind them, coming between the armies of Egypt and Israel. Throughout the night the cloud brought darkness to the one side and light to the other.'[6]
- Exodus 23:20: '… an angel [will go] ahead of you to guard you along the way and to bring you to the place.'[7]
- Exodus 23:23: '[the] angel will go ahead of you and bring you into the land.'[8]
- Exodus 24:15–18: 'When Moses went up on the mountain, the cloud covered it and the glory of [Yahweh] the LORD settled on Mount Sinai. For six days the cloud covered the mountain, and on the seventh day [Yahweh] the LORD called to Moses from within the cloud … Then Moses entered the cloud.'[9]
- Exodus 24:9–11: 'Moses and Aaron, Nadab and Abihu, and the seventy elders of Israel went up and saw [Yahweh] the God of Israel … they saw [Yahweh] God, and they ate and drank.'[10]

The biblical text occasionally includes a phrase such as, 'I am sending an angel,' indicating that God is speaking, but this is the result of the interpretations of later translators. The angel *was* the communicator who promised to guide them.

With regard to the seventy-four people who observed an ethereal manifestation on Mount Sinai, this is arguably a mediumistic physical phenomenon. This event would have powerfully convinced the scores of onlookers that they could witness the physical appearance of their angelic or spirit guide, rather than witness the presence of God. The manifestation of Yahweh was described as being observed by many people simultaneously. This is not in keeping with distinctly personal experiences of "God."

Mystical experiences of God, the Divine, are characterized by singular, personal experiences. Such experiences are not group experiences of physical manifestations. They are further characterized by a sense of ineffable union with all creatures, who are interpenetrated by the Divine and in whom an aspect of the Divine permanently resides. Indeed experiencers feel at one with all aspects of the natural world and with God, the Divine.

The materializations and conversations with the supernormal entity known as Yahweh evidently had an otherworldly quality about them. Yahweh's specific spiritual focus is evidenced by the biblical accounts which tell us of Yahweh's desire to liberate the oppressed slaves and their receipt of a moral code in the form of, the Ten Commandments.

Later, however, the Hebrews fought battles with other peoples in order to secure a land of their own. These were not spiritual acts. It should be pointed out that spiritual guidance is inevitably interpreted by the experiencer. The level of interpretation is often shaped by the spiritual maturity of the experiencer, who in turn, is shaped by the historic era in which communications were received.[11]

It is also possible, as previously alluded to, that there was more than one communicator guiding Moses the medium. 'Yahweh' might be something of an umbrella term for those various 'messengers of the lord' who spoke with humanity. These communicators may each have demonstrated a different level of spirituality. Certainly, historic and present-day mediums and those who work with electronic voice phenomena hear and record the voices of many non-physical communicators including those of animals and birds!

Indeed it is rare to access only a single communicator, at any one time, though a single communicator may become the most dominant speaker. Some modern mediumistic communications have a very clear spiritual focus which has obvious parallels with the spiritual aspects of historic phenomena.

The Ten Commandments, received through psycho-spiritual mediumistic conversations with Yahweh, represented a relatively elevated code of conduct, even though there was an ebb and flow in their adoption by the people. The Hebrews were given morally superior laws including all forms of sacrifice were condemned, fairer treatment of servants and slaves, property dealings, compensation for personal injuries, idols were banned and annual festivals were established to commemorate the spiritually transformative events of the past.

It was believed that these mediumistic events were evidence of a spiritually orientated plan for the lives of the people. The ancients were evidently familiar with demonstrations of mediumistic phenomena, and the biblical references to 'angels' should be viewed in terms of the intervention of spirits or angels, messengers of the Divine, rather than the Divine itself.

Present-day psychical researchers have observed countless demonstrations of precognitive knowledge, clairvoyance, clairaudience and lectures given by mediums in trance, yet such phenomena may always baffle humankind. We may never have a complete explanation for them. However, the phenomena described in the Old Testament accounts can regularly be fitted and better understood in a mediumistic context. Many mediums today would have no difficulty understanding the intentions of the biblical authors.

After receiving the Ten Commandments, Moses experienced many further angelic or spirit communications. These are documented in the book known as the Book of the Covenant. It is most revealing when the narratives are interpreted literally and in close connection with contemporary psychical research; they evidence the people's long-term, close and responsive relationship with their celestial guide. This guide was of an anthropomorphic and authoritative nature who, at clear intervals, sought to elevate the Hebrews' moral code.

Exodus 23:20–23 states: 'See, I am sending an angel ahead of you to guard you along the way and to bring you to the place I have prepared. Pay attention to him and listen to what he says ... he will not forgive your rebellion, since my Name is in him.'[12] Similarly, the theme running throughout the Book of Hebrews in the New Testament is that a ministering otherworldly messenger named Yahweh (and possibly other messengers) was sent to guide humankind forward spiritually. He communicated through the prophets' mediumistic abilities, not through priests, as typically the priests did not have these gifts.[13]

Hebrews 1:1–2 evidences the belief, that Yahweh and possibly other non-physical beings were angelic messengers of God The Hebrews believed that these angels spoke to humankind through the mediumistic prophets and later communicated through Jesus: 'In the past God spoke to our forefathers through the prophets at many times and in various ways, but in these last days he has spoken to us by his Son.'[14]

In a later chapter we will look at evidence that Jesus was mediumistic and of an elevated spiritual nature. This again will prove that the paranormal and religion are intricately intertwined.

## Spirit Manifestations in the Ark

Returning to Moses, Exodus 25 records Yahweh's instructions to Moses. The following account is not written in the third person as some translations appear to be:

... make a sanctuary for me, and I will dwell among them ...
Have them make a chest of acacia wood [the Ark] ... Insert the
poles into the rings on the sides of the chest to carry it ... put in
the ark the Testimony, which I will give you ...

There, above the cover between the two cherubim that is over
the ark of the Testimony, I will meet with you and give you all my
commands for the Israelites.[15]

Moses was required to build a Tabernacle, which was to be located
among the people. Due to the frequent manifestations of Yahweh's
presence in the Tabernacle, it was believed that this angelic being
actually lived there.

Significantly, the Hebrews' laws were to be kept inside the Ark in
close proximity to the location where Yahweh manifested his
presence. Yahweh as guide and protector was also the lawgiver. The
Ark was the Hebrews' most sacred possession and was kept in the
most holy place beside the Inner Shrine, situated behind a curtain of
an adjoining darkened room. Yahweh's permanent presence lived in
the Ark and traveled with the Hebrews. Many biblical accounts have
recorded for posterity the regularity with which Yahweh communicated and manifested his presence to Moses and the people. Yahweh
was typically observed between the two carved cherubim situated
on top of the Ark.

Over time, Yahweh began the practice of communicating and
manifesting in the presence of a small group of tribal elders who
accompanied the prophet Moses. This practice continued
throughout the years. When Moses passed away, a succession of
later spiritual leaders, accompanied by tribal leaders, continued to
receive Yahweh's communications in the Ark.

The Tabernacle was built and furnished in accordance with exact
descriptions given to Moses by Yahweh. Moses was told to create a
dark room within the Tabernacle which was to be considered most
holy. As we have seen, the Ark of the Covenant was placed in this
dark room behind a curtain which was also designated as most holy.

This area was also to contain a golden table for the 'bread of the presence', a golden lampstand, an altar of incense, a further bronze altar and a basin for washing. The entire Tabernacle was to be 150 feet long and 30 feet wide. In later years, the Tabernacle became a permanent structure.

We are given detailed descriptions in Exodus chapters 25 to 40[16] regarding the Tabernacle, the Ark and the above ancient Semitic artifacts. Remarkably similar artifacts, which seem to have been used for similar psycho-spiritual purposes and date back to the same era, have been unearthed in the remains of neighboring cultures. We are already aware of the mediumistic and psychic necromancer known as the 'witch of Endor' who utilized sacrificial murder to support her craft, she lived in a neighboring society.

Interestingly, the Endor event, discussed earlier, is historically later than the lifetime of Moses, revealing the continuation of these paranormal, ritualistic, religious practices. The Endor narrative evidenced the barbaric, foreign practices involvinghuman and animal sacrifice and the use of the victims' entrails. Murder accompanied the divinatory and mediumistic practices of the neighboring cultures.

Clearly, the mediumistic and divinatory practices of the surrounding cultures had marked differences from those of the Semitic tribes. Yahweh had condemned these foreign, abhorrent forms of mediumship and divination, and had delivered the Ten Commandments to the Hebrews. Certainly, these measures demonstrated a more spiritually orientated mediumship.

It is interesting to note that:

The Ark of the Testimony [Ark of the Covenant] compares with the roughly contemporary shrine and funerary furniture of King Tutankhamun (c.1350 BC) ... The table holding the bread of the Presence was made of wood covered with thin sheets of gold. All the objects were portable and were fitted with rings and carrying poles, practices typical of Egyptian ritual processions as early as the Old Kingdom ... The symbolism of God's redemptive covenant was preserved in the tabernacle, making each element an object lesson for the worshipper.[17]

As a result of being born and educated in Egypt, certainly, Moses would have been fluent with ancient Egyptian mediumistic practices. Moses spent a large part of his life in Egypt including his formative years. He was nurtured as a member of the royal Egyptian family and would inevitably have been influenced by the earlier practices of both royal and public members of the Aten cult. These people followed the revolutionary beliefs of the presumably mediumistic Pharaoh Akhenaten. This innovative pharaoh was the first person in recorded history to experience and teach the singularity of God.

Akhenaten may have had a mystical experience of the Divine. However, it is quite possible that he was a psychic sensitive who received the spiritual insight into the singularity of God as a result of spiritually transformative communications from a non-physical communicator. If so, this indicates that the pharaoh had spiritually transformative mediumistic experiences. Akhenaten's writings are of a spiritually elevated nature, indicating that if he was in contact with an angelic or spirit communicator, that entity too was of a spiritually elevated, compassionate nature.

Akhenaten was fiercely loyal to his very real, living God. However, it is worth remembering that a non-physical communicator was typically considered to be a god. It has been shown that confused deification practices of non-physical communicators has had a long history. This unique pharaoh moved his capital in order to overthrow the existing, powerfully entrenched religious practices.

This was an inimitable, distinctive, revolutionary and exceedingly bold step to take, which was presumably supported by regular mediumistic communications. In the same way, Moses was also a revolutionary figure who was fiercely loyal to his singular non-physical communicator named Yahweh.

In later years, after Solomon had authorized the building of a permanent structure, which would be known as the Temple, the Ark of the Covenant was taken into its most holy dark area. Importantly, here, in this holy area, regular mediumistic conversations with Yahweh continued to take place. Biblical references testify to this fact, for example: 'There above the cover between the two cherubim that are over the Ark of the Testimony [known as the Ark of the Tabernacle or Covenant], I will meet with you and give you all my commands for the Israelites.'[18]

## Predicting the Future with Divination Stones

Moses' brother Aaron became a priest among the Hebrews. It was known that Aaron did not possess the mediumistic abilities of Moses. The mediumistic prophet and the priest performed very different functions. Priesthood became a hereditary process, the role being passed down from father to son over successive generations. The call to prophecy, alternatively known as mediumship, also ran in families, arguably due to inherited mediumistic abilities. However, this was not inevitable. If the next generation was unsuitable due to a lack of mediumistic abilities, then the call to prophecy was delivered to a member of another family.

Aaron was told to wear a garment which had small pockets in it to house the small divination stones. Arguably, the priest was the keeper of the divination stones as he was not a medium. Unlike Moses, he did not possess the gifts of clairvoyance or clairaudience, so could not directly hear or see Yahweh at will. When Yahweh did not manifest in the form of physical phenomena, for all to see, the priest would cast the stones in order to guide tribal decision-making.

The two main small pebbles were known as Urim and Thummim and were thrown frequently as a method of accessing future information, known as finding out 'Yahweh's will.' The manner in which the pebbles fell answered questions with a 'yes' or 'no.' The predictive stones were used to provide a quick method to discover whether Yahweh was in support of a particular course of action or not.

Significantly, the answers provided by the regular use of these stones were responsible for many pivotal decisions that affected the Semitic tribes as they evolved into a nation. It is possible that the less spiritually elevated decisions they made were influenced by use of the stones, as the results were more open to human interpretation.

Exodus 28:3–30 describes the priest's garment which housed the divination stones. My extensive biblical research has uncovered the fact that, apart from Urim and Thummim, there were twelve other stones which were used for the same divinatory practice.

> ... they are to make garments for Aaron ... so that he may serve me as priest ... for your brother Aaron and his sons, so that they may serve me as priests ...
>
> Fashion a breastpiece for making decisions ... There are to be twelve stones, one for each of the names of the sons of Israel ...
>
> Whenever Aaron enters the Holy Place, he will bear the names of the sons of Israel over his heart on the breastpiece of decision ... Also put the Urim and the Thummim in the breast-piece ... Thus Aaron will always bear the means of making decisions for the Israelites over his heart before the LORD [Yahweh].[19]

The commentary to the *NIV Study Bible* offers further clarification regarding the use of:

> [the] Urim and the Thummim ... The Hebrew word Urim begins with the first letter of the Hebrew alphabet (aleph) and Thummim begins with the last letter (taw). They were sacred lots and were often used in times of crisis to determine the will of God. [See Numbers 27:21] It has been suggested that if Urim (curses) dominated when the lots were cast, the answer was no, but if Thummim (perfections) dominated, it was yes. In any

event, their every decision was from the Lord [Yahweh].[20]

The Hebrews held the experience-based belief that Yahweh conveyed his knowledge of the future timing of natural events to the people in order to protect and guide them. It was an extension of the same belief that the all-powerful Yahweh was also seen to act through natural world events including the small divination stones. The Hebrews' believed that Yahweh utilized both the major and very minor events, such as how the pebbles fell, to convey his will.

Apart from being used in times of crisis when the Hebrews needed speedy guidance from Yahweh, the stones may also have been thrown when the leaders did not have either the time or peaceful atmosphere necessary to carry out mediumistic conversations in the holy sanctuary.

The biblical Book of Proverbs provides evidence that the Hebrews believed Yahweh manipulated how the stones fell in order to make his will known. For example, Proverbs 16:33:

> The lot is cast into the lap,
> but its every decision is from the LORD.[21]

The Bible commentary explains: 'The lot may have been several pebbles held in the fold of a garment then drawn out or shaken to the ground. It was commonly used to make decisions. Every decision is from the Lord; God, not chance, is in control.'[22] Similarly, Proverbs 16:1 and 16:9 state:

> To man belong the plans of the heart,
> but from the LORD comes the reply of the tongue.[23]
> In his heart a man plans his course,
> but the LORD determines his steps.[24]

The use of the divination stones is clearly revealed in a later account of events that took place after the Hebrews lost the Battle of Ai. These events are described in Joshua 7:14.[25] Yahweh told Joshua, Moses' successor, that they had lost this battle as a form of punishment because one of their people was a thief. Through the use of the divination stones the leaders asked for the whereabouts of the thief. Tribe by tribe was called out. Once a tribe was singled out by the stones, the leaders called out clan by clan, then family by family. Finally, the stones singled out the guilty person.

## Yahweh Speaks in the Tent of the Meeting

There are many biblical references to the Tent of the Meeting. They are always found in connection with 'enquiring of the lord' (Yahweh). It was in the Tent of the Meeting that the prophets of the Semitic tribes made regular mediumistic contact with Yahweh. The following biblical quotations will demonstrate that the psychically sensitive Moses was chosen predominantly because he possessed highly developed clairaudient and clairvoyant abilities and could perform automatic writing. Moses was born a powerful, natural medium.

It was normal practice for individuals to visit Moses and request that he contact Yahweh in the Tent of the Meeting to help them solve their problems. In the earliest days of Moses' leadership, the Hebrews were a nomadic people, newly liberated from slavery. At that time, the Tent of the Meeting was a simple tent, set apart from the noise and the crowd, for the purpose of making contact with Yahweh. Exodus 33:7–11 describes Yahweh's manifestations of his presence and Moses' conversations with him:

Now Moses used to take a tent and pitch it outside the camp some distance away, calling it the 'tent of meeting'. Anyone enquiring of the LORD would go to the tent of meeting outside the camp. And whenever Moses went out to the tent, all the people rose and stood at the entrances to their tents, watching Moses until he entered the tent. As Moses went into the tent, the pillar of cloud would come down and stay at the entrance, while

[Yahweh]the LORD spoke with Moses. Whenever the people saw the pillar of cloud standing at the entrance to the tent … [Yahweh] The LORD would speak to Moses face to face, as a man speaks with his friend.[26]

In later years when the people were less nomadic, the Tent of the Meeting became a more durable fixture in a separate area of the Holy Tabernacle in the Temple, as evidenced in Exodus 29:29–44:

Aaron's sacred garments will belong to his descendants … The son who succeeds him as priest and comes to the Tent of Meeting to minister in the Holy Place is to wear them …

For the generations to come this … offering … is to be made regularly at the entrance to the Tent of Meeting before [Yahweh] the LORD. There I will meet you and speak to you; there also I will meet with the Israelites and the place will be consecrated to my glory.

So I will consecrate the Tent of Meeting … Then I will dwell among the Israelites and be their God. They will know that I am [Yahweh] the LORD their [angelic guide] God, who brought them out of Egypt so that I might dwell among them.[27]

It is worth remembering that when the biblical accounts describe Yahweh talking to Moses in a face-to-face manner, later biblical translators use the words 'Lord' and 'God' instead of Yahweh. Frequently, Moses was not alone when he visited the Tent of the Meeting. Many tribal elders witnessed Yahweh's materializations and Moses' conversations with Yahweh. Arguably, these biblical accounts are clearlydescribing negotiations with, and manifestations of, a non-physical communicator, such as an angel or spirit, rather than with God [the Divine].

Exodus 39:32 to 40:32 tells us that

all the work on the tabernacle, the Tent of Meeting, was

completed ...

Then [Moses] spread the tent over the tabernacle and put the covering over the tent as [Yahweh] the LORD commanded him.

He took the Testimony and placed it in the ark, attached the poles to the ark and put the atonement cover over it. Then he brought the ark into the tabernacle and hung the shielding curtain and shielded the ark ... as [Yahweh] the LORD commanded ...

He placed the basin between the Tent of Meeting and the altar and put water in it for washing, and Moses and Aaron ... used it ... They washed whenever they entered the Tent of Meeting.[28]

Exodus 30:36 tells us that Yahweh 'said to Moses, ... "Grind some [incense] to powder and place it in front of the Testimony in the Tent of Meeting, where I will meet with you. It shall be most holy to you."'[29] Similarly Leviticus 1:1 tells us that Yahweh 'called to Moses and spoke to him from the Tent of Meeting,'[30] and Numbers 1:1 says that Yahweh 'spoke to Moses in the Tent of the Meeting in the Desert of Sinai on the first day of the second month.'[31]

The NIV Bible commentary does not look deeply into these accounts and does not appear to appreciate that it was not God that materialized in the Tent of the Meeting for all to witness. Consequently, Yahweh is translated to mean God: 'It was not a place where God's people met for collective worship but one where [Yahweh] God himself met – by appointment, not by accident – with his people.'[32]

As further evidence of Moses' clairvoyance and clairaudience and his ability to facilitate mediumistic physical phenomena, Yahweh's presence at this time was again described as a cloud-like manifestation which was observed by all the people. Again, translators use the term 'the lord,' meaning 'God,' to describe Yahweh, who is an angel or spirit. Exodus 40:34–36 tells us:

Then the cloud covered the Tent of the Meeting ... the LORD filled the tabernacle. Moses could not enter the Tent of Meeting because the cloud had settled upon it ...

In all the travels of the Israelites, whenever the cloud lifted from above the tabernacle, they would set out.[33]

Moses' face is described in Exodus 34:29–35 as being radiant for a considerable time after his face-to-face conversations with Yahweh.[34] These accounts are clearly indicative of Moses' gifts of clairvoyance and clairaudience. The radiant phenomenon was observed when Moses returned from Mount Sinai, immediately after receiving the Ten Commandments from Yahweh: 'He was not aware that his face was radiant because he had spoken with the LORD.'[35]

The importance of this event is born out by the fact that today, several millennia later, many Jews and Christians, seek to obey the Ten Commandments. It is fascinating to discover from this account that at intervals, Moses wore a veil in order to hide his radiant face. This radiance has parallels with accounts investigated by contemporary psychical researchers. Kirlian photography is a sensitized photographic technology that photographs and videos the constantly moving, colored energy vibrations which emanate from and permeate all living creatures and plants.

Notably, energy cannot be destroyed, instead energy transmutes in form, it makes a transition rather than ceases to exist. All living creatures and indeed, all life forms are animated by energy alternatively known as the soul/spirit. People may prefer to think of the colored auric energy around all creatures as the soul, spirit or consciousness which leaves the physical body of all creatures at death.

At death, this energy or soul may transmute in form, giving birth to a non-physical replica of those who have passed away. In plants (which are also observed in the non-physical realms), this energy represents the life force. Today, digital cameras are able to photograph orbs, which are possibly a photographic fragment of this auric energy.

## Prophets Were Shamans/Mediums/Channels

The 15th-century mistranslations found in contemporary bibles prohibit all forms of spiritual mediumship. This has had an enormous detrimental effect on the beliefs of countless people over the centuries, causing them to oppose all forms of spiritual mediumship. It is ironic that these mistranslations have existed for so long without being clearly exposed. The research in this book is doing exactly that by progressively revealing that the mistranslations directly contradict the mediumistic practices of many esteemed spiritual leaders historically known as prophets.

It has been shown that Moses was one such medium; his whole life, as a prophetic leader of the Semitic tribes, was one in which predictive divination and communication with a spirit/angel was at the core. Without the contact typically initiated by a non-physical communicator, Moses' spiritual leadership and that of many other prophets would not have occurred. Such was the paramount importance of the non-physical communicator.

Significantly, Moses taught the Semitic tribes that they should test the prophets to see if they were false prophets. This proves that there were many lesser prophets, namely mediums, in Moses' day.

The same is true today, revealing that mediumistic gifts are an intrinsic part of animal nature, human and non-human. To test for false prophets, Moses taught the people to check the accuracy of these mediums' predictions. Only those mediums whose predictions were accurate were confirmed by Moses as having Yahweh working with them. According to Moses, if they were inaccurate, Yahweh did not work with them.

Clearly, Yahweh was seen to work with lesser mediums than Moses as well as with Moses himself. Clearly, Yahweh was perceived asthe reliable non-physical communicator. However, it is evident that Yahweh was regarded as being one, among many other non-physical communicators, some of whom were reliable and many were not.

Moses' teachings clearly demonstrate that the Semitic tribes believed that Yahweh could communicate through many prophets or mediums, not just one. This is further proved by the fact that Yahweh himself said that he had spoken with a succession of people, generation after generation, who became prophetic leaders as a result of his communications. The first of these was Abraham.

We now have an improved context for viewing all spiritually orientated mediumship. The biblical text below demonstrates the 'correct context in which the Deuteronomic Prohibitions' against sorcery, not mediumship were delivered. (Deuteronomy 18:8–14). The mistranslations are exposed.

This text reveals that the mediumship of Moses and other prophets was not condemned, as the powerful Endor mistranslations would logically indicate, if they were correct. It also proves that Yahweh communicated for all to hear and see, through physical phenomena, until the people asked that such communications should come through a designated medium instead (1 Samuel chapter 28).

Deuteronomy 18:14–21 states:

The nations you will dispossess listen to those who practise sorcery ... the LORD ... has not permitted you to do so. The LORD ... will raise up for you a prophet like me [Moses] ... You must listen to him. For this is what you asked of the LORD [YAHWEH] ... you said, 'Let us not hear the voice of the LORD [Yahweh] ... nor see this great fire any more ...'

The Lord said to me: '... I will raise up for them a prophet ... I will put my words in his mouth and he will tell them everything I command ... If anyone does not listen to my words that the prophet speaks in my name, I ... will call him to account.'

You may say to yourselves, 'How can we know when a message has not been spoken by the LORD [YAHWEH]?' If what a prophet proclaims in the name of the LORD [YAHWEH] does not ... come true, that is a message the LORD [YAHWEH] has not spoken.[36]

Deuteronomy chapter 18 contains many other prohibitions, none of which prohibited spiritually orientated mediumship. The 15th-century mistranslations which condemn mediumship are in sharp contrast to the daily mediumistic practices of the great spiritual leaders of the Bible. A strange dichotomy is being exposed here: spiritual mediumship is condemned as evil in powerfully mistranslated narratives that have had long lasting consequences over many centuries, yet all the prophets of note were mediums.

Mediumship and predictive divinatory practices are being progressively evidenced as being integral features of ther beliefs and practices. Of the great spiritual mediumistic prophets. The realm of the paranormal and that of religious beliefs and practices are clearly interdependent and interrelated, bound together at a very deep level.

## Yahweh the Spirit Communicator

After Yahweh established contact with Moses, communications between the two became frequent and extensive. A number of features of Moses' mediumship echo characteristics of contemporary mediumship. Biblical accounts inform us that Moses was able to hear Yahweh, i.e. Moses possessed the gift of clairaudience. Likewise, Moses could see Yahweh – he possessed the gift of clairvoyance. Moses' receipt of the Ten Commandments may suggest he also possessed the ability to take down information, the descendant of this mediumistic practice is known today as automatic writing. Moses may also have had the ability to enter into altered states of consciousness such as entranced states in which he received commandments, instructions and other guidance.

Inevitably, Moses' mediumistic abilities helped facilitate the observable public demonstrations of physical phenomena such as the daily responsive, guiding, cloud-like manifestation of Yahweh. These events were accompanied by Yahweh's audible communications. Again, many members of the tribes were witnesses to them. Moses was also able to access precognitive information. He negotiated with Yahweh, which implies that Yahweh was perceived as a highly respected celestial being, a messenger of God rather than God.

Yet modern-day individuals are advised to disregard the references to 'Yahweh,' and follow the incorrect translations which refer to Yahweh as 'the lord' and 'God.' Terms such as 'the lord' imply great respect, like the more contemporary terms 'sir' and 'my lord,' frequently used by dutiful, loyal servants. Instead, we should focus on the more accurate translations which refer to Yahweh as 'the angel of the lord.' Evidently, God, the Divine, was not the non-physical communicator who materialized and spoke for all to see and hear.

## Spirituality of Content

Towards the close of Moses' life, he wavered in his trust, either in Yahweh's instructions or Yahweh's predictions. After Moses' death his biographer records that Yahweh punished Moses for this lack of trust by prohibiting Moses from entering the fertile land at the edge of the wilderness, known as the 'Promised Land.' During their years in the desert, guided by Yahweh's spiritual leadership, Moses had welded together a disparate rabble of slaves into a cohesive community and through his mediumship had helped them make enormous spiritual progress.

The spiritual significance of the foundation of monotheism (the belief in one God) propagated by the Mosaic Doctrine cannot be overstated. Moses learned from his angelic/spirit communicator of the singularity and transcendence of God. Also of revolutionary importance was a further concept: Moses learned that Yahweh demanded, at the behest of God, that the Hebrew Semite tribes progressively demonstrate morally superior behavior.

This was in stark contrast to the amoral, idolatrous and murderous sacrificial necromancy of the neighboring peoples with whom Moses' tribes interacted during the exodus from Egypt. A great responsibility fell on the Hebrew tribes when they were asked to become role models, lights or beacons, for others to follow.

The tremendous spiritual significance of the teachings of the angelic/spirit communicator is indicated by the spiritual growth which occurred through Moses' mediumship. Yet, as the following quotation reveals, theologians continue to demonstrate ongoing confusion between Yahweh's teachings regarding how the prophets should work with him, and Yahweh's teachings regarding the nature of God.

> Exodus was not intended to exist separately but was thought of as a continuation of a narrative that began in Genesis and was completed in Leviticus, Numbers and Deuteronomy. The first five books of the Bible are together known as the Pentateuch ... [many] references strongly suggest that Moses was largely responsible for writing the book of Exodus ...
>
> Exodus lays a foundation theology in which God reveals his name, his attributes, his redemption, his law and how he is to be worshipped. It also reports the appointment and work of the first covenant mediator (Moses), describes the beginnings of the priesthood, defines the role of the prophet and relates how the ancient covenant relationship between God and his people came under a new administration (the Sinai covenant).
>
> Profound insights into the nature of God are found in Chs. 3; 6; 33 – 34. The focus of these texts is on the fact and importance of his presence ... But emphasis is also placed on his attributes of justice, truthfulness, mercy, faithfulness and holiness ... The foundation of biblical ethics and morality is laid out first in the gracious character of God as revealed in the Exodus itself and then in the Ten Commandments (20:1–17) and the ordinances of the principles of the commandments.[37]

We have viewed the lives of the early prophets in the context that they became spiritual leaders due to their conversations with Yahweh. Moses, in particular, led his people by virtue of his mediumistic conversations with Yahweh. Many of these conversations appear to have had a profound, revolutionary and deeply spiritual focus that advanced human spirituality during that era.

This book does not seek to prove that survival after physical death occurs or to unravel the exact workings inherent in demonstrations of historical and present-day mediumship. However, it does provide evidence that mediumship has had, and continues to have, an enormous spiritual impact. This evaluation of biblical accounts suggests that the scribes' biblical reports are meaningless if they are not revivified in the light of mediumistic experiences.

Arguably, the historic, spiritually orientated mediumistic legacy has enormous implications for humankind's contemporary spiritual quest and current psycho-spiritual practices. If today, individuals sincerely asked for the most spiritually elevated celestial guides to inspire their lives, the non-physical world might rain down upon humankind, the spiritual and compassionate integrity we so badly need. Present-day societies are overwhelmingly exploitative and callously indifferent in the way we humans treat each other, our animal relatives and the earth.

Murder has become a daily way of life that few people notice. Billions of flesh-and-blood animal relatives are murdered every year. The daily genocide of sentient, flesh and blood animals cannot be condoned without cheapening the value of all life and creating tragic and murderous consequences for humanity. Insensitive attitudes which lack compassion may even bring about the future cessation of humanity, all other related life-forms and the planet herself.

Many psychic sensitives are born mediums. Others find that their mediumship occurs spontaneously creating a turning point in their lives. Other individuals meditate, seeking to develop as mediums. Echoing fragments of the warnings Moses gave to the tribes, it is vital that in each case all mediums should test their communicators. It is important to receive communications exhibiting the most elevated spiritual content. People should also be aware of the differences between genuine communicators and those that are not.

Psychic or memory systems are not surviving intelligences. Put simplistically, they are left over energy systems. False communicators are mischievous spirits who lie about their identities, using the reputations of others in order to cause harm and manipulation.

Due to the psychically sensitive faculty which facilitated the receipt of spiritually orientated communications, it appears that the historic mediums grew spiritually as they accepted the responsibility of guiding their people. The prophets led them in accordance with the instructions of the invisible spiritual guide. Their obedience to the angel/spirit communicator was also demonstrated by the fact that the prophets' own planned courses of action were frequently overturned by the celestial communicator.

The prophets were frequently set shamanic vision quests that had little chance of success, yet they did succeed. Consequently, the prophets' increasing trust in the angel/spirit's commands deepened over the years.

Yahweh's leadership and protection at intervals worked hand in hand with raising the spiritual conduct of the evolving nation. Cumulatively, it has been revealed that since historic times many instances of mediumship have had a strong spiritual focus. These pages have evaluated examples of related human experiences of many historic spiritual figures.

They have provided evidence that phenomena that feature communications with otherworldly sources are best understood as a continuum of mediumistic experiences. Unfortunately this discussion clearly reveals the extent to which western, materialist, reductionist, modern day society has become divorced from understanding the importance of personal 'experiential' testimonies associated with spiritual mediumship.

Evidently, many of these angelic/spirit communications lay at the source of humankind's evolving spiritual awareness, reflected in the birth and development of the world's revealed religious traditions. The spiritual focus of mediumistic experiences continues to furnish and develop religious beliefs regarding the existence of after-death landscapes and their non-physical animal inhabitants, human and non-human.

If a person applied contemporary, fragmented, materialist belief systems to the birth of the revealed religions, all of humankind's inspired spiritual philosophy would be rejected out of hand – because it arose from transformative spiritual-mediumistic experiences! Materialist parapsychologists wrongly believe that mediumistic experiences are merely the result of imagination and distortions of chemicals in the brain. Surely this unconstructive, simplistic belief system has a negative influence.

These pages are cumulatively providing evidence of the long established tradition of reports of communications between the inhabitants of the material world and those of the co-existent, diversely populated, non-physical world. Significantly, Yahweh told the people not to listen to the necromantic murderous mediums from neighboring communities and their non-physical communicators. Arguably, the reason for this prohibition was that these mediums were not of the same spiritual caliber as the many mediumistic prophets. Yahweh warned against such mediums and their horrendous accompanying practices such as human and animal sacrificeand the utilization of their entrails.

Inevitably, Yahweh would also have been aware that 'like would attract like.' As a result, their communicators would not have the same elevated spiritual mission as Yahweh and the people would inevitably have fallen victim to psychic systems and lower level spirits including mischievous false communicators. It is possible, however, that at intervals the people did listen to the wrong teachings of spiritually inferior communicators and through misguided judgments carried out misguided acts.

## The Spirit Yahweh Spoke Face to Face

Apparently, both Moses himself and his biographers tell us that Moses regularly spoke 'face to face' with Yahweh in the same way as a person talks to another person. These communications increasingly took place in the Tent of the Meeting, and the accounts of them cannot be describing anything other than Moses' physical mediumship. We are told in Deuteronomy 34:10 that: 'Since then, no prophet has risen in Israel like Moses, whom [Yahweh] knew face to face.'[38]

Numbers 12:5–8 tells us:

Then the LORD [Yahweh] came down in a pillar of cloud; he stood at the entrance to the Tent [of the Meeting] and summoned Aaron and Miriam ... [then] he [Yahweh] said ...

When a prophet of [Yahweh] is among you,

I reveal myself to him in visions,

I speak to him in dreams.

But this is not true of my servant Moses;

he is faithful in all my house.

With him I speak face to face,

clearly and not in riddles;

he sees the form of [Yahweh].[39]

It cannot be stated more forcefully that biblical descriptions of a willful, animated, communicative manifestation is not describing aberrant volcanic ash as some materialists believe.

The next chapters will evaluate historically later biblical material and prove that these accounts also possess the shamanic mediumistic features shared by present-day mediumship.

*Chapter 9*

# Later Spiritual Prophets were Mediums

We have established the fact that a number of early historic prophets carried out psychic and mediumistic practices which were inter-woven with their evolving religious beliefs. Consequently, it has been verified that there was an extremely close relationship between the paranormal and religion in this long lasting era. Notably, these prophets practices had many shamanic mediumistic features and parallel contemporary mediumistic practices.

It will be demonstrated that the later spiritual prophets and their biographers were equally fluent with psychic and mediumistic practices. They provide us with evidence that these later generations of prophets, judges and seers likewise performed divinatory and mediumistic practices in close conjunction with their unfolding religious quest.

Due to mistranslation, suppression and distortion of the context of the biblical texts these ancient reports became unclear and left people confused as to their real meaning. Again we will decode the biblical accounts clarifying and verifying the fact that the lives of these spiritual leaders were consumed by mediumistic communica-tions with non-physical communicators. Protection, guidance, laws, customs and spiritual progression each had their source in accounts of Yahweh's communications with humankind. These ancient testi-monies continue to describe faculties known today as clairaudience and clairvoyance.

I accept the integrity of the biblical authors' descriptions and reports. It would be wrong to deny the value of personal experiential testimony whether it is ancient or modern. Many mediumistic and divinatory events were witnessed by large numbers of our ancient forefathers, giving further credence to the reports. Notably, many biblical accounts have now been verified for their historic, political, sociological and geographic accuracy. Consequently, the biblical reports of divinatory and mediumistic events should also be accepted for their truthfulness. Experts in fields such as archaeology, theology and history have testified to the integrity of countless biblical narratives. Likewise, each chapter of the present book contributes to amplifying contemporary understanding concerning the context into which these ancient testimonies can be fitted.

The following biblical accounts will confirm the ancient prophets' customary divinatory and mediumistic tradition, interlaced with their religion. Certainly, it will become increasingly clear that knowledge of the psychically sensitive faculty which facilitates mediumship enhances our understanding of spirituality. The clarification of the following biblical accounts will continue to bridge the gap between contemporary materialist parapsychology and the realm of humankind's transformative, spiritual-mediumistic experiences.

Progressively, the reader will become aware that these invaluable experiences gave rise to core features of the world's spiritual philosophy. It is from this realm that many of the world's religious teachers received their spiritual teachings and their spiritual missions. It fell on them to disseminate this knowledge among a typically fiercely reluctant, non-spiritual, rebellious world.

When reading the following decoded biblical accounts the reader is reminded that these pages are cumulatively revealing that transformative spiritual mediumistic experiences are not simply a modern day phenomenon. Instead, they are shown to represent a continnuum of experiences from the most anicent of times and have far reaching implications for the world's spiritual knowledge.

Due to the fact that transformative spiritual mediumistic experiences occur throughout all ages and cultures of the world, it is a fact that these paranormal phenomena can be seen to unite all races, creeds and cultures together. For those unfamiliar with the phenomena experienced by mediumstic individuals, they are reminded that although they lie outside the range of the five physical senses, they are very real. Inevitably, they do not lie beyond the realm of animal experiencing, human and non-human.

To arrive at an enriched perspective of human wholeness, the wholeness of the animal nature, it is necessary to accept and make sense of genuine experiences and incorporate them into an improved context of understanding. As previously alluded to, skeptics should be aware that progressively, quantum physicists are indeed unraveling the complexities and very real natural laws that relate to mediumistic experiences.

These pioneering scientists who are establishing the science for future generations reveal the inadequacies of Newtonian, mechanistic science. This limited science cannot explain the realm of the experiential including mediumship. People need to be reminded that Newtonian physics, born in the 17th century, has goverened and shaped our more materialistic understanding of the natural laws of the universe. People need to be aware when they read the following clarified biblical accounts that they are a product of this limited science which needs to be supplemented by the latest pioneering scientific discoveries.

The psycho-spiritual practices of the religious leaders, respected by more than half the world's population need to be understood and accepted as such. These leaders included Joshua, Moses' successor. Joshua's successors were oracles or seers, known as 'the Judges.' These psychics and mediums included Deborah, Gideon and Jephthah, who were succeeded by the prophet Samuel and then King David. Life will be breathed back into these psychic and mediumistic accounts, by revivifying them in the way the biblical writers expected them to be understood.

The reader should be reminded that mediumistic and psychic phenomena include clairvoyance, clairaudience, clairsentience, telepathy, precognition, retro-cognition, levitation, divination, sensing people's inner natures, auras and atmospheres, psychometry (sensing information from objects), spiritual healing, knowledge of events at vast geographic distances away, and mediumistic trance states, during which the medium gives spiritual lectures.

Psychic and mediumistic gifts can best be viewed as tools with which a person can commit good or bad actions, in the same way that a knife can be used by a murderer to kill, or by a surgeon to save lives. Utilizing psychic and mediumistic abilities without a spiritual objective is of a lower order than the use of mediumship to gain elevated spiritual insights.

Mediumistic communications can help to heal the bereaved and alleviate distress; this is obviously a spiritual practice. However, some mediumistic people may not be spiritual at all. Alternatively, many spiritual people do not possess a developed mediumistic gift. A life that has included a great deal of personal suffering may teach a person compassion, thereby advancing their spirituality, however, such disruptions can act as an obstacle to the development of the mediumistic ability. Peace of mind, a calm environment and meditation are catalysts to developing mediumship.

Reverend E. Garth Moore, the president of the Churches' Fellowship for Psychical and Spiritual Studies from 1963 to 1983, writes:

> It is to my mind quite absurd in the face of the evidence to deny ... the existence of ghosts ... the fact of telepathy ... [and] precognition, or retro-cognition (post-cognition) ... and indeed some of the remarkable phenomena of mediumship ... it is idle in my opinion to deny their existence ... The importance of the existence of these phenomena to most religious faiths is enormous. The Bible ... is full of stories of the miraculous.
>
> The hard bitten atheist or agnostic tends to dismiss such stories as mere fables whilst the materialists say that such things couldn't have happened because they cannot happen ... the survival of bodily death is ... common to a great many religions, [such as] Christianity ... Judaism ... Islam, Buddhism and Hinduism ... let us take mediumistic experiences ... either the

medium really is in contact with the dead ... or ... exhibiting ... extrasensory perception, either telepathic or precognitive ...

If it be the first ... there is ... a strong case for survival (not necessarily for immortality). If it be the second ... this at least shows something which all these religions are claiming, [that] ... there is a dimension beyond the purely material ... You could call that dimension the psychic or the spiritual and the two probably merge into each other. But to show that there is this non-material dimension provides an enormous prop for certainly Christianity, Judaism, Islam, Buddhism and Hinduism.[1]

## Joshua, Moses' Successor

After Moses' death, Joshua was appointed as his successor, as reported in the biblical accounts. Moses' legacy to the Semite tribes included the Ten Commandments as received from Yahweh. Many other laws had also been mediumistically transmitted, as described in the Book of Deuteronomy, some of which, Moses may have received in the form of trance and/or automatic writing.

Moses' mission had been to free the Hebrew slaves from oppression. It included welding together these newly liberated, rebellious, instinctively idolatrous peoples into the beginnings of a monotheistic Jewish nation. As a result of teachings received from Yahweh, Moses had taught his people the revolutionary concept of monotheism, which asserts the singularity and supremacy of God.

Joshua, a very different type of man from Moses, was to take the helm and follow in the vein of Moses' spiritually orientated mediumship. It is important to remember that typically, in this era, it was common to deify non-physical communicators. As a result of Yahweh's verbal teachings, increasingly, the name 'Elohim' was used to describe the Hebrews' growing understanding of the One God, the Divine.

The blending into one and confusion between God and non-physical communicators is revealed by tracing the original use of the term Elohim. It was originally used to describe experiences of

Yahweh, ghosts, gods/angels/spirits and humans who had passed into the higher spheres after death. This reveals the confusion associated with spirits, angels and God and how they merged and blended into one in people's understanding. A further reason why people over the centuries have believed Yahweh to be God is due to the use of this somewhat confused umbrella term, Elohim. They have overlooked the fact that Yahweh, the non-physical communicator, was presumably an angel or spirit and that the name may have been applied to many different communicators. All mediumistic contact with such entities bore witness to an otherworldly realm.

This range of non-physical figures was often deified due to their ancient, as yet uniformed understanding. Yahweh was understood to be a heavenly messeger yet historically Yahweh also came to be equated with 'a god' and God. Later translators made the same mistake due to their lack of understanding of authentic mediumistic experiences. The following examples clearly show predictive and mediumistic features.

It was inside the Tent of the Meeting that Yahweh commanded Moses to nominate Joshua as his successor and leader of the Semitic Hebrew tribes. Communication with Yahweh typically took place at this holy place. It can be suggested that the following biblical narrative reveals Yahweh's concern that the Hebrews would inevitably consult with and worship spiritually inferior spirits/gods including those contacted by the Hebrews' idolatrous mediumistic neighbors.

These spiritually inferior mediums murdered their victims and were idolatrous because they did not worship Yahweh or recognize his exclusivity. It will be seen that this account yet again demonstrates translation errors. Instead of stating 'angel or spirit,' the terms 'god' and 'the lord' have been used.

In earlier centuries in Britain, gentlemen or gentry were called 'my lord' as a term of respect. This is probably similar to the terms of respect used by the Semitic tribes to describe Yahweh.

Deuteronomy 31:14–23 tells us that Yahweh called a group together so that he could speak and materialize in front of them. Yahweh then said to Moses and the tribal leaders:

> The day of your death is near. Call Joshua and present yourselves at the Tent of Meeting, where I will commission him ...
>
> Then [Yahweh] the LORD appeared ... in a pillar of cloud, and the cloud stood over the entrance to the Tent ... And [Yahweh] the LORD said to Moses: '... Now write down ... this song ... so that it may be a witness for me against [the Israelites]. When I have brought them into the land flowing with milk and honey ... they will turn to other gods [spirits] ... rejecting me and breaking my covenant. And when many disasters ... come upon them ... I know [already] what they are [going] to do ...'
>
> [Yahweh] The LORD gave this command to Joshua: 'Be strong and courageous, for you will bring the Israelites into the land I promised them.'[2]

Each of the several versions of the Bible expresses the same clear statement that Yahweh selected Joshua because, 'the spirit resided in Joshua' or 'the spirit could be found in Joshua.' Evidently, Yahweh chose Joshua because he had divinatory and mediumistic abilities. In the New International Version (NIV) of the Bible, in Numbers 27:18–21, this fact is made clear:

> So the LORD said to Moses, 'Take Joshua ... in whom is the spirit, and lay your hand on him ... He is to stand before Eleazar the priest, who will obtain decisions from him by enquiring of the Urim before the [Yahweh] LORD. At his command he and the entire community ... will go out, and at his command they will come in.'[3]

The divination stones, including Urim and Thummim, which provided predictive information, were given to Joshua to use and protect. He was to be the new mediumistic prophet in receipt of

Yahweh's instructions, continuing Moses' mediumistic legacy. Inherent in mediumistic beliefs, both ancient and modern, is the idea that the non-physical communicators guide, protect and enhance spiritual progress.

The biblical Book of Joshua records Joshua's countless conversations with Yahweh. Notably, several phrases are used to describe Joshua's mediumistic receipt of communications from Yahweh. Typically, they commence with: "[Yahweh] the lord said to Joshua" ...' Further examples of Joshua's mediumistic understanding of Yahweh's wishes can be found in Joshua 7:10,[4] 8:1[5] and 8:18.[6]

Instead of being a peaceable, compassionate angelic communicator, the communicator who spoke to Joshua appears to have guided his war efforts. Alternatively, Joshua misinterpreted the communications and believed this was the course of action Yahweh instructed. Significantly, the NIV Bible commentary refers to Yahweh as God:

[Yahweh] God commissioned his people, under his servant Joshua, to take Canaan in his name out of the hands of the idolatrous and dissolute Canaanites whose measure of sin was now full (Gen. 15:16). Joshua is the story of the kingdom of God breaking into the world of nations ... Thus [Yahweh's] the Lord's triumph over the Canaanites testified to the world that [Yahweh] the God of Israel is the one true and living God, whose claim on the world is absolute. It was also a warning to the nations that the irresistible advance of the kingdom of [Yahweh] God would ultimately disinherit all those who opposed it.[7]

Of the author and date of the Book of Joshua, the Bible commentary explains that the:

Earliest Jewish traditions (Talmud) claim that Joshua wrote his own book except for the final section about his funeral ... On at least two occasions the text reports writing at Joshua's command or by Joshua himself ... Moreover the author's observations are accurate and precise. He is thoroughly at ease with the antiquated names of cities.[8]

The following examples illustrate Joshua giving commands to his people (see Joshua chapters 3[9] and 4[10]). We are informed that these predictive instructions were conveyed to Joshua by the non-physical communicator, Yahweh. He advised Joshua how best to lead the Hebrews across the River Jordan en route to Jericho, a task that seemed impossible as descriptions suggest that the River Jordan was in high flood.

Despite this, Joshua led his people safely across the river. Joshua did not carry out feats that defied the natural laws of nature; instead, it is strongly indicated that Joshua had accessed precognitive knowledge from Yahweh regarding the timing of future events. This is deduced as Joshua knew precisely where and when the people should cross the river.

It is probable that Joshua knew when a future landslide would occur and at which particular stretch of the tumultuous waters. If this prophetic information had not been gained from direct communications with Yahweh, Joshua would have accessed it from the divination stones (it was the Hebrew belief that the divination stones were controlled by Yahweh). The Hebrews' arduous journey to Jericho, known as 'the promised land' and 'the land of milk and honey', was again supported by Yahweh.

Joshua 3:5–13 reports:

Joshua told the people, '... tomorrow [Yahweh] the LORD will do amazing things among you ... Come here and listen to the words of [Yahweh] the LORD your God. This is how you will know that [Yahweh] the living God is among you ... as soon as the priests who carry the ark of [Yahweh] the LORD – [Yahweh] the LORD of all the earth – set foot in the Jordan, its waters flowing downstream will be cut off.[11]

Joshua, like Moses, his prophetic predecessor, taught his people that the non-physical communicator Yahweh clearly lived among them. In these nomadic days, Yahweh's otherworldly dialogues took place in the Tent of the Meeting. This sanctuary, where witnessed manifestations and communications took place, was housed in later years in the most sacred area of the permanent structure of the Temple building.

Joshua's interpretation of Yahweh's teachings led him to convey to the tribes that this evolving Hebrew nation was a chosen people. They were commanded to live increasingly spiritually mature lives, as guided by the Ten Commandments and were tasked with setting an example for others to follow. They were severely reprimanded if they were tempted to join in or copy the idolatrous sacrificial rituals and ceremonies of the barbaric neighboring settlements.

They were progressively taught to demonstrate spiritual integrity and how best to follow the leadership of Yahweh, their protector and teacher. Increasingly, there were strong spiritual components involved in the prophets' mediumistic experiences.

Evidently, Yahweh selected future leaders because, as mediums, they possessed the faculties that enabled them to see and hear this otherworldly messenger. Mediums became the nation's seers, judges, prophetic leaders and spiritual teachers. Included in the long list of famous spiritual leaders who were mediums are Moses, David, Solomon, Samuel, Daniel, Elijah, Elisha, Ezekiel, Jeremiah, Isaiah, John the Baptist and Jesus. They each progressively exhibited spiritual leadership and each had experiences of and communications from non-physical beings. Their lives were encompassed by the angelic and spirit world.

Fighting for their survival under Joshua's leadership, the evolving Hebrew nation lost the Battle of Ai. Joshua chapter 7[12] describes Joshua's interpretation of these events and the mediumistic communications from the non-physical world. Joshua understood this loss to be a punishment as the tribes had a thief among them – a robber who had stolen Yahweh's sacred property.

The divination stones, including Urim and Thummim, were used to discover the identity of the thief. This verifies that the divination stones were used both in a spiritual and predictive way, and further proves that the leadership and protection of Yahweh was interwoven with raising the spiritual conduct of the nation.

However, as previously stated, communications have to be interpreted by the spiritual level of those who receive them.

In turn, interpretations are shaped by the morals of the historic epoch in which they occur. It is also worth remembering that although Joshua was a medium, he may not have received communications from the same otherworldly communicator as Moses.

Significantly, Joshua's leadership was defined by the fact that he was a military leader. Joshua's mediumship did not reach the profound and superior level of Moses' mediumship, this was undoubtedly due to the markedly different characters and mediumistic abilities of these two men. Furthermore, Joshua did not have the benefit of Moses' advanced Egyptian education, which would have helped when interpretation was needed.

## The Book of Judges

The title 'Judge' was given to Joshua's mediumistic successors. The biblical Book of Judges[13] provides historical accounts of the lives of these psychic and mediumistic individuals. Daily, these men and women offered valuable guidance both pertaining to the leadership of the Semitic tribes and for individuals. The historic epoch of the Judges ranged from the time of the elders who outlived Joshua until the decision to instate a hereditary monarchy. The foundation of a hereditary monarchy was inevitably influenced by, and followed in the fashion of, the pagan neighboring settlements.

The accounts found in the Book of Judges describe the Semitic tribes' repeated pattern of unfaithful behavior. Repeatedly, they are reprimanded by Yahweh for straying away from the mediumistic practice of communicating with him. They are further castigated for worshipping their neighbors' gods. It is probable that some of these gods were deified non-physical communicators whose images took the form of idols.

As a consequence of this diluting, foreign influence, the Hebrews began to lead spiritually inferior lives. The pagan gods, some of whom were presumably spirit communicators, were not of the same caliber as the Yahweh of Moses, who had provided leadership and protection interwoven with raising the spiritual standards of the Semitic tribes.

Repeatedly, this evolving Semitic nation faced attacks and oppression from the neighboring powers. This adversity was interpreted as Yahweh's punishment of his people because they had turned to foreign gods and spirit guides. When Yahweh heard the people's sincere plea for help, he intervened by offering mediumistic guidance and with great compassion repeatedly liberated them from their enemies. In order to do this, Yahweh chose a succession of mediumistic figures known as 'the judges,' each of whom followed Yahweh's guidance, which successively led the Hebrews to freedom.

The judges came to the fore after the loss of both Moses and Joshua, both of whom were revered mediumistic leaders. The people sought new mediumistic leaders to guide them and answer tribal and individual needs, consequently, there followed the period of the mediumistic judges. In the following biblical quotation, the name Yahweh has again been mistranslated as 'the Lord,' when inevitably, the original text referred to Yahweh as 'the angel of the lord' or 'messenger of the lord.'

Through ignorance and/or condemnation of mediumship, the correct term for Yahweh, the non-physical communicator, has been lost in translation. The biblical record may have referred to Yahweh using an alternative reverential term, which was perhaps wrongly translated as LORD. Both in former centuries and contemporary times, the name 'lord' gives the reader the false impression that the scribes were at all times referring to God and not Yahweh, the non-physical communicator.

All those, including angels and spirits, who were highly

respected and/or deified were inevitably given titles similar to 'lord.' Through inaccurate translation the whole context of the account has been lost. Significantly, Yahweh as guide and spiritual teacher taught the Hebrews that there was a single God and that he should be considered as a messenger of God.

The period of 'the Judges' is described in Judges 2:10–11 as a time when a 'whole generation had been gathered to their fathers [passed to spirit, in heaven] [and] another generation grew up, who knew neither [Yahweh] the LORD nor what he had done for Israel. Then the Israelites did evil in the eyes of the LORD [Yahweh] and served the Baals.'

Judges 2:1–4 records for posterity that the angel or spirit, Yahweh, moved from one place to another and spoke for all the people to hear. On many occasions Yahweh also physically manifested in a form best described as resembling a cloud, but significantly, this manifestation spoke in a clearly audible manner. The Semitic tribes were told that Yahweh had decided to leave the Hebrews' enemies unscathed as a punishment, in direct response to their disloyalty. In this particular passage, 'Yahweh' has been correctly translated as 'the angel of the lord.'

> The angel of the LORD [Yahweh] went up from Gilgal to Bokim and said, 'I brought you out of Egypt and led you into the land that I swore to give to your forefathers … Yet you have disobeyed me … I tell you … I will not drive them out … they will be thorns in your sides and their gods will be a snare to you.[15]

Many biblical accounts such as these tell us of a moving, talking, anthropomorphic manifestation. This non-physical leader is demonstrably an angelic or spirit communicator. Yahweh is otherworldly in nature; however, he is certainly not Almighty God, the Divine.

Judges 2:16 tells us that Yahweh 'raised up judges, who saved them out of the hands of these raiders.'[16] We learn of a man named Gideon, who became a judge. Guided by Yahweh, Gideon saved the

Semitic tribes from the fierce attacks and oppression mounted by their idolatrous neighbors. As a result of his mediumistic leadership and the people's fears and insecurities, Gideon was asked to become a hereditary monarch.

Judges 8:22–23 records this request for future generations: 'The Israelites said to Gideon, "Rule over us – you, your son and your grandson – because you have saved us ..." But Gideon told them, "I will not rule over you, nor will my son ... [Yahweh] The LORD will rule over you."'[17]

Evidently, Gideon clearly understood that leadership through hereditary succession would create an enormous obstacle for Yahweh's leadership. Gideon appears to have been aware that traditionally, Yahweh selected individuals from successive generations, as a result of their mediumistic gifts. If this evolving nation had appointed a hereditary ruler, Yahweh's selected mediumistic prophets, 'raised up' to lead the people, would have been 'lone voices' against the powerful establishment.

Repeatedly throughout the history of the Semitic tribes, Yahweh had initiated contact with mediumistic individuals. Generation after generation had had mediumistic prophets who ruled them in accordance with their interpretation of Yahweh's wishes.

Yahweh was believed to communicate his spiritual leadership and protection through his conversations with the judges. The following biblical accounts make no sense if they are not revivified by an improved understanding, namely that they reveal clear examples of historic mediumship: Deborah the judge: Judges chapters 4 to 5;[18] Gideon the judge: Judges chapter 6 to 9;[19] Jephthah the judge: Judges 10:6 to 12:7.[20]

## Judge Deborah the Medium

Judges 4:1–9 tells us that:

> After Ehud [the judge] died, the Israelites once again did evil in the eyes of the LORD. So the LORD sold them into the hands of ...

a king of Canaan. The commander of his army was Sisera ... Because he had ... cruelly oppressed the Israelites for twenty years, they cried to the LORD for help. Deborah, a prophetess [a medium] ... was leading Israel at that time. She held court under the Palm ... and the Israelites came to her [to receive predictions and guidance] ... She sent for Barak ... and said to him, '[Yahweh] the LORD, the God of Israel, commands you, "Go, take with you ten thousand men ... [Yahweh] will lure Sisera ... with his chariots ... and give him into your hands."'

Barak said to her, 'If you go with me I will go; but if you don't go with me, I won't go.'

'Very well,' Deborah said, 'I will go ... But ... [Yahweh] the LORD will hand Sisera over to a woman.'[21]

This judge called Deborah counseled people under a palm tree in the highlands of Ephraim. Daily, people visited Deborah in order for her to ask Yahweh for predictive information and guidance to help solve their problems. This practice was known as 'enquiring of the lord [Yahweh].' Deborah, therefore, clearly practiced mediumship, exactly the same practice that has continued throughout the centuries to this day.

By conducting her mediumship under a tree in the highlands, Deborah was following in the same fashion as her predecessors, the ancient mediumistic shamans. As we have noted, mountains, hills, steps and trees were viewed in the shamanic tradition as having special powers which enhanced mediumistic communications. These physical locations were viewed as symbols of the steps which could be ascended and descended, bridging the interconnecting physical and non-physical worlds.

Deborah's advice and predictions were highly respected for their wisdom and accuracy. The provision of accurate predictions proved to the Israelites that she received her guidance from Yahweh. Deborah had been told by Yahweh to ask the people to find a man named Barak and inform him that he would lead the Israelite army to victory against their enemies.

The respect for her mediumistic role as Yahweh's voice was clearly demonstrated when Barak, the general, who was given 10,000 men to command, would not accept his mission unless Deborah accompanied them. This event has much in common with the occasion when the young female medium known as Joan of Arc accompanied the French army against the English in the early 15th century AD.

## Judge Gideon the Medium

The historic accounts tell us that Gideon, while working in the fields, suddenly saw Yahweh manifest in front of him. Yahweh told him of his future vision quest to save Israel from the oppression of the Midianites, who were attempting to starve the Israelites out of existence. Following in the familiar shamanic tradition, Yahweh had initiated his first meeting with Gideon under an oak tree and had set him a shamanic vision quest at the onset of his mediumship.

It has been noted that similarly, vision quests were given to the ancient mediumistic shamans when they first discovered their mediumship. Gideon had been selected as a mediumistic judge. Judges were understood to be seers, alternatively known today as mediums, due to their transfer of information from their angelic or spirit guide.

Judges 6:6–12 tells us that:

Midian so impoverished the Israelites that they cried out to [Yahweh] the LORD for help.

... he sent them a prophet, who said 'This is what [Yahweh] the LORD ... says ...

[Yahweh] The angel of the LORD came and sat down under the oak in Ophrah ... where ... Gideon was threshing wheat.[22]

Evidently, apart from the physical manifestations described of Yahweh, presumably for all to witness, it would appear that Gideon inevitably possessed the ability to see and hear Yahweh: he had the gifts of clairvoyance and clairaudience. This is clear from phrases such as '[Yahweh] the angel of God said to him ... the angel of the LORD touched ... the unleavened bread ... the angel of the LORD disappeared.'[23]

Although Gideon showed great respect for Yahweh, he questioned this angel of the lord. This does not describe an experience of ineffable union with God (the Divine). Some individuals who have experiences that are believed to be of God (the Divine) describe seeing a formless luminous light or blaze of living light, whereas Gideon's experience is characterized by seeing a form, and negotiating with an audible voice, as in present-day mediumship.

Gideon even tested the otherworldly spirit or angel by placing a specific wool fleece outside, and asking for it to become wet while the ground around it stayed dry. Risking the anger of the celestial communicator, Gideon then had a second request – this time that the fleece should stay dry while the ground around it became wet. Gideon needed physical signs to prove to him that the non-physical communicator was authentic and had paranormal abilities.

Judges 6:34 tells us that when he was preparing to attack the Midianite oppressors, 'the Spirit of the LORD came upon Gideon.'[24] The literal Hebrew translation is most revealing. We learn that the 'Spirit clothed himself with this vivid figure [which] emphasises that the Spirit of the Lord empowered the human agent and acted through him.'[25]

The accurate translation of the Hebrew tells us that the angel or spirit 'wore,' 'put on,' 'clothed itself in Gideon.' This establishes the fact that the Hebrews believed the angel or spirit manifested itself through the use of the medium's body – in this case, Gideon's body. The accurate translation of the Hebrew text describes forms of altered states of consciousness that are observed and investigated today. Contemporary mediums demonstrate entranced states, – altered states of consciousness,– in which they appear to be overshadowed.

There are many cases of spirits speaking through the medium in a variety of languages unknown to the medium, including ancient languages. Male and female voices have been heard to speak through mediums or emanate from mediums. These phenomena have occurred while mediums' hands have been tied and their mouths gagged by investigators. Books have been written at remarkable speeds while mediums have been in these altered states of consciousness.

One remarkable example from the 20th century was Mrs Curran, a poorly educated American housewife, who, while entranced, had a communicator named Patience Worth communicate through her. Patience Worth held conversations, answered questions, and wrote in-depth historical books and poetry at a phenomenal speed. Patience was intensively investigated by professionals from many academic backgrounds for several decades, and they concluded that Patience was a separate entity from Mrs Curran and that Mrs Curran was not responsible for the spoken and literary outpourings.

Returning to the parallel Hebrew phenomena, the Hebrew phrases which were used with great regularity to describe them included: 'the spirit clothed himself,' 'wore' and 'acted through the judge.' – These descriptions demonstrate an observable and witnessed change in the personalities and abilities of the mediumistic judges when the otherworldly guide or guides overshadowed them. These psycho-spiritual leaders believed that they received instructions from the angelic or spirit guide, so that they could in turn offer prophetic leadership to the Israelites.

Another example of Yahweh powerfully overshadowing a mediumistic figure relates to David in 1 Samuel 16:13: 'So Samuel took the horn of oil and anointed him in the presence of his brothers and from that day on the Spirit of the LORD came upon David in power.'[26] We are also told in Judges 14:6 that Yahweh powerfully overshadowed Samson: 'The Spirit of the LORD came upon him in power;'[27] Judges 14:19 offers a further example.[28]

The mediumship of a judge named Othniel can also be seen clearly. Judges 2:18 tells us that: 'Whenever the LORD raised up a judge for them, he was with the judge and saved them out of the hands of their enemies as long as the judge lived.'[29] In chapter 3:10 we read: 'The Spirit of the LORD came upon him so that he became Israel's judge.'[30] In Jeremiah 1:9 Yahweh tells Jeremiah: 'I have put my words in your mouth.'

Descriptions such as these verify that the Hebrews believed that a celestial communicator acted through the human agent. Evidently, the judges, in succession, all possessed mediumistic gifts. They were guided by their ability to see and hear otherworldly communications and due to these profound abilities and their willingness to use them to help others, they were revered as spiritual leaders. We see again the intermeshed relationship between the realm of the spiritual and the realm of the psychic and mediumistic.

Some judges, also known as seers, lived in particularly dangerous times. They experienced hostilities and oppression from the neighboring cultures and were frequently forced to defend the Semitic tribes from annihilation. Each time, the judges sought support and guidance from their spirit or angelic communicator(s). These otherworldly beings spoke through the mediumistic judges in order to guide the people to safety.

Gideon was astonished when, through his mediumistic communications with Yahweh, he learned about a new battle plan. He was incredulous when Yahweh told him to reduce his troops from 30,000 men to 300 men. Yahweh's intervention reversed Gideon's plans in the same way that otherworldly communications had reversed the plans of both Abraham and Moses. Abraham was told that he had misunderstood Yahweh's wishes and that he was wrong to attempt to sacrifice his son; he learned that Yahweh did not look for sacrifices.

Wanted for murder, Moses was told against his wishes to return to Egypt and oppose Pharaoh single handedly. After reducing the number of his troops, Gideon was told by Yahweh to listen to the enemy's conversations during the night. The results of this encouraged Gideon to divide his 300 men into three groups, and they successfully defeated the Midianites. This brought the past seven years of hostilities from the Midianites to an end.

## Judge Jephthah the Medium

Judges 11:29 tells us that 'the Spirit of the LORD came upon Jephthah.'[31] We are told that Jephthah received his calling from the 'the angel of the lord' (Yahweh). Significantly, at that time Jephthah was a notorious robber. This offers convincing proof that Yahweh selected leaders primarily because of their mediumistic abilities rather than for their initial moral integrity or spirituality. Without mediumistic abilities, they could not participate in the innumerable reported conversations with their ethereal spirit or angelic communicators. Evidently, these mediums were progressively molded into mediumistic leaders with an ever-growing spiritual maturity.

## Samuel the Medium

Eli was a high priest who tutored a child named Samuel, a young boy who had been dedicated by his mother Hannah from birth to the service of the Temple. One night, Samuel was awakened by a voice which called out his name. The boy slept besides the Ark, which in these more settled times was situated in a most sacred area in the permanent Temple building. 1 Samuel 3:1–7 tells us:

> In those days the word of [Yahweh] the LORD was rare; there were not many visions ...
>
> Samuel was lying down in the temple ... [by] the ark ... Then [Yahweh] the LORD called Samuel ... he ran to Eli ... But Eli said, 'I did not call ...'
>
> Again [Yahweh] the LORD called, 'Samuel!' ...
>
> Now Samuel did not yet know [Yahweh] the LORD: The word of [Yahweh] the LORD had not yet been revealed to him.[32]

This account tells us that the Israelites had entered a period in history when mediumistic prophets could not be found. This is partly the reason why Samuel thought the distinctly audible voice belonged to Eli his teacher. Samuel was called three times, and each time, he ran dutifully to Eli. The old man realized that as no one else was there, the voice belonged to the angel of the lord, Yahweh. Eli was aware that the boy had been called while he slept by the sacred Ark, where Yahweh was believed to live.

Samuel's initial mediumistic experience has distinct parallels with those of Moses in an earlier age. Yahweh spoke and manifested with great regularity for Moses, and Moses incessantly asked for Yahweh's advice. These manifestations took place between the two cherubim on the Ark and were witnessed by tribal elders who accompanied Moses.

Eli told Samuel that the next time he heard his name called out by the voice, he should reply courteously, 'Speak, for your servant is listening.'[33] Clearly, Eli believed that Samuel had begun his mediumistic mission that night. Yahweh is described in 1 Samuel 3:10 as a clear manifestation which called out Samuel's name[34] and in 1 Samuel 3:15 Samuel's new acquaintance with Yahweh is described as a vision.[35]

These experiences, which continued for the rest of Samuel's life, establish the fact that Samuel had clairaudient and clairvoyant mediumistic abilities. This famous historic mediumistic figure is highly respected today as a prophet and spiritual leader; Samuel clearly combined his mediumship with his spirituality.

In later years, Samuel was told by the non-physical communicator to anoint Saul as the future king of Israel. We are told that Yahweh had given Samuel predictive information regarding his forthcoming meeting with Saul. He was told that Saul would come to him and request his mediumistic guidance. In keeping with the prediction, while searching for some lost donkeys, Saul visited Samuel. He wanted the mediumistic prophet 'to enquire of the lord,' and ask where his lost donkeys could be found.

1 Samuel 9:9 makes clear that in the past prophets used to be called seers. Like the judges, they performed a predictive mediumistic and spiritual leadership role; one role was intertwined with the other. These psycho-spiritual leaders took the people's problems and questions to Yahweh when they 'enquired of the lord': 'Formerly in Israel, if a man went to enquire of God, he would say, "Come, let us go to the seer," because the prophet of today used to be called a seer.'[36]

1 Samuel chapter 9 describes Samuel anointing Saul as the future king.[37] Chapter 10[38] then informs us that the prophet Samuel predicted a succession of events that would occur to Saul as he returned home. If Samuel's predictions proved accurate, this should confirm to Saul that Yahweh had indeed chosen him to be the future king. Accurate predictions confirmed that Samuel was acting on behalf of Yahweh and the authenticity of Samuel's anointment of Saul.

Each of Samuel's predictions for Saul did prove to be accurate. One such prediction was that 'the spirit of the lord' would overshadow Saul and from that moment on, Saul would become a medium for Yahweh. Samuel had told Saul that this event would occur when he met a group of traveling prophets on his way home. Samuel had informed Saul that; 'The Spirit of the LORD will come upon you in power and you will prophesy with them; and you will be changed into a different person.'[39]

This prediction was accurate. When Saul met the traveling prophets, he began to dance and sing; Saul gained the gift of mediumistic prophecy at that time. The fact that there were lesser prophets traveling around the country indicates that mediumistic and psychic practices were common at that time.

These psycho-spiritual practices echo those of the ancient mediumistic shamans who also utilized ecstatic, rhythmic dancing and singing as a catalyst for entering into trance states. In altered states of consciousness, the shamans were empowered to receive predictive information and guidance for others. Biblical 'mediumistic prophecy' clearly possessed the same characteristics as that of ancient mediumistic shamanism.

1 Samuel 10:19–21 tells us that after Samuel had privately anointed Saul as Israel's first king, he later used a second method of selection: the divination stones, including Urim and Thummim. Yahweh was reluctant to establish a hereditary monarchy and only did so in response to the people's request:

> But you have now rejected [Yahweh, your spirit communicator] your God, who saves you out of all your calamities ... And you have said, 'No, set a king over us. So now present yourselves before the LORD by your tribes and clans.'
>
> When Samuel brought the tribes of Israel near, the tribe of Benjamin was chosen. Then ... clan by clan ... Matri's clan was chosen. Finally Saul son of Kish was chosen.[40]

Although the people chose to have a hereditary monarchy, the role of the prophet in Israel was considered to be superior to the role of kingship. Yahweh, the non-physical communicating messenger of the lord, was believed to be the otherworldly guide who spoke through his mediumistic prophets:

> Moses had anticipated Israel's desire for a human king (Deut. 17:18–20) but Israelite kingship was to be compatible with the continued rule of [Yahweh] over his people as their Great King ... The request for a king constituted a denial of their covenant relationship with [Yahweh], who was their king ... The problem was resolved when Samuel called the people to repentance and renewal of their allegiance to [Yahweh] on the very occasion of the inauguration of Saul as king ... By establishing the kingship in the context of covenant renewal, Samuel placed the monarchy in Israel on a radically different footing from that in surrounding nations.
>
> The king in Israel was not to be autonomous in his authority

and power; rather he was to be subject to the law of [Yahweh] and the word of the prophet (10:25; 12:23). This was to be true not only for Saul but also for all the kings who would occupy the throne in Israel in the future. The king was to be an instrument of [Yahweh's] rule over his people, and the people as well as the king were to continue to recognise [Yahweh] as their ultimate Sovereign (12:14–15).[41]

Although Saul at intervals demonstrated mediumship and predictive knowledge, Samuel was the greater and most consistent medium of the two. Daily, people came to Samuel, requesting that he 'enquire of the lord' on their behalf, to alleviate their problems by offering predictions and mediumistic guidance. 1 Samuel chapter 13[42] tells us that the practice of 'enquiring of the lord' continued despite Saul becoming the king. It is impossible to prevent people being born with or developing mediumistic gifts.

This account also tells us of an occasion when King Saul was waiting for guidance from Yahweh through the mediumship of Samuel. When Samuel did not arrive when expected, Saul became impatient and took decisions without Samuel's help. When Samuel arrived later, he fiercely condemned Saul for his disobedience to Yahweh. Significantly, the Israelite king was prohibited from taking certain decisions without Yahweh's instructions as conveyed through the prophet Samuel.

This reported event further clarifies the importance of divination and mediumship at that time. Samuel's disappointment with King Saul for his disloyalty to Yahweh also provides further information regarding the historical background to the Endor event. That event was clearly mistranslated, misinterpreted and taken out of context, as was discussed earlier.

Samuel learned that Yahweh was going to punish Saul for his willful disobedience. So he informed Saul that Yahweh would no longer guide him and that all future generations of his family, including his respected son, Jonathan, would not inherit the throne.

1 Samuel chapter 31 tells us that this prediction was accurate as Saul and his sons were later killed in battle.[43]

Significantly, there are no biblical accounts that describe Jonathan as having the ability 'to enquire of the lord' (Yahweh). This suggests that although Jonathan had many spiritual characteristics, he was not a medium. Today, we find that the reverse can also be true, that some mediums are not spiritually orientated people.

## King David the Medium

1 Samuel chapter 16[44] tells us of further conversations between Yahweh and the prophet Samuel. These led to Samuel's private anointing of David as an alternative king to Saul. Significantly, David continued the mediumistic practices of the earlier psycho-spiritual leaders, especially from the time of his anointment. 1 Samuel 16:13 notes: 'So Samuel took the horn of oil and anointed him in the presence of his brothers and from that day on the Spirit of the LORD came upon David in power.'[45] It is possible that from the anointing day onwards, David's mediumship was strengthened.

When important decisions needed to be made, David was known to 'enquire of the lord,' that is, he asked Yahweh, the otherworldly being, for guidance, in stark contrast to the willful and disloyal behavior of Saul. 2 Samuel 2:1[46] provides an example of David's mediumistic practice: 'David enquired of the LORD. "Shall I go up to one of the towns of Judah?" he asked ... [Yahweh] The LORD said, "Go up." David asked, "Where shall I go?" "To Hebron," [Yahweh] the LORD answered.'

Another example is found in 2 Samuel 7:18: 'King David went in and sat before [Yahweh] the LORD and he said ...'[47] To clarify the phrase 'went in,' the NIV biblical commentary tells us that it referred to going into 'the tent in which the ark was kept.'[48] David was therefore carrying out the same mediumistic practices as those of his predecessors, all of whom had entered the Tent of the Meeting 'to enquire of the lord.' It was in this most sacred area that historic mediums found the atmosphere conducive to facilitating mediumistic manifestations and communications, here they saw and spoke with Yahweh.

It is interesting to speculate as to the reason why Yahweh chose David to become king. We find that he was the youngest of Jesse's eight sons, yet it was the eldest son who by tradition had the superior right to inherit money and title. We also learn that David spent much of his time away from the family, working alone as a compassionate shepherd. 1 Samuel chapter 16[49] tells us that upon arrival at Jesse's home, Samuel spontaneously thought that the tall, older son, named Eliab, was the man to be anointed as the next king of Israel. However, Yahweh intervened and told Samuel that this was not the son he had selected. This account gives further evidence of human decisions being changed by Yahweh's intervention.

Evidently, David was chosen because he had mediumistic abilities and compassion for animals. These gifts were probably unwittingly cultivated during his solitary, meditative days and nights in the countryside where he tended to, cared for and protected the family's animals. From then on, David was to use his mediumship throughout the rest of his life, 'enquiring of the lord.'

We learn that even before David met Samuel and was chosen as king, David had already spoken with Yahweh, the angel of the lord. Yahweh guided all of David's actions and they already had a close relationship. We are told of David's earlier meeting with Goliath, a giant of a man who had issued a challenge to the Israelite army some time before. Everyone feared Goliath's challenge, but it was taken up by the brave young boy named David.

David's faith in Yahweh is demonstrated in 1 Samuel 17:45 where he says to Goliath: 'Who is this that dares to defy the armies of the living God [Yahweh]?'[50] Significantly, David's solitary meditations in the peaceful countryside among the animals, for whom he cared, would have been the catalyst for the onset and development of his mediumship. These featues echo those that facilitate mediumship and a relationship with spirit guides today.

David's mediumship, in turn, facilitated his close relationship with Yahweh, whom he saw as a living angelic presence. An enormous amount of researched evidence has been provided to prove that generation after generation of psycho-spiritual leaders had experienced a similar relationship; their mediumship was spiritually orientated, elevating themselves and the people they led.

In the next chapter I will evaluate evidence of mediumistic and psychic phenomena predominantly in the biblical New Testament. These will include examples of trance states, the use of dreams as psychic tools, visionary and manifestation (physical phenomena) experiences, extrasensory perception and clairvoyance.

Chapter 10

# Angelic Materializations and
# Jesus' Mediumship

The following research will prove that the Bible contains many
accounts that describe mediumistic trance states, observations of
materializations of angels or spirits and the mediumship of Jesus
Christ. These represent ancient precedents of the mediumship
which continues to this day. Modern mediumship which is global is
observed by psychical researchers and the general public alike. The
following evidence continues to show that mediumship was born at
the dawn of time, has continued throughout the ages, is found in all
cultures of the world and is closely intermeshed with evolving spirituality.

When some present-day mediums go into trance, they give
profound direct-voice trance lectures which provide information on
natural laws of which we are normally unaware. However, discoveries made in the realm of quantum physics are progressively in
harmony with much of the phenomena and information received.
Direct-voice trance lectures edify us with inspired spiritual
philosophy and the descriptions of the non-physical landscapes
which we will inhabit after death are most illuminating.

Much of this information has been recorded over the years.
Arguably, this research proves that generations of biblical writers
recorded their observations of entranced mediumistic, spiritual
leaders. These ancient psycho-spiritual trance experiences have
profound parallels with the psycho-spiritual experiences of other
historic and contemporary trance mediums.

## Mediums in Trance in the Bible
As we have seen, the biblical biographers were completely

conversant with the various features of mediumship. Understanding the narratives in this clarified mediumistic context breathes life and authentic meaning into the ancient accounts. The events in the lives of the mediumistic prophets can then be understood in exactly the same way as the way the biblical authors intended.

While experiencing varying degrees of altered states of consciousness, mediums throughout the centuries believed they received spiritual guidance and information from otherworldly beings, and they conveyed these spiritual insights and advice to observers. Trance states demonstrated by contemporary mediums vary throughout the centuries, each believed they received spiritual guidance and other information from otherworldly beings.

They conveyed these spiritual insights to observers. Trance states, demonstrated by contemporary mediums, vary enormously with regard to the spiritual quality and quantity of the communications received. During mediumistic trance states, mediums frequently access a remarkable degree of precognitive and/or retro-cognitive knowledge.

Arguably, this is received from angels and spirits who are in a non-physical dimension transcending mundane, linear time and space. This state of being enables them to access such information and communicate it to mediums. It is true that psychics can access past and future information without contacting angelic and spirit personalities; however, mediumship provides much more than the obtaining of predictive and retro-cognitive information.

It is important to clarify the term 'trance,' which is frequently reported and described in biblical passages. The practice of going into genuine trance, with the sincere intention of receiving spiritual guidance from tested angelic or spirit communicators, is vindicated in the Bible, as is revealed when the biblical text is translated accurately. The mediumistic spiritual teachers and leaders known as seers, prophets and judges certainly received mediumistic information in a spiritual context. This is verified by the use in the biblical text of the Hebrew word for 'trance,' *tardemah*. It is frequently translated as 'deep sleep.'

Of trance, Donald J. Bretherton writes: 'The Hebrew form is tardemah ... [it] is used ... to describe a divinely-induced condition in order to carry out some supernatural purpose or to reveal hidden truth.'[1] Gerhard von Rad further clarifies the accurate meaning of *tardemah*, which signifies a trance state: '*A deep sleep* falls upon man, a kind of magical sleep that completely extinguishes his consciousness.'[2]

R. Davison comments: 'The man is in a trance or deep sleep, a word used elsewhere in the Old Testament to describe a condition in which man receives a vision or message.'[3] The first use of the word 'trance' in the Bible is in Genesis 2:21: 'God caused [Adam] to fall into a deep sleep; and while he was sleeping, he took one of the man's ribs ...'[4]

Further evidence to prove that biblical writers were describing trance states is demonstrated by the following examples:

Genesis 15:12: 'Abram fell into [*tardemah*] a deep sleep and a thick ... darkness came over him. Then [Yahweh] the LORD said to him ...'[5]

Job 4:12–16:

A word was secretly brought to me,
my ears caught a whisper of it.
Amid disquieting dreams in the night,
when [*tardemah*] deep sleep falls on men,
fear and trembling seized me ...
A spirit glided past my face ...
A form stood before my eyes,
and I heard a hushed voice.[6]

(Biblical references to mediumistic trance states are plentiful, this is demonstrated once a person knows which terms to look for. Trance states are being described whenever the biblical text uses a term such as: 'when deep sleep falls on men.' )

Job 33:14–15 (Elihu comforting Job):

For [Yahweh] God does speak – now one way, now another – though man may not perceive it.
[But it can be perceived] In a dream, in a vision of the night, when [*tardemah*/trance] deep sleep falls on men …[7]

1 Samuel 26:12: '… the LORD had put them into a deep sleep [*tardemah*/trance].'[8] This trance state came over King Saul's soldiers, allowing David to spare the life of King Saul and escape.

Daniel 8:15–18 verifies tht Daniel was in a trance state:

While I, Daniel, was watching the vision and trying to understand it, there before me stood one who looked like a man. And I heard a … voice … calling, 'Gabriel, tell this man the meaning of the vision.' …

While he was speaking to me, I was in a deep sleep [*tardemah*/trance], with my face to the ground.[9]

With reference to the condition a mediumistic person must be in, in order to receive communications from Yahweh the otherworldly guide, Bretherton adds:

The Hebrew forms (*tardemah*) and the Greek equivalent (*ékstasis*) are not always used to express the trance-experience as such. This condition is sometimes described in other terms, or is implied by the very context in which it is placed … Several Hebrew terms are used both of 'uncovering' the ears so as to 'hear' that which is concealed by normal hearing and 'uncovering' the 'eyes' in order to 'see' that which is hidden from normal sight.

For instance, the word galah ('to strip,' 'to uncover') when used with 'ozen (ear) means 'to make known,' 'to reveal,' but literally to 'uncover the ear' … and when [Yahweh] God is the subject, to suggest a special revelation … This supernatural form of disclosure in which the recipient is enabled 'to see' … and 'to hear' … finds parallels elsewhere in the Old Testament. When

Samuel was told by [Yahweh] that he was sending to him the man he had chosen to be anointed king, the text reads: 'Now [Yahweh] had told Samuel in his ear a day before Saul came,' that is literally, '[Yahweh] the Lord had uncovered the ear of Samuel.' [1 Samuel 9:15][10]

The biblical descriptions in the above quotation parallel descriptions of clairaudience and clairvoyance. Hans Hertzberg reveals that the accurate translation of the original Hebrew was, in effect, describing clairaudience, proving that the ancient biblical writer was fluent with this form of mediumship: 'Samuel received a revelation, a revelation perceptible to the ear, as the literal rendering of the Hebrew shows.'[11]

In another Old Testament account, describing the siege of the city of Dothan by the king of Syria, the prophet Elisha asked Yahweh to give his fearful servant a clairvoyant vision in order to alleviate his distress. This is translated as a request 'to open the eyes' of the servant. Elisha asked that his servant be granted this form of mediumship to enable him 'to see' the angelic protection that was around them, so that he would calm down: 'Elisha prayed, "O [Yahweh] LORD, open his eyes so that he may see." Then [Yahweh] the LORD opened the servant's eyes, and he looked and saw the hills full of horses and chariots of fire all round Elisha.'[12]

The servant duly experienced a vision. John Skinner in *The Century Bible* states that when the servant's eyes were 'opened,' he saw: 'The greater host, invisible to mortal eyes – horses and chariots of fire that protected Elisha.' This event is documented in 2 Kings 6:17.[13]

In his book *Prophecy and the Prophets in Ancient Israel*, T.H. Robinson writes about the Old Testament prophet Amos. He confirms that the biblical accounts are emphatic that Amos had the ability to clairvoyantly and clairaudiently see and hear non-physical communicators:

One of the visions of Amos ... is introduced with the words: 'I saw;' the rest by the phrase 'Yahweh made me hear.' It appears that in this case the prophet is reporting an experience which is now past ... Just as in one case an abnormal power of sight had been developed in the prophet, so in the other case he has obtained abnormal powers of hearing.[14]

In the Book of Ezekiel, we learn about another prophet who regularly entered into the trance state.[15] Ezekiel 1:1 to 3:22 graphically describes Ezekiel's vision while he was in an altered state of consciousness:

> ... the heavens were opened and I saw visions of God ...
> I looked, and I saw a windstorm coming out of the north – an immense cloud ... surrounded by brilliant light ... in the fire was what looked like four living creatures ... their form was that of a man, but each of them had four faces and four wings ... Then there came a voice ...
> As he spoke, the Spirit came into me ...
> Then I looked, and I saw a hand stretched out to me ...
> Then the Spirit lifted me up ... The hand of the LORD was upon me there, and he said to me ...[16]

To help clarify the above translation, John Weaver informs us that a: 'Vision of God ... is a technical term for an ecstatic vision ... [and] the hand of the Lord [describes] ... the ecstatic state.'[17] An 'ecstatic state' is an altered state of consciousness known today as a mediumistic trance state. Descriptions such as 'the spirit entered into me' and 'the spirit lifted me up' similarly describe mediumistic trance states. Discussing the first three chapters of the Book of Ezekiel, John B. Taylor states: 'All this took place while Ezekiel was in his state of trance.'[18]

In Ezekiel 8:2[19] we read that Ezekiel experienced himself being transported away from Babylon and from the people with whom he was seated. Ezekiel's consciousness or soul observed atrocities being carried out in Jerusalem, which was many miles away from Ezekiel's inert physical body.

This biblical account makes better sense if we use modern-day psychical research terminology to describe Ezekiel's experience. In contemporary language we would say that Ezekiel was in an out-of-body or remote-viewing state. We can also use the ancient shamanic term to describe Ezekiel's experience: he 'soul-journeyed' geographic distances away to observe events.

Ezekiel chapter 8 illustrates the mediumistic nature of Ezekiel's out-of-body experiences during which his soul journeyed to Jerusalem and his visions of angels when he was in exile in Babylon:

> ... while I was sitting in my house [with] ... the elders ... the hand of the Sovereign LORD came upon me there ... I saw a figure like that of a man ... He ... took me ... The Spirit lifted me up between earth and heaven and in visions of God he took me to Jerusalem.[20]

Ezekiel believed that he was both accompanied and guided by an angel or spirit who showed him these sights and visions. The same phenomenon has been repeated throughout the centuries. An 18th-century example of this phenomenon will be provided in the next chapter, which describes Emanuel Swedenborg's accompanied soul-excursions to the many levels and landscapes found in the non-physical realms.

Professor Wheeler Robinson supports the belief that many biblical accounts describe mediumistic experiences. Of Ezekiel, Robinson states:

> Psychical phenomena are described ... he remains dumb after his call, he is to lie in one position for a lengthy period; he is conscious of being transported from Babylon to Jerusalem, that he might describe to the elders what he had seen in the Temple

apparently during a trance state.[21]

Bretherton[22] confirms that enlightened biblical scholars accept that the biblical phrase of 'falling down on the face' describes a visionary experience gained through a mediumistic trance state. These may include 'visions of the glory of the lord.' During the altered state of consciousness, mediumistic prophets experienced visions, heard voices and experienced their consciousness being transported to distant locations. The following biblical writings describe Daniel and Ezekiel in an entranced state, speaking with angels, spirit communicators or otherworldly beings.

Daniel 8:15–18:

While I, Daniel, was watching the vision ... I heard a man's voice ... calling ...

I ... fell prostrate ...

While he was speaking to me, I was in a deep sleep, with my face to the ground. Then he touched me and raised me to my feet.[23]

Daniel 10:7–18:

I, Daniel, was the only one who saw the vision; the men with me did not see it ... So I was left alone, gazing at this great vision; I had no strength left, my face turned deathly pale and I was helpless. Then I heard him speaking and as I listened to him, I fell into a deep sleep, my face to the ground ...

I bowed with my face towards the ground and was speechless. Then one who looked like a man touched my lips, and I opened my mouth and began to speak. I said to the one standing before me, 'I am overcome with anguish because of the vision ... How can I, your servant, talk with you ...? My strength is gone and I can hardly breathe.' ...

Again the one who looked like a man touched me and gave

me strength.[24]

Ezekiel 3:22–24:

The hand of the LORD was upon me [I was in a trance] there, and he said to me; 'Get up and go out to the plain and there I will speak to you.' So I got up and went out to the plain. And the glory of the LORD was standing there [trance] ... and I fell face down [trance].

Then the Spirit came into me and raised me to my feet. He spoke ...[25]

Further phrases such as 'the hand of Yahweh was upon me' have been described by theologians and linguists as 'the onset of ecstasy, visions, trance, seeing with the inner eye or hearing with the inner ear.' During such mediumistic trance experiences, the prophet believes that he or she is in receipt of spiritual inspiration, predictive information and/or experiences soul journeys to the many levels of heaven and its animal inhabitants, human and non-human. David Paterson defines ecstasy as the trance condition. He states: 'Ecstasy [is] more precisely termed trance ... behaviour.'[26]

The shamans are described as ecstatics due to their psycho-spiritual use of the trance state in order to access otherworldly communicators and supernormal knowledge. The results of such experiences helped to develop the shamanic holistic and spiritual worldview. As previously revealed, the beliefs and practices of many of the biblical seers, prophets and judges have strong parallels with those of their more ancient shamanic predecessors. Clearly, mediumistic shamanism was geographically widespread in the ancient world.

Bretherton confirms the use of spiritual mediumship in the Bible:

Thus the 'glory of the Lord,' 'the hand of the Lord,' 'the visions,' 'the word of the Lord' ... the activity of the spirit (breath or wind) are all terms involved in expressing the supernatural activity ... invoking the trance state. This sometimes included the prophet falling down on his face during this condition whilst he was enabled to 'see,' 'hear' and receive ... Such terms as ecstasy, prophetic ecstasy, dream-vision, seeing with the inner eye ... are used at times to disguise the perhaps rather unwelcome fact as far as Biblical scholars are concerned that many prophetic visions were received when the prophet was in a trance condition.[27]

## New Testament Trance Mediumship

Examples of the use of trance states by biblical prophets can also be found in later years, as described in the New Testament. The Hebrew term *tardemah*, which means 'trance,' has a Greek equivalent, *ekstasis*, which is employed by the New Testament scribes.[28] This term, describing the mediumistic trance state, is found frequently in the Acts of the Apostles, providing further evidence of the spiritual focus associated with this form of mediumistic communication.

If it was true in the past, there is no reason to believe that spiritual information cannot be accessed today through the use of the mediumistic trance state. In contemporary times, direct-voice trance-state lectures on many spiritual subjects have been recorded.

An example of the description of trance state is found in Acts 10:9–20:

About noon ... Peter went up on the roof to pray ... he fell into a trance. He saw heaven opened ... Then a voice told him ...

The voice spoke to him a second time ...

While Peter was still thinking about the vision, the Spirit said to him ...[29]

The NIV Bible commentary on Acts 10:10 informs us that: 'Fell into a trance [is] a state of mind ... produced and used to communicate with Peter. It was not merely imagination or a dream. Peter's consciousness was heightened to receive the vision.'[30] Peter attempted to describe his experience in Acts 11:5: 'I was in the city of Joppa praying, and in a trance I saw a vision.'[31]

Some biblical scholars make linguistic distinctions between that which is experienced during the trance state and visions experienced when the medium is not in a trance state. Arguably, a person has to enter some form of altered state of consciousness, however lightly, in order to receive any form of mediumistic experience.

Acts 10:3 uses different terminology to describe Cornelius' *vision*, rather than a *trance*: 'One day at about three in the afternoon he had a vision. He distinctly saw an angel of God, who came to him and said ...'[32] In the Book of Acts this account comes just before the description of Peter's trance state.

With reference to the descriptions of 'trance,' if they are to be translated faithfully, they cannot be interpreted as anything other than descriptions of 'mediumistic trance.' Bretherton confirms this:

> It is significant that the Latin Vulgate renders this passage as follows: *cecidit super eum mentis excessus*. The word *excessus* means *departure from life, decease* or *death*. With *mentis* it means *loss of mental powers* ... or *trance* ... In any case it means implied loss of normal faculty and a condition of suspended consciousness or *trance*. Attempts to rationalise the experience in terms of purely mental impressions or the projection of his inner thoughts ... do not do justice to the actual Greek of the passage, to Jerome's Latin Version, or to the intention of the author of Acts.
>
> The fact that Luke is reputed to have been a physician and is regarded as being very much a part of the authorship of Acts, gives the use of the medical/psychological slant of *ekstasis* special importance in this and other passages in Acts. The writer seems to have taken special care to distinguish Peter's experience [trance] ... from that of Cornelius (Acts 10:1–8) who in a vision [an angel spoke to him] was told to send messengers for Peter.'[33]

Cornelius' experience of an angel speaking to him is described as a vision. That experience was in contrast to Peter's trance-state, when heaven opened and a voice spoke to him and he saw creatures. Mediums today can be observed communicating with non-physical beings in a manner that is markedly different from when the medium is in a direct-voice trance state. Significantly, the distinct features of mediumship are clearly recognized and differentiated in the biblical accounts, which indicates the ancient scribes' fluency with spiritual mediumship.

Paul is described as being in a trance state in Acts 22:17–18: 'When I returned to Jerusalem and was praying at the temple, I fell into a trance and saw [Yahweh] the Lord speaking. "Quick!" he said ... "Leave Jerusalem immediately, because they will not accept your testimony about me."'[34]

The above description of *trance* is contrasted with Paul's initial *visionary* experience. Paul informed others that he had experienced a transformative spiritual vision, after which, Paul converted to Christianity. After Paul's announcement he no longer had Christians persecuted and executed, but instead sought to lead and direct the course of the burgeoning Christian movement. Acts 9:3–8 states: 'As he neared Damascus ... suddenly a light from heaven flashed around him. He fell to the ground [had a vision] and heard a voice ... The men travelling with Saul ... heard the sound but did not see anyone.'[35]

Bretherton states that the Apostle Paul

quite clearly differentiates between what happened to him on the Damascus road, which led to his conversion (Acts 9:1–9) and the trance in the Temple. In the trance he experienced no apparent physical effects. The various descriptions of the Damascus road (Acts 22:6; 26:12; 1 Cor. 15:8) suggest a more objective vision.[36]

Paul's traveling companions did not share the entirety of Paul's experience. We learn that Paul described himself as feeling alone and blinded for several days after the experience. Descriptions such as these clearly demonstrate that the biblical writers possessed fluent-knowledge of different types of mediumistic phenomena and help 'to confirm the point that great care was taken to differentiate between a vision "openly" received and a vision received in a trance state.'[37]

## Jesus' Spiritual Mediumship

The following brief exploration of the psychic aspects of human personality in conjunction with their spiritual focus, provides further evidence that the realm of the spiritual and the science of psychical research are interweaved. The two should not be divorced from one another. Events described in Jesus Christ's life provide evidence that psychic and mediumistic gifts can be closely associated with spirituality. The two are intertwined and should not be divorced from one another.

Certain people possess psychically sensitive faculties which facilitate mediumistic experiences of angelic or spirit manifestations; these encounters can profoundly enhance the spiritual growth of the experiencer and those associated with them.

In the following sections we will explore the psycho-spiritual aspects of the three Synoptic Gospels. These books are believed to be written by Matthew, Mark and Luke, men who were among the twelve disciples of Jesus. The accounts in each of these Synoptic Gospels support and harmonize with each other. As these early writings were written by men who lived with Jesus, they represent some of the most valuable accounts describing the mediumistic life and spiritual ministry of Jesus.

## Dreams as Psychic Tools

Angelic and spirit communications appear to convey both literal and symbolic messages, including predictions. These frequently occur during the sleep state, which is an altered state of consciousness. As noted previously, the Old Testament patriarch

Joseph was famous for his ability to interpret sleep-state experiences. In 1 Samuel 28:6 the prophet Samuel tells King Saul that due to his lack of trust in Yahweh, this angelic, spirit guide is going to punish Saul. Significantly, we are told that Yahweh would no longer use the sleep state or any other means to communicate with Saul: when king Saul 'enquired of [Yahweh] the Lord, [Yahweh] ... did not answer him by dreams or Urim [the divination stones] or prophets [other mediums].'[38] It is important to remember that later translators interpreted the name Yahweh, the angelic or spirit guide, to be 'the Lord,' implying he was God (the Divine). References to Yahweh in the early biblical records may also indicate that this otherworldly messenger(s) was erroneously deified by the ancient Hebrews.

Two New Testament examples of visions and angelic/spirit communications received during the sleep state can be found with regard to Joseph, who became the father of Jesus. Matthew recorded these for posterity in the Book of Matthew. The first experience occurred at the time when Joseph was planning to break off his betrothal to Mary after discovering that she was pregnant.

While Joseph slept, an otherworldly communicator gave him instructions to name his future son Jesus. The non-physical communicator who visited Joseph is called 'the angel of the Lord' in the following translation of Matthew 1:20–21: 'an angel of the Lord appeared to him in a dream and said, "Joseph ... what is conceived in [Mary] is from the Holy Spirit ... you are to give him the name Jesus."'[39]

A second example of an angel or spirit personality appearing during the sleep state follows. This otherworldly being is described as warning Joseph to flee, because King Herod had given the order to have all male babies executed. Matthew 2:13 tells us that 'an angel of the Lord appeared to Joseph in a dream. "Get up," he said, "take the child and ... escape to Egypt."'[40]

Many examples of visions and angelic or spirit communications during the sleep state can be found in both biblical and other historic writings. Matthew, who lived in New Testament times, proves through his writings that he was fully conversant with experience-based beliefs in sleep-state visions and communications from angels and spirits.

## Materializations of Angels and Spirits

The following psychic and mediumistic events are reported to have occurred during Jesus' life and also affected those associated with him. They reveal the spiritual focus of Jesus' mediumship and how his spirituality and mediumship are intertwined. Of necessity, loose definitions of the various categories of psychic experience will be applied to these biblical examples.

The following examples prove, however, that the Gospel writers believed predictive information was conveyed to humankind through mediumistic experiences. Our ancestors believed these messages were sent to humankind by spiritually evolved angels. These encounters were experienced as either manifestations or visions. Typically when confronted with an otherworldly manifestation or vision, the experiencer is described as being afraid and filled with awe.

The following quotation describes the experience of Zechariah, a priest in the Jewish Temple; he and his wife Elizabeth had no children despite their mature years. Luke 1:9–19 tells us that Zechariah

was chosen by lot [Urim and Thummim] according to the custom of the priesthood to go into the temple ... and burn incense ... all the assembled worshippers were praying outside. [The] angel of the Lord appeared to him, standing at the right side of the altar ... the angel said to him: '... Your wife ... will bear you a son ... [to be named] John ... he will be filled with the Holy Spirit ... from birth ... [John] will go on before the Lord, in the spirit and power of Elijah ...'

... The angel [said], 'I am Gabriel.'[41]

Significantly, this non-physical communicator was known as the angel Gabriel, proving that it was not only Yahweh who communicated with people in biblical times. Mary, the young woman who was destined to become the mother of Jesus, also experienced a non-physical communicator believed to be the angel Gabriel. Luke 1:26–31 tells us that: 'God sent the angel Gabriel to Nazareth, a town in Galilee, to a virgin pledged to be married to a man named Joseph ... The angel said to her, "You will be with child and give birth to a son."'[42]

Later, we learn that a group of shepherds visited the infant Jesus, soon after his birth. In the fields near Bethlehem, the shepherds each had a shared, simultaneous experience of a non-physical communicator who told them Jesus had been born. This event is described in Luke 2:9–13:

> An angel of the Lord appeared to them, and the glory of the Lord shone around them ... the angel said to them, '... I bring you good news of great joy ... You will find a baby ... in a manger.' Suddenly a great company of the heavenly host appeared ...[43]

A further example of a vision, which possibly Jesus alone experienced, was that of a dove descending from heaven while Jesus was being baptized by John. (John was the son of Zechariah and Elizabeth mentioned above and had become known as John the Baptist.) The dove symbolizes creativity and peace. Luke 3:21–23 tells us: 'When all the people were being baptised, Jesus was baptised too. And as he was praying, heaven was opened and the Holy Spirit descended on him in bodily form like a dove. And a voice came from heaven ...'[44]

Luke 4:1–13[45] provides a graphic description of the visionary temptation experiences of Jesus. This testimony is generally believed to have originated with Jesus himself, as he was alone when he had these vivid, symbolic visions. Luke recounts the successive temptations put to Jesus by an otherworldly communicator who personified the forces of evil, namely the devil.

The devil is thought to use and manipulate negative human emotions and frailties for his own evil purposes. Jesus experienced these non-physical encounters after he had fasted and meditated alone in the desert. By meditating and fasting, Jesus was sharing in an ancient shamanic custom practiced by mystics, ascetics and other esteemed spiritual teachers since ancient times.

## The Materialization of Moses and Elijah

My research into the event known as 'The Transfiguration on the Mount' proves that the acclaimed spiritual leader known as Jesus Christ was a medium. During this event, Jesus had the experience of speaking to the spirit manifestations of both Moses and Elijah. These mediumistic prophets had both died and passed to spirit centuries before. Jesus' experience on the mountain was witnessed by his close companions, known as his 'disciples.' They shared Jesus' daily life and recorded information about his paranormal abilities for posterity in the Synoptic Gospels.

The psychic and mediumistic experiences of this highly respected spiritual teacher were of paramount importance in his life. They also have enormous parapsychological and spiritual significance for humankind, as the life, practices and spiritual teachings of Jesus gave rise to the Christian religion, in its original, undistorted form. Here again we see evidence of the interwining of the realm of the paranormal and that of spirituality.

Sincere Christians throughout the ages have tried to follow Jesus' practices and teachings. However, due to distortions and mistranslations of the original accounts, resulting in different versions of the Bible much about him has been manipulated and corrupted through the ages. It is reasonable to assume that vitally important uncorrupted early religious texts describing Jesus' practices have also tragically been lost.

One of the several accounts of the 'Transfiguration on the Mount' can be found in Matthew 17:1–8.[46] We are told that three of Jesus' disciples, named Peter, James and John, accompanied Jesus up a mountain. Ascending a mountain must have involved both time and effort; it would have been easier to have simply gone out into the countryside. Importantly, this event echoes the shamanic actions of Moses who, likewise went up a mountain in order to contact the angelic or spirit communicator, Yahweh. Moses received the Ten Commandments from Yahweh at the top of a mountain.

The choice to ascend a mountain by both Jesus and Moses also has close parallels with the practices of the their more ancient shamanic predecessors. As noted earlier they ascended mountains when they wished to speak with angels and spirits. Mountains, hills, trees and steps were believed to possess special properties that enhanced mediumistic experiences; their physical features were symbols that reminded the mediumistic 'prophets' and 'judges' of the stairway that could be ascended or descended by angelic messengers or by those who had passed to the spirit realms.

To verify the accuracy of the Gospel account, religious historians have named the mountain that Jesus' small party climbed together with the intention of making closer contact with the inhabitants of the invisible world. They believe the biblical reports refer to Mount Hermon, which is situated northeast of Caesarea Philippi in present-day Israel.

The disciples described Jesus' face as shining radiantly during the experience on Mount Hermon and they observed that his clothes were as bright as light. Interestingly, Moses' face, many generations before, was also described as shining with radiance after he had been spoken to by Yahweh.

Jesus is described on this occasion as being transformed or 'trans-figured' into a glorified state of light. Manifesting besides Jesus were the two recognizable non-physical spirits of Elijah and Moses. As noted, these earlier mediumistic prophets had died and passed to spirit many years before. The three disciples who accompanied Jesus reported that they heard an ethereal voice from a communicator, declaring that Jesus was his son.

They are then described as entering into an altered state of consciousness; this is indicated by the description: 'they fell face down to the ground.'[47] It is highly significant that Paul's face was not described as radiant after he reported his vision of Jesus on the road to Damascus. The lack of this feature is in sharp contrast to that of both Moses and Jesus. Paul rose to fame as the persecuter of early Jewish Christians. His actions proved to be fruitless against the unstoppable faith. When he ceased having the early Jewish Christians tortured and executed, he sought instead, to lead this burgeoning movement. He was bitterly hated by the disciples who had shared their lives with Jesus. Before they were suppressed and executed, they continued for many years to struggle against Paul who had never lived with Jesus or heard Jesus' spiritual philosophy in person.

The disciples accused Paul of dilluting and suppressing Jesus' vegetarian teachings in order to make the movement more popular to the Romans and other foreigners and Paul's position more powerful! The disciples would not even sit at the table with those who ate animal flesh and bitter disputes with Paul ensued.

Jesus demonstrated boundless compassion for all those victims who suffered as outcasts and much evidence proves this was extended to animals. It is known that James the Just, Jesus' own brother was raised as a vegetarian since birth. Consequently, Jesus' own family followed the widespread vegetarian teachings of his day. Vegetarian teachings were democratized by Pythagoras, followed by many generations of Greek spiritual philosophers also by Hinduism, Buddhism, Jewish sects and cults led by leaders of the Egyptian priesthood.

As a result of travel and popular trade routes vegetarian influences were pervasive in Jesus' day. At the time of Jesus' birth, Hellenism (Greek) had been a long-lasting and dominant force in his land and had comparatively recently been usurped by the contrasting Roman occupation.

To discuss this further would be to digress, however, proof for the vegetarianism of Jesus and the undistorted vegetarian teachings of much of the world's spiritual philosophy is the subject of my forthcoming book.

We have learned that during modern-day mediumistic demonstrations of trance phenomena, mediums, in order to produce the phenomena, receive supportive energy from those who accompany them. Arguably, Jesus selected these three particular disciples because each of them possessed mediumistic gifts. In turn, as mediums, they would have been able to offer the most conducive, supportive energy possible to enable the whole group to experience the physical materializations of two long-'dead' mediumistic prophets.

Evidently, by taking his disciples to witness and participate in this event, Jesus was teaching spiritual mediumship to his followers. Inevitably, Jesus was also teaching his disciples that life continues after physical death. This demonstration of physical mediumship would have helped to prepare the disciples for their future loss of Jesus at his forthcoming crucifixion and for their reunion with Jesus after his physical death.

I will continue to provide proof that there was a whole range of psychic and mediumistic phenomena operating in Jesus' spiritual mediumship and the lives of his companions. The key events surrounding the ministry of this revered spiritual teacher are written in the context of mediumistic and psychic experiences.

For this reason, it is ironic that current mediumistic and psychic experiences, which so closely echo those of the past, as researched today by psychical researchers are condemned as imaginings by materialist parapsychologists. The evidence is clear that people associated with Jesus believed that they received communications from angels, and that Jesus' small party witnessed mediumistic manifestations and communications from the spirit bodies of Elijah and Moses.

Arguably, Jesus did not physically rise from the dead but was seen and heard by his companions after his crucifixion due to their clairvoyant and clairaudient gifts. Jesus demonstrated his psychic abilities on a number of reported occasions, particularly when he gave his disciples predictions and appeared to know the souls of individuals. Jesus predicted that his companions would have the ability to heal people and that they would be followed by other healers in future generations.

Healing can be described as another form of mediumship, as mediums with this gift channel healing energy to the sick rather than conveying spirit or angelic messages. If Jesus knew his disciples could channel healing, it could be argued that he also knew his disciples had other mediumistic abilities. Presumably, they were each chosen by Jesus to continue Jesus' spiritual-mediumistic legacy after his death.

Jesus taught the disciples to teach others that life continues after physical death and that God is the creative parent of all animals, human and non-human. Jesus emphasized this message when he explained that God, as the Father, knows of all events that befall all creatures, even the fall of the tiniest sparrow from the sky. The ever-compassionate Jesus taught that nothing we think or do is unseen or unjudged in some form.

## Extrasensory Perception in the New Testament

The following New Testament examples demonstrate the pronounced and refined psychic and mediumistic sensitivities of Jesus. These equipped him with a profound insight into a person's deepest feelings, allowing him to access the hidden or masked thoughts, emotions and intentions of others. Such abilities might be classified in modern-day terminology as telepathy and/or extrasensory perception. It is also possible that the knowledge Jesus had about others was conveyed to him mediumistically from non-physical communicators.

Certainly, the psychic and mediumistic abilities of Jesus overlapped with his highly evolved spiritual personality and enhanced his spiritual ministry. Arguably, when people become more fully evolved, whole individuals, they come to possess elevated spirituality, accompanied by highly developed psychic and mediumistic gifts. Because people evolve on all levels, however, we find today that some people exhibit remarkable mediumistic and psychic abilities yet are not spiritual people. The reverse is also true: highly spiritual, sensitive people may find that they are not overtly mediumistic.

The following examples demonstrate that Jesus had either mediumistic or psychic awareness of the hidden thoughts of the powerful men known as the Pharisees. Some of these influential men either observed or heard about Jesus' healing abilities and accomplishments. Jesus knew that the Pharisees feared his abilities and his growing influence, and that they secretly accused him of receiving his wonderful healing power from the evil devil known as Satan. Yet they were also aware that the compassionate Jesus alleviated suffering whenever and wherever he could. Jesus was drawn to the downtrodden and the vulnerable, all who were rejected, disrespected or abused by society; he did nothing but good to all vulnerable creatures.

Jesus' mediumistic healing practices echoed those of the ancient shamans. Both sets of healers channeled healing, and both claimed that they had driven out the devil when they accomplished a healing feat. Matthew 12:24–25 tells us that Jesus knew the thoughts of others: 'Jesus knew their [the Pharisees'] thoughts ...' Later he said to the Pharisees: 'If Satan drives out Satan, he is divided against himself.'[48] We are told in Luke 11:17 that when Jesus was healing the sick, while some people were astonished and grateful for his success, others reacted with hostility and suspicion. Sadly, this is typically the nature of many people. Luke's account of this event also emphasizes that Jesus 'knew their thoughts ...'[49]

The following example demonstrates the highly advanced level of Jesus' psychic sensitivity, which gave him the ability to have a deep and profound awareness of the unspoken thoughts and feelings of others. Jesus was described as knowing the emotional contents of people's hearts and, during one particular healing process, he is reported as saying 'Your sins are forgiven,' indicating that the patient was now well.

Immediately he said this, Jesus was aware of the spontaneous reaction his words had evoked in the minds of the Pharisees who observed him. Matthew 9:4–5 states: 'Knowing their thoughts, Jesus said to the Pharisees, "Why do you entertain evil thoughts in your hearts? Which is easier: to say, 'Your sins are forgiven,' or to say, 'Get up and walk?'"'[50] Jesus told them that his words were not blasphemous but that he was simply telling the patient that he was now healed.

Further examples of Jesus' mediumistic or psychic awareness of the hidden thoughts of others can be found in the following quotations:

Mark 2:8: 'Immediately Jesus knew in his spirit that this was what they were thinking ...'[51]

Luke 5:22: 'Jesus knew what they were thinking and asked, "Why are you thinking these things in your hearts?"'[52]

Luke 6:78: 'The Pharisees and the teachers of the law ... watched him closely ... But Jesus knew what they were thinking ...'[53]

## Precognition in the New Testament

The role of prophecy, foretelling the future, is found with regularity in the Synoptic Gospels, which were originally written by a number of Jesus' disciples. Predictions are particularly pronounced in the Book of Matthew, which emphasizes that Jesus' life was the fulfillment of many earlier predictions. This concept was crucial for the Jews in order for them to believe that Jesus was the Messiah foretold in ancient prophecy.

The literal biblical meaning of the word 'prophet' is 'one who speaks for another.' Evidently, the biblical prophet or medium spoke for Yahweh – he or she received Yahweh's guidance and conveyed it to the people. Frequently, the information mediumistically received and conveyed to others contained predictions about future events. Hence, 'to prophesy' is to mediumistically transmit otherworldly guidance to humankind. This process became interrelated with providing accurate predictive guidance.

Precognitive or predictive knowledge can be obtained through the use of psychic abilities or through mediumistic communications from otherworldly beings. Spirits are sometimes described by mediums as being seen in an externalized manner; for example, the spirit may be seen sitting on a chair or standing by a person with whom they wish to communicate.

Alternatively, spirits are described as being seen in the window of the medium's mind, in the form of a miniature image, similar to those of people and animals seen during the sleep state. Alternatively, some mediums see spirit images in the mind's eye in a manner similar to seeing images at the end of a kaleidoscope.

Some people loosely use the word 'clairvoyance' to describe both deep psychic insights and predictive psychic abilities. Alternatively, the term refers to seeing non-physical communicators. The profound level of knowing that is repeatedly documented about Jesus is further illustrated by the following biblical examples, which also tell us that Jesus had the ability to give people information about the future.

Mark 12:41–44 tells us of Jesus' psychic sensitivity and awareness when he caught sight of an old woman contributing a small amount of money to the Temple treasury. Jesus demonstrated that he had a profound insight into the hidden nature of the old lady. He said: 'I tell you the truth, this poor widow has put more into the treasury than all the others. They gave out of their wealth; but she, out of her poverty, put in everything ...'[54] Jesus' insightful psychic sensitivity is recorded in Luke's account of the same incident in Luke 21:1–4.[55]

It is important to remember that there are blurred boundaries between psychic and mediumistic phenomena. It is sometimes difficult to see where one ends and the other begins. Categories and definitions created by psychical researchers and parapsychologists are merely a guide to understanding the phenomena. It is more accurate to clarify the full nature of the psychic or mediumistic experience by speaking to the person who has had the experience.

Many definitions are also colored by the pre-existent mindset of the people who have devised them. Many parapsychologists would not agree that a vision can be put into a person's mind by spirits or angels, yet many people recognize the fact that spirits or angels can inspire our thoughts. Mediumistic symphonies have been written by some of the world's leading composers. Each of whom said their music was produced as a result of hearing the music either during their sleep or when awake; they then simply wrote it down in the form of dictation.

To give one example, Amadeus Mozart's manuscripts are arguably examples of his dictation of the music he heard in his head. There are no crossings-out in his manuscripts, reflecting the fact that he did not change his mind and that the music poured through his pen. Inspiration is arguably another form of mediumship.

In Luke 19:41–44 it is recorded that one day Jesus became saddened. He explained to his disciples that he was upset because he knew that the Jerusalem Temple would be destroyed in the future. Evidently, Jesus demonstrated his ability to offer precognitive knowledge. His prediction regarding the fall of the Jerusalem Temple was proved accurate some time later when it was destroyed by the Roman general Titus.

We can only speculate as to whether Jesus received this information in the form of a mediumistic clairaudient (audible) or clairvoyant (symbolic) message from spirits or angels. Alternatively, Jesus had this precognitive knowledge as a result of his psychic awareness. It can also be argued that spirits and angels inspire humankind's thoughts and offer symbolic pictures and dreams even when they do not talk to us directly. This is, perhaps, an easier form of communication.

The following two reports record Jesus' predictions concerning

Jerusalem. Luke 19:41–44 tells us that as Jesus 'approached Jerusalem and saw the city, he wept over it and said, "The days will come ... when your enemies ... will dash you to the ground."'[56] Matthew 24:1–2 tells us of another prediction: 'Jesus left the temple ... his disciples [brought] his attention to its buildings. "Do you see all these things?" he asked. "... not one stone will be left."'[57]

A further example of Jesus' knowledge of future events is his prediction that Judas, one of his disciples, would betray him to the authorities, and that this would lead to his death through crucifixion. We are told in Matthew 26:2: 'When Jesus had finished saying all these things, he said to his disciples, "As you know, the Passover is two days away – and the Son of Man will be handed over to be crucified."'[58] Jesus' precognitive knowledge regarding his betrayal follows in Mathew verses 21–25:

> ... he said, 'I tell you the truth, one of you will betray me.'
>
> They were very sad ...
>
> Jesus replied, 'The one who has dipped his hand into the bowl with me will betray me ...'
>
> Then Judas, the one who would betray him, said, 'Surely not I, Rabbi?'
>
> Jesus answered, 'Yes, it is you.'[59]

Jesus Christ's precognitive knowledge is described also in the books written by Mark and Luke: see Mark 14:17–21,[60] Luke 22:14[61] and Luke 22:21–23.[62]

Further examples of Jesus' predictive abilities follow. The first is found in Luke 22:47–48: 'While he was still speaking a crowd came up, and the man who was called Judas, one of the Twelve, was leading them. He approached Jesus to kiss him, but Jesus asked him, "Judas, are you betraying the Son of Man with a kiss?"'[63] Jesus had already informed his disciples that soon Judas would betray him. Therefore, he knew that Judas' kiss was the agreed signal to identify him to the authorities for arrest. Another example is found in

Matthew 26:45–48: 'Then he returned to the disciples and said to them, "... the hour is near, and the Son of Man is betrayed ... Here comes my betrayer!" ... Now the betrayer had arranged a signal ... "The one I kiss is the man; arrest him."'[64] The historic records in Mark 14:41–43 also confirm the above accounts.[65]

The following discussion draws attention to the frequent use of terms such as 'filled with the Holy Spirit' or 'the Spirit came upon him' and 'experiences of the Holy Spirit.' Through the use of these phrases, the ancient writers believed that they authenticated the spirituality of the communications conveyed to a mediumistic prophet from an angel or spirit.

Luke demonstrates the predictive abilities of Simeon, an old man who knew before meeting the infant Jesus and again, later, when he held the baby, that Jesus would become an eminent spiritual teacher. This event is described in Luke 2:25–28:

> Now there was a man in Jerusalem called Simeon, who was righteous and devout. He was waiting for the consolation of Israel, and the Holy Spirit was upon him. It had been revealed to him by the Holy Spirit that he would not die before he had seen the Lord's Christ. Moved by the Spirit he went into the temple ... When the parents brought in the child Jesus ... Simeon took him in his arms and praised God.[66]

Matthew 21:1–5 describes the adult Jesus instructing two of his disciples where and when they would find both a colt and a donkey. He described the predicted scene with great accuracy. '[Jesus said:] "Go to the village ahead of you, and at once you will find a donkey tied there, with her colt by her." ... This took place to fulfil what was spoken through the prophet.'[67]

At the close of Jesus' earthly spiritual ministry, he made further predictive references, known as prophecy. These foretold of his last days on earth, the future fate of his disciples immediately after his death, and their later works beyond that. Matthew 10:19 tells us that

Jesus told the disciples that they would have spirits or angels mediumistically speaking through them when they were arrested. This
again confirms that the disciples had mediumistic faculties. Jesus'
prediction indicates their future direct-voice trance mediumship:
'But when they arrest you do not worry what to say ... for it will not
be you speaking, but the Spirit ... speaking through you.'[68]

During the event known as the Last Supper, Jesus gave predictions to those who ate and drank with him regarding events
associated with his forthcoming death. He predicted that his body
and blood would be shed, and compared his body and blood to the
bread that was being broken and the red wine that was being drunk.
The Gospels of Luke and Matthew also record Jesus' demonstrations
of precognitive knowledge during the final days of his spiritual
ministry – in Luke 22:34: 'I tell you, Peter, before the cock crows
today you will deny three times that you know me,'[69] and in
Matthew 26:31: 'Jesus told them, "This very night you will all fall
away on account of me."'[70]

Other psychic abilities of Jesus are reported in the writings of his
disciples. They were obviously familiar with the psychic phenomena
that engulfed Jesus'life, including examples of his psychokinetic,
levitation, and healing abilities. These followers, who lived with
Jesus, inform us that crowds often observed these phenomena.

A person with psychokinetic abilities can affect the movement of
an object with their mind, causing it to move or stop moving.
Levitation abilities involve ascension, such as a person rising off the
ground. These psychic phenomena have been observed and recorded
of others throughout the centuries and have been videoed in more
recent years by psychical researchers. Matthew 8:23–27[71] describes
Jesus' psychokinetic ability to calm a storm; Matthew 14:25[72] tells of
Jesus' levitation abilities as he walked on water; and Luke 24:50–53[73]
also confirms Jesus' levitation abilities as he is described as
ascending to heaven.

Jesus' acclaimed ability to heal the sick was evidently a mediumistic ability. He channeled healing energy into the recipient rather

than channeling otherworldly communications to them. Certainly, mediumistic healing has an intrinsic spiritual focus due to the obvious spirituality and compassion involved in the desire to heal another's pains.

Matthew 15:30 has preserved for posterity the record of Jesus' mediumistic healing phenomena: 'Great crowds came to him, bringing the lame, the blind, the crippled, the mute and many others, and laid them at his feet; and he healed them.'[74] Jesus predicted that his (mediumistic) disciples and later generations of (mediumistic) people would also perform mediumistic spiritual healing. All later generations of mediumistic spiritual healers are following Jesus' example in practicing this form of mediumship.

It is of enormous significance that probably the most momentous events in the spiritual ministry of Jesus are described in the many reports of people having experiences of him after his physical death from crucifixion. In the context of psychical research, those people who experienced Jesus after his physical death seem to have provided convincing experiential testimonies of clairaudience and clairvoyance.

Alternatively, their transformative spiritual mediumistic accounts may have been describing the materialization or manifestation of the non-physical Jesus who appeared in a recognizable etheric form, known as a spirit or ghost. These experiences had parallels with the materialization of Moses and Elijah during the Transfiguration on the Mount.

The following three quotations demonstrate the mediumistic experiences of Jesus' companions after his physical death:

Luke 24:13–30:

... two of them were going to a village ... They were talking ... about everything that had happened ... Jesus himself came up and walked along with them; but they were kept from recognising him ...

When he was at the table with them ... their eyes were opened and they recognised him, and he disappeared from their sight.[75]

Luke 24:36–45:

> While they were still talking about this, Jesus himself stood among them and said to them, 'Peace be with you.' They were startled and frightened, thinking they saw a ghost ...[76]

Mark 16:9–20:

> [After death] Jesus ... appeared first to Mary Magdalene ... When they heard that Jesus was alive and that she had seen him, they did not believe it.
>
> Afterwards Jesus appeared in a different form to two of them ... These ... reported it to the rest; but they did not believe them either.
>
> Later Jesus appeared to the Eleven as they were eating; he rebuked them for their lack of faith and their stubborn refusal to believe those who had seen him after [his death] ...
>
> Then the disciples went out and preached everywhere, and the Lord worked with them and confirmed his word by the signs that accompanied it.[77]

These sightings and conversations with Jesus were experienced by groups of people and individuals alike. In the main, they included those who were closest to Jesus during his physical life.

Later biblical translators have used the word 'resurrected' to describe Jesus' physical return after his physical death. Unfortunately, the use of this word has grossly distorted our understanding of these reports, which actually describe mediumistic experiences proving life continues after physical death.

The result of this inaccurate translation has caused many people around the world to have confused beliefs. Some Christians and non-Christians have been left with the false belief that Jesus alone was able to live after physical death; others have the false belief that because Jesus was murdered everyone has gained immortality. Evidently, demonstrated by the Transfiguration on the Mount, Jesus was trying to teach humanity that life continues for humans and all other creatures after physical death.

He was emphatic that the creative parent God is ever aware of the sorrows of any member of his earth family, including the smallest sparrow. Jesus taught that God knows of the most minute event in the lives of all of his creation which includes all animals, human and non-human, birds, aquatic creatures and so forth.

Arguably, the Transfiguration on the Mount, involving the manifestation of the surviving spirit intelligences of the physically long-dead Moses and Elijah, gave emotional support to Jesus before his transition to the non-physical realms. It also provided a demonstration of physical phenomena to his mediumistic disciples who were being trained by Jesus to teach humanity, after Jesus' physical death. The materialization of these two physically recogniseable, long dead, mediumistic, spiritual prophets was a prelude to the disciples' experiences of Jesus after he passed to spirit.

Arguably, an intrinsic feature of Jesus' teachings was to provide evidence of survival after physical death. Importantly, a person's misdeeds would have future consequences in relation to the 'many mansions' they would encounter in the after death realms. The disciples sought to take this message, along with Jesus' other compassionate spiritual teachings, to the wider populace.

If Jesus had shown boundless love and compassion for social outcasts, how much more would he have had for homeless, vulnerable, innocent people and animals? Schooled with years of highly elevated spiritual tuition from Jesus himself and now certain that life continues after physical death, equipped the disciples to deliver Jesus' message, 'to do no harm to any living creature,' as the benevolent creator-parent God loves His/Her entire family!

Jesus obviously wanted his disciples to participate in, and learn from, these experiences. They learned that spirit communicators speak to humankind and that life continues after physical death. Jesus did not tell his disciples, "If you believe in me you will live after physical death," and "if you do not, you will not survive physical death." Rather he emphasized that the compassionate and ever-merciful parent God knows the hearts and emotions of all members of his creature family, and every event in their lives.

Jesus wanted his disciples to know and teach others that Moses and Elijah had survived physical death. (Significantly, neither of these mediumistic prophets knew Jesus as they had lived many years before his birth. This fact indicates that the spirits or consciousness of the long dead can observe those who are still in the material body.) Jesus taught his disciples that they too would go to heaven after their death. Indeed he told them that he would take them to heaven, thereby teaching that heaven was not exclusively for him. Through this promise, Jesus continued the ancient shamanic tradition. The mediumistic shamans believed that they, too, escorted the souls of the dead to the invisible realms; they were adepts at soul-journey exploits.

Evidently, Jesus' teachings have been misinterpreted over the years by the powerful organized, institutionalized church. Historically, the church manipulated and distorted Jesus' spiritual ministry. Its leaders claimed that only through the church could people access Jesus, and only through Jesus could a person go to heaven. This gave the institutionalized church an all-powerful monopoly on Jesus and heaven. In previous historic periods, the church asked people to pay money to the clergy in order to buy letters that acted as tickets to heaven. Such is the power of distortion of the original scriptures.

To provide one crucial example of the 'lost original Christianity' that is typically not practiced today: the church, through both Paul and the Roman usurpation of this growing religion, quashed knowledge of the vegetarianism of Jesus and his family. It is a fact that Jesus and his siblings were vegetarians since birth. This compassionate practice was widespread across the ancient world.

Vegetarianism had spread across borders, oceans and continents, promoted in the Hindu scriptures known as the Vedas, in Buddhism, in Jewish cults, in Egyptian teachings and by a succession of great Greek spiritual philosophers, to name but a few influences. The many generations of vegetarian Greek spiritual philosophers followed the teachings of Pythagoras and those who had taught him. These included Pherecydes/Pherekydes and his Egyptian teachers of Thales.

Vegetarianism had been adopted by some Jewish sects due to their insightful interpretation of the original scriptures including the records in Genesis when God uttered his preferred commands to Adam and Eve, for humanity to live vegetarian lives. The 8th century prophets had also believed they had been commanded by God to condemn all forms of animal sacrifice, revealing God's compassion for all His/Her family.

The term Essene is believed to be an umbrella term for a number of Jewish sects, some of whom were vegetarian. Jesus' family was obviously an adherent of vegetarianism. There was a strong Greek/Hellenic influence in the lands of Jesus before his birth, where extensive trade routes brought in cultural influences from other countries.

Those people throughout the ancient world who practiced vegetarianism were confronted with an alien culture whose traditions were set in sharp contrast to their own compassionate lifestyle. This was the rapidly expanding, fierce Roman empire. Romans were gross animal flesh eaters. Rome and Paul usurped Christianity at a very early stage. The disciples of Jesus hated Paul for this and for Paul's corruptions and distortions of Jesus' original teachings and practices. They were keenly aware that Paul, the self-appointed apostle, had never known or lived with Jesus, nor had Paul learned Jesus' compassionate message as they had done.

Over the centuries, animal genocide has become a multibillion-dollar industry. Billions of our living, breathing animal brethren are slaughtered every year. Their mass murder has become a profitable production line. These thinking, feeling, emotional, traumatized creatures are treated like inanimate commodities, not the sentient flesh-and-blood relatives they are. They suffer wasted lives of pain, misery, heartbreak and grief, all to provide their bodies for people's dinner plates.

We are taught today by mediums, as we were by Jesus, that life continues after physical death. This being so, a person's thoughts and actions in the material life do not die either. They have inescapable consequences, shaping the ideo-plastic, non-physical landscapes encountered after death. We are taught that like attracts like. Jesus described heaven as 'many houses' or as a 'house' having 'many rooms.'' This can be interpreted to mean that many levels and landscapes exist in the non-physical realm. Near-death experiencers and mediums in trance describe this alternate world in a similar way. Jesus also taught his disciples that God knew everything about the lives of His/Her creation, down to the life of the smallest bird. Consequently, God as parent, in His/Her compassion, empathizes with and shares in the suffering of all His/Her creatures.

Near-death experiencers and mediums in trance also talk of life reviews. Throughout these, a person feels the pains they have inflicted during their earthly lifetime on any other creature, whether by neglect, thought or deed. This perfect form of justice is in harmony with Jesus' teachings. However, the profundity of these teachings can be better understood today.

In the past, people would not have understood about the deeper significance of the life reviews which near-death experiencers witness. During these, each person sees their true self and is drawn to a matching landscape. As like attracts like to it, our earthly life determines the nature of the non-physical landscape in which we will find ourselves after death.

Certainly, the integrity of human testimonies on this matter should be accepted. Deathbed visions of loved ones and similar phenomena reveal recurring features or patterns of experience. These have been reported from the beginning of time to the present day, crossing all cultures and global boundaries.

Consequently, many historic accounts echo present-day observable spiritual mediumship and other transformative spiritual experiences. The further evidence provided in the historic accounts of the New Testament vindicates the authenticity of the ancient testimonies of communication between the physical and non-physical realms, as one interpenetrates the other.

The mediumistic experiences of the disciples after Jesus' death, in which they saw and spoke with him, had a transformative spiritual impact on them: '[They] went out and preached everywhere, and the Lord worked with them and confirmed his word by the signs that accompanied it.'[78] We are told that 'signs and wonders' supported the spiritual teachings of Jesus' followers. Notably, their 'signs and wonders' would have been demonstrations of psychic and mediumistic phenomena, echoing those produced by Jesus to edify his disciples.

The disciples would have become familiar with psychic and mediumistic phenomena as these were integral to the life and spiritual teachings of Jesus. This again establishes the fact that the realm of the paranormal, that of the psychic and mediumistic, is closely interlaced with the realm of humankind's evolving religious quest.

Core themes underlying Jesus' life and spiritual teachings prove that Jesus had a very close relationship with the invisible celestial world. He was encouraged by the non-physical inhabitants of this after-death realm. Jesus also had knowledge of the hierarchical landscapes experienced by all creatures after death.

During his spiritual-mediumistic ministry, he taught: 'I do nothing on my own but speak just what the Father has taught me.'[79] 'I am telling you what I have seen in my Father's presence.'[80] 'I know that his command leads to eternal life. So whatever I say is just what the Father has told me to say.'[81] 'In my Father's house are many rooms ... I will come back and take you to be with me.'[82] Jesus offered to act as the disciples' escort when it was their time to make their transition to the imperceptible realms.

We have seen throughout this book that many ancient biblical writers recorded for posterity mediumistic transmissions of information that were an integral part of the prophets' lives. 'Yahweh' was the name usually given to the non-physical communicator, but various angels were also cited as giving information to the people, some of whom were associated with Jesus. Increasingly, these countless communications from a variety of non-physical communicators were ascribed to one single communicator, who became known as the Holy Spirit or Spirit of Truth.

Jesus taught that the 'Holy Spirit' would act as a 'Counselor,' offering future generations of humankind spiritual guidance from the non-physical dimension. Biblical translators used phrases such as 'Holy Spirit' and 'the Spirit of Truth' in a confused attempt to depict the beings to whom Jesus referred. The institutionalized church teaches that Jesus was referring to a singular non-physical angel or spirit. The following discussion offers a comprehensive and improved insight into Jesus' teachings.

Evidently, Jesus taught the concept that spiritually elevated angelic or spirit personalities could be contacted mediumistically by all, throughout future centuries. Certainly, he taught the value of genuine spiritual mediumship. It is important to remember that Jesus himself spoke with at least two spirit personalities, those of Moses and Elijah.

Jesus was aware that angels and spirits can communicate with all animals, human and animal alike, and this was the purpose of the demonstration for the disciples known as the Transfiguration on the Mount. The Holy Spirit or Spirits is/are therefore an umbrella term for all those elevated souls who seek to communicate in order to advance human spirituality.

Clearly, Jesus taught that all of humanity can receive spiritual guidance and inspiration from elevated spiritual guides. At Christmas time in particular, people sing hymns about the 'Holy Counselor' and the 'Spirit of Truth.' It appears that most people are unaware of the true meaning of the concept they are singing about. The term 'Holy Counselor' indicates a singular being, whereas the term the 'Spirit of Truth' appears to refer to those spiritually elevated truthful beings who speak to humanity.

Significantly, Jesus also taught humanity about the interrelatedness and therefore the interdependent nature of all of creation, that each of us and God too dwells in the smallest of creatures. God therefore knows the smallest detail about the smallest creature. The ancient shamans too believed in the concept of interrelatedness, and recent discoveries in quantum physics are proving this profound insight to be true. In the passage quoted below, Jesus explains this concept while teaching about the non-physical, spiritually elevated angel or spirit communicators:

> I will ask the Father and he will give you another [other] Counsellor[s] to be with you for ever – the Spirit of truth. The world cannot accept him [them], because it neither sees him [them] nor knows him [them]. But you know him, for he lives within you and will be in you. I will not leave you as orphans; I will come to you. Before long, the world will not see me any more, but you will see me ... you will realise that I am in my Father, and you are in me, and I am in you ...
>
> But the Counsellor, the Holy Spirit, whom the Father will send in my name, will teach you all things and will remind you of everything I have said to you.[83]

As commented upon earlier, biblical translators interpreted the ancient scripts to mean the Holy Spirit and the Spirit of Truth. The ancient writers, closer to actual events, were evidently describing non-physical, spiritually elevated communicators who deliver mediumistic information to humankind. The concept of the Holy Spirit, the Spirit of Truth, was arguably adopted to authenticate spiritually orientated mediumship which provided spiritual insights and guidance.[84]

Over the centuries, the organized Christian church has accepted that the Holy Spirit, also named the Holy Ghost, is a non-physical spiritual communicator who can be accessed by spiritually orientated mediumistic individuals. Ironically, today, when mediums believe they have accessed spiritual guidance from such a being or beings, many Christians react with hostility towards them. Their confused ignorance is highlighted when such prejudiced people will not listen to or evaluate the spiritual philosophy received.

It appears that an unfortunate confusion has developed, blurring together several concepts. The first is the concept prohibiting the worship of more than one God. The second relates to accessing more than one highly spiritually evolved non-physical angelic or spirit communicator. The third is the ancient, mistaken pattern of deification of non-physical communicators, confusing them with a god due to their otherworldly nature.

Historically, as understanding grew, people increasingly spoke of non-physical communicators as God's messengers. Unfortunately, the mistaken deification of spirit messengers was perpetuated by biblical translators who erroneously omitted the original term 'angel of the lord' and replaced it with God (the Divine). They had now named that being God (the Divine). This leaves people throughout the centuries and today believing that the ancients regularly held audible conversations with God, who also materialized for all to see.

Throughout the millennia, a number of fortunate people have reported profound spiritual experiences of the ineffable oneness of all of creation. They experience the fact that all of creation is interdependent, interrelated and indeed part of one another. To hurt an animal, bird or tree is, therefore, to hurt ourselves and the parent, God. Millions of global near-death experiencers report that during their life review they felt the emotional and physical pains of other creatures who had been adversely affected by their previous thoughts, actions and inactions.

Similarly, Jesus taught that the loving parent God empathized with the plight of all His/Her creation. He was emphatic that the suffering of animals does not go unnoticed by the invisible realm. This is also the subject of many present-day direct-voice trance lectures. Animals think, dream and demonstrate the emotions of a vulnerable, innocent child throughout the entirety of their lives. The celestial world can empathize with animals' emotions and they, too, can have their emotions uplifted by spiritually elevated angels or spirits.

Humankind's ancestors were once four-legged creatures, and humans, like other animals, continue to evolve physically, mentally, spiritually and emotionally. Many animals show more love, loyalty and devotion than many humans. Dogs, for example, have laid down their lives to save their beloved owners. Acts of self-sacrifice in warfare are rewarded with the Victoria Cross in the United Kingdom, but similar medals have been awarded to animals, posthumously, who have also selflessly given their lives for others.

Cosmologists tell us that all of creation is made of the same original cosmic source material derived from the Big Bang. Consequently, experiences of the ineffable oneness of all of creation are indeed scientifically accurate. Mediums in trance and near-death experiencers describe their visits to populated, non-physical landscapes inhabited by the whole range of animals, birds, trees, plants and spirit people. Logically, if these diversely inhabited landscapes are not an after-death reality, we humans at death would arrive in ugly, deserted, barren, non-physical landscapes. In the next chapter I will discuss experiences of these myriads of non-physical regions.

## The Ancient Semitic Cultural Heritage

The following information provides a brief cultural background to the beliefs about the invisible realms which were an integral part of Jesus' Hebrew heritage. Jesus' ancient Semitic ancestors believed that diverse types of spirits lived on in some form after physical death and that they were more informed than people in the physical body. The concept of monotheism burgeoned around 1000 BC and, progressively, people stopped worshipping other gods. However, they continued to hold on to their experience-based beliefs in the existence of spirit and angel communicators.

It has been shown that throughout successive generations, the prophets who taught monotheism each believed that Yahweh was their ongoing non-physical communicator. Over the centuries and including today, the same is the case: many mediums believe that they have a predominant spirit guide. Spirit and angelic communicators are not necessarily thought of as Yahweh, nor are they conceptually confused with God, the Divine.

Often when a medium is in trance, the non-physical communicator informs those listening that having a name reflects ego and as a consequence is unimportant. As a result, the communicator's name is not always given; it is the spiritual message that matters. If this is the case today, it has arguably been the case historically too. Many communicators, over many generations, may have been given the same umbrella name, notably that of Yahweh.

Both in the past and today a person has to evaluate the spirituality of the information conveyed through spiritual mediumship. If the message conveys forgiveness, love and compassion for all creatures, each of whom are interrelated, then it has spiritual contents. If the idea of violence, harm or neglect to any creature, in any form, is transmitted, then the non-physical communicator should be totally ignored and the message discarded.

Also it is worth remembering that contemporary observable mediumistic demonstrations show us that there are many types of communications that can be unwittingly accessed. Not all communications are from surviving personalities.

Inevitably, sincere spiritual mediums over time gain some experience of the otherworldly realms, much in the same way as our shamanic predecessors. However, few modern day mediums are similarly adept at soul journeying to this labyrinthine co-existent world. Contemporary mediums and their sitters also need to be aware of the existence of malevolent and false communicators and psychic memory systems.

Likewise, the advice found in 1 John 4:1–6, one of the later books of the New Testament, is that people should discern between non-spiritual communicators and those who offer elevated, enlightened spiritual and ethical guidance. This provides further evidence that historic spiritual teachers either practiced or were fully conversant with all the features of spiritual mediumship:

Dear friends, do not believe every spirit, but test the spirits to see whether they are from God, because many false prophets have gone out into the world. This is how you can recognise the Spirit of God ...

This is how we recognise the Spirit of truth and the spirit of falsehood.[85]

Paul demonstrated his fluency with diverse forms of spiritually orientated mediumship. He saw mediumship as a 'spiritual gift' or a 'gift of the spirit.' He offered guidance and warnings regarding how easy it is to be misled by the wrong non-physical communicators. Just as there are many 'rooms/mansions' or levels in the non-physical spheres, equally there are diverse inhabitants there, who range from the most spiritual to the most depraved.

Paul tells us in 1 Corinthians 12:1–11:

Now about spiritual gifts ... I do not want you to be ignorant. You know that when you were pagans ... you were ... led astray to mute idols. Therefore I tell you that no-one who is speaking by the Spirit of God says, 'Jesus be cursed,' and no-one can say, 'Jesus is Lord,' except by the Holy Spirit.

There are different kinds of gifts, but the same Spirit. There are different kinds of service, but the same Lord. There are different kinds of working, but the same God works all of them in all men.

Now to each one the manifestation of the Spirit is given for the common good. To one there is given through the Spirit the message of wisdom, to another the message of knowledge by means of the same Spirit, to another faith by the same Spirit, to another gifts of healing by that one Spirit, to another miraculous powers, to another prophecy, to another distinguishing between spirits, to another speaking in different kinds of tongues, and to still another the interpretation of tongues.[86]

Significantly, Paul, taught his followers fluency with spiritual mediumship. He informed them that many non-physical communicators make contact through mediumship and that they should be evaluated for their level of spirituality. Paul warned that those communicators who taught love were good and that those who did not should not be trusted. The terminology used by Paul is: 'there is given through the Spirit ... [the gift of] distinguishing between spirits.' 'Spirit' may have originally been a plural term for those who help to distinguish between the many levels of good and bad spirits.

## Summing-Up

This biblical research has proven that, according to many Old and New Testament accounts, the Semites were schooled in the many features of mediumship. Many of the populace were either adept at mediumship themselves or fluent with this practice as a means of obtaining spiritual guidance. Spiritual guidance and predictive information was frequently conveyed through varying depths of altered states of consciousness known as trance, the sleep state, materializations and visions.

Evidently, as the mediums evolved spiritually throughout the ages, so did their interpretation of the teachings they received. This was reflected in their maturing understanding of their encounters with spirits and angels. However, due to human misinterpretations, deliberate and otherwise, spiritualization is not inevitably a totally progressive process, but one that is characterized by features of ebb and flow; sometimes different human cultures regress spiritually.

Many experiences of spirits and angels have had a transformative spiritual impact on of the spiritual education of humankind. This continues today through the work of modern spiritually orientated mediums and through understanding the profoundly descriptive testimonies of near-death experiencers. This book contributes to bridging the divide between the realm of parapsychology and the realm of human testimonies which confirm the authenticity of spiritual mediumship.

*Chapter 11*

# The Medium Emanuel Swedenborg

Emanuel Swedenborg was an 18th-century writer and inventor who over the course of his life became well acquainted with royalty, emperors and heads of state. During the last 30 years of his life he described to the rulers of Europe both his soul-journey excursions to the non-physical planes and his experiences of angels visiting him.

Swedenborg is an excellent example of more contemporary mediumship due to his fine intelligence and the great extent of his ethereal encounters. This genius analyzed his experiences of the meta-geographic realms (the realms beyond the threshold of ordinary three-dimensional time and space) into three classifications: 'Heaven,' 'Hell,' and 'the Intermediate Realms.'

Swedenborg had lengthy discussions with the angels he encountered in these multifaceted realms. Some of them informed him that in the distant past they had once lived physical lives on earth, but due to their spiritual progression they had ultimately become angels.

John Klimo paints a vivid picture of this prolific writer:

One of the true giants of channelling literature [is this] Swedish scientist turned mystic ... A middle-aged, well-respected scientist with nearly one hundred publications to his credit, Swedenborg seemed in every way a well-adjusted professional. He wrote, at age fifty-six, that he began to have extremely vivid and prolonged visions, voices, sojourns and visitations. By his own prolific accounts, he probably spent more hours channelling than anyone before him. Time and again, he reported angels visited him and also took him in his spiritual body into the non-physical realm.[1]

Swedenborg believed that he was taught by angels, some of whom he described as spirits. These angels asked him to record the spiritual philosophy which he learned and to describe the after-death realms for the benefit of humankind. They taught him that life is a continuous process and that each animal, human and non-human, makes its transition at death from the physical plane to the non-physical planes.

He was made aware that this transition is part of a natural law. As a result of his soul-journey excursions and conversations with otherworldly beings, Swedenborg accumulated a vast amount of information about the countless levels of the non-physical dimension and the natural laws which govern it. He supplemented the angels' teachings with his own experience-based insights and the knowledge he received from his meditations and studies.

As a result of Swedenborg's transformative spiritual-mediumistic experiences, yet another religious movement was born. Swedenborg called his movement the New Church or the Church of the New Jerusalem.[2] The New Church is dedicated to the dissemination of the spiritual philosophy and information about life after physical death that he believed was communicated to him from angelic and surviving personalities inhabiting the invisible spheres.

When Swedenborg began teaching others all that he learned, it was not his original intention to establish an alternative religious movement. However, after receiving further angelic and spirit teachings, he passionately came to believe that his mission was to cleanse people's minds. His task was to free people from the errors, distortions, corruptions, dogmas and doctrines that had accumulated over the millennia among the teachings of the institutionalized church.

Progressively, Swedenborg understood that the institutionalization and organization of many of the world's religions had resulted in the suppression of a great deal of the original spiritual philosophies. He was taught that spiritual truths can still be found at the core of the world's spiritual philosophies (religions) and that each is an expression of the Divine. However, he learned that the profound truths have become clouded by the dogmas and corruptions devised by leaders of organized religious institutions. Consequently, we are dealing with a lost Christianity and many other lost and clouded religions.

The earlier discussions of biblical mistranslations verify the claims of Swedenborg's angelic teachers. They explained that misunderstandings regarding spiritual teachings arose when spiritually revealed messages were distorted and organized into official compilations by translators who expressed the beliefs of those in power. People were then falsely informed that the writings were the exact, undistorted word of God.

Arguably, it these spiritually orientated mediumistic messages were interpreted at the level of understanding of the prophetic medium who received them, and again at the current level of human spiritual maturity. They would have been further influenced by the cultural, political and religious climate of the historic epoch in which the otherworldly messages were received and disseminated. Consequently, it would appear to be impossible for humanity to receive the undistorted word of God due to inevitable human interpretation.

Communications from angelic and spirit beings may inadvertently be distorted by the medium's sensory filters when he or she tries to make sense of their clairaudient, clairvoyant or visionary experience. As a consequence, over the millennia, the original message and its deepest meaning, already unwittingly corrupted, can become increasingly lost and out of date – if it is not accurately and dynamically reinterpreted at each stage of humankind's evolution in spiritual understanding.

There is also the question of which celestial communicator is conveying the information. The source needs to be evaluated as to the spirit's level of spirituality, as they could be from any of the countless hierarchical levels found in the non-physical world.

Swedenborg learned from his angelic communicators that they

wished to encourage spiritual maturity and spiritual liberation among the earth's populace. This would greatly assist all human beings as they seek to understand the authentic spiritual truths. Swedenborg's otherworldly communicators guided him to teach the universality of spiritual thought. The current ecumenical movement shares this objective, as it progressively works to weld all members of different world religions together. True spirituality is in harmony with the most elevated spiritual teachings, at this highest level aspects of all religions can potentially merge.

The following pages will provide a valuable summary of Swedenborg's voluminous writings which detail his soul journey experiences to the many levels of the non-physical world and the teachings of its inhabitants. As a result of approximately three decades of otherworldly experiences, Swedenborg compiled an encyclopedic body of writings detailing the advanced spiritual philosophy which he had been taught. This spiritual philosophy also contains many of Swedenborg's experience-based spiritual insights, some of which, in turn, contributed to his theoretical and scientific discoveries.

Due to the enigmatic nature of the broad range of Swedenborg's experiences he has been described as a sage, a prophet, a seer, a mystic and a medium. He has been described as a medium because he demonstrated clairvoyant, clairaudient and soul-journey abilities. However, he can be described as a spiritual medium of the highest order. He was also a leading 18th-century psychical researcher, exploring beyond the physical realm into that of the non-physical. His first objective in this inadequately researched area was to seek out the location of the soul in the physical body.

Swedenborg uses the term 'spiritual realms' in his writings to describe the many levels or landscapes he encountered during his soul-journeys to the implicit, unseen, non-physical continents. His experiences have many parallels with the soul-journeys described by the shamans of antiquity and likewise with that of Muhammad, the prophet of Islam, who experienced a soul-journey to Jerusalem.

As a result of Swedenborg's soul journey explorations of these unknown metaphysical shores Swedenborg returned with fascinating details about the nature of existence after physical death.

Swedenborg taught that the landscapes encountered after death manifest in accordance with the deepest levels of a person's psyche. The mental, emotional and spiritual state of the person arriving in the ethereal spheres attracts to it an environment and spirit inhabitants in keeping with it. The type of spirit people and animals met, and the landscapes encountered, can be perceived as resulting from a natural law, representing a perfect form of divine justice as opposed to wrathful, vengeful punishment. The scenarios we find ourselves in are a direct consequence of our predominant personality, a result of our deeds and thoughts during our physical existence.

The reports of near-death experiencers and the information provided during mediumistic direct-voice trance lectures both independently describe the non-physical landscapes in the same way. They confirm that these meta-geographic realms are fluid in the sense that they are malleable to thought (ideoplastic), but become objective realities once a person has entered them. The predominant aspects of a person's personality, thoughts and feelings, whether good or bad, become externalized and made manifest.

Like a mirror, the landscape reflects the true nature of a person – their soul – rather than the social facade or mask they have worn during their earthly life. Progression to improved landscapes is possible, however, in accordance with a person's spiritual growth. This is achieved through the work they do while based in any one of these countless fluid landscapes. We learn that a person can be in the most hell-like landscape or in the most sublime or at any relevant point on the gradient of hierarchical realms.

## Historical Background

Emanuel Swedenborg was born on 29 January 1688 in Stockholm, Sweden. His father, Jesper Svedberg, was raised among a farming community based in Dalecarlia that was known for its strong, independent spirit. Jesper had studied theology at the universities of Lund and Uppsala, had traveled extensively in Europe, and held successive positions as court chaplain, Dean of Uppsala and Bishop of Skara. Swedenborg's mother was Sara Behm, who had married Jesper in 1683. Swedenborg's maternal grandfather was a wealthy mine owner. Due to his family's contributions to society they were ennobled and the family name was changed from Svedberg to Swedenborg.

During Swedenborg's early adult life he lived with his sister and uncle, both of whom had an extensive influence on him. Erik Benzelius, his uncle, progressively held the posts of librarian, professor of theology at Uppsala University and Bishop of Linkoping, and ultimately became the Archbishop of Uppsala. Swedenborg's upbringing, due to the religious vocations of both his father and uncle, was marked by the deep influence of both academia and religion.

At the age of 21, after studying at Uppsala University, Swedenborg left Sweden and traveled extensively in Europe to supplement his formal education. Deeply interested in Isaac Newton's works, he had pursued a wide range of academic, theological and practical studies and skills. His studies ranged from mathematics, natural history and astronomy to practical pursuits such as watch-making, engraving and the design and construction of mathematical instruments.

By 1714 the depth and range of his genius was demonstrated by his fourteen mechanical inventions. These included a prototype for a submarine, a giant siphon which facilitated the raising of large volumes of water from a river to a higher locality, designs for the construction of sluices where there is no fall of water, a water clock, a method for engraving by fire, a method of synchronizing the firing of a number of air-guns, and a device to help an untrained person to play music.

By 1715, in a journal entitled *Daedalus Hyperboreus*, Swedenborg commenced publishing his mathematical inventions and experiments. These even included a design for a flying machine. Shortly after, King Charles XII of Sweden gave him the position of 'extraordinary assessor' of the College of Mines. At the approximate age of 30, Swedenborg had published or was in the process of publishing books and research papers on subjects such as chemistry, metallurgy, astronomy, navigation, mining science, the construction of dock embankments and the compilation of tables predicting future eclipses of the sun and moon.

From 30 to 50 years of age, Swedenborg studied natural philosophy and published his findings in 1727. The first volume translated into English was *Principia: The First Principles of Natural Things*.[3] He was also deeply involved in research into human physiology and anatomy, publishing his theoretical findings in 1740 under the title *Oeconomia Regni Animalis*.[4] This was followed by *Regnum Animale*.[5]

However, much of the voluminous material of the latter was left in manuscript form, including Swedenborg's extraordinarily advanced understanding of the structure of the human brain. Swedenborg advanced the theory that the cortical substance of the brain housed the higher psychical activities and concluded that it was the seat of the soul.

Swedenborg wrote in Latin, the language universally used throughout the academic world at that time. His fame as a highly acclaimed scholar in an extensive range of subjects spread throughout both academia and political circles. Swedenborg's life is characterized by his enormous mental prowess.

He was a scientist of considerable stature and throughout his life constantly searched to add to his already considerable knowledge and practical skills. He utilized each of these for the benefit of all. However, he did not feel that his mission would be achieved by accepting the university chairs of astronomy or mathematics at Uppsala University. Consequently, he declined both of these positions.

A distinct turning point in Swedenborg's life occurred in 1743. The marked transition in his thinking is revealed in a letter he wrote in 1769 to an Anglican priest, Reverend Thomas Hartley, in which he said: 'I have been called to a sacred office by the Lord Himself, who in the year 1743 most graciously manifested Himself in person to me, His servant, and then opened my sight into the spiritual world and granted me to speak with spirits and angels.'[6]

Swedenborg has left diaries containing accounts of the initial powerful temptations and struggles that he experienced during the sleep state. He believed these prepared him for the spiritually elevated mediumistic work that lay ahead of him (after 1743). This form of preparation occurred in order to rid him of his self-conceit, born of his international fame as a genius.[7]

After successfully rejecting this self-conceit, he reportedly began to have vivid experiences of a range of angelic and spirit beings. He entered into long and lively debates with them, and they educated him about the many different hierarchical levels of non-physical existence and the natural laws which govern these realms.

In 1747, as a result of Swedenborg's experiencesof the multi-faceted non-physical realms and their inhabitants, he resigned from his eminent position in the Royal College of Mines. He took this step despite the fact that this post had been personally given to him by the King of Sweden. To become ready for the work that lay ahead of him, Swedenborg became fluent in Hebrew and made an intensive study of the Bible.

He believed that his earlier academic prowess was merely a preparation for the more important work which he was yet to complete. He was extremely grateful for his new, privileged spiritual position. This allowed him to access deeper spiritual insights and knowledge of the nature of life after physical death from celestial communicators.

Among Swedenborg's transformative spiritual mediumistic experiences there were times when he believed that it was in fact God who revealed His/Her true nature to him. He therefore occupies a unique position in spiritual history as he described both his mystical experiences of God and his mediumistic experiences of spirits and angels. He wrote about his many enigmatic encounters with characteristic vigor.

The following is a brief survey of a number of his most important works, which offer insights into the nature of his experience-based beliefs.

Swedenborg's first theological publication was *Arcana Coelestia* (in English: *Heavenly Secrets*). This work consisted of eight volumes and was published in London between the years 1749 and 1756.[8] It was popularly described as revealing the secrets of the world of spirits and of the heaven of angels. On the introductory page Swedenborg wrote:

> The Word of the Old Testament contains heavenly arcana, with every single detail focusing on the Lord, His heaven, the Church, faith and what belongs to faith ... nobody views it as anything more than a record ... of external features of the Jewish Church... it can be disclosed that in the Lord's Divine mercy I have been allowed constantly and without interruption for several years now to share the experiences of spirits and angels and to listen to them speaking and to speak with them myself.[9]

Swedenborg was emphatic that it had been revealed to him by the highest angelic sources that every detail of the Old Testament relates on a deeper level to spiritual matters. *Arcana Coelestia* represents his detailed word-by-word exposition of the spiritual sense of the Books of Genesis[10] and Exodus.[11] Accompanying this, he provided the Hebrew translation of the text of each chapter, a summary of the spiritual sense of the meanings, and then his inter-chapter material. The latter provided descriptions of his observations during his many soul-journeys to the non-physical realms.

In 1746–1747, before the end of his many experiences of the non-physical realms of amplified time and space, Swedenborg wrote *The*

*Word of the Old Testament Explained.*[12] In this work, which was published posthumously, he provided a detailed exposition of the biblical books known as Genesis,[13] Exodus,[14] Leviticus,[15] Numbers,[16] Deuteronomy,[17] Isaiah[18] and Jeremiah[19] and discussed a variety of other miscellaneous verses from other Old Testament texts. The publication known in English as *Heaven and Hell* (the full original title, translated from the Latin, was *Heaven and Its Wonders and Hell: From Things Heard and Seen*) was first published in 1758.[20]

Over half a million copies have been sold and it has been translated into seventeen languages. In it Swedenborg discussed at great length the teachings that he learned from his countless conversations with spirits and angels. Swedenborg described many of the sights, sounds and conversations of the past thirteen years of tangible experiences, which evidently confirm his clairaudient, clairvoyant and soul-journey abilities. The following statement by the Swedenborg Society in London explains Swedenborg's personal understanding of the purpose of his experiences. He believed that his visits

> into the spiritual world [were] divinely intended ... so that knowledge of that world might be revealed to mankind. We are shown how we enter the next world; the spiritual character of our surroundings there; where and how judgement is effected; the life of heaven; the training of children; marriage; the universal language; recreations; the orderly arrangement of heaven into societies; these and many other matters are described in great detail.[21]

*Heaven and Hell* is a travelogue of Swedenborg's experiences of the non-physical dimension. He discusses the landscapes, architecture, spirit animals, people, angels, birds, minerals and plants in the heavenly, intermediate and hell-like dimensions. It is a magnificent attempt to help the reader understand the whole spiritual world as an outward image portraying the soul, the Divine and the ego's distortions.'[22]

Swedenborg taught that when any creature dies, they awaken as a spirit. They see other spirits as they move into the non-physical realm of spirits. His writings are emphatic that all living creatures on earth awaken in this way as a non-physical being after death. This transition of life is an inevitable consequence of universal natural laws. The spirit realms are populated with animals, human and non-human, birds, marine life, plants and minerals. He taught that a person's spirit can progress to ultimately become an angel, if it becomes highly spiritually evolved, or equally, it can deteriorate and regress. This would occur if the individual rejected spiritual principles. He described such a person as becoming a devil.

Swedenborg's personal belief, perhaps as a result of his upbringing was that Jesus was God, the Divine. He described Jesus as the bright light of the Sun of heaven. The laws of physics state that energy cannot be destroyed; rather it transmutes in form. This fact supports Swedenborg's experiences of the continued after-death state of all of creation.

Transmuted energy could be said to be another term for the spirit, soul, consciousness or auric orb which survives physical death. If we scrutinize nature to learn its lessons, we see that nature in its physical form on earth physically dies away in the winter, only to be reborn in the spring. Incredibly, lifeless, brittle, inert vegetation is revivified every year. In the same way, lifeless bodies reawaken as spirits. Clearly, Swedenborg's insights and experiences indicate that the same pattern of events awaits all after death, all awaken and become inhabitants of the non-physical world.

Swedenborg's book *The Last Judgment*[23] discusses his under-standing of the meaning of the term the 'Last Judgment,' an event predicted in the biblical Book of Revelation.[24] He believed that the term does not refer to a future tragedy on earth but rather describes events observed by Swedenborg himself in the non-physical realms during the mid to late 18th century. After his observation of these events, there followed the process of judgment, the reordering of the world of spirits and the restoration of peace.

Swedenborg believed that these events led to the development of the New Heaven. He believed tht this reordering in the non-physical realms did not cause corresponding changes in our physical world in relation to external forms. However, as a result of this Judgment, he taught that the Church on Earth (which he uses as a symbolic term for all religious faiths) would gradually allow individuals to have greater autonomy of spiritual thought. Swedenborg was certain that given this freedom, people would increasingly access and internalize the original, authentic and profound spiritual truths for themselves.

Swedenborg's book *The New Jerusalem and Its Heavenly Doctrine*,[25] written in 1758, clearly describes the doctrines of the New Church and summarizes his most important theological teachings. He tells us that the doctrine 'is for the New Church, which because it has been revealed to me from heaven, is called Heavenly Doctrine. To deliver that doctrine is the purpose of the present work.'[26]

*Apocalypse Explained*,[27] written during the years 1757–1759 and published posthumously, provides a detailed verse-by-verse exposition of the Book of Revelation up to chapter 19 verse 10.[28] *Divine Love and Wisdom*[29] was first published in 1763. This book 'outlines his mature understanding of the doctrine of creation in emanations, spheres (or auras), series and degrees. It concludes with a section devoted to the interplay of will and understanding in the mind and its correspondence as mirrored in the interaction of the heart and lungs in the body.'[30]

In *Divine Providence* (1764) Swedenborg 'outlines how the Divine Nature inevitably involves an inviolate order in its operation, which governs all that It has created ... The early chapters contain some of Swedenborg's endeavours to express the deeper mystical relationship of finite man to his infinite source in God.'[31]

*Conjugial Love*[32] (1768) discusses the importance of the marriage bond and how a husband and wife become unified on some levels:

The love, which is the soul of marriage, originates from the union of the Divine Love ...This love is therefore celestial, spiritual and holy above all other loves and after death remains ... The second part of the book deals with disorderly loves opposed to conjugial love and the deplorable spiritual states resulting from such evils.[33]

Evidently, Swedenborg taught that if a husband and wife become unified on some levels, their energy harmoniously blends with each other. Therefore, when positive events occur in one partner's life, positive events will also occur in the other partner's life. Due to their shared positive energy, positive events would happen to both around the same time period.

Swedenborg also taught that the reverse would be true: shared negativity would draw negativity to both around the same time. I have experienced many personal examples underlining the accuracy of this concept. I believe it also embraces companion pets (who so closely live their adopted human parents' lives) and if there is harmony in the family, it also includes other family members.

Regarding Swedenborg's insights into 'conjugial love,' the Reverend Dr Michael Stanley tells us that:

Swedenborg turned his attention to an area which has been so poorly understood, if not misunderstood, by ... Christianity – sexuality and the union of man and woman. Similar though it may appear in some ways to alchemical teachings concerning the union of masculine and feminine in the soul, it differs in its practical application of deep spiritual fundamentals to the actual situation of men and women faced with sexual urges, eros and deeper longings for soul union with a mate.[34]

As has been discussed, Swedenborg's soul-journey excursions and conversations with otherworldly beings taught him that predominant aspects of the personality draw corresponding after-death landscapes, inhabitants and events. This model is in keeping with the principle of 'like attracting like:' positive, compassionate, selfless personalities would predominantly draw positive after-death scenarios, with the reverse being true for personalities which possess more negative features.

However, Swedenborg also learned that the same natural laws govern our lives on earth. During our physical lives our positive or negative thought patterns, emotions, homes and working environments create corresponding energies, which draw to us equivalent positive or negative people and events. Significantly, many direct-voice trance lectures corroborate Swedenborg's insights into the workings of these natural laws. Interestingly, modern-day life coaches and other therapists have also learned the truth underlying this phenomenon. They teach the importance of positivity.

*Apocalypse Revealed*[35] (1766) is a detailed verse-by-verse exposition of the last book of the Bible, Revelation:

> Swedenborg expresses his insights in relation to the life and teachings of corporate religions such as the Catholic and Reformed churches, showing how subtle evils and falsities develop in disguised forms in churches, until a crucial point is reached when, according to Divine Order, a Last Judgement takes place, which spiritually separates the matured good from the fully grown evil within those within the churches.[36]

*The True Christian Religion* was first published in 1771, the year before Swedenborg's physical death,[37] and contains the complete theology of his 'New Church.' Swedenborg believed that the New Church had been predicted by God, the Divine, as recorded in the Bible in Daniel 7:13–14[38] and Revelation 21:2–3.[39] In this work, Swedenborg taught that the Christian belief in 'the second coming of Jesus' should be understood in symbolic, not physical terms. He believed that Jesus' 'second coming' had already occurred through the revealed spiritual teachings contained in Swedenborg's own writings. In contrast, many Christian churches still claim that Jesus will return to earth to teach humankind.

Swedenborg had a clear vision of the (predicted) forthcoming new, reformed church. Many insights into the nature of his teachings can be gleaned from the chapter headings which include: God the Creator; The Lord the Redeemer; The Holy Spirit and the Way God Works; The Sacred Scripture or the Word of the Lord; The Catechism or the Ten Commandments Explained in Both the External and Internal Senses; Faith; Charity or Love Towards the Neighbor and Good Deeds; Free Will; Repentance; Reformation and Regeneration; Imputation; Baptism; The Holy Supper; The Ending of the Age, the Lord's Coming, the New Heaven and the New Church.

All of Swedenborg's writings can be obtained from the Swedenborg Society, which has several international bases, including those in London, UK, and Philadelphia, Pennsylvania in the USA. His writings were first published in the 18th century in either or both London and Amsterdam, locations he chose due to the comparative religious freedom that could be found there. He avoided writing his name on most of his books as an act of modesty.

Swedenborg died in London on 29 March 1772 at the age of 84, and was buried in a Swedish church situated near the Tower of London. His remains were later moved to a sarcophagus in Uppsala Cathedral, Sweden, where a memorial was unveiled by the King of Sweden in 1910. Significantly, as he faced physical death, Swedenborg possessed 'the full mental vigour that had been his gift all his life [and died] ... calmly and happily looking forward to an unending life in a universal spiritual world which had grown very familiar to him.'[40]

Swedenborg wrote his spiritual, experiential, mediumistic, theological works during the last 30 years of his life. It should be emphasized that throughout these decades, he continued his work attending to the affairs of the world. He frequently attended the House of the Nobles in Stockholm where he and other governmental ministers debated complex affairs of state, including the reform of the currency. During this last 30-year period of his life, he did not become a recluse but remained active until the time of his death.

Swedenborg commanded a great deal of respect. Amongst his close friends were the Swedish king himself and chief ministers in the government. Klimo concludes that Swedenborg wrote about his experiences of the non-physical world 'with all the analytical care and descriptive prowess of his earlier technical works [and that he wrote] at least sixteen books on these experiences.'[41] The quotation from Swedenborg's writings below vividly portrays his awareness that some spirit communicators cannot be trusted. It also graphically describes an array of his mediumistic abilities, including his clairvoyant, clairaudient and soul-journey experiences, each of which became the subject of his prolific writings:

I am well aware that many will say that no one can speak with spirits and angels so long as he lives in the body ... [but] I have seen, I have heard, I have felt ... When spirits begin to speak with man, he must beware lest he believe in anything; for they say almost anything; things are fabricated of them, and they lie ... And as I desired to know in what manner [biblical prophets] were actuated by spirits, I was shown by means of a living experience ... for a whole night possessed by spirits who took possession of my body ... A thousand times I have seen them [spirits], heard them, and talked with them – even about the fact that people in the world do not believe that spirits are what they are ... The spirits were heartsick at the persistence of this ignorance on earth, especially within the Church.[42]

Evidently, Swedenborg was a leading post-death survival researcher. He was trained as a mathematician and scientist yet spent the last 30 years of his life in experiential exploration and methodical research into the continuous nature of consciousness after physical death. In many respects, he was a experiential theoretical scientist who plumbed the eternal depths of the many levels of the non-physical world and its relationship with the physical world.

Swedenborg's prolific writings which described his enigmatic, ethereal experiences were met with extraordinary hostility when they were first published. Some adversarial individuals attempted to label this eminent genius as insane. Yet his ongoing active professional career proved to everyone that he was not at all insane. As stated, at the same time as Swedenborg was experiencing soul-journeys to the countless levels of the non-physical world and meeting spirits and angels, he was demonstrating his genius and worldly analytical reasoning in his professional life. For example, eleven years before Swedenborg's death in 1761, he was commended by the prime minister of Sweden for submitting the most solid and best-written commentaries on the financial state of the country.[43]

## Royalty Observed Swedenborg Soul-Journeying

Some of Swedenborg's exceptional experiences occurred in the presence of observers. They would happen spontaneously in many places, including when he was at dinner with other guests. Witnesses spoke of watching Swedenborg's lips move, as though he was speaking, yet the words were inaudible. He had obviously moved into an altered state of consciousness. In this state, he believed, he was speaking with imperceptible surviving personalities and angels. Swedenborg's experiences began at approximately 55 years of age and spanned almost three decades, ranging from 1743 to 1772. In 1772 he himself passed to spirit.

David Lorimer, the former president of the International Swedenborg Society in London, and former director of the Medical and Scientific Network and editor of their journal, provides the following information on some of Swedenborg's famous experiences. These occurred while Swedenborg was in the company of aristocrats, government ministers and other highly respected professionals. These people witnessed the events.

[Swedenborg had] a spectrum of experiences ... from clair-voyance to perception into a different order of reality ... one of these incidents took place in 1759 when he was one of fifteen guests at dinner in the Gothenburg Mansion. At six o'clock in the evening he became very alarmed. He explained that there was a fire burning in Stockholm three hundred miles away and that the fire was in danger of reaching his house ... then he told the company that the progress of the fire had been halted not far from his house ... He related the details to the Governor and two days later, messengers arrived with reports that corresponded to that which Swedenborg had *seen* at the time and with the same timing ... This incident was so famous that this is one of the particular incidents that was investigated by the philosopher Immanuel Kant.[44] Kant satisfied himself that it had happened ... and that the witnesses were reliable witnesses, so he could not dismiss it. Consequently, it put Kant in an awkward situation of not being able to believe or disbelieve.[45]

Lorimer tells us of a further fascinating incident that was reported of Swedenborg in 1770 which involved

a manufacturer called Bollander who owned extensive cloth mills. Swedenborg suddenly addressed him and, without any explanation, he said that he [had] better go quickly to his mills because there was a disaster unfolding. When the manufacturer arrived at his mill, he discovered that a large piece of cloth had fallen down near the furnace. It had started to burn, so the whole property would have been razed to the ground, if Swedenborg had not given that advice. The man came back to the dinner and thanked Swedenborg who, in turn, explained that he was abrupt with him earlier as he knew that there was no time to be lost ...[46]

In Amsterdam another remarkable event associated with Swedenborg was witnessed. Lorimer adds:

just after the Russian ... Peter III had fallen from power and had been replaced by Catherine ... Swedenborg had a change of expression on his face and looked very shaken. When a guest asked what had happened, he said that Peter III had just been assassinated. He urged his fellow guests to note the date and his account. The newspapers then featured [the Russian event] ... a few days later.[47]

A person's normal field of consciousness usually covers only the room in which they are seated. Lorimer supports the view that some people have a capacity to have their normal field of consciousness greatly extended, so that events at a distance, happening to somebody else, can be sensed by the third party. The advance of quantum physics is helping us to understand how such experiences happen. Lorimer notes that from the point of view of the experiencer, such as Swedenborg, it is actually a perception, something that registers in their field of consciousness.[48]

Lorimer refers to Swedenborg's predictive abilities. These were demonstrated when he was asked if he knew which of the 'assembled company would die first ... after a few moments of silence, he said it would be Olafson and that he would die at four forty-five the next morning ... This actually happened and his clock stopped.'[49]

Proof that Swedenborg visited the non-physical realms and spoke with angels and spirits was provided when a merchant tested his claims. The merchant informed Swedenborg that he had shared an important discussion with a friend immediately prior to his friend's death. He asked Swedenborg to learn from spirits or angels the nature of the subject they had discussed.

Lorimer points out:

A few days later, Swedenborg returned and told him that the discussion had been about the restitution of all things. This turned out to be correct ... you could say that he [acquired it from his] mind ... but this is certainly not the way it was constructed by Swedenborg. If Swedenborg had done this [telepathically] he could have given him the answer straight away ... Swedenborg added that his friend was still tormented by this subject ... after he had died.[50]

The Queen of Sweden also tested Swedenborg's claim that he could speak with spirits and angels. She was emphatic that she was not easily duped. During his private audience with the queen, she asked him to find out some information regarding her dead brother. It was reported that when Swedenborg transmitted the information to her, she gasped and, in shock, felt compelled to leave the room. The queen was so astounded because only she and her 'dead' brother knew the information Swedenborg gave her.[51]

Yet another enquiry came from a baroness who also sought to verify whether Swedenborg could speak to spirits and angels or not. The lady was troubled, as she had been asked to pay a bill that she believed had already been paid by her 'dead' husband. She asked Swedenborg if he could genuinely assist her and ask her spirit husband if he had proof regarding this matter. Several days later Swedenborg had some information for her. Lorimer states:

Yes [the account] had been paid and ... the receipt was in a secret drawer in the back of the bureau ... The interesting thing about this particular incident is that she did not know of the existence of the receipt or of the secret drawer of the bureau ... Here you have an instance that is either super-ESP or survival ... Swedenborg told her that her husband had given him the information ... This was a matter of months after [the husband's physical] death.[52]

Significantly, Swedenborg accurately predicted the date of his own death. Writing to Swedenborg in 1772, Wesley asked him for a meeting in April or May of that year. Swedenborg's written reply to

Wesley informed him that he would have passed to spirit by then, so they would have to meet earlier. Aware of the date of his own death, Swedenborg decided to pay his rent only to the end of March. It is on record that on 29 March 1772 he bid farewell to his landlady and then went upstairs and passed away; presumably he passed to spirit.

Lorimer classifies Swedenborg as a 'first person investigator of consciousness, examining these things for himself ... [and then trying] to make sense of them for other people.'[53] Lorimer is aware that people

> can get completely stuck in ... terminology and cease to relate it to something concrete ... if you take a first person view they are convinced by their own experiences and the interaction of the scientist helps with interpretation ... after looking at ... [the spectrum of experiential evidence] such as mystical experiences, out of body experiences, altered states of consciousness.[54]

Perhaps Swedenborg's experiences will be better appreciated in future years when the latest pioneering discoveries of quantum physics are more fully understood by the general public. These illuminating breakthroughs are progressively explaining the reality of laws that govern the non-physical realms. At that future time, the world may be more receptive to Swedenborg's discoveries, and will wish to learn about his descriptions of the non-physical realms, the laws that operate there, and his spiritual insights.

The next chapter will explore some of Swedenborg's teachings. Most of these were gained from his transformative spiritual-mediumistic experiences and his soul-journeys to the celestial dimension.

# Chapter 12

# Major Features of Swedenborg's Teachings

## The Mysteries of the Non-Physical World

Emanuel Swedenborg provided humanity with a great profusion of detail regarding the non-physical realms. Sadly, today, only a minority of people are aware of this. Information regarding the after-death realms is of enormous significance. When a person plans to emigrate to another country, they learn about the conditions, the regions and the laws that govern the place. Naturally, they are enthusiastic to know as much as possible about the future area in which they are going to live. The knowledge gained by Swedenborg should be considered in the same way.

Upon arrival at our destination, the first thing any of us would want to do is to make contact with our loved ones and report that we had arrived safely. Both parties are deeply comforted by the opportunity to communicate. Anxiety is resolved for those who departed and those who are left behind. In the same way, a medium facilitates an 'after-death trans-dimensional telephone call.'

He or she transfers a message from the spirit person or spirit animal to their loved ones, providing much-needed mutual emotional support. Both parties feel the loss of their loved ones, both those on the spirit side of life and the broken-hearted bereaved who have been left behind.

The post-death non-physical world can best be understood as a 'shared mind-dependent world' or 'the world of mind.' Generally, if two people watch an event, there are differences in their descriptions of it. Inevitably, they each focus to different degrees upon different aspects of the scene, for example, sights, sounds and smells. However, for the benefit of future generations, Swedenborg did his utmost to report his experiences in a scientific, coherent and systematic way.

As discussed, Swedenborg taught that after death the predominant aspects of personality, the deeper-most psyche or inner self, draws energy to it which is malleable to thought, creating landscapes and drawing comparable inhabitants and events. This energy becomes manifest in the form of non-physical landscapes which are objective to all who share this level of reality. Inhabitants of the same level of reality each see the same scenes and spirit inhabitants.

Swedenborg taught that through the law of attraction, like attracting like, people and animals draw to themselves persons, animals and events which are in harmony with their state of spirituality. Loving people and animals share a landscape with other compassionate spirit people and spirit animals. They live among breathtaking scenes of beauty, including trees, skies, rivers and birds.

The 1998 film *What Dreams May Come*, starring Robin Williams, is worth watching as it graphically illustrates some of Swedenborg's findings (however, some features of the film have been the subject of poetic license). Robin Williams plays a man who finds himself, after death, in the non-physical realms. He lives in idyllic, colorful landscapes with his son and daughter, who had passed to spirit as the result of a car accident some years before his own demise.

Williams' wife in the movie is an artist – a kindly, creative, sensitive woman. She becomes profoundly depressed for a lengthy period of time and, tragically, finally committs suicide. She can no longer bear to live her physical life without her children and her husband.

She arrives in the after-death realms prostrate with grief. As a consequence of this attitude and emotion, she becomes a fearful, solitary figure, trapped in a dilapidated duplicate of her own earthly house. This new abode is in stark contrast to the home she has left behind; it is derelict, bitterly cold, dark and shadowy. In her realm there are no neighbors, no sunshine, color or warmth. The film tries to show that as a result of the woman's predominantly depressed thoughts during her earthly life, she has been drawn to this ugly, isolated, hostile landscape. This state of affairs is particularly sad as she had been a kindly soul during her physical life.

Direct-voice trance lectures confirm that like attracts like in both the material and non-material realms. However, it is comforting to know that they also inform us that all animals, human and non-human, are met by loving souls when they die. These accompany them to the next realms, whatever their state, and tend to their needs. It is on this point that the film digresses from original spiritual teachings.

As the woman's emotions heal, she leaves the house. The new scenes which she observes are filled with vibrant colors, from the vibrant blue sky to the vibrant green grass. In this non-physical world she moves from one level of mind to the next. Finally, at the end of the movie, she regains the wonderful, loving company of her husband, children and other similar good souls.

The story line relates how this reunion comes about: Initially, upon arrival in the non-physical realms, Williams' character did not recognize his children as they had taken on different bodies and appeared as wise adults. If they had not done so, he might not have taken their much-needed advice concerning navigating these realms. As it is, they help him to set out to visit his wife, in order to rescue her from the realm she finds herself in.

He is warned not to stay there long, as her reality would then become his own long-term reality. He crosses many bleak realms in order to find her. When he eventually meets her, she is reluctant to leave her realm and so he decides to stay with her. His selfless act of love seems to ignite her positivity and benevolent emotions again, and they leave that dark realm together. The account ends with the two living happily in a heavenly realm for a while. They later reincarnate and meet each other again as chidren!

Commenting on Swedenborg's experience-based view of the after-death environment, Stanley adds:

Whatever appears in the spiritual world is a representation or correspondence of the spiritual state of the observer. All spirits who are in a state of inner peace, harmony and desire to co-operate, appear ... in peaceful, harmonious and co-operative communities which form the heavens. Their groupings reflect the similarity of their spiritual condition, or, as, one of the great universal spiritual laws is commonly expressed, 'like attracts like.[1]

Regarding the post-death, non-physical landscapes, Swedenborg taught that non-physical animals, human and non-human, plants and minerals are experienced in accordance with a spirit's inner nature. He taught that over time, spirits can achieve spiritual progression, some ultimately become angels. 'The angels of one heaven are not together in one place, but are distinguished [divided] into societies, larger or smaller, according to the differences of the good of love and faith in which they are. They who are in similar good, form one society.'[2]

In the book *Heaven and Hell*[3] Swedenborg discusses his conversations with discarnate beings, covering a wide range of religious and after-death issues. Swedenborg categorizes heaven into two main kingdoms, each of which has many subdivisions, which are in turn composed of countless societies. Swedenborg emphasizes that there is a correspondence in heaven with all things of the earth. By this he means that everything found on earth is similarly found in heaven.

He describes changes that occur among angels occupying specific heavenly realms. As they achieve spiritual progression from lower to higher levels, their form is altered. He describes the changes in their faces, garments, dwellings and speech when the transition to a higher level occurs. He learned that many angels had experienced countless incarnations on earth and/or other planets.

All who form one angelic society have a common resemblance of face, with individual differences ... It is well known that every

race of people has some common likeness in the face and eyes ...
but this is more perfectly the case in the heavens, because there,
all the interior affections appear and shine forth from the face.
The face in heaven is the external and representative form of
those affections.[4]

Regarding the angels' clothing, Swedenborg tells us that:

Their garments correspond to their intelligence ... and because
some excel others in intelligence ... they are more beautifully
clad. The most intelligent have garments that glow as with flame,
and some, those that shine as with light; the less intelligent have
garments that are bright and white without splendour and the
still less intelligent have garments of various colours; but the
angels of the inmost heavens are not clothed ... Since the
garments of the angels correspond to their intelligence, therefore
they correspond also to truth, because all intelligence is from
Divine Truth; so that whether you say that angels are clothed
according to intelligence, or according to Divine Truth, it is the
same thing.[5]

Swedenborg's detailed descriptions of the heavenly regions include:

The nature of the things seen by the angels in the heavens ... for
the most part they are like things on the Earth, but more perfect
as to form and more abundant in number. That there are such
things in the heavens may be evident from those which were
seen by the prophets: as by Ezekiel, where he speaks of the New
Temple and the New Earth (chapter xi) ( ( ) and by John (from the
first chapter of the Apocalypse to the last) and from the things
seen by others ... in the historical and the prophetic books
...They saw these things when heaven was opened to them ...
when the interior sight, which is the sight of the spirit of man, is
opened. For what is in the heavens cannot be seen by the eyes of

man's body, but with the eyes of his spirit.[6]

Swedenborg describes the source of the origins of the light and heat in heaven as follows:

> All things in the heavens exist from the Lord, according to their correspondence with the interiors of the angels ... the angels have heat according to the quality of their love and light according to the quality of their wisdom and the case is similar with all other things which appear to the senses of the angels.[7]

In his *Apocalypse Explained*, Swedenborg describes the abundance of life-forms and landscapes in the various heavenly realms:

> In general, whatever appears in heaven is wholly similar to what exists in our material world in its three kingdoms ... Gold, silver, copper ... mountains, hills, valleys ... the mineral kingdom ... parks, gardens, forests ... [and] the vegetable kingdom.
>
> Animals of the earth, fowls of the heaven, fishes of the sea, reptiles and these of every kind appear there; and they are so much like those on our Earth that they cannot be distinguished ... But still there is this difference, that the things that appear in heaven are from a spiritual origin; while those in our world are from a material origin.[8]

In *Heaven and Hell*, Swedenborg tells us that there are

> two distinct loves in heaven, love to the Lord and love towards the neighbour. In the inmost or third heaven is love to the Lord; in the second or middle heaven, is love towards the neighbour. Both proceed from the Lord and both make heaven ... I have sometimes talked with angels on this subject.[9]

Swedenborg's discoveries are most illuminating. He informs us that good and evil spirits influence, in perpetuity, the thoughts and actions of physical people on earth. Evidently, drug addicts, alcoholics, depressed people and those with negative characteristics would be most vulnerable to an escalating range of negative, mischievous and evil spirits. Kind and positive people would be more likely to attract the influence of positive, creative and good spirits.

Due to our free will, we need to ask these spirits to intervene in our lives and offer us assistance. Some people may be familiar with aspects of Swedenborg's teachings without being aware that the teachings originated with him. Over the years, certain features of his teachings have progressively infiltrated people's minds.

In *Heaven and Hell*, under the subheading 'The Conjunction of Heaven with the Human Race,' Swedenborg wrote:

With every man there are good spirits and evil spirits: by good spirits man has conjunction with heaven and by evil spirits with hell. These spirits are in the world of spirits, which is in the midst between heaven and hell ... When these spirits come to man, they enter into all his memory and thence into all his thought; evil spirits, into those things of the memory and thought which are evil, but good spirits, into those things of the memory and thought which are good.[10]

Evidently, it is very important to keep our thoughts and emotions spiritually orientated and positive. In turn, this will help draw to us a range of positive experiences both in the physical and non-physical life. When we feel depressed and lonely, it may help to go for a walk by the beautiful ocean or in the countryside. We could listen to uplifting music, watch comedy programs, or help charitable causes.

We might choose to adopt a homeless, vulnerable, devoted animal companion who is a child-like innocent in a hostile world, callously indifferent to their suffering. Thinking of the needs of others, causes us to give of ourselves, when a person gives, in turn, they will also receive! Such uplifting experiences would serve to elevate our thoughts and emotions, and help create a positive energy or vibration around us. This, in turn, will draw to us even more positivity.

According to Swedenborg's teachings, there is a hierarchical range of good and bad spirits who are attracted to company that corresponds with themselves. Apparently, good and bad thoughts and emotions can be expanded upon by different degrees of good or evil entities. People with negative characteristics and occupations could find themselves spiralling downwards in terms of happiness and success in their physical and non-physical lives.

Those working in all types of slaughterhouses and animal experimentation laboratories are working in environments of deplorable suffering creating negativity in their own lives and drawing to them yet more negativity in their pre and post death existence. Conversely, compassionate and creative pursuits such as supporting charitable or health care organizations, or producing art, music and writing, are supported by those spirits with similar interests and abilities.

Entranced mediums teach a similar lesson; for example, if a person becomes interested in Chinese art or medicine, they may draw to themselves a likeminded Chinese spirit who will work to inspire their thoughts and enhance their abilities. This mediumistic information confirms the teachings of Swedenborg.

## Swedenborg's Insights into Spirits and Angels

The Reverend Dr Michael Stanley offered some pertinent insights into Swedenborg's teachings in his lecture 'Swedenborg, Prophet of the New Age' delivered at the Churches' Fellowship for Psychical and Spiritual Studies' Annual Conference in September 1988.[11] The theme of the conference was Inspiration and Prophecy. Stanley, who has written a helpful book, *Emanuel Swedenborg: Essential Readings*,[12] was ordained as a minister of the Church of the New Jerusalem in England in 1971.

Since his ordination, he has presented lectures on philosophy, psychology, comparative religions, and symbolism in sacred scriptures. He has also provided psycho-spiritual counseling based upon Swedenborgian principles in the UK, Australia and the USA. Rev. Stanley has now retired.

In his 1988 lecture, Stanley wished to clarify a number of themes found in Swedenborg's teachings. He suggested that Swedenborg's view of creation can be better understood by use of a symbolic mandala analogy. He suggested that a person should think in terms of two symbolic concentric circles, one inner and the other outer, with a dot in the absolute center.

The central dot represents God who can also be understood as the 'source of life' 'within all aspects of all of creation.' (The creative parent God dwells in all living creatures, harming them harms God.) The inner circle represents the heavens and the inner life in creation. This comes from that source which is whole, pure and unified.

It is the heaven within each aspect of creation. The outer circle represents the earth and can be described as being ordinary, natural life. This represents natural thoughts and feelings and the way one sees and understands the world. Around this outer circle, Stanley suggested a person think of a skin, which represents the physical bodies around all aspects of creation.

Stanley used the mandala symbol to illustrate Swedenborg's teachings regarding the original flow of inspiration from God to all physical creatures on earth. He explained the concept that life flows out of the central dot, which represents God. It then flows freely through the inner circle of the heavens and through the outer circle, right through to the earthly part of creation and shines through the physical body. Stanley suggested that when that flow is connected, it is like the opening of a window or door, through which the flow of life manifests from the central source. This can then be felt by all of creation.

Regarding the mandala symbol, Stanley described the real meaning of the New Age as a new breakthrough in consciousness to the inner circle domain. This is the domain of the inner heavens, which are a unified whole. His personal belief is that this consciousness is a re-emerging, holistic consciousness. It is an experience of the wholeness and inner purity and 'oneness of life.' It comes from the Source and manifests through all creatures, human and non-human.

Stanley sees all of creation as being interconnected and part of the whole. There may be many distortions in the outer appearance of this non-physical world due to the distortions in hearts and minds. However, behind all that, he believes that there is the 'one life,' around which is the 'one heaven.' However, he accepts that heaven might be seen as having many facets, composed of many heavens, stemming from one 'Single Source of Life.'

It is in this way that Stanley understands some of Swedenborg's experience-based beliefs, many of which were based upon his conversations with spirits and angels from the non-physical spheres. Swedenborg had learned how to repeat these encounters at will. Swedenborg was emphatic that he experienced the geo-psychic realms and its diverse non-physical inhabitants as if he was one of them. This was despite the fact that he was still living in the physical body. Stanley describes Swedenborg as the leading 'prophet of the New Age,' the new, dawning, holistic consciousness.

He believes that this is being sensed by people from diverse religions in a myriad different ways. One of which is that some people are becoming aware of the existence of the universal relationship of all creatures; that all creatures are indeed, interrelated, interconnected and interdependent. This is a fact of which leading scientists from a broad range of disciplines are acutely aware, underlining the sisterhood and brotherhood of all creatures.

This interdependent relationship supersedes and crosses the boundaries that separate religions and creeds. Stanley described this in terms of the Christ, Buddha or Krishna Consciousness. He believes that the most important aspect of Swedenborg's teachings relates to the new breakthrough in consciousness which is currently affecting the contemporary world.

True to his scientific training, Swedenborg was so encouraged by being able to see, hear and touch the inhabitants of the non-physical realms that he followed their advice and studied the scriptures. The spirit or angelic beings then used the knowledge which he gained as a basis for providing him with further knowledge and inspiration. Swedenborg taught that every person has the potential to receive direct inspiration from God. This is not simply through the process of communication with spirits and angels, though these can be of the utmost spiritual importance.

Stanley clarifies Swedenborg's use of the term 'angels':

Angels are children of God who have become open and transparent ... to the Divine Life that flows from their centre. Just as they have heaven in them so do we also ... we too are angels deep inside of us. Unfortunately, we can also be devils. It may be the devilish distortion of the Divine Life that we manifest, hence we see that which is distressing coming from others and *out of* ourselves, because we have the whole of the spiritual world within us, which contains the whole range from Heaven and God at the highest to the lowest regions of the hells beneath. All that spectrum is within everyone's spirit and we are all linked together as denizens of that same spiritual world. The physical body veils over that awareness from us, so that normally we are unable to be aware of this common spiritual unity that binds us.[13]

Stanley suggests that in a sense Swedenborg saw a world within a grain of sand:

In a symbolic sense, he sees the visionary aspect which everyone can share and that is to see the inner world, which resides within every outer visible form which we see in this life or in the life to come. The unspiritual can see only the outside. They see nothing but the grain of sand, which, to them is relatively worthless. To the truly spiritual, the whole of the heavens and the whole of the Divine can be revealed within that grain of sand.[14]

In Swedenborg's early work, *The Principia*,[15] he outlines the process by which he, as a theoretical scientist, believed the Divine brought the physical world into being. Stanley describes Swedenborg's theory.

[He] saw God as being a point that has no dimensions, that is not in space as space does not exist yet and yet this point contains an infinity of life and in physical terms an infinity of energy ... this point is infinitely dynamic. It moves in such a way that the creative process starts to bend round on itself and begins to form a limited form ... Swedenborg believed that this new form that is developed by the movement of this dimensionless point ... contains something of the energy and dynamic of the point that forms it, but it is no longer infinite but finite. So it is no longer this infinitesimally small particle ... It is dynamically moving itself, and it moves in a way to constrain or limit the area or volume that it describes, so that it moves in such a way that it forms a denser, more gross particle, which does not have quite as much energy as the little particle out of which it was made.[16]

Swedenborg believed that it was as a result of a series of the above processes that created what we now call electrons. These finally came to rest and are the building blocks of all of creation. Contained within the center of every single particle is the energy of God. Swedenborg talked in analogous terms, describing some angels as fulfilling the role of the hands, the feet and so on.

He termed this 'the Grand Man.' The Grand Man represented the whole of humanity. Swedenborg used this analogy to describe all physical and non-physical spirits. They are ultimately part of one single body, even though the bad spirits may act as a distorted, bad or cancerous cell within the whole.

Swedenborg applied this same analogy to his description of the relationship between the mind and body. He taught that both the mind and body are interconnected and form the whole; all the thoughts and feelings of all physical creatures are inspired and influenced by diverse spirits and angels; everything that becomes visible in the non-physical realms reflects each individual's own unique, personal, inner, spiritual state.

This includes the tangible manifestation in the ethereal spheres of landscapes and all aspects of creation such as animals, mountains, lakes and vegetation, for in the non-physical realms, Swedenborg observed duplicates of all aspects of the earth.

He noted that all life-forms make their individual transitions to these realms at death. Swedenborg experienced three, basic subdivisions in the afterlife realms. He called these Heaven, the Intermediate World and the Infernal World. Within each of these, Swedenborg visited a whole spectrum of subdivisions.

Swedenborg learned that within every person there is a complexity of good and bad. After arriving in the non-physical world, Swedenborg tells us, each creature explores their own inner states. These are made manifest in the non-physical landscapes. Ultimately, a person has the potential, through spiritual progression, to meet the more heavenly aspects of their own spirituality and psyche. These would be mirrored in the diverse landscapes in harmony with the concept of 'like attracting like.' Different hierarchical levels of existence would include corresponding spirit animals, spirit birds and spirit people.

The following summarizes Swedenborg's insights regarding the after-death landscapes. He learned that people who experience beautiful, non-physical environments which include pets, animals, trees, vegetation, lakes and mountains, had a beautiful, peaceful, inner spiritual nature. He believed that many people would observe a whole spectrum of good and bad, non-physical landscapes.

During time spent at different levels, all have the opportunity to heal and spiritually progress their inner emotional and mental states. Everything visible in the non-physical world mirrors the person's inner spiritual, emotional and mental state. Evidently, this natural law governing the non-physical world represents a perfect form of divine justice.

Swedenborg learned from his out-of-body, shamanic, soul-journey excursions to the non-physical realms, and from those who escorted him, that there are three types of heavenly angels. They appear to reflect three different levels of spiritual progression, although as we have seen there are many subdivisions in each realm. Swedenborg was taught that the 'celestial angels' are moved by love and the unity of all of creation. Importantly, all of creation, which includes all creatures and vegetation, is viewed as the external manifestation of God, the Divine.

It was revealed to Swedenborg that the second type of angels, the 'spiritual angels', are moved primarily by their love for their neighbors. The third type of angels, known as the 'natural angels', obey the guidance of the more spiritually elevated angels who inhabit the heavenly hierarchies.

Swedenborg's beliefs were born of a blend of his detailed discussions with spirits and angels, his soul-journey excursions to many non-physical spheres, his meditations on the Bible, his understanding of the ancient wisdom literature and Neoplatonic-Gnostic teachings. His powerful intellect synthesized all of these, which in turn, furnished and empowered his profound insights.[17]

Swedenborg applied his insights into the workings of the non-physical world to his understanding of the workings of all aspects of physical creation. He also spent time theorizing and analyzing the differences between right- and left-brain function. He was an exceptional pioneer and a gifted traveler in destiny.

Sadly, many people today are ignorant of the results of his soul-journey discoveries and their relevance for their own post-death destinations. It was from this experiential, spiritually orientated mediumship that Swedenborg offered his profound spiritual understanding of the Unity and Source of all Things.

## Major Themes

Several major themes can be found in Swedenborg's teachings. Each of these is associated with his mediumistic experiences and soul-journeys to the alternative non-physical realities. 1. Universality, 2. Spiritual Freedom, 3. Union with the Lord and the Neighbor, 4. Doctrine of Use, 5. The Fall, 6. Incarnation and Redemption, 7. Regeneration, 8. Life after Death, 9. Conjugial Love (with the 'i') and 10. The New Age.[18] It is important to remember that the following spiritual revelations discovered in the 18th-century as a result of paranormal means have now to be expressed in 21st century language:

## Animals, human and non-human and vegetation are interconnected

Swedenborg's pioneering research and paranormal experiences taught him that at a deep level of existence, all of creation is unified. This is the meaning of his concept of universality. He discovered that all life-forms are interrelated and part of the whole. This concept has been conclusively verified by a number of scientific disciplines. Swedenborg learned that if a person harms any living creature, they harm themselves and God.

Such an act would markedly shape their energy, their surviving soul, spirit or consciousness. Consequently, it would also adversely affect the quality of the non-physical landscape to which the person will be drawn at death. He taught that all life-forms owe both their life origins and continued existence to their interconnected relationship with God, the Source, from which everything emanates. He described God as the single, infinite Source alternatively known as 'Love.'

He taught that:

All life is on different discrete levels and in forms which are ...

part of an overall form ... which he calls the Grand Man or Universal Human ... The higher mind, or spirit, is itself an integral part of the Universal Human ... Thus in essence, *humankind is one community and every religion a part of the one timeless universal religion.* Man's inmost thoughts and feelings, therefore, are not from himself, but part of a flow of life at the higher levels of the Divine emanation. Yet at each of these levels, each man or spirit has a distinct personality enabling him to take his place, if he is willing to allow the higher inner levels to govern him, in the perfection of the whole.[19]

## Spiritual freedom

Swedenborg taught that at the innermost level, all creatures are interconnected, for eternity, with God, the Source. Regarding the outer levels of the nature of creation, he was aware that human beings are free to choose to act in accordance with their higher self or not. He taught that the higher self is interconnected with God. He believed that historically, humankind chose not to act in accordance with the higher self and this led to the birth of evil.

The superior inner levels are the 'heaven within.' Basically two in number, there is a higher level called 'celestial,' which is essentially a love ... of the whole ... or Good Itself, God – and a lower level, 'the spiritual,' which is essentially a love ... of the goodness of all the parts of the whole, the neighbour. The celestial ... is holistic and mystical, the spiritual ... [is] more analytic and structured.[20]

## The unity of all creatures

Swedenborg taught that at first human beings lived in accordance with the non-heavenly realms of their spirit. They were oblivious to the inner heaven which he described as 'Divine Sonship.' He believed that in this spiritually bereft state, humans feel they are alienated from each other, all other creatures and God. They feel no love for people and other creatures. In this state they are ignorant of the interconnectedness and interdependence of all of creation with God.

Living in this state of separation is described by Swedenborg as 'living in a hell.' He taught that within this state of hell there exists a great range of experiences, from the mild to the terrifying. Consequently, he believed different people live in hell to different degrees. In this unfortunate lowly spiritual state, a person is unable to experience the inexpressible unity of love between themselves, all other creatures and God, the Source.

Swedenborg taught that only through a revelation from God can a person's spiritual darkness be illuminated, thereby rescuing them from this hell-like state of existence. He explained that revelations from God can occur in two ways. Using Swedenborg's terminology, the revelation or spiritual insight can take the form of 'an external light above' or as 'an internal aspect from within the soul.' He clarified the meaning of a spiritual awakening 'from within' in the following words:

> The Divine Word calls to the soul through manifested forms or images – through the beauty of nature [animals] through music or dreams ... in Swedenborg's case through the written form of sacred scripture. When the Word is received, the Divine or Holy Spirit ... awakens the separated depths in man and stirs his heart (or will) to ... seek union with the whole [all creatures, nature and God][21]

### Vegetarianism and Mother Earth

The following summarizes Swedenborg's 'doctrine of use.' He taught that spiritual reunion occurs when a person's lower will becomes elevated and is in harmony with, therefore uniting with, the will of God. This occurs when a person has free will, yet freely chooses to do good in order to serve. This choice to act in unison with God's will ultimately brings happiness to all of creation.

To exemplify the point, we might consider vegans and vegetarians who live by ecological principles. Such people seek to do no harm to any creature and to protect the ecology of the planet. They demonstrate love and compassion in all their dealings with all of creation. This has much in common with the spirituality demonstrated by devout Buddhists. The Buddha's original, undistorted teachings clarified that the spiritual journey commences when a person vows to do no harm to any living creature.

Authentic Buddhists appreciate that all life-forms are precious. The Buddha taught them that living a vegetarian life (doing no harm) represents a starting point on their spiritual journey. From this first step, they begin to value, then learn to love all creatures, as the related brethren they are. Progressively, in this way, they advance their spirituality, becoming increasingly selfless, compassionate people.

Swedenborg would class such spiritual behavior as the union of the individual with God. Due to the fact that spiritual sensitivity is growing in some people, both the vegetarian and ecological movements are progressively gaining ground today. Significantly, members can be found among spiritually awakened people from all religions of the globe. However, large numbers of vegetarians can be found in particular, in the religions of Hinduism, Buddhism, Judaism, Christianity and Spiritualism.

> The highest awareness of the truth is linked with the motivation to serve the true spiritual interests of all the parts [all creatures and the planet] in spiritual and practical ways. Far from the individual feeling lost through union with [God], on the contrary it feels most distinctly and uniquely itself, whilst sensing itself as belonging as a part of the whole.[22]

Swedenborg learned that humankind can never 'fully' understand or empathize with God's parental love for all of His/Her Creation. Nor can humankind offer to God the highest form of love. The full appreciation of both issues will always be beyond human comprehension. However, the human higher mind, once spiritually developed, can express humankind's highest form of love. It can, at least, relate to some of the spiritual teachings that Jesus tried to teach the world. Jesus taught that love should quench all hatred.

Ever compassionate, Jesus supported all those who suffered as social outcasts. His mission was to teach the importance of allevi-ating the suffering of all individuals, the most defenseless and vulnerable of which are innocent, homeless animals. These infants, who offer devotion, loyalty and unconditional love, are so at the mercy of the vicissitudes of human attitudes. Their loving parent God created them to share this planet with us.

## The illusion of being alone and separate

Swedenborg uses the word 'proprium' to describe the human condition of experiencing life as if all individuals are separate and alienated from God. Proprium has much in common with the contemporary term 'the ego.' This term expresses I-ness and self-identity, and is frequently used today in the field of consciousness studies.

The ego (proprium) interprets the world, and its place in it, through the faculty of the bodily senses. It provides the illusions which govern humankind's understanding of life. It misinforms human beings that they are alienated, independent, separate and alone in a vast, often hostile world. Swedenborg teaches that as a result of people's self-deception and credulity, they believe themselves to be separate and alone.

Unfortunately, some people in this spiritually bereft condition demonstrate negative personality traits, including jealousy, fear, hatred, guilt and shame. Consequently, using Swedenborg's termi-nology, humankind's world is 'a fallen world' into which 'Redemption' comes.

## Powers of Light

The teachings of Swedenborg's spirit and angelic communicators enlightened him enormously. They informed him that at one period in humankind's history, spiritual degradation had become so pronounced that it almost precluded any person from 'seeing the light.' He learned that God is 'the light' and that the creative parent God lives within all creatures; because they are part of God and God is a part of every living being, God feels their contentment and suffering as His/Her own.

Interestingly, he learned that God can incarnate as a being and express Him/Herself in order to redeem the world. Similarly, research into sightings of angels reveals that they too, can manifest, being fluid and malleable in form. They take the form most needed at the time of crisis, a form that is in keeping with a person's deepest needs and expectations of them.

Swedenborg believed that at that ungodly period in history, God caused the birth of Jesus, whose constitution was markedly divine. Jesus acted as 'the light' in order to steer humankind away from the dangerous degree of spiritual degeneration and darkness that had been created. Swedenborg described Jesus of Nazareth as a most special incarnation of God.

This can be understood in terms of the belief that aspects of God manifest and dwell in all creatures. Swedenborg taught that the war between the powers of light and darkness were carried out within the person of Jesus and that Jesus '"overcame the hells through temptation combats" in his soul.'[23]

Swedenborg taught that the battle between the forces of good and evil continues in perpetuity. As a consequence, each individual's thoughts and emotions are constantly influenced by good and bad non-physical personalities. This battle is part of every individual's personal process of spiritual growth. The fallen individual has the 'light' enter them.

Using Swedenborg's terminology, this is the 'Incarnation' or the birth of the Christ within. An individual can alternatively choose to see this process as God's light entering them. That which follows is the 'recognition and acknowledgement of proprium [egoic self-centredness]; repentance – to return to [God] within love and freedom; redemption – the Divine rescue of the soul from the hellish bonds of the 'proprial' illusion and selfishness.'[24]

## The eternal purifying process

Swedenborg uses the word 'regeneration' to describe 'spiritual growth.' Spiritual growth is also described in terms of 'a rebirth' or 'a return.'

> The seed, as remnant states of heavenly experiences, is implanted in [humanity's] natural awareness from physical birth onwards. Regenerating man goes through cycles of enlightenment, alternating with an emerging awareness of some evil ... tendency, lurking – often well disguised – in a deeper part of his mind or life. The ensuing battle, called temptation combat, is between [the Light] ... and the powers of darkness [the hells].[25]

Swedenborg taught that all individuals can achieve victory over evil when they choose to do good. In doing so, they accept the power of God. The power of God is within them, although they feel that the victory is their own.

> In this way, the Divine and [humanity] are as one and united in the inner struggle and afterwards [humanity] enjoys the inner peace, humility and joy that is God's within him and he is then in the state of heaven. This purifying process is repeated eternally, since total purification of the natural consciousness and life is never completely attained.[26]

## Eternal energy: all animals, human and non-human, survive death

Swedenborg was aware that he was supremely privileged to be

tutored by angelic and spirit communicators, many of whom accompanied him during his soul-journey excursions to the many levels in the non-physical realms. As stated earlier, Swedenborg learned that after the death of the physical body, each new arrival's inner spiritual, emotional and mental condition creates an energy that attracts to it corresponding, objective, non-physical landscapes and non-physical inhabitants.

These after-death landscapes range from the celestial to the infernal with many hierarchical sub-strata regions in between. Depending on the characteristics of the individual, they find themselves in a corresponding sub-strata region. These correspond to the person's level of spiritual maturity which is also reflected in a person's emotional state at the time of their soul's transition into the world of energy or spirit.

This transition at death is a rite of passage for all creatures because all creatures are composed of energy. Significantly, energy cannot be destroyed. Energy is malleable: when it changes, it simply transforms or transmutes in form. As noted earlier, energy is another way of understanding what is meant by the terms 'soul,' 'spirit' or 'consciousness.' The soul, spirit or consciousness, having a constitution of energy, leaves the physical body at death and continues to survive, having transmuted in form.

Swedenborg taught that all living beings after their physical death experience the hierarchical subdivisions, different levels or landscapes depending on their continued pre-death and post-death soul-growth. It is as though all landscapes are present but only those that mirror an individual's soul become visible, objective, externalized shared worlds or shared dimensions.

This feature was explained earlier using the analogy of the ink that was present in the glycerine but became unseen (enfolded, implicate, implicit in structure). For those living in physical bodies, the co-existent realm of spirits and angels is best understood in this way. However glimpses of those beyond the veil, in another room, can be accessed and mediums do this most proficiently.

In the post-death realms a person meets others who were formerly living at a similar level of inner spiritual, mental and emotional condition. Like is drawn to like and together they inhabit the same landscape. Significantly, these findings are clearly endorsed by Jesus' teachings. This is evidenced in the writings of Didymos Judas Thomas. Incredibly, this man was the author of the previously lost Gospel of Thomas.

Included in his writings are 114 of 'the secret sayings that the living Jesus spoke.' This invaluable find was unearthed during the 20th-century archaeological discovery of the ancient Nag Hammadi Library. In keeping with Swedenborg's findings, Thomas tells us that Jesus said: 'The kingdom of heaven is inside of you, and it is outside of you ... there is nothing hidden which will not become manifest.' This doctrine taught by Jesus vindicates Swedenborg's discoveries in the physical world and non-physical landscapes.

Everything is interrelated and interdependent, no thoughts and emotions are hidden, and one's energy draws to it like energy. In the non-physical world, appropriate landscapes being composed of energy, become manifest. This process determines the landscapes a person will inhabit as everything is composed of energy, including the landscapes.

The author of the Gospel of Thomas did not consider it important to tell us of the birth, life or death of Jesus. Instead, Thomas' overriding concern was to preserve for posterity Jesus' spiritual teachings, many of which had hitherto been long since lost and unknown. Thomas tells us that Jesus taught that all creatures have their origins in 'the light' and that it is the destiny of all creatures to return to 'the light.'

Eternal life, as a natural law of nature, is the meaning of salvation. The goal of all is to live a spiritual life and to inhabit the idyllic landscapes with like-minded companions. In order to do this all beings must rise above negative characteristics.

The contents of this ancient Gospel prove that early Christian communities had original, authentic collections of Jesus' spiritual teachings. The emphasis and content of many of these teachings was later suppressed, lost or destroyed by the institutionalized church. Jesus' profound spiritual teachings have remarkable parallels with those of Swedenborg, near-death experiencers and the spiritual communications received by entranced mediums.

Swedenborg was aware that people typically create obstructive barriers between themselves and enlightened knowledge. This is because humans incarnate into a physical body and possess a preoc-cupation with the material life. They unwittingly prevent themselves from gaining any conscious awareness of the workings of spiritual laws of nature or spiritual paranormal phenomena. However, at intervals, human awareness bridges the divide between the two worlds, the non-physical and the material.

In these instances, conscious communications are facilitated between humankind, spirits and angels. Using Swedenborg's termi-nology, those spirits who live in the celestial regions of their spirit are 'angels' and those who are living in the infernal zones of their spirit are 'evil spirits' or 'devils.'

Both Jesus and Swedenborg were emphatic that all living creatures, in keeping with laws of nature and their constitution, make their transitions at death to the immaterial co-existent spheres. I have verified this information for my own personal satisfaction. I have spent 3 decades conducting tests of mediums throughout the UK. The following examples offer proof of this assertion. I visited Paignton Spiritualitst Church, Devon, UK soon after my beloved Jack Russell had passed to spirit. A visiting medium named Sally Stocker gave messages to individuals in the congregation then she spoke to me. "I can see a small, brown and white dog sitting by your feet. I am being told that the dog had an unusual name yet I am also hearing the name Jack, which is not an unusual name."

She informed me she had recently made her transition and that she was still very much around me in the house and would wait for our reunion at death. After the service I informed Sally that my name is Jackie and my female Jack Russell was named Jac, an unusual name and that she was indeed, tan and white.

Some time after I was awoken in the night with a dog licking my face and as I woke my husband, we both witnessed a nearby area on the duvet cover go down as a result of the weight of my invisible dog.

Twenty years later, when teaching leisure classes at Paisley University, Glasgow, UK I invited Jean Brown, a medium to demonstrate her abilities to my class. She provided remarkable evidence to many individuals then she came to me saying: "I can see a small, female, brown and white dog with you who used to lift her leg up to go to the toilet like a male dog." This medium described a park I used to take Jac to, two decades ago! Jean continued by telling me how passionate my dog was and how I used to feed her something that made her feel much better and that my dog would communicate with her all day!

Jac used to sit in a begging position 3 times a day requesting her heart medication, it was clear to me that she knew it made her feel better afterwards. One day I had given her, her tablet and she came to beg soon after for another one. Obviously I did not readminister it for fear of an overdose. Shortly after she had a heart attack, I gave it then, realizing she knew she needed it to make her feel better. Apparently she had chewed or lost the one I had given her. The evidence provided by Jean Brown on all counts was indeed correct.

When I haemorrhaged some years ago and lost more than 5 units of blood, my dog Jac, who had passed to spirit one month before, lay across my right calf. I could distinctly feel the weight and warmth of her body and fur. I was aware of her when I awoke discovering I could not breathe. At that time a kindly male voice told me I had fluid going onto my lungs and that I should try to sit up to make it clear. No person or animal was physically in my hospital room. Days later we learned that I had developed a deep vein thrombosis in the calf where Jac had been sitting. I believe she had been giving me healing. Whenever I could not breathe I sat up, taking the advice of the benevolent male spirit. I later discovered that a deep vein thrombosis had formed in my right calf as a result of being bedridden, due to the haemorrhage, which was embolising blood clots to my lungs. Doctors commented on how quickly I healed.

When Sioux my 16 year old Jack Russell passed to spirit (at the vetinary hospital) I kissed her and sent my prayers out to my deceased father, nana and granddad asking them to take care of her for me. Tragically, though she fought gallantly, she and I had lost her battle with cancer and I had nursed her for several weeks.

Obviously none of the mediums below had been informed of events in my life. Ann Mc Cutcheon president of Langside Halls and Cambuslang Spiritualist Churches, (Glasgow, UK), Aileen Wallace, Ricky Martin, (also Glasgow-based mediums), Mhairi, Mary and Brian Pitt who run the Bathgate Spiritualist Church (near Edinburgh, UK), Virginia Swann (Coventry, UK), Jean Hole (Cornwall, UK) and Kay Cook (Bath, UK) independently of each other, told me that they could see and hear my dog, Sioux, and that she is with my father, grandparents and another terrier. (Jac went to spirit before her). Each of them were described giving ample proof.

They conveyed gratitude from Sioux for her life with us and her heartbreak at having to leave us and her request that we look after Edward for her. He is the other rescue Jack Russell whom she had mothered. Jean Hole added that it would be arranged for my dog to visit me in the fashion of physical phenomena. This indeed occurred several weeks later as she manifested, touched me and became smaller and smaller, finally vanishing apparently into the skirting board. This might reflect evidence of her changing her dimension as she disappeared.

The personal proof reported above is but a brief extract from the masses of evidence I have collected over 3 decades regarding the loss of my beloved childlike pets, family and friends. I am convinced as a law of nature that all living beings, who are indeed all composed of energy and related, do make their transitions at death to the next stage of existence. Many psychical research investigations into evidence of survival after death gained through mediumship and near-death experiences, do prove the reality of the experience-based beliefs of Jesus, Swedenborg and many others.

## Loving partners become one angel

As a result of Swedenborg's mediumistic communications with angels and spirits, combined with his inspired meditations and enlightened understandings of the Bible, he developed a theological system, known as a theocracy. The Swedenborgian or New Church was founded upon his teachings and flourishes to this day. Swedenborg was a fascinating medium and prophet. He fulfilled a remarkable mission: to teach humankind that life continues after physical death, that many levels exist in the post-death reality, and that there are laws that govern these after-death realms.

Swedenborg was acutely aware that it was vital for him to purify the scriptures of mistranslations, distortions, corruptions and the dogmas of faith propagated by the powerful, institutionalized church. Over the centuries, Jesus' original, authentic teachings had progressively become lost, distorted, clouded and unrecognizable. Swedenborg followed in the footsteps of our most ancient shamanic ancestors, successive generations of mediumistic prophets, and the Gnostics.

These men and women who lived throughout the millennia sought to teach that all animals, human and non-human, can make their own personal contact with God, angels and spirits. All can strive to have their lives uplifted, inspired and guided by those of the highest spiritual caliber. These enlightened beings are filled with compassion for the sufferings of the vulnerable innocents among God's entire earth family, many of whom are our related animal brethren who suffer dreadfully at the hands of humanity.

In his teachings Swedenborg made distinctions between reality and illusion, between heaven and hell, and also between heart and mind. He divided heart and mind into subjective feelings (heart) and objective thought (mind). He believed that the 'aspect of objective thought' is more conscious in the male and that the male can rationalize and comprehend patterns in the world around him.

He believed that the 'aspect of subjective feeling' is more unconscious in the male. The attributes of the female were in reverse: the 'aspect of objective thought' in the female is more unconscious and the 'aspect of subjective feeling' is more conscious.

Some of these insights would have been given to him directly by the inhabitants of the non-physical realms. Others were received as a result of his interpretations of further inspirations that came to him as a result both of meditation and of reading the Bible. All information and communications are open to interpretation by the experiencer who has to make sense of the information they receive.

In Swedenborg's day, women did not receive the education that men received, as they spent a large part of their lives bearing and rearing children. Consequently, women would not have actualized their potential with regard to education and career. This fact would inevitably have influenced some of Swedenborg's understanding of women.

According to Swedenborgian thought,

> the unconscious elements in one sex resonate with and stir the more overt elements in the other. When a truly deep fundamental uniting of both aspects takes place through the union of man with his appropriate female counterpart, Swedenborg calls it a conjugial union. And the human pair who are in conjugial love essentially form one angel – not in body or outer mind but in inner heart, mind, and soul.[27]

In his book *Conjugial Love*[28] Swedenborg explored the meaning of the true marriage relationship and its implications for the non-physical realms. His interest in this area was unique, particularly in his day. In order to classify his understanding of the relationship between the sexes and the true spiritual bonds represented by marriage between one man and one woman, brought into being through the Divine, he adds the letter 'i' to the usual term 'conjugal.'

Fundamentally, Swedenborg perceived 'man' and 'woman' as being two halves of a single whole. He believed in the complementarity of the feminine and masculine minds. There would be a drawing together, then the uniting of one man and one woman in the non-physical realms. Swedenborg witnessed weddings taking place in the non-physical dimensions.

Significantly, he learned that males and females who were harmoniously married to each other came to form one single united angel. They would thus live in eternity together. Evidently, this is the true meaning of the term 'soul-mates.' Soul-mates would progressively unite as one single angel in the spirit world. However, they would be two united aspects of the whole.

## Institutionalized religions' distortions removed

Regarding Swedenborg's concept of the 'dispensations of the ages,' Stanley notes that:

The inner transformative (regenerative) cycles in the individual spirit have their collective counterpart in groups (such as churches), both small and large ... and more general or global. With the most general of these spiritual dispensations of the ages, there have been four since the beginning of humankind on earth, with a fifth (the age of the New Jerusalem) about to begin.[29]

According to the enlightenment he received, Swedenborg believed that each of these ages was born of a unique divine (Godly) revelation, which ended because the spiritual message had, over time, become progressively corrupted and distorted. Swedenborg taught that each era is judged, after which the corruptions of that age are removed. As a result, only the pure spiritual concepts remain and these become the seeds from which the next spiritual era is born.

## Spirituality without religious dogmas

Swedenborg predicted that a New Age was yet to be born. This New Age would be characterized by people outgrowing religious authoritarianism. As a result, they would reject the religious dogmas and articles of faith of the institutionalized churches and instead seek out spiritual knowledge and information about life after death for themselves. They would obtain this knowledge for themselves in the form of direct personal experiences and from those with whom they discussed such matters.

Swedenborg's communicators taught him that God preferred and desired this change. He was convinced that this spiritual liberation leading to enhanced spiritual maturity would permeate the deepest levels of each and every individual. The thirst for spiritual knowledge represents true spirituality which is superior to the man-made corruptions of world religions. Significantly, the direct personal, transformative, spiritual, mediumistic and revelatory experiences of the shamans, the world's mediumistic prophets and the Gnostics, have close parallels with the future, experiential New Age which Swedenborg predicted.

Evidently, the forthcoming New Age will be a return to historic spiritual experiences, including spiritual, mediumistic experiences. Progressively, institutionalized religion condemned personal spiritual, experiential exploits. The receipt of such ongoing spiritual inspirations and revelations would inevitably have challenged the institutionalized religion's fixed, static, dogmatic claim to authority. Swedenborg's prediction has come to pass. With the global recognition of worldwide near-death experiences, an enhanced spiritual maturity is being born.

Progressively, increasing numbers of people are discovering spiritual truths for themselves. Transformative spiritual experiences are being democratized as increasing numbers of people are having, or learning about, entranced spiritual-mediumistic and near-death experiences. Both have in common the conviction that universal spirituality and love for all creatures and the earth are superior to the dogma propagated by organized, sectarian religion.

Historically and today, organized religions have bred hostility in the name of religion. Swedenborg expressed his prediction that humankind's spiritual liberation and progression would be like the enlightenment and sagacity gained in old age. It is 'inner freedom that only wisdom in mankind's old age can bring, the freedom that God's Will brings.'[30]

## Higher spirituality will create the peaceful union of all religions

Swedenborg believed that spirits, angels and God had enlightened him over many decades. They had commissioned him to illuminate humankind regarding the forthcoming birth of a global 'new religion.' This worldwide religion would respect and unite all elevated spiritual philosophies. Some of the revelations and insights that Swedenborg received pertained to the organized Christian church itself.

The reader is reminded of the historical background to the Christian church below. Initially founded by the Apostles in the 1st century AD, the Christian church was usurped by Paul and his personal interpretation of Christianity at a relatively early stage. Due to Paul's corruptions and negations of many of Jesus' teachings, he was vehemently hated by Jesus' disciples. He had previously had Christians murdered and persecuted, yet assumed leadership of this growing religious movement.

Paul had never met Jesus when he was alive; he had never lived with Jesus, nor had he ever discussed Jesus' teachings with him, as was the case with Jesus' disciples. He was a self-appointed apostle who negated Jesus' compassionate vegetarianism. Disputes between Paul and the disciples increasingly broke out, particularly in relation to this central issue.

In view of the above facts it is highly significant that Swedenborg's communicators taught him that the institutionalized church had suppressed, distorted or lost many of Jesus' original, authentic teachings. He was told that the church had, in effect, collapsed during Swedenborg's own lifetime. Swedenborg was convinced that a 'new church,' interpreted as a 'new religion,' was being formulated in the non-physical realms.

He learned that this eventuality, in the non-physical, higher side of life, would have repercussions on the earthly plane of existence. He believed that this event would begin to revivify and liberate spirituality in the physical world. Swedenborg named this church the 'Church of the New Jerusalem.' Significantly, this was his umbrella term for all elevated spiritual thought.

He adopted this term due to its use in the last two chapters of the biblical Book of Revelation.[31] Matthew 24:29[32] also indicates that a New Jerusalem would represent a time when aspects of the celestial realms would descend from the heavens and begin a whole new chapter for humankind on earth. Evidently, the word 'descend' is a symbolic metaphor for a metaphysical event and was not used in a literal, physical sense.

Swedenborg taught that the spiritual transition brought in with the New Age from the 18th century onwards would take considerable time to be absorbed into humankind's spiritual thought and consciousness. He believed that the changes with regards to spirituality that were occurring in the non-physical realms would have corresponding repercussions in the material realms. For Swedenborg, these changes represent the true meaning of the concept of the Last Judgment.

Brian Kingslake explains:

The human race, by education, had developed rationally to such a degree that the kind of teachings and manner of worship which had been adequate in the past were no longer serving men's needs. The Lord therefore liquidated the old church (a temporary one at best) by making certain drastic changes in the spiritual realm, which [were] ... the long-awaited Last Judgement.[33]

Swedenborg's predictions are being vindicated. From his day onwards, and most particularly since the 20th century, there has been a progressive movement away from organized religion. Increasing numbers of people have become aware that organized religion has corrupted, distorted and lost original teachings. As a consequence of this, many are rejecting dogmas of faith and moving towards a more universal, elevated spirituality.

Kingslake supports this view. He notes that the

distinctions between various denominations are apparently on their way out, with what is called the ecumenical movement. The first heaven and the first earth are passed away ... [and] there is probably more genuine spiritual life in the world today than there has been for centuries ... A new era is beginning, which is ... the New Church. Taken in this broad sense, everybody in the whole world, who believes in God and tries to live a good life, belongs to the New Church, whether he knows it or not.[34]

It was never Swedenborg's objective to create a rival religion to that of institutionalized Christianity. However, this did occur as a result of his primary mission, which was to bring in a new spiritual maturity, to liberate people from religious dogmas. His new church was born as a consequence of creating a tolerant, genuinely spiritual new era. It was Swedenborg who named the dawning of this new era the 'New Age.'

He was aware that all of humankind, like himself and other spiritual, mediumistic prophets, would learn how to find God and spiritually elevated spirits and angels for themselves. Then they would progressively learn true spirituality.

As a result of Swedenborg' profound and extensive teachings, the church of the New Jerusalem was founded, with the goal of preserving and publicizing his spiritual discoveries for future gener-ations. The church was established after Swedenborg himself had passed to spirit. Numerous societies and organizations across the globe have also been established in Swedenborg's name, one of which is the London branch of the Swedenborg Society, which was founded in 1810 in the United Kingdom. The objective of the London Swedenborg Society and presumably others is to continue to publish Swedenborg's writings and to encourage readership.[35]

## Summing-Up

Swedenborg taught that survival after physical death occurs. He assured us that all animals, human and non-human and all other creatures make a transition of consciousness at death. All survive with their recognizable personality in tact. Swedenborg witnessed conversations taking place among spirits and angels, all of whom inhabit diverse hierarchical societies in the invisible realms.

He was aware that non-physical communicators spoke with him and inspired his thoughts. Swedenborg realized that most individuals are unaware of the positive and negative spirit inspirations and influences that they attract to them.

This occurs in both the physical and non-physical spheres as a result of their own spiritual, emotional and mental level. Swedenborg was convinced that God exists. He knew that enlightened spiritual truths and knowledge of the natural laws of the non-physical world can be gained from spiritually elevated other-worldly communicators.

Swedenborg's teachings regarding the non-physical realms and the natural laws that govern them are being progressively verified by the vast array of experiential evidence amassed from mediums and out-of-body and near-death experiencers. Many near-death experiencers have been blind from birth and include blind children. Some of the most watertight evidence confirming post-death survival has been gained from blind children and adults. They experience their consciousness, soul, spirit or 'extended mind' providing them with an 'extension of experience,' geographically distant from their physical body.

Near-death experiencers are found across the globe. These people

confirm that they experienced their consciousness survive independently of their physical bodies. Many describe their meetings in the
non-physical realms with beings of light and with spirit animals,
human and non-human. The latter had passed to spirit some time
before.

Significant evidence has been gathered regarding near-death
experiencers who report meeting the spirits of those whose deaths
they had been unaware. They had not been told of the passing of
loved ones for fear that the tragic news would worsen their own
critical health. Volumes of excellent, powerful, incontrovertible
evidence vindicate the authenticity of the soul-journey accounts of
countless near-death experiencers.

Some near-death experiencers do not meet a variety of spirits.
However, they meet a 'being of light,' while their inert body lies in
the hospital morgue awaiting burial. Animal spirit bodies, human
and non-human, appear to possess a faster energy or frequency than
the denser, physical body. Near-death experiencers soul-journey to
their earthly homes, geographic distances away. Here, they may
hear their families discussing their funeral arrangements.

Typically, most family and friends cannot see them in the room.
Most out-of-body and near-death experiencers who have experienced their consciousness separate from their physical body claim
that 'physical death' is simply a permanent near-death experience.
The transition at death is a soul-journey to the non-physical realms
from which the experiencer does not return.

Swedenborg's discoveries are further substantiated by the vast
amount of recorded communications received by mediums.
Information conveyed through the medium frequently provides
extraordinary proof to sitters of recognizable surviving animal spirit
intelligences, human and non-human. Evidently, their souls at
physical death have made the transition of consciousness from the
physical to the non-physical realm.

Although Swedenborg's transformative spiritual-mediumistic
experiences are most persuasive, they may not be universally

compelling. This is because many people have a personal material-istic belief system. Most would be unaware that their beliefs are born of overwhelming materialistic conditioning and indoctrination. Materialism dominates in our present reductionist age.

Unfortunately, many people evaluate all evidence of mediu-mistic, out-of-body and near-death experiences within the limited parameters of traditional materialist science rather than the latest dynamic findings of quantum physics. Sadly, the quantum physi-cists' discoveries regarding hitherto unknown natural laws have not percolated into schools and general society yet.

Despite volumes of overwhelming evidence for post-death survival, some would claim that the survival of consciousness cannot be wholly proved or disproved. Consequently, beliefs and conclu-sions are the responsibility of each individual. For many people, these issues cannot be addressed as a matter of certainty. People's opinions are based upon their previously held spiritual beliefs, personal mediumistic experiences and their materialist or non-materialist worldviews.

Their beliefs are also shaped by their knowledge (or lack of knowledge) regarding the libraries of experiential (paranormal) reports of spirit and/or angelic communications. Many of these have been collected for more than a century by numerous organizations including the Society for Psychical Research (SPR). The SPR is based in many countries of the world, including the UK and the USA.

Swedenborg's intention was to convey to others, the teachings which he believed were communicated to him from spiritually elevated non-physical messengers. His mission was to advance the spiritualization of all peoples of the world and unite them in spiritu-ality. He wished to unify religious beliefs under the umbrella of a higher universal spirituality, breaking down the illusory boundaries between religions and creeds.

Swedenborg was used as a mediumistic prophet. He followed in the footsteps of the long succession of shamans, historic mediumistic prophets and Gnostics before him. There were many mediumistic shamanic features demonstrated throughout his life as there were in the lives of the prophets before him. As a more contemporary spiritual medium, his purpose was to purify organized religion by ridding it of accumulated distorted teachings. He sought to advance humankind's spirituality by offering to others the contents of his mediumistic communications and experiences in the non-physical realm.

His prophecy or mediumship, which is the same thing, was used to herald the birth of a New Age. This is an age which is currently dawning on human spiritual consciousness. Arguably, this New Age is an epoch in which people will progressively follow the most spiritually elevated religious teachings found in a number of religions. They will then discard teachings of a lower spiritual level that do not teach love for all creatures and the planet herself.

People will cumulatively appreciate the richness of human religious diversity as elevated spiritual pathways leading to the same place. On a global scale they will develop personal relationships with God and spiritually elevated spirits and angels, rather than blindly following the dogmas of the world's institutionalized religions. The changes brought in by the New Age are progressively being integrated into peoples' spiritual consciousness.

Swedenborg was aware that it would take a considerable length of time for the advanced universal spiritual thought of the New Age to permeate into humankind's spiritual life. A large proportion of humankind is frequently insecure, intolerant and fearful of change, preferring to be tightly and securely bound by authoritarian religious dogmas.

Swedenborg's spiritually inspired celestial messengers gave him revelations and unique experiences of the non-physical spheres in order for him to begin the process of liberating people's minds from dangerously naïve, intolerant religious fundamentalism. His communicators' mission was to educate Swedenborg so that he could progressively empower humankind to discover for themselves profound, spiritual truths, so that they could judge all 'religions' by a spiritually elevated yardstick.

Spiritually liberated and evolved thinkers will grow to respect all elevated spiritual ideologies that teach us to love and protect all living creatures, including animals, human and non-human, birds, marine life, reptiles and the earth herself. According to Swedenborg's privileged paranormal conversations and experiences of the celestial and infernal realms it is right action such as this that determine a positive environment for all those who make their transition at death to the non-physical dimension.

The spiritual truths Swedenborg learned revealed that no harm, neglect, exploitation, emotional or physical pain, should be directed directly or indirectly against any creature who shares this planet with us. Significantly, we are all interrelated, interconnected and interdependent at a very deep divine level.

Spiritual thinkers will appreciate that animals should not be overbred or slaughtered as there are so many healthier, more compassionate alternatives to eating animal flesh. There is an ever-increasing profusion in our markets of low-fat, low cholesterol, vegetarian alternatives. Many offer tasty vegetarian replicas of beef, chicken, turkey, bacon, ham and sausages. The manufacturers of these ever increasing multifarious vegetarian alternatives are committed to halting animal genocide and make their products using delicious proteins made from quorn, tofu and soya.

As humans spiritually evolve and return to their idyllic vegetarian beginnings, such as they enjoyed in the Garden of Eden, their health and souls also benefit. By eating low-fat vegetarian alternatives, weight gain and bad cholesterol is reduced, thereby decreasing the risk of developing a wide range of cardiovascular diseases such as coronary artery disease, peripheral vascular disease, cerebral vascular disease which can manifest as strokes and Parkinson's disease.

Studies have shown that vegetarians halve their chances of developing a number of cancers, including breast and prostate cancers, some forms of dementia, and the above 'animal flesh related' diseases.

Spiritual thinkers will also oppose animal experimentation, which is cruel and produces inaccurate results. There is an emerging potential to culture stem cells from human adults. This process may be able to produce isolated human organ tissue which can then be subjected to a diverse range of toxicological drug testing. This is a much more accurate substitute for animal experiments. However, any forms of genetic engineering, carrying out artificial selection and manipulating specific genes, should be heavily monitored for compassionate and ethical reasons.

A tragic and inevitable result of that type of experimentation can be the birth of hybrid monstrous animal creations. Such hybrids have been washed up on the seashores in parts of America. These sentient creatures must have daily, led tormented, agonized lives of tortured suffering. The evolution of a particular species has taken millions of years and cannot be replicated in a laboratory without disastrous results. Such hybrid creations would inevitably harm all life on this planet as they would infect the global gene pool and open up a Pandora's Box, the results of which would be beyond our worst imaginings.

Stem cell research should be limited to stem cells, thereby preventing experimentation on any living animal, especially those that have become semi or fully developed. The results of stem cell research can provide much more accurate results. It represents a more positive, compassionate development as long as the stem cells are used only to culture isolated organs and are not allowed to develop and mature into tragic creatures that would perpetually suffer as hybrid monstrosities.

Computer modeling is another more accurate substitute for animal experimentation. It simulates and investigates the action of drugs on human tissues without harming animals. Our ancient human ancestors had four legs, and all creatures are on earth to evolve physically and spiritually. We should not make an industry out of breeding and then conducting wholesale slaughter on animals when we have countless healthier vegetarian protein food alternatives.

Adopting vegetarian alternatives would rid the world of the filthy, overcrowded, dark, damp, hellish housing of animals and poultry. Vegetarianism would end the overuse of hormones and chemicals in rearing animals. These inevitably end up in the human body with little understood disasterous effects. Vegetarianism would also end the force-feeding of animals to produce foods such as foie gras. Through this process their bodies become bloated as food is mechanically poured down their esophagus. Geese, who in the wild mate for life, suffer this fate, which fortunately is banned in some countries.

Cows spend a short time in the fields. The rest of their lives they are tied to rape racks. Cows are kept pregnant for the rest of their lives producing milk, which is filled with hormones which inevitably adversely affect the human body. Male calves and male chicks are killed after birth. Calves endure the deprivation of light and indeed life. Veal calves are trapped in boxes in which they cannot move or sit down to rest. Leaders of humanity sanction the convoluted, nightmarish journeys involved in live animal transportation and the barbaric, painful, slow, torturous experimentation and/or mass slaughter of our animal companions.

It is difficult to teach compassion to those who daily commit slaughter in this multibillion-dollar industry. The factory conveyor-belt system, which enables murder to be committed piece by piece, knows no mercy as animals cry out in agony, terror and disbelief. These practices cannot be policed to ensure painlessness throughout the world, but one day this degradation of our fellow animals will be seen on a par with other murderous atrocities, such as that committed on the Jews in the Nazi concentration camps.

Many humans have come to disregard the sacred sanctity of all life. If we respect animal life, how much more will we learn to respect human life? A wise person once said, 'A nation can be judged for posterity by the way it treats its animals.' The genius Leonardo

Da Vinci foretold that: 'A time will come when men will look upon the murder of animals as they look upon the murder of men.'

Instead we should allow all animals, human and non-human, to evolve physically, mentally, emotionally and spiritually. Animals, including human animals, have evolved from fish to four-legged creatures. Some branched off and became humans. Many people who own a pet know that their beloved animals regularly demonstrate all the cute adorable childish emotions of innocent, vulnerable children throughout their entire lives.

They are often devastated when their pet passes to spirit; they miss their devotion, loyalty, companionship and unconditional love. Many animals would choose to give up their lives to protect their human family. Taking a spiritually enlightened vegetarian path would be wholly in keeping with the teachings of Swedenborg. Such compassion would fulfill his concept of the true meaning of 'union' between a person and God. Union is attained when a person aspires to love all creatures and the planet in the same way as the ever-compassionate, creative, loving parent God.

*Chapter 13*

# The Bible's Power as Perennial Bestseller

Throughout the ages, this ancient composite of books, written over many centuries, prejudicially chosen by those in authority, has continued to be the most widely circulated book of all time. The Bible is a perennial world bestseller despite the fact that biblical scholars know it is full of mistranslations and misconceptions. For spiritual truth-seekers, this is a sad state of affairs. The Bible's accounts of the lives of prophets and kings, the people's oppression, and the rise and fall of pharaohs and ancient empires, have inspired the world's finest writers, poets, painters and composers.

Due to the magnitude of the Bible's influence, it is vital to expose suppressed, mistranslated and misrepresented biblical records. Consequently, it has been the task of this book to put the record straight. Many people may have a changed perspective as a result of reading the revelations provided here.

Over half the world's population reveres the writings in the Bible. It is sacred to 2 billion Christians and 14 million Jews. 1.3 billion Muslims also accept the Bible as a holy book. The prophet Muhammad taught Muslims to respect the religions of Jews and Christians as both are 'Peoples of the Book.' The decoded biblical information provided in this book should therefore be of immense interest to countless people who seek truth.

The impact the Bible has had and continues to have on human civilization cannot be overstated. Throughout the ages and still today, the biblical accounts are manipulated with good and bad intent to justify or condemn many aspects of human activity. The Bible has strongly influenced the foundation of humanity's laws, created ethics, and shaped the way global society is governed. The message of its pages is powerfully pervasive.

To give one example of the widespread circulation of the Bible, societies such as the American Bible Society (ABS), founded in 1816 with its headquarters in New York City, has published, distributed and had linguistic scholars translate the Bible (in part or in whole) into more than 1500 languages. This represents over 97% of the world's nations. The ABS produces the modern translations known as the Good News Bible and the Contemporary English Version. They have reproduced the biblical scriptures on records, cassettes, compact discs and in Braille.

In 2001 the ABS distributed over 4 million bibles and over 8 million copies of the New Testament throughout the world. By 1934 the ABS had distributed 70 million volumes of scriptures to China alone! There are many other international Christian societies which also co-ordinate the translation and global distribution of the Bible. They supplement the millions of bibles circulated by the ABS throughout the world with yet many more millions.

Individuals have been oppressed, persecuted, tortured and condemned to death due to non-spiritual and ignorant interpretations of the Bible's words. Likewise, open warfare has found its excuse in biblical misinterpretations. Consequently, improving our understanding of the correct context for biblical and other spiritual teachings is imperative for the progression of humanity, all creatures and the earth herself.

Many Jews, Christians and Muslims see their scriptures as being the pure word of God. Some believe the words are therefore sacrosanct and unchanging. They may be unaware of the fact that religio-political intrigues have ensued over the centuries, causing religious texts to have been either lost or suppressed. There has also been much religio-political manipulation of the scriptures.

The prophet Muhammad taught his followers to demonstrate compassion for all creatures. This is exemplified by the fact that he taught that those people who give food, water and shelter to helpless creatures such as dogs and cats would go to Paradise. Approximately six centuries earlier, Jesus taught that compassion was expected of his followers as every creature is precious to the parent God. This is clearly indicative of Jesus' belief in one single earth family. It is highlighted by his teaching that God is aware of and shares the suffering of even the smallest bird. Both Muhammad and Jesus, like the famous Greek philosophers, the Buddha and the Hindu sages, taught compassion and expected it to be practiced by their followers. Each of these traditions, except Islam, specifically taught vegetarianism as a means of demonstrating compassion.

Such original uncorrupted teachings are in sharp contrast to the murder, cruelty to animals and warfare that are carried out in the name of religion. Erroneous interpretations of the prophets' teachings as recorded in the scriptures remain explosive issues. Poor interpretations of these are used to legitimize violence, sectarianism, intolerance, land grab and the wholesale breeding, merciless slaughter, abuse and misuse of animals. Our related fellow animals are living feeling members of the single Earth family. Such issues highlight the tremendous importance attached to clarifying mistranslations and corruptions of spiritual texts.

The abuse and murder of animals through cruel factory-farming methods and in slaughterhouses is abhorrent. Their vulnerable bodies are turned into tinned products in supermarkets. Incredibly, many people have become oblivious to the pain and suffering each innocent individual animal suffers. In countless laboratory experiments these flesh-and-blood relatives of ours are wracked with pain as they are used as though they are a mass of inanimate chemicals.

This is relentless genocide which knows no mercy. Though related, their bodies are different and the experimental results would surely reflect their bodies not human bodies. As noted earlier many alternatives to animal experimentation exist which are considered to produce more accurate results.

These practices are in direct contravention of the prophets' teachings regarding the spirituality of compassion. Eating animals and cruelty to animals is in stark contrast to the widespread vegetarianism in the world preceding and during the birth of Christianity, and in the early centuries of that religion. Early Christians followed the vegetarian practices of Jesus' disciples, who were the individuals who had been the closest to Jesus and the first followers of his teachings. This can be understood as Jesus' authentic uncorrupted brand of Christianity.

Progressively elevated spiritual guidance received by mediumistic prophets from celestial incursions into the material plane continue to make their presence known today. Arguably, their teachings imply that a lifetime spent without compassion and sensitivity to animal suffering would determine a negative post-death reality. When describing the after-death domains, Jesus said there were many 'rooms/mansions' or levels in his Father's house. Buddhism, shamanic, out of body and near death experiences, Swedenborg and other mediums confirm this belief.

Jews, Christians and Muslims treat their religious texts with ritual reverence. Even today the Torah scroll is housed in the sacred Ark in Jewish synagogues. Catholics follow a procession which escorts the Bible into church services. The Koran is placed on top of all books and no Muslim should smoke in front of it. The holy books of all the great global religions teach that true spirituality is reflected in demonstrating compassion to all human and non-human animals and to Mother Earth herself. Yet how little are these teachings followed in our daily affairs when we have developed an industry that murders billions of animals every year?

If adherents to religion fail to express compassion as an act of true spirituality they fail the very scriptures which they proselytize. Living in harmony with each other and all creatures is the scenario to which humankind needs to return. This state of living was symbolically reflected in the ancient biblical account of the first of humankind who lived in the idyllic Garden of Eden. Adam and Eve were told to eat many things but not to eat the animals. Respected archaeologists following biblical directions to the harmonious Garden of Eden have located it in present-day Iran.

## Successive Misrepresentations of the Bible

People today have a vague knowledge that over the centuries the Bible narratives have been successively interpreted, revised and translated from different languages. However, many believe these writings are the pure, undiluted, revealed word of God. Accurate translation and interpretation is a work of great responsibility, requiring diverse specialist knowledge.

Those scholars able to carry it out would need to be unconcerned with political, institutionalized theology. They would need a correct historical, sociological and political understanding of the context in which something was said.

They would need to know what the original author was clearly inferring. Looking beyond the confusion to the greater truth, translators over the centuries would need to understand historic beliefs, practices and customs. They would need to have knowledge of psychical phenomena and research, as revealed in this book. Evidently, most translators did not possess all these attributes and this has led to many subjective misconceptions and mistranslations.

Without fail, all the biblical records were written against the background of their author's personal level of spiritual maturity and understanding. They also reflect the spiritual understanding of the age in which the revelations were received and interpreted. The disparate religious teachings contained in the Bible's pages have become understood by the yardstick of institutionalized politico-religious and materialist interpretations.

Materialism has consciously and unconsciously colored many biblical accounts which are then fed to the people. Materialism dismisses mediumistic and psychic phenomena as irrelevant and non-existent, hence these invaluable phenomena have become marginalized and their significance has been lost.

Many people are brainwashed by manipulators of religion into believing that the Bible tells us certain things. This fact makes it imperative that biblical research unearths the truth underlying many biblical accounts. This is a grave responsibility and a task that must be carried out with diligence and sensitivity in the same way as an archaeologist delicately unearths ancient artifacts and in so doing clarifies popular misconceptions about ancient truths.

It is vital for the spiritual researcher to act as a spiritual archaeologist and uncover the true meanings and contexts of the Bible's depictions. This task is vital because the Bible has changed the world. Throughout history to the present day it has been perceived as a spiritual roadmap by billions of people. Our interpretation of it therefore shapes the way people live and perceive their existence, and how they treat each other, animals, and our home the earth.

## Background to the Bible

Earlier chapters have clarified a number of important biblical accounts. It is useful, therefore, to be aware of how the composition of the Bible came into being. Approximately 40 men, over an approximate period of 1,600 years, contributed to writing the 66 books which are contained within the Bible. The text was written between 1450 BC and 100 AD, but the biblical accounts describe lives, historical events and discuss matters dating from approximately 2000 BC to 100 AD.

The Bible was written in three continents: Asia, Africa and Europe, and in three languages: Hebrew, Aramaic and Greek. Many believe that at least the first book of the Bible was written by Moses, who lived approximately 1,400 years before the time of Jesus Christ. The last book was written about 70 years after Jesus passed to spirit. Authors of the Bible refer to it as 'the word of God' (Hebrews 4:12; 1 Thessalonians 2:13, NIV), 'the Holy Scriptures' (Romans 1:1–2, NIV) and the 'sacred writings' (2 Timothy 3:15, Revised Standard Version).

The Bible is composed of a number of literary genres including poetry, myth, wisdom literature, prophecy, letters and narratives, many of which describe historically based events. Many of the historical biblical records reflect a schematized chronology rather than a literal historical record as it was not written in the same way as a history book is today. The word 'bible' is derived from the Latin word *biblia* which means 'books,' so when we say 'Bible' we are in fact saying 'Books.' The Bible is divided into two sections known as the Old and New Testaments. The word 'testament' means 'covenant,' which means 'promise.'

The following facts help illustrate something of the human element which has given us the Bible today. Many religions have been impacted by the human element, and the same can be said of many of the world's religious scriptures.

The Bible was divided into chapters by Cardinal Hugo in 1250. It holds the distinction of being the first book in the world to be printed, in 1454. The first English translation of the whole Bible was published in 1535 by Miles Coverdale. Its text was divided into verses by Sir Robert Stephens in 1551, and the first Bible to show chapters and verses was published in 1560.

The King James Version of the Bible was first published in 1611, the Revised Version in 1885, and the American Standard edition in 1901. The Bible has been translated into 2,000 languages, more languages and dialects than any other book in the world.

## The Old Testament Writers

The commencement of the writing of former oral traditions is believed to have begun at the time of Moses. Moses was a Hebrew educated in the royal court in ancient pharaonic Egypt. Most scholars believe he lived in approximately the 13th century BC, which in archaeological terms is classed as the later Bronze Age. Many people believe that Moses wrote the first five books of the Bible known to Jews as the Torah and to Christians as the Pentateuch or Books of Moses.

These books are named Genesis, Exodus, Leviticus, Numbers and Deuteronomy. Moses may not have been their sole author, and editorial updating by a person or persons who lived after Moses may have occurred. However, the authenticity of many events and characters described in the biblical Pentateuch has been shown earlier to have been proven by the findings of historians and archae-ologists.

The Old Testament contains 39 books (not counting further scrip-tures known as the Apocrypha). Significantly, the Christian Old Testament is virtually the same as the Jewish Tanakh. This book was originally written in Hebrew and tells of the mediumship of the biblical prophets revered by Jews, Christians and Muslims. The names of the Old Testament books in Hebrew are derived from the first prominent word or phrase found in that book. The names of the Old Testament books in Greek (and English) are derived from the general topic of that book.

## The New Testament Writers

The New Testament contains 27 books, originally written in Greek. Its authors used a Greek translation of the Old Testament known as the Septuagint, which was a translation of the Hebrew Bible into Koine Greek. The Septaguint is the most ancient of a number of ancient translations of the Hebrew Bible into Greek (356–323 BC). The text was successively translated from the 3rd to 1st centuries BC in the city of Alexandria in Egypt.

Significantly, the Septuagint contains books that are not included in the Hebrew Bible; this provides an example of the variations that exist between biblical texts. Jews have not included these books in their religious scriptures since the 2nd century AD. The New Testament is approximately the same length as the Islamic holy scriptures known as the Koran.

## Finding Lost and Unknown Ancient Sacred Texts

Due to the wonderful archaeological discoveries of ancient sacred texts in the mid-20th century, a renewed passion has emerged to search out original authentic teachings, including those of Jesus Christ. Jesus' original teachings are reflected in the beliefs and practices of those closest to him, his faithful early followers. Significant passages in the Hebrew contents of these previously unknown sacred manuscripts support the findings of this book regarding biblical prophetic mediumship.

Discoveries of lost or unknown ancient scriptures are of momentous importance. They raise people's awareness of biblical textual corruptions and mistranslations and of the fact that many hitherto lost or unknown ancient scriptures were deliberately omitted from the future canonized Bible (i.e. containing only the books that were permitted by the church).

This was done by ambitious men who belonged to the developing powerful politico-religious orthodoxy. These discoveries have included the Dead Sea Scrolls and the lost or unknown ancient Gnostic Christian scriptures known today as the Nag Hammadi Library.

## The Dead Sea Scrolls 250 BC – 100 AD

The Dead Sea Scrolls were found in a series of discoveries from 1947 to 1956 in eleven caves in the Khirbet Qumran area of the Judean desert. This area is outside of Jerusalem at the north end of the Dead Sea. In total, 800 manuscripts have been identified among these badly disintegrated, poorly preserved scroll segments. For many centuries 'Cave 4' had secretly housed 1,500 scroll fragments. These are thought to be all that survives of 574 ancient manuscripts that had been previously lost to humanity.

These invaluable documents have been dated to the intertestamental period (250 BC to 100 AD). The textual formation of the Old Testament had been carried out by this time. However, Christianity and rabbinical Judaism had not yet been standardized. Impressively, a copy of the ancient Old Testament Book of Isaiah, relevant in particular to Jews, Christians and Muslims, was found among the scrolls. It represents the most ancient complete manuscript of a Hebrew scripture and dates back to 100 BC.

The 'Community Rule' scroll details the rules of conduct and beliefs of a Jewish community, dated around 150 BC to 70 AD. The hypothesis is still contentious, though strongly supported by many respected scholars, that the scrolls belonged to an ascetic Jewish community known as the Essenes. Notably, the 'Essenes' is an umbrella term for many differing groups. Ancient ruins located near the Qumran caves may have been the buildings in which this community lived.

The scrolls, written by the hands of hundreds of scribes, reveal the heated debates between competing Jewish sects. These diverse ancient religious Hebrew scrolls express differing perspectives and interpretations, each of which competed to monopolize the opinions of future generations. Importantly, they provide us with a window into the past, spotlighting a time when Christianity was enduring its gestation period. The scrolls also enrich our understanding of early Christian debates regarding the decisions to establish Jesus as both 'the Messiah' and 'the Divine.'

They take us to a time which clearly reveals the human element in the interpretation of religion and the human choices of what was acceptable regarding the teachings of long-dead prophets. The debates and decisions taken at that time crystallized the form that Christianity would take for posterity.

The future generations who were not privy to these discussions might not have accepted the dogmas systematized by religio-political church leaders at that time and may not have adered to the unquestioning faith that was subsequently born.

### Nag Hammadi: 200–300 AD

In 1945, ancient sacred texts written on papyrus were unearthed in the Egyptian village of Nag Hammadi, near Luxor, in Upper Egypt. The thirteen brown, leather-bound volumes or codices were discovered near an ancient grave by a Bedouin. They had been sealed in a large, red earthenware jar. It is thought that they were hidden in 390 AD by monks from the neighboring monastery of St Pachomius. These codices represent approximately 55 sacred texts which represent lost or unknown early Christian sacred scriptures.

They have been dated to approximately 200–300 AD and consist of gospels written by the early Gnostic Christians, who sought to protect them from destruction. They are known today as the Nag Hammadi Library.

The Coptic Gospel of Thomas was found among these concealed manuscripts. This Gospel is considered to be older than the four canonical Gospels of Matthew, Mark, Luke and John (those included in the Bible). Importantly, it is thought that the Gospel of Thomas actually provided the source material for the Gospels of Matthew and Luke. Despite this fact, the Gospel of Thomas was obviously condemned and sought after by the greater church, with the intention of destroying it.

Jesus is shown in the Gospel of Thomas encouraging others to become like him. Ironically, Jesus' own teachings would have been considered heretical by the developing powerful religious orthodoxy as they can be interpreted as undermining Jesus' unique position.

Astonishingly, these ancient writings inform us that this Gospel was written by Thomas, the twin brother of Jesus! The orthodox church successfully suppressed this information until now, presumably because they believed that this truth would reduce the primacy of Jesus.

The Gospel of Thomas contains 114 previously lost secret sayings of Jesus regarding life after death. Consequently, documents such as these ancient precious artifacts have created renewed interest in searching out the authentic teachings of Jesus so that they can be compared with the dogmas of the orthodox church. These include the assertions that Jesus is God and that Jesus had to die so that others could go to heaven. It appears Jesus did not teach this, which again reveals the human element affecting original teachings and scriptures.

## Background and Beliefs of the Gnostics

The term *gnosis* is a Greek word that means 'the act of knowing.' Significantly, it does not refer to rational knowledge, but to the direct personal, interior experience of absolute knowing. This is diametrically opposed to following dogmas with blind faith and very different from rational, logical knowledge. The Gnostics claimed that they were the most authentic followers of the uncorrupted teachings and practices of Jesus. Importantly, they claimed that they were the custodians of sacred esoteric Christian gospels, traditions and rituals.

Around 100–150 AD, when we first learn of the Christian Gnostics, Christianity was in its formative stages and had not yet been standardized into one set of articles of faith. Once set in stone, these were never to be disputed for all time. During this period there were diverse struggling Christian groups declaring their own individual expression of Christianity. For some of these groups, to varying degrees, Christianity was absorbed and blended with previously held religious convictions.

Records indicate that the highly educated and respected Gnostic teacher Valentius, from Alexandria, was nearly made Bishop of Rome around 150 AD. The results of this decision represented a pivotal turning point for the future destiny of Christianity. Amazingly, if Valentius had become Bishop of Rome this experiential 'lost Christianity' might have survived and been practiced by Christians today. However, when Valentius lost this influential opportunity to become bishop, opponents in Rome, in the developing greater orthodox church gained politico-religious sway.

Instead of gaining power and acclaim the decision went against him. This resulted in Valentius as a Gnostic being expelled as a heretic for not accepting their particular developing orthodox brand of Christianity. Some of Valentius' core beliefs differed from those of the other ambitious church leaders who were fast monopolising power. Inevitably, members of the greater church would have been challenged by the fact that, as a Gnostic, Valentius could regularly access new scriptures containing a continuous stream of elevated spiritual truths that differed from the orthodox fossilized version.

Evidently, Valentius was able to take advantage of the Gnostic experiential psychic and mediumistic practices which were of a spiritually transformative nature. The threat he presented to those seeking total authority was unimaginable hence the church leaders banded together to have him expelled as a heretic; their legacy changed Christianity for all time.

From the 2nd to 4th century AD, politically powerful bishops and early church Fathers mounted passionate verbal and physically violent attacks on the Gnostics. This resulted in the destruction of precious Gnostic scriptures and the exile of their devotees. People should be aware that many aspects of later Christian theology were created by powerful men in antagonistic response to Gnosticism. Later Christian theology was significantly misrepresented or diluted compared to earlier teachings and certainly condemned the Gnostic spiritually experiential beliefs and practices.

Regarding the beliefs of the Gnostics, they had an unshakeable belief in one God. However, they accepted the existence of other infernal and celestial beings who could influence all living creatures. These might be described today as wicked and mischievous spirits who were at that time thought of as demons, and spiritually advanced angels and spirits. The Gnostics did not believe that Jesus' death bought people the keys to eternal life.

Rather, they taught that immortality was there for all as a fact of life. Pursuing spiritual truths and acting upon them during life would positively affect the type of after-life a person would experience. The spiritual truths sought by the Gnostics included discovering who we truly are, the authentic origin of all of creation, and how the spiritual quality of a person's life can lead them at death to shape their non-physical home.

The Gnostics sought dynamic, ongoing, direct, personal, spiritual, revelatory, inspirational knowledge from God and the spiritually elevated angelic realm. They were not interested in mindlessly accepting and reciting institutionalized, standardized creeds and articles of faith as they judged these to have no value. Instead the Gnostics advised all people to strive during their earthly lives to access the celestial source of elevated spiritual knowledge.

Such Gnostic beliefs were dramatically and directly opposed to the acceptance of rigid religious dogmas and religious affirmations that were being progressively laid down by the increasingly powerful religious orthodoxy.

Rational, religio-political and legal considerations cumulatively drowned the Gnostic creative, inspirational and revelatory free spirit. The Gnostics did not have a static creed but supplemented their beliefs by means of ongoing spiritually elevated revelations, insights and information, presumably received mediumistically from the celestial world. The Gnostics lost the battle. Their teachings were suppressed and replaced with static religious dogmas and articles of faith, which came to dominate Christian theology to the present day.

The Gnostic goal was to seek various forms of direct, personal, transformative spiritual experience to cumulatively progress their knowledge of a wide range of spiritual truths. This led to the ongoing production of religious scriptures which recorded their spiritual insights regarding the authentic nature of humanity, our relationship with other sentient creatures, and life after death. Importantly, Gnostic experience-based beliefs taught others that all people can seek to attune to God and the inhabitants of the celestial realms.

They believed that recording spiritual truths is an ongoing process, not a static preserve of the past.

Within this ancient Christian tradition they taught that all living creatures have the seed of God within them and that it is vitally important to do no harm to any creature. The Gnostics were ascetics who sought to know themselves at the deepest level of inner knowing, in an attempt to experience God and the angelic inhabitants of the celestial world. Such beliefs and practices were anathema to the orthodox church which simplistically perceived God and humanity as two disunited entities.

Because members of the orthodoxy could not mediumistically access celestially inspired teachings, they claimed that the angelic realm had stopped communicating. They closed their doors on the angels' fountains of spiritual wisdom, one of the sources of knowledge that the Gnostics regularly accessed. Their goal was to close humankind's doors to the celestial realms for all time. Experiential meditative and mediumistic practices were firmly condemned. Such was the power of these men that their beliefs and influence control many people to this day.

Importantly, the Gnostics learned from celestial sources to perceive God as a 'Father Mother God.' The institutionalized church responded with the decree that this concept was blasphemous. Indeed before the discovery of the Nag Hammadi Library, much of what was known of Gnostic Christianity was gleaned from the misrepresentations and passionate attacks hurled at them by the politically powerful bishops and early church Fathers. These were powerful religio-political members of the developing orthodox church. These included attacks by Tertullian of Carthage (200 AD) and Hippolytus of Rome (200 AD).

By the 4th and 5th centuries AD, Gnostic Christianity, composed of those who claimed to be the most accurate followers of Jesus and custodians of early esoteric Christian scriptures, had been violently swept away. Some early Gnostic groups hid their scriptures to prevent their destruction, trusting that their writings would one day be found, miraculously, by others in a more spiritually liberated era. Thanks to them, the discovery of the ancient, sacred texts at Nag Hammadi is continuing to enrich our understanding of the beliefs and experiential practices of the Gnostics who claimed to be the most faithful followers of Jesus.

They believed they closely followed Jesus' original teachings including his beliefs and practices, yet many of these are in sharp contrast to some of the main tenets that became present-day Christianity. This fact acutely raises our awareness that our traditional bibles contain mistranslations and omit many original Christian teachings. Considerable interest has thus been reawakened in spiritual archaeology: learning the original truths and teachings of the uncorrupted scriptures. The results of this spiritual archaeology have been clarified throughout this book.

## Early Christianity's Divergent Beliefs

In the first centuries after Jesus passed to spirit, as yet there was no official New Testament for the early Christians. The doors had not yet been firmly closed on ancient sacred writings that reflected views that men in the developing orthodox church opposed; canonization of the New Testament books came later. Early Christians held beliefs that were to be quashed by a succession of later powerful church leaders. These men threw out early Christian Gospels and other contemporaneous sacred scriptures in order to streamline and standardize their creed. This was to be the official, unquestioned version of Christianity for all future generations.

Therefore, in this formative period, Christians had far more scriptures than we have today. However, all religious writings which held a different view to the newly standardized, consistent, religious creed were excluded from the canon. The prejudicially chosen canon became the approved books of the Bible. Writings revered by diverse groups were branded as heretical, forgeries and the work of dissidents. These scriptures were then destroyed by the authorities or hidden for safety and so became lost to future generations.

In effect, those ruling the developing institutionalized church decided which ancient scriptures they would preserve, which they would destroy and which of Jesus' teachings they would accept. Jesus' teachings had been filtered by man-made preferences and choices resulting in omissions and distortions deliberate and otherwise. They decided that Jesus should be viewed by all as both the Messiah and divine.

Their doctrine with a most powerful impact commanded people to believe that Jesus had to die as a sacrifice in order for others to enter heaven. They taught that the precious gift of eternal life could be gained only through belief in Jesus, which meant accepting their dogmatic decisions about him. The opinions of politically ambitious men became standardized religious teachings for all future Christians.

The early Christian Gnostics did not believe that there was any part of Jesus' teachings that stated that his future death would buy people a place in heaven. Guided by their knowledge of his teachings, they understood that a life after death was inevitable for all creatures. They were aware that the after-death state would be enhanced if a person followed Jesus' beliefs and practices and lived a compassionate spiritual life. For them, it was not heretical to follow the role model of Jesus as they believed Jesus had asked people to follow him, as stated in the suppressed Gospel of Thomas.

Although Jesus was greatly revered, the Gnostics did not believe that he ever taught that he was literally one and the same as God. They believed that a person works their way back to heaven through various forms of direct spiritual experience, which underlines the importance they attached to accessing spiritual knowledge and guidance from celestial, angelic beings.

The Gnostics believed they gained many spiritual insights from the celestial realms regarding the mysteries of the non-physical realms and spirituality. Importantly, they learned that it was best to live a vegetarian life. Such a life demonstrates spirituality in the form of compassion, as they did no harm to any of God's creatures. All flesh-and-blood creatures know emotional, mental and physical pain and suffering.

An ancient prayer of thanksgiving has been discovered in the Gnostic Gospels in the Nag Hammadi Library. Notably, it demonstrates the command that led to ancient vegetarianism. The Manichaeans, who were the largest Gnostic group and almost gave birth to one of humankind's major religions, were vegetarian. Many Hermetic, Jewish and Gnostic Christian groups over 2,000 years ago were also vegetarian. The Hebrew Christians who supported James the Just (Jesus' brother) in Jerusalem possessed vegetarian Ebionite gospels and lived a vegetarian lifestyle.

The same prayer can be found in the Corpus Hermeticum, which is another Egyptian religious text. The last sentence of the Hermetic translation of this prayer particularly reflects strong vegetarian values: 'When they had said these things in the prayer, they embraced each other and they went to eat their holy food, which has no blood in it.' Scholarly opinion accepts that the whole context of this prayer and the last sentence reflects the Divine command for vegetarianism.

'The Epilogue of Asclepius,' in *Hermetica* by Brian Copenhaver (Cambridge University Press) translates the last sentence as: 'With such hopes we turn to a pure meal that includes no living thing.'

The G.R.S. Mead translation has: 'With this desire we now betake us to our pure and fleshless meal.'

A third translation of the 'Epilogue of Asclepius' in *Hermetica*, translated by Sir Walter Scott, states: 'Having prayed thus, let us betake ourselves to a meal unpolluted by flesh (animalia) of living things' (see http://agochar.livejournal.com/23084.html).

The term 'blood' therefore, refers to 'animal flesh' itself. It is impossible to separate blood from flesh, flesh and blood are permanently interwoven in the capillary structure of flesh. There is always blood within the capillary structure of flesh which cannot be removed by bleeding, also plasma, which is one of the main components of blood, actually perfuses and interchanges with the contents of the cells proving flesh and blood are inseparable parts of the whole; 'blood' being an abbreviated term referring to a 'flesh and blood creature.'

It is unfortunate that the struggles between early Christian groups and the increasingly powerful orthodox church caused various scriptures to be suppressed and destroyed. These lost religious texts would have revealed so much more about Jesus' original teachings, leading to a more profound version of Christianity. Notably, the religion would have been very different on key spiritual, compassionate issues as it would have promoted vegetarianism. Notably, this is sharp contrast to the version that has come down to us today in the current biblical New Testament. We are dealing with a lost Christianity.

Of this lost Christianity, we learn from early church writings that Matthew, Peter and the brother of Jesus, named James (alternatively called 'James the Just)' were all vegetarian. James was selected to become the first leader of the New Jerusalem Church. All these disciples had known Jesus well and closely followed his teachings after he passed away. From the writings of the early church father Eusebius, it becomes clear that many leaders of the early church were likewise vegetarian.

The fact that James was a vegetarian from birth proves that at least the immediate family of Jesus must have been vegetarian: Mary and Joseph, Jesus' parents, taught the children vegetarianism. The ever compassionate Jesus and his brothers and sisters chose to continue as vegetarians. Consequently, the whole of, at least the immediate family of Jesus must have been vegetarian. John the Baptist, who had prepared the way for Jesus, was also his relative, he too, was and a vegetarian. John was among many others who followed the vegetarian lifestyle.

The early Christian writings, which were based on spiritual-mediumistic practices, were barred from preservation by being excluded from the Bible. This was done as the result of prejudicial 'choices' made by powerful men. This fact may indicate that some less authentic books took their place in the canonized bible because they supported the orthodox position or were adapted to do this.

Until recently, we were predominantly limited to the prejudicially selected biblical canon; such is the influence of humankind over prophetic religious teachings. Some early Christian writings appear to have been based on spiritual mediumistic practices which produced transformative spiritual revelations-knowledge of the celestial realms and spirituality.

It appears that most of these accounts were suppressed or destroyed by orthodoxy who preferred dogma, creeds and articles of faith which dramatically shaped the New Testament we have today.

458

People were told to recite creeds and dogma and they were not open for question or discussion. Those who wished to point out their shortcomings either lived in fear of execution or exile as a heretic.

The early Christian church was tragically fragmented due to the suppression of its origins and the ambitions of key figures from an exceptionally early date. Criticism of those who sought to cultivate altered states of consciousness in order to commune with spiritually elevated non-physical beings has persisted to this day.

The Gnostics claimed that they were the most faithful followers of Jesus. As Jesus has been proven to have carried out psychic and mediumistic practices, in direct succession from the spiritually orientated mediumistic prophets, there is no reason not to believe that integral to both Jesus' and the Gnostic way of life was the use of both psychic and spiritually elevated mediumship. Both gifts are closely interrelated.

Meditation cultivates altered states of consciousness which act as catalysts to the facilitation of mediumship. Meditation was practiced intensely by the ascetic Gnostics as was the case with other prophetic figures. Moses would have meditated consciously or unconsciously while in exile, working alone in the countryside as a shepherd.

These practices would have been used to attune to God and to spiritually advanced, celestial beings. Gnostics actively sought, through clairvoyance, clairaudience and clairsentience, spiritual wisdom for the soul's spiritual progress. The spiritual insights gained as a result of these activities were progressively recorded in their ongoing sacred scriptures.

Consequently, the Gnostics represent the lost revelatory, inspirational, dynamically alive version of Christianity. Gnostics challenged the early institutionalized church who won the battle and officially closed the doors to the angelic realm. In the longstanding mediumistic spiritual tradition, the Gnostics believed that the angelic realm continually sought to assist humankind's spiritual advancement. Many of the insecure early church fathers felt their decisions would be threatened by this ancient tradition, as angelic communications severely challenged and undermined their arrogant human claim to authority.

The orthodox church sought to halt the ongoing, dynamically alive, progressive acquisition of spiritual wisdom by the Gnostics. Intent that these spiritual-mediumistic practices would not weaken their position, the bishops and church fathers tightened their control over the people. Their attacks on the experiential practices of the Gnostics became increasingly virulent. Through fierce suppression, the Christian Gnostic groups who rejected the dogmas of the orthodox church and held divergent beliefs eventually died out.

However, Gnostic practices have survived to this day in esoteric, spiritual-mediumistic environments among the world's psychic sensitives. Many mediums may not be familiar with Gnosticism nor would they call themselves a Gnostic. Although the Gnostics were gone, this direct, personal, ever advancing approach could not be totally wiped out by violent suppression. This is because psychic and mediumistic abilities have continued to spring forth among humankind, globally and throughout the ages. They are a natural part of animal nature, human and non-human.

Many non-human animals are known for their heightened senses over and above those of their human relatives. The transformative spiritual-mediumistic experiences of the prophets have become increasingly democratized over the millennia, exemplified by modern-day near-death experiences.

However, the information acquired through mediumistic means should only be accepted if it teaches love of humankind, all animals and the planet. If it does not, the non-physical communicator is not of a sufficiently advanced spiritual level and their communications should be discarded.

As Gnosticism suffered under the full force of suppression by the orthodox church, so too did that integral mediumistic strand of their practices. Historically, those Gnostic features of spiritual mediumship also suffered biblical suppression and mistranslation.

Mediumistic references in the Bible were either recorded out of context or condemned.

Gnostic practices of attuning to direct spiritual experience of celestial and spirit beings in order to acquire spiritual truths were violently quashed. Throughout the passage of the centuries, all similar expressions of mediumship or channeling have suffered the same fate. The spirituality of their purpose was divorced from the psychic and mediumistic gifts, yet the two are closely intertwined, as this book has proven.

Carl Gustav Jung, the Swiss psychiatrist (1875–1961), was the founder of analytical psychology and an eminent explorer of the inner world of the psyche. Jung carried out Gnostic practices which provided results that paralleled those of the Gnostics. He had much sympathy with Gnostic teachings, including those regarding the human mediumistic ability to attune to the non-physical realms.

As a psychiatrist, Jung understood some of the spiritual insights he gained from his mediumistic practices in psychological terms. It might be suggested that symbols received in altered states of consciousness can be understood in terms of both the language of the soul and symbolic communications from non-physical beings.

## Biblical Translation is Not Infallible

The following brief overview shows in a simplistic but very real sense the influence of flawed humanity on recording religious texts for posterity. It lists some basic, commonly known historic mistranslations which occurred due to human misinterpretations and errors. The first is known as the 'Treacle Bible.' This name was given to Beck's Bible of 1549 which used the word 'treacle' instead of 'balm' in Jeremiah 8:22. This was followed by a translation in 1579 by Whittingham, Gilby and Sampson which became known as the 'Breeches Bible.' Their translation instructed Christians that Adam and Eve made themselves 'breeches.'

In 1562 the second edition of the Geneva Bible became known as the 'Place Makers' Bible,' due to its mistranslation of 'peacemakers' found in Matthew 5:9. The Rosin Bible of 1604 is associated with known mistranslations of Jeremiah 8:22. The 'Debased Bible' of 1815 translated Philippians 2:7 as 'Christ debased himself,' rather than 'emptied' or 'exinanited' himself.

There has been a succession of printings of the King James Version of the Bible. As the translation errors became apparent, these editions were also given a succession of derogatory names. The first was the 'Blasphemous Bible' and the 'Judas Bible' of 1611. This was followed by the 'Wicked, Adulterous or Sinner's Bible' of 1631. This particular edition was given this name because Barker and Lucas translated Exodus 20:14, producing, 'Thou shalt commit adultery.' Errors continued to be found including those in the so-called 'More Sea Bible' of 1641, the 'Unrighteous Bible' of 1653, the 'Printer's Bible' of 1702, and the 'Sin on Bible' of 1716 which said, 'Go and sin on more' rather than 'Go and sin no more.'

The 'Vinegar Bible' of 1717 followed, as did the 'Fool's Bible' of 1763. Further biblical mistranslations continued to become apparent in successive King James Versions of the Bible. The details of these translation and misinterpretation errors do not need to be discussed in detail here. For our purposes it is sufficient to point out that many known mistranslations have inevitably occurred in religious scriptures due to human errors, deliberate or otherwise. They occurred in 1792, 1801, 1804, 1805, 1806, again in 1806, 1809, 1810, again in 1810, 1820, 1823 and 1944.

This information has been included to make the reader aware that when information, religious and otherwise, is committed to processes over many centuries, errors do occur, some of which are deliberate. These include writings by countless prophets and scribes, translations and publications, falsities and a range of misinterpretations. These occur due to innocent but mistaken human error, misunderstandings through various forms of ignorance of the facts, and manipulation of the biblical narratives due to the social, politico-religious leaning of the leaders of the institutionalized church.

Biblical narratives have also been misrepresented due to the fact

that they have been interpreted by individuals whose understanding has been shaped by the historic epoch in which they lived
and their personal level of spiritual maturity. This book has revealed
other suppressed, condemned and misinterpreted biblical information which has been taken out of context concerning the psychic
and mediumistic gifts of many famous, revered prophetic figures.

# Conclusion

This book has established the fact that the lives of successive generations of mediumistic spiritual prophets are archaeologically verifiable. Particular research substantiated the authenticity of the life of Moses, the mediumistic shamanic spiritual leader. I have proved that there is a very clear and close relationship between transformative spiritual psychic and mediumistic experiences and the birth and evolution of spirituality on this planet.

Spirituality then became coined by the most powerful religious orthodoxies, and independent separatist world religions were founded. This fact is something of a shock in this materialistic age. People who have psychic and mediumistic experiences are informed by our limited, non-quantum scientists that such experiences cannot exist and must be imagined. This is because our traditional Newtonian physics, unlike quantum physics, cannot explain and accommodate such experiences.

Those who try to apply our limited traditional science then fall into the old error that things that cannot be fully understood, cannot be allowed to exist. The reason for this is that they highlight the glaring inadequacies in our knowledge. Ironically, science itself was born as a result of trying to explain the experiential, trying to explain and understand all we experienced and encountered.

The paradox is that we are left with the fact, revealed by the research in this book, that transformative, spiritual, psychic and mediumistic experiences which are powerfully condemned as 'imagined and non-existent experiences' have actually given birth to the world's religions!

It has been irrevocably evidenced that spiritual-mediumistic experiences throughout the ages have had a profound transformative impact on all prophetic experiencers. Long ago, through theoretical research accompanied by observation of demonstrations of diverse forms of mediumship and personal mediumistic experiences, I became aware that psychic and mediumistic experiences are facts. These facts have created phenomena that have endlessly occurred from the dawn of time to the present day, crossing all religio-political national boundaries and cultures.

It has been noted that some people believe that mediumship demonstrates authentic communication with surviving personalities who inhabit non-physical realms. Other people believe that mediumship does not prove survival beyond physical death and is nothing more than the result of a convoluted range of psychic abilities. This book has revealed the inadequacies of the 'psychic' argument by uncovering the powerful and pervasive impact mediumship has had on humankind.

It has revealed that highly spiritually evolved spirits and angels have communicated over the millennia with humankind. Their mission was/is to cumulatively and progressively lead humankind spiritually forward. They sought to elevate and advance humankind's state of spirituality.

My research has explained how materialist paradigms of thought have covertly shaped many people's worldviews. This brainwashing makes it almost impossible for them to evaluate objectively the volumes of accumulated evidence for the survival of consciousness after physical death. Many cannot allow themselves to entertain the concept that communication takes place between inhabitants of the physical and non-physical spheres, nor can they allow themselves to believe that God exists.

These chapters have demonstrated that spiritually orientated mediumistic experiences gave birth to humankind's spirituality, which laid the foundations for the development of the world's religions. The inspiration of spiritual truths through the mediumistic faculty is ongoing and dynamic in nature. Both psychic and mediumistic experiences have spanned the millennia and the globe and, evidently, will never cease. The mediumistic faculty appears to be an animal attribute, a gift that animals, human and non-human share.

Chapter 1 provided fascinating information about mediumistic and paranormal phenomena and supplied definitions of key terms to clarify these complex concepts. Chapter 2 summarized the predominant debates and explanations regarding these phenomena. Chapter 3 provided an historical, cross-cultural review of examples of mediumship, showing that mediumship has spanned all ages, cultures and creeds. Chapters 4 and 5 explored the ancient shamanic origins of mediumship, proving that mediumship is as old as life on earth. Chapter 6 provided extensive archaeological evidence vindicating the accuracy of biblical accounts, particularly those relating to Moses. Moses' mediumship was explored in depth. Chapters 7 to 10 presented research to highlight the fact that ancient biblical texts were describing mediumship. It revealed that the Old and New Testament spiritual leaders known historically as seers, sages, judges and prophets were spiritual mediums who, following the same pattern as the shamans, provided people with predictions about the future, offered healing, spoke with non-physical beings and cumulatively progressed humankind's spiritual understanding.

It was through the mediumistic receipt of communications from the world of angels and spirits that monotheism, the worship of One God, became the spiritual focus. I explained that many people have been misled into believing that the name Yahweh was originally used as a name for God, whereas the term Yahweh originally referred to 'the messenger of the lord,' 'the angel of the lord' and 'the spirit of the lord.'

Chapters 11 and 12 explored the spiritual experiences and soul-journeys of the 18th-century medium Emanuel Swedenborg, whose mediumistic visions profoundly shaped his spiritual philosophy. Significantly, he shared the same pattern of experiences as the ancient shamans and gained insights into the existence of innumerable celestial, infernal and purgatorial spheres in the realms of sacred time and space. Swedenborg learned that in the same way as we draw to us the influence of spirits and angels before and after death, so our positive and negative energies draw to us positive or negative conditions before and after death. This reflects a perfect form of justice.

I once observed a medium informing a man in the audience that he saw hundreds of dead rabbits around him in his aura. The man replied that he had shot countless rabbits over the years. Evidently, this man would experience the tragic suffering of the rabbits during his near-death experience. His energy was undoubtedly interwoven with theirs, otherwise the medium would not have observed the rabbits around him. Inevitably, he would experience aspects of the consciousness of his vulnerable, innocent victims in his after-death landscape. The rabbits' terror and agony would profoundly affect his energy and the conditions he would attract to himself in this life and the next.

In contrast, the rabbits would make their transition to the non-physical realms, but due to their innocent psyches their expectations would be fulfilled. They would run freely in the countryside in the sunshine in the non-physical realities. Compassionate people who enjoy the enchanted pleasure of watching rabbits, foxes, birds and other creatures would inevitably share their vibrant and beautiful non-physical landscapes.

Swedenborg taught that an increasingly mature spiritual philosophy that is liberated and free from institutionalized religious dogma would be brought in with a 'New Age.' Swedenborg's mediumistic legacy indicates that all individuals should evaluate how they might spiritualize their lives on all levels rather than following institutionalized teachings that have become distorted by humankind's preference for creating traditions, creeds and dogmas.

Chapter 13 explained the human element involved in compiling the Bible and the man-made nature of much of institutionalized religion. It showed that the Bible is composed of books chosen by those in power, while countless other authentic religious texts were condemned and discarded.

We saw how the successful excavation of hitherto-unknown sacred texts, such as the Dead Sea Scrolls and the Nag Hammadi

Library, has helped to highlight the original spiritual voices of the New Testament era who cried out in the wilderness against the religious establishment and prevailing erroneous, human social traditions. Jesus' original undistorted teachings are being unearthed.

Despite the existence of divergent beliefs in early Christianity, historical vicissitudes led to the domination of the form of Christianity we have today and the suppression of some of Jesus' original teachings. The Roman establishment was particularly opposed to Jesus' vegetarianism, hence this original Christianity became lost to future generations until today. The beliefs and practices of the Gnostics in that period were seen to share many parallels with transformative spiritual-mediumistic experiences.

From the above research, we have learned that it is vital to assess the spiritual level of all religious philosophies and mediumistic communications as there is a diverse range of communicators in the non-physical world. Communications which teach compassion and forgiveness, telling us to love and protect our fellow infants – the vulnerable animals who share the earth with us – are indicative of a spiritually elevated spirit or angelic teacher. Unfortunately such revelations and commands, though delivered many times throughout the millennia, have repeatedly been overturned by humanity's preferences.

Vegetarian teachings appear in the Hindu Vedas, in the works of the Greek spiritual philosophers, and in God's first and preferred commands found in Genesis, the first book of the Bible, in writings that are holy to Jews and Christians. Both the Buddha and Jesus continued the vegetarian commands, yet both were aware that their teachings would be corrupted to fit human desires. This valuable message has not yet permeated the senses of all people, yet we have been clearly taught that as guardians of the planet, it is our duty to care for it and all our fellow animals, many of whom are often our spiritual superiors.

There has always been, and still is, a very strong pivotal relationship between spiritually orientated mediumistic communications and the growth of spirituality on this planet. The utilization of our mediumistic sensitivities and receptors, which we all possess to varying degrees, can access the spiritual realm and inspire us with new creativity, insights, communications and revelations.

As we have learned that like attracts like, it is important that we attempt to attune to the highest and the best, the most spiritually elevated non-physical communicators. Arguably, spirits, angels and God, when invited to intervene in our lives, work through people and events in unexpected ways. This is made easier when we drop our skeptical preventative filters and accept that there are other-worldly forces beyond our mundane perception.

Jesus' spiritual insights recorded in the hitherto lost ancient spiritual writings of Didymos Judas Thomas corroborate the findings of Swedenborg, other mediums and near-death experiencers regarding the nature of the non-physical realms. Thomas informs us that Jesus taught: 'The kingdom is inside of you and it is outside of you; there is nothing hidden which will not become manifest.'

As we have learned, in the after-death realms all thoughts, emotions and deeds are laid bare, and create an energy that cannot be hidden. This energy will attract to each one of us corresponding landscapes and companions. Swedenborg, trance mediums and near-death experiencers are all profoundly aware of the infinite diversity of the 'many rooms/mansions in my Father's house' to which Jesus referred.

# Appendix

## Figure 1: The Computer-Modem Model of the Psycho-Spiritual Function by Professor A.E. Roy

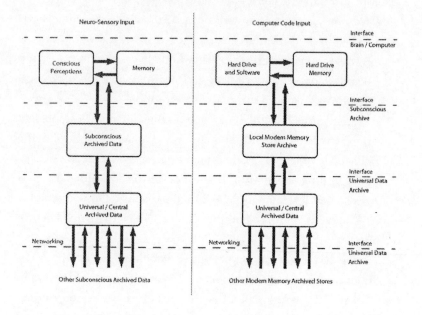

Figure 2: Historic Timeline compiled by Dennis Bratcher

# Summary Chronology of the Bible Period

The Patriarchal Era 1800–1290 BC

Exodus – The Judges 1290–1050 BC

Early Israelite Monarchy 1050–750 BC

The United Kingdom

Saul 1029–1000 BC

David 1000–961 BC

Solomon 961–922 BC

Rebellion of the North and its Aftermath

The Southern Kingdom

Assyrian Dominance 750–605 BC

Babylonian Era and Exile 605–538 BC

Waning Assyrian Power

The Fall of Jerusalem and its Aftermath

The Peak of Babylonian Power

The Persian Period and Return from Exile 538–323 BC

The Decline of Babylon

The Greek Wars/Maccabean Period 323–663 BC

The Rise of Rome 63–3BC

With thanks to Dennis Bratcher, the executive director of CRI/Voice Institute, who compiled this timeline displayed at www.crivoice.org /othistory.html Copyright © 2008

The historic timeline has been included to provide as clear a time frame as possible regarding ancient biblical historical events. As indicated, many accounts in the Pentateuch in the Bible, Torah and Koran have been shown to be genuine events largely proven by archaeological excavations.

# References

## Chapter 1 Mediumship: Definitions and Complexities

1 E.M.Kirkpatrick (ed.), *Chambers Twentieth Century Dictionary*, Chaucer Press, UK, 1983, p. 1039.

2 Hal N. Banks, STD, *An Introduction to Psychic Studies*, The Seminary of the church, Alaska, USA, 1980, p. 1.

3 *The Compact Edition of the Oxford English Dictionary*, vol. II, P–Z, Book Club Associates, London (by arrangement with Oxford University Press), 1979, p. 2347.

4 Helen Hemingway Benton (pub.), *Encyclopaedia Britannica: Micropaedia*, 15th edn, vol. IV, UK, 1974, p. 13.

5 Banks, *Introduction to Psychic Studies*, p. 1.

6 Ibid., p. 1.

7 A. Angoff (ed.), *The Psychic Force*, New York: G.P. Putnam's Sons, 1970, p. 337.

8 Kirkpatrick (ed.), *Chambers Twentieth Century Dictionary*, p. 1329.

9 A.E. Roy, *The Archives of the Mind*, SNU Publications, UK, 1996.

10 Benton (pub.), *Encyclopaedia Britannica: Micropaedia*, p. 751.

11 A. Campbell Holms, *The Facts of Psychic Science*, University Books, New Hyde Park, New York, 1969, p. 38.

12 O.W. Stevens, *Psychics and Common Sense*, E.P. Dutton, New York, 1953, p. 77.

13 U. Roberts, *Hints on Mediumistic Development*, Almoris Press, London, 1980, p. 1.

14 Kirkpatrick (ed.), p. 231.

15 Benton (pub.), *Encyclopaedia Britannica: Micropaedia*, p. 961.

16 Roy, *Archives of the Mind*, p. 300.

17 Ibid.

18 Ibid.

19 Ibid., pp. 300–301.

20 Ibid., p. 301.

21 Benton (pub.), *Encyclopaedia Britannica: Micropaedia*, p. 511.

22 Kirkpatrick (ed.), *Chambers Twentieth Century Dictionary*, p. 776.

23 Ibid., p. 1248.

24 Benton (pub.), *Encyclopaedia Britannica: Micropaedia*, p. 429.

25 Ibid., p. 429.

26 Robert Audi (ed.), *The Cambridge Dictionary of Philosophy*, Cambridge University Press, 1995, p. 755.

27 Benton (pub.), *Encyclopaedia Britannica: Micropaedia*, p. 511.

28 The Spiritual Frontiers Fellowship International (SFFI), PO Box 7868, Philadelphia, Pennsylvania 19101-7868, USA.

29 The English Churches' Fellowship for Psychical and Spiritual Studies, The Rural Workshop, South Road, North Somercotes, Nr Louth, Lincolnshire, LN11 7PT, UK.

30 The Society for Psychical Research (London), 49 Marloes Road, Kensington, W8 6LA, UK.

31 The American Society for Psychical Research, Inc., 5 West 73rd Street, New York, New York 10023, USA.

32 *The Spiritualists' Hymn Book*, 19th edition, The Headquarters Publishing Co., London, 1985, p. 1.

33 Benton (pub.), *Encyclopaedia Britannica: Micropaedia*, p. 512.

34 H.C. Moolenburg, *Meetings with Angels*, C.W. Daniel Co., Essex, UK, 1992.

35 Benton (pub.), *Encyclopaedia Britannica: Micropaedia*, p. 512.

36 Ibid. p. 513.

37 J. Klimo, *Psychics, Prophets and Mystics*, The Aquarian Press, UK, 1991, p. 17.

38 Roy, *Archives of the Mind*, p. 325.

39 'Report by Mrs Henry Sidgwick on the Psychology of Mrs Piper's Trance Phenomena', *The Proceedings of the SPR*, vol. 28, 1915, ch. 3, p. 437.

40 A.E. Roy, *A Sense of Something Strange*, Dog and Bone, Glasgow, UK, 1990, p. 260.

41 Roy, *Archives of the Mind*, p. 328.

42 Ibid., p. 339.

43 Ibid., p. 134.

44    31 April 1989, The Arthur Findlay College, Stansted, Mount Fitchett, Essex, England; Mary Duffy (clairaudient) and Coral Polge (psychic artist).

## Chapter 2 The Predominant Explanations and Debates

1    A.E. Roy, *The Archives of the Mind*, SNU Publications, UK, 1996.

2    Ibid., p. 330.

3    Ibid., p. 319.

4    Ibid., p. 330.

5    Ibid., p. 316.

6    H.F. Saltmarsh, *Evidence of Personal Survival from Cross Correspondences*, Bell, London, 1938; O. Lodge, *Raymond; or Life and Death*, Methuen, London, 1916; S. Smith, *The Mediumship of Mrs Leonard*, University Books, Hyde Park, New York, 1964.

7    Roy, *Archives of the Mind*, pp. 316–317.

8    Ibid., pp. 317–318.

9    Ibid., p. 317.

10   Ibid.

11   Ibid.

12   Roy, *Archives of the Mind*.

13   Ibid., p. 318.

14   Ibid., p. 319.

15   Ibid.

16   Ibid., pp. 322–323.

17   Ibid., pp. 100–103.

18   Ibid., p. 105.

19   Ibid., p. 105.

20   Ibid.

21   Ibid.

22   Ibid..

23   Ibid., pp. 124–125.

24   Michael Talbot, *The Holographic Universe*, Harper Collins, UK, 1996.

25   Ibid.

26  Ibid., pp 11–14, 18–20, 28–31, 163.

27  Ibid, pp. 11–14, 18–20, 163.

28  D. Bohm, *Wholeness and Implicate Order*, Routledge & Kegan Paul, UK, 1982.

29  Talbot, *Holographic Universe*, pp. 47–50, 121; (earlier edn, Grafton Books, 1991).

30  Ibid., p. 2.

31  A.E. Roy, *A Sense of Something Strange*, Dog and Bone, Glasgow, UK, 1990, p. 260.

32  Ibid.

33  Roy, *Archives of the Mind*.

34  Roy, *Sense of Something Strange*, pp. 35–36, 260–261.

35  Ibid.

36  C.G. Jung, *The Archetypes and the Collective Unconscious*, Collected Works, vol. 9, part 1, Routledge & Kegan Paul, London, UK, 1959.

37  Roy, *Archives of the Mind*, p. 327.

38  Ibid. p. 360.

39  Ibid.

## Chapter 3 Global Mediumship Throughout the Ages

1  J. Klimo, *Psychics, Prophets and Mystics: Receiving Information from Paranormal Sources*, The Aquarian Press, Grafton Books, UK, 1991, p. 76.

2  Ibid., p. 79.

3  Ibid.

4  Wallace E.A. Budge (ed.), *The Egyptian Book of the Dead*, Dover Publications, UK, 1985.

5  J. Klimo, *Psychics, Prophets and Mystics*, p. 79.

6  J.D. Ray, Michael Loewe and Carmen Blacker (eds), *Ancient Egypt in Oracles and Divination*, Shambhala, Boulder, Colo., Boston and London, 1981, p. 179.

7  Ibid., pp. 185–186.

8  Klimo, *Psychics, Prophets and Mystics*, p. 80.

9    Ibid., pp. 80-81.

10   Ibid., p. 81.

11   Ibid.

12   Lewis, Bayles, Paton, *Spiritism and the Cult of the Dead in Antiquity*, Macmillan, New York, 1921.

13   H.P. Blavatsky, *Isis Unveiled*, Theosophical University Press, USA, 1972 (original edition, 1877).

14   A. Besant, *Man and His Bodies*, Theosophical Publishing House, Adyar, India, 1971.

15   *Plato, Theagetes, Theaetetus*, Loeb Series (trans. by H.N. Fowler, bound with *Sophist*), W. Heinemann, London, 1921.

16   D.C. Knight, *The ESP Reader*, Grosset & Dunlap, New York, 1969, p. 257.

17   Lewis, Bayles, Paton, *Spiritism and the Cult of the Dead in Antiquity*, p. 83.

18   Klimo, *Psychics, Prophets and Mystics*, p. 84.

19   John Cournos, *A Book of Prophecy: From the Egyptians to Hitler*, Bell, New York, 1942, pp. 135– 136.

20   Henry James Forman, *The Story of Prophecy: Hildegarde of Bingen*, Farrar and Rinehart, New York, 1936, pp. 130–131.

21   Ibid.

22   Ibid., pp. 134–138.

23   Ibid., p. 194.

24   Saint Teresa of Avila, *Interior Castle*, Image/Doubleday, Garden City, New York, 1961, p. 72.

25   Saint John of the Cross, *Ascent of Mount Carmel*, Image/Doubleday, Garden City, New York, 1958, pp. 242–248.

26   Charles E. Ward, *Oracles of Nostradamus*, Scribners, New York, 1941.

27   George Fox, *The Journal of George Fox*, ed. Rufus M. Jones, Friends United Press, Richmond, Ind.: 1976, pp. 74–75.

28   Klimo, p. 93.

29   H.E. Palmer (ed.), *The NIV Study Bible*, New International Version, Hodder & Stoughton, UK, 1987: 1 Corinthians 12:1–11,

p. 1716; 1 Corinthians 14, p. 1718ff.

30  E. Swedenborg, *Heaven and Its Wonders and Hell: From Things Heard and Seen* (a translation of *De Caelo et ejus Mirabilibus, et de Inferno ex Auditis et Visis*), The Swedenborg Society, London, 1958, p. 9.

31  Ibid., p. 3.

32  Ibid., pp. 5–6.

33  Ibid., pp. 6–7.

34  Ibid., p. 12.

35  Ibid., p. 14.

36  E. Swedenborg, *Principles of Nature* (originally published by) The Swedenborg Society, 20–21 Bloomsbury Way, London, 1958.

37  E. Swedenborg, *Death and After*, The Swedenborg Society, 20–21 Bloomsbury Way, London, 1958.

38  E. Swedenborg, *Heaven and Its Wonders and Hell*, The Swedenborg Society, 20–21 Bloomsbury Way, London, 1958.

39  E. Swedenborg, *Arcana Coelestia*, The Swedenborg Society, 20–21 Bloomsbury Way, London, 1958.

40  E. Swedenborg, *Divine Love and Wisdom*, The Swedenborg Society, 20–21 Bloomsbury Way, London, 1958.

41  Michael Stanley, *Emanuel Swedenborg: Essential Readings*, published by the Swedenborg Lending Library and Enquiry Centre, New South Wales, Australia, 1993.

42  Helen Hemingway Benton (pub.), *Encyclopaedia Britannica: Macropaedia*, 15th edition, vol. XII, UK, 1973–1974, pp. 442–444.

43  *The Doctrine of Tenrikyo*, 2nd edn, Headquarters of the Tenrikyo Church, printed in Tenri Jihosha, Japan, 1958.

44  W.H. Evans, *Twelve Lectures on The Harmonial Philosophy of A.J. Davis*, published by the Spiritualist National Union Ltd, Manchester, UK, 1924.

45  Ibid. (unnumbered opening title page).

46  Ibid., p. 1.

47  Sir A.C. Doyle, 'Professor of Hebrew: Dr. George Bush, University of New York', in *The History of Spiritualism*, vol. 1,

Psychic Press, London, 1989, pp. 41–42 (first impression 1926).

48  Ibid., p. 49.

49  Sir A.C. Doyle, *The History of Spiritualism*, vol. 1, Arno Press, New York, 1975 (first pub. George H. Doran Co., 1926), p. 57.

50  *Hydesville Millennium Magazine*, published by *Psychic News* for The Spiritualist National Union, The Coach House, Stansted, Essex, UK.

51  Nandor Fodor, 'The Birth of Spiritualism: The Fox Sisters and the Hydesville Rappings', *The ESP Reader*, ed. David C. Knight, Grosset & Dunlap, New York, 1969, p. 27.

52  Nettie Colburn Maynard, 'Séances with Abraham Lincoln', *The ESP Reader*, 1969, p. 36.

53  A. Kardec, *The Gospel According to Spiritism*, The Headquarters Publishing Co. Ltd, London, 1987 (original edition, 1864).

54  Trevor H. Hall, *The Spiritualists: The Story of Florence Cook and William Crookes*, Helix Press/Garrett, New York, 1963, p. 170.

55  Rev. William Stanton Moses, *Spirit Teachings and Higher Aspects of Spiritualism*, London Spiritualist Press, UK, 1949, 1976.

56  *OAHSPE: A New Bible in the Words of Jehovih and his Angel Ambassadors*, Oahspe Pub. Assoc., New York, 1882.

57  Frederick S. Oliver, *A Dweller on Two Planets*, Alhambra, Bordon, Calif., USA, 1952 (first pub. 1899).

58  Alta Piper, 'Professor William James and Mrs Piper', *The ESP Reader*, p. 80. Also, Alta L. Piper, *Life and Work of Mrs Piper*, Kegan Paul, Trench Trubner, London, 1929.

59  Madame H.P. Blavatsky, *Isis Unveiled*, Theosophical University Press, USA, 1972 (original edition, 1877).

60  James Robert and Eva Lees, *The Life Elysian*, Leicester, England, 1905.

61  Printed on inside cover of the *Journal of the Society for Psychical Research*, 49 Marloes Rd, London W8 6LA, UK.

62  F.W.H. Myers, *Human Personality and Its Survival of Bodily Death*, edited and abridged by S.B. and L.H.M. Longmans, Green and Co. Ltd, London, Toronto, 1927 (original version edited by R.

Hodgson and A. Johnson, 2 vols., New York, 1903, reprinted New York, 1961).

63   Ibid., pp. 14-17.

64   Klimo, *Psychics, Prophets and Mystics*, p. 95.

## Chapter 4 The Ancient Shamanic Origins of Mediumship

1   Mircea Eliade, *Shamanism: Archaic Techniques of Ecstasy* (trans. from French by Willard R.Trask), Arkana/Penguin Books, London, 1989, pp. xix–xx (first pub. in UK by Routledge, 1988).

2   Mircea Eliade, 'Shamanism', in Mircea Eliade (ed.), *Encyclopaedia of Religion*, Macmillan, London, 1987, p. 205.

3   Ibid., p. 203.

4   Holger Kalweit, *Dreamtime and Inner Space*, Shambhala, Boston and London, 1988, p. 98.

5   Eliade, *Shamanism: Archaic Techniques of Ecstasy*, pp. xi–xii.

6   Ibid., p. 27ff.

7   E. Ackerknecht, 'Psychopathology, Primitive-Medicine, and Primitive Culture', *Bulletin of the History of Medicine*, USA, 1943, 14:30–67, p. 46.

8   J. Silverman, 'Shamans and Acute Schizophrenia', *American Anthropologist*, USA, 1967, 69:21–31, p. 23.

9   Jean Houston, Jean, Foreword to 'The Mind and the Soul of the Shaman', in *Shamanism*, ed. S. Nicholson, Quest Books, USA, 1987, p. viii.

10   S. Shirokogoroff, S., *Psychomental Complex of the Tungus*, Routledge & Kegan Paul, London, 1935, pp. 268, 271.

11   R. Firth, 'Shamanism', in *Dictionary of the Social Sciences*, p. 338, ed. J. Gould and W. Kolb, Free Press of Glencoe, New York, 1964, pp. 638–639.

12   Larry G. Peters and D. Price-Williams, 'Towards an Experiential Analysis of Shamanism', *American Ethnologist*, USA, 1980, 7:397–418.

13   Larry G. Peters, 'The Tamang of Nepal', in *Shamanism*, ed. S. Nicholson, Quest Books, Theosophical Publishing House,

Illinois, USA, 1993, p. 174.

14  Eliade, *Shamanism: Archaic Techniques of Ecstasy*, pp. xii–xiii.

15  Ibid., p. xiv.

16  Ibid., pp. xiv–xv.

17  Ibid., pp. xv–xvi.

18  Ibid., pp. xvi–xvii.

19  Ibid., p. xvii.

20  Ibid., p. xviii.

21  Ibid., p.xix.

22  Ibid., pp. 7–8.

23  Ibid., p. 9.

24  Peters, 'The Tamang of Nepal', p. 171.

25  Ibid., p. 167.

## Chapter 5 Shamanic Mediums as Ancestors of Cultures

1  S. Nicholson, 'Shamanism and the Perennial Philosophy', in *Shamanism*, ed. S. Nicholson, Quest Books, Theosophical Publishing House, Illinois, USA, 1993, p. 211.

2  Eliade, Mircea, 'Shamanism', in *Encyclopaedia of Religion*, ed. Mircea Eliade, Macmillan, London, 1987, p. 205.

3  Nicholson, ' Shamanism and the Perennial Philosophy', p. 212.

4  Larry G. Peters, 'The Tamang of Nepal', in Nicholson (ed.), *Shamanism*, pp. 172–173.

5  Ibid., pp. 173–174.

6  Robert Ellwood, 'Shamanism and Theosophy', in Nicholson (ed.), *Shamanism*, pp. 259–260.

7  W.Y. Evans-Wentz (ed.), *The Tibetan Book of the Dead (Bardo Thodol)*, trans. Lama Kazi Dawa-Samdup, London, 1927 (2nd edn, 1949; 3rd edn, 1957).

8  Mircea Eliade, *Shamanism: Archaic Techniques of Ecstasy*, trans. by W.R. Trask, Arkana/Penguin Books, 1989, p. 440.

9  H.E. Palmer (ed.), *The NIV Study Bible*, New International Version, Hodder & Stoughton, London, 1987: 1 Corinthians 12:1–11; 1 Corinthians 14:5–6, 18, pp. 1716–1719.

10    Eliade, Mircea, *Shamanism*, p. 438.

11    Serge King, 'The Way of the Adventurer', in Nicholson (ed.), *Shamanism*, pp. 192–193.

12    Jean Achterberg, 'The Shaman: Master Healer in the Imaginary Realm', in Nicholson (ed.), *Shamanism*, pp. 107– 108.

13    Ralph Metzner, 'Transformation Processes, Alchemy and Yoga', in Nicholson (ed.), *Shamanism*, p. 233.

14    Rabbi Yonassan Gershom, 'Shamanism in the Jewish Tradition', in Nicholson (ed.), *Shamanism*, p. 182.

15    Palmer (ed.), *NIV Study Bible*, 2 Kings 2, 4, 5, pp. 514, 517, 520.

16    Ibid., Ezekiel p. 1206ff.

17    Ibid., Genesis 17, p. 32ff.

18    Ibid., Genesis 30:25–31:13, p. 53ff.

19    Ibid., Genesis 32:23–33, p. 57ff.

20    Ibid., Genesis 33, p. 58ff; also Gershom, 'Shamanism in the Jewish Tradition', pp. 182–183.

21    Palmer (ed.), *NIV Study Bible*, 1 Samuel 9:1–15, pp. 380–381.

22    Ibid., 1 Samuel 9:9, p. 380.

23    Ibid., 1 Samuel 10, p. 381ff.

24    Gershom, 'Shamanism in the Jewish Tradition', p. 184.

25    Ibid., pp. 184–185.

26    Ibid., p. 185.

27    Ibid., p. 186; Palmer (ed.), *NIV Study Bible*, 2 Kings 2, p. 514ff.

28    Gershom, 'Shamanism in the Jewish Tradition', pp. 186–187.

29    Ibid., p. 187.

30    Ibid., p. 188.

31    D. Scott Rogo, 'Shamanism, ESP, and the Paranormal', in Nicholson (ed.), *Shamanism*, pp. 134–135.

32    Ibid., p. 135.

33    Ibid., p. 135.

34    Ibid.

35    Ibid., p. 136.

36    Ibid.

37    Ibid.

38  Joan Halifax, *Shamanic Voices*, Dutton, New York, USA, 1979.

39  Marlene Dobkin de Rios, *Visionary Vine*, Chandler Publishing Co., San Francisco, USA, 1972.

40  Vladimir Bogoras, *The Chukchee*, Memoirs of the American Museum of Natural History, New York, USA, 1904–1909.

41  David Read Barker, 'Psi Phenomena in Tibetan Culture', in *Research in Parapsychology*, 1978/9, Scarecrow Press, Metuchen, NJ; David Read Barker, 'Psi Information and Culture', in *Communication and Parapsychology*, ed. Betty Shaplin and Lisette Coly, Parapsychology Foundation, New York, 1980.

42  Diamond Jenness, *The Life of the Copper Eskimo, Ottawa*, Report of the Canadian Arctic Expedition, USA, 1922, p. 12.

43  Adrian Boshier, 'African Apprenticeship', *Parapsychology Review*, 5 (4), 1–3, 25–27.

44  Irving A. Hallowell, *The Role of Conjuring in Saulteaux Society*, reprint, Octagon Books, New York, USA, 1971.

45  P. Phillips, and W.L. MacLeod, *Here and There: Psychic Communication Between Our World and the Next*, Corgi/Transworld, London, 1975, pp. 144–145.

46  Rogo, 'Shamanism, ESP, and the Paranormal', p. 139.

47  Mircea Eliade, *The Myth of the Eternal Return*, Routledge & Kegan Paul, London, 1955, pp. 6–7.

48  Henri Corbin, Seminal Paper, *Mundus Imaginalis: The Imaginary and the Imaginal*, Gogonooza Press, Ipswich, UK, 1976.

49  Metzner, 'Transformation Process in Shamanism, Alchemy and Yoga', p. 235.

## Chapter 6 Archaeology Supports Biblical Accounts

1  Dennis Bratcher, 'The Date of the Exodus: the Historical Study of Scripture' www.crivoice.org/exodusdate.html.

2  Ibid.

3  Ibid.

4  Ibid.

5  Ibid.

6    Ibid.

7    Ibid.

8    Ibid.

9    Ibid.

10   Ibid.

11   Ibid.

12   Ibid.

13   Ibid.

14   Ibid.

15   James K. Hoffmeier, *Israel in Egypt: The Evidence for the Authenticity of the Exodus Tradition*.

16   Dennis Bratcher, 'The Yam Suph: "Red Sea" or "Sea of Reeds", Copyright © 2006.

17   Ibid.

18   Ibid.

19   Ibid.

## Chapter 7 Ancient Spiritual Prophets Were Mediums

1    H.E. Palmer (ed.), *The NIV Study Bible*, New International Version, Hodder & Stoughton, London, 1987, Genesis, p. 8; Exodus, p. 88; Leviticus, p. 147; Numbers, p. 187.

2    The Churches' Fellowship for Psychical and Spiritual Studies (CFPSS), Lincolnshire UK; The Society for Psychical Research (SPR), London, UK; The Arthur Findlay College for Psychical and Spiritual Research, Essex, UK.

3    Harold Knight, *The Hebrew Prophetic Consciousness*, Lutterworth Press, UK, 1976, p. 53.

4    A.H. Haddow, *The Paranormal in the Synoptic Gospels*, The Churches' Fellowship for Psychical and Spiritual Studies (CFPSS), UK, 1988.

5    Ernest G. Wright, *Isaiah: Layman's Bible Commentary*, SCM Press, UK, 1964, p. 23.

6    T.H. Robinson, *Decline and Fall of the Hebrew Kingdoms*, Clarendon Press, UK, 1944, p. 234.

7   H.W. Robinson, *Religious Ideas of the Old Testament*, Duckworth, UK, 1968, p. 115.

8   R.C. Johnson, *Teach Yourself Psychical Research*, EUP, UK, 1955, p. 127.

9   J.G.S. Thomson, *The New Bible Dictionary*, IVP, UK, 1962, p. 1312.

10  D.J. Bretherton, *Holy Scripture and the Trance-State: Part 1: The Old Testament*, The Churches' Fellowship for Psychical and Spiritual Studies (CFPSS), UK, 1988, p. 32.

11  'Psychical Studies and the Bible', mission statement of The Churches' Fellowship for Psychical and Spiritual Studies, UK,

12  D.J. Bretherton, *Holy Scripture and the Trance-State, Part 1: The Old Testament*, p. 22.

13  D.J. Bretherton, 'Psychical Research and the Biblical Prohibitions', in *Life, Death and Psychical Research*, ed. J. Pearce-Higgins and G.S. Whitby, Rider, UK, 1973, pp. 110–124; *The Christian Parapsychologist*, vol. 5, no. 6, June 1984.

14  Palmer (ed.), *NIV Study Bible*, 1 Samuel chapter 28, p. 409.

15  Bretherton, *The Christian Parapsychologist*, vol. 5, no. 6, June 1984, p. 203.

16  Ibid., pp. 203–204. (See Judges 6:25; Exodus 34:13; 1 Kings 15:13; 2 Kings 18:4; 23:14; 2 Chronicles 15:16; Micah 5:13; Nahum 1:4, etc.); (Leviticus 26:1; 19:4; Exodus 34:17; Isaiah 2:20).

17  Dr Edward Langton, *Good and Evil Spirits*, SPCK, UK, 1982, p. 184.

18  Bretherton, *The Christian Parapsychologist*, vol. 5, no. 6, UK, June 1984, p. 204.

19  Osterley, *Immortality and the Unseen World*, SPCK, UK, 1976, pp. 132–133.

20  Osterley and Robinson, *Hebrew Religions*, SPCK, UK, 1974, p. 104.

21  H.P. Smith, *1 and 2 Samuel*, ICC, UK, 1984, p. 239.

22  Bretherton, *Christian Parapsychologist*, p. 204. (Deut. 18:10-12 cf. 2 Kings 21:11; 1 Kings 21:26); (cf. Lev. 19:31, 20:3–6, etc); (cf. Isa. 19:3, 2 Kings 21:6).

23 Ibid., pp. 205–206.

24 Ibid., p. 204.

25 Bretherton, 'Psychical Research and the Biblical Prohibitions', p. 110; the reference to 'therefore he slew him' is found in 1 Chronicles 10:13–14.

26 Rev. L. Argyll, *Nothing to Hide*, CFPSS, UK, 1971.

27 Bretherton, 'Psychical Research and the Biblical Prohibitions.'

28 Ibid., pp. 110–111. (See the *Malleus maleficarum*, 'The Hammer of Witches', ed. Summers.)

29 Ibid., pp. 111–112.

30 Ibid.

31 R. Ahmed, *Black Art*, Arrow Books, UK, 1970, p. 50.

32 Bretherton, 'Psychical Research and the Biblical Prohibitions', pp. 121–122.

33 Ibid., pp. 122–123.

34 Ibid., p. 124.

35 'Letter of Introduction to all Members', The Churches' Fellowship for Psychical and Spiritual Studies, Lincolnshire, UK.

36 Palmer (ed.), *NIV Study Bible*, Genesis 12, p. 26

37 Ibid., Genesis 12:1, 6, 7, 8, pp. 26-27.

38 Ibid., p. 26.

39 Rev. M. Elliott, *Spiritualism in the Old Testament*, Psychic Book Club, UK, 1940, p. 24.

40 Palmer (ed.), *NIV Study Bible*, Genesis 16, p. 31.

41 Ibid., Genesis 21, p. 38.

42 Ibid., Genesis 16:7–9, pp. 31–32.

43 Ibid., Genesis 16:13, p. 32.

44 Ibid., Genesis 21:17–19, p. 39.

45 Ibid., Genesis 17:17, p. 33.

46 Elliott, *Spiritualism in the Old Testament*, p. 32.

47 Palmer (ed.), *NIV Study Bible*, Genesis 22:11–12, p. 40.

48 Elliott, *Spiritualism in the Old Testament*, p. 32.

49 Palmer (ed.), *NIV Study Bible*, Genesis 24, pp. 42–44.

50   Ibid., Genesis 24:12, p. 42.

51   Ibid., Genesis 24:27, p. 43.

52   Ibid., Genesis 25:22, p. 45.

53   Ibid., Genesis 25:23, p. 45.

54   Ibid., Genesis 27 – 28, pp. 47–50.

55   Elliott, *Spiritualism in the Old Testament*, pp. 41–42.

56   Ibid., p. 43.

57   Palmer (ed.), *NIV Study Bible*, pp. 63–77.

58   Ibid., Genesis 44:5, p. 73.

## Chapter 8 Moses and his Spirit Guide Yahweh

1    Palmer (ed.), *The NIV Study Bible*, New International Version, Hodder & Stoughton, London, 1987, Exodus 1ff., p. 88.

2    Ibid., Exodus 3:14–15, p. 91.

3    Rev. M. Elliott, *Spiritualism in the Old Testament*, Psychic Book Club, UK, 1940, pp. 52–53.

4    Palmer (ed.), *NIV Study Bible*, Exodus 4:16, p. 92.

5    Ibid., Exodus 13:21, p. 105.

6    Ibid., Exodus 14:19–20, p. 107.

7    Ibid., Exodus 23:20, p. 120.

8    Ibid., Exodus 23:23, p. 120.

9    Ibid., Exodus 24:15–18, p. 122.

10   Ibid., Exodus 24:9–11, pp. 121–122.

11   Ibid., Exodus 20ff., p. 114ff.

12   Ibid., Exodus 23:20–23, p. 120.

13   Ibid., Hebrews, p. 1819.

14   Ibid., Hebrews 1:1, p. 1819.

15   Ibid., Exodus 25ff., pp. 122–124ff.

16   Ibid., Exodus chapters 25 – 40, pp. 122–144.

17   Ibid., p. 124.

18   Ibid., Exodus 25:22–23, p. 124.

19   Ibid., Exodus 28:3–30, pp. 127–128.

20   Ibid., p. 128.

21   Ibid., Proverbs 16:33, p. 951.

22   Ibid.

23   Ibid., Proverbs 16:1, p. 949.

24   Ibid., Proverbs 16:9, p. 950.

25   Ibid., Joshua 7:14, p. 296.

26   Ibid., Exodus 33:7–11, p. 135.

27   Ibid., Exodus 29:29–44, p. 130.

28   Ibid., Exodus 39:32 – 40:32, pp. 142–P143.

29   Ibid., Exodus 30:36, p. 132.

30   Ibid., Leviticus 1:1, p. 147.

31   Ibid., Numbers 1:1, p. 187.

32   Ibid., p. 127.

33   Ibid. Exodus 40:34–36, pp. 143–144.

34   Ibid., Exodus 34:29–35, p. 137.

35   Ibid., Exodus 34:29, p. 137.

36   Ibid., Deuteronomy 18:14–21, pp. 263–264.

37   Ibid., pp. 84–85.

38   Ibid., Deuteronomy 34:10, p. 283.

39   Ibid., Numbers 12:5–8, p. 206.

## Chapter 9 Later Spiritual Prophets were Mediums

1    E. Garth Moore (president of the Churches' Fellowship for
     Psychical and Spiritual Studies from 1963 to 1983 and former
     chancellor of the dioceses of Durham, Southwark and
     Gloucester), 'The Frontiers of Religion and Psychical Research',
     *The Christian Parapsychologist*, vol. 5, no. 6, June 1984, pp.
     178–180.

2    H.E. Palmer (ed.), *The NIV Study Bible*, New International
     Version, Hodder & Stoughton, London, 1987, Deuteronomy
     31:14–23, pp. 277–278.

3    Ibid., Numbers 27:18–21, p. 228.

4    Ibid., Joshua 7:10, p. 296.

5    Ibid., Joshua 8:1, p. 297.

6    Ibid., Joshua 8:18, p. 297.

7    Ibid., Revelation 19:11–16, p. 286.

8    Ibid., Joshua, p. 284.

9    Ibid., Joshua 3, p. 290.

10   Ibid., Joshua 4, p. 291.

11   Ibid., Joshua 3:5–13, pp. 290–291.

12   Ibid., Joshua 7, pp. 295–296.

13   Ibid., Judges, p. 321.

14   Ibid., Judges 2:10–12, p. 327.

15   Ibid., Judges 2:2–4, p. 326.

16   Ibid., Judges 2:16, p. 327.

17   Ibid., Judges 8:23, p. 338.

18   Ibid., Judges 4 – 5, pp. 329–333.

19   Ibid., Judges 6 – 9, pp. 333–338.

20   Ibid., Judges 10:6 – 12:7, pp. 341–344.

21   Ibid., Judges 4:1–9, pp. 329–330.

22   Ibid., Judges 6:6–12, pp. 333–334.

23   Ibid., Judges 6:20–21, p. 334.

24   Ibid., Judges 6:34, p. 335.

25   Ibid., Judges 6:34, p. 335.

26   Ibid., 1 Samuel 16:13, p. 392.

27   Ibid., Judges 14:6, p. 346.

28   Ibid., Judges 14:19, p. 347.

29   Ibid., Judges 2:18, p. 327.

30   Ibid., Judges 3:10, p. 328.

31   Ibid., Judges 11:29, p. 343.

32   Ibid., 1 Samuel 3:1–7, p. 373.

33   Ibid., 1 Samuel 3:9, p. 374.

34   Ibid., 1 Samuel 3:10, p. 374.

35   Ibid., 1 Samuel 3:15, p. 374.

36   Ibid., 1 Samuel 9:9, p. 380.

37   Ibid., 1 Samuel 9, p. 380.

38   Ibid., 1 Samuel 10, p. 381.

39   Ibid., 1 Samuel 10:6, p. 382.

40   Ibid.,1 Samuel 10:19–21, p. 382.

41   Ibid., p. 367.

42    Ibid., 1 Samuel 13, pp. 386–389.

43    Ibid., 1 Samuel 31, p. 412.

44    Ibid., 1 Samuel 16, p. 392.

45    Ibid., 1 Samuel 16:13, p. 392.

46    Ibid., 2 Samuel, 2:1, p. 416.

47    Ibid., 2 Samuel 7:18, p. 426

48    Ibid., 2 Samuel 7:18, p. 426.

49    Ibid., 1 Samuel 16, p. 392.

50    Ibid., 1 Samuel 17:45, p. 395.

## Chapter 10 Angelic Materializations and Jesus' Mediumship

1    Rev. Donald J. Bretherton, *The Holy Scripture and the Trance-State: Part 1 – The Old Testament*, The Churches' Fellowship for Psychical and Spiritual Studies (CFPSS), Kent, UK, 1988, p. 22.

2    Gerhard von Rad, *Genesis*, Old Testament Library, SCM Press, UK, 1964, p. 81.

3    R. Davison, *Genesis 1 – 11: The Cambridge Bible Commentary on the New English Bible*, 1973, p. 37.

4    H.E. Palmer (ed.), *The NIV Study Bible*, New International Version, Hodder & Stoughton, London, 1988, Genesis 2:21, p. 11.

5    Ibid., Genesis 15:12, p. 30.

6    Ibid., Job 4:12–16, p. 722.

7    Ibid., Job 33:14–15, p. 752.

8    Ibid., 1 Samuel 26:12, p. 407.

9    Ibid., Daniel 8:15–18, p. 1291.

10   Bretherton, *The Holy Scripture and the Trance-State: Old Testament*, p. 25.

11   Hans Hertzberg, *1 & 2 Samuel*, OT Library, SCM Press, 1964, p. 82.

12   Palmer (ed.), *NIV Study Bible*, 2 Kings 6:17, p. 522.

13   J. Skinner, *1 & 2 Kings: The Century Bible*, Nelson, 1969, p. 303.

14   T.H. Robinson, *Prophecy and the Prophets in Ancient Israel*, Duckworth, UK, 1967, pp. 42–43.

15  Palmer (ed.), *NIV Study Bible*, p. 1211.

16  Ibid., Ezekiel 1:1 – 3:22, pp. 1211–1213.

17  John Weaver, *Ezekiel: The Century Bible*, Nelson, 1969, p. 43. (Also p. 24, new series.)

18  John B. Taylor, *Ezekiel*, Tyndale Commentaries, Tyndale Press, 1969, p. 67.

19  Palmer (ed.), *NIV Study Bible*, Ezekiel 8:2, p. 1217.

20  Ibid., Ezekiel 8:1–4, p. 1217.

21  Prof. Wheeler Robinson, *The Religious Ideas of the Old Testament*, Duckworth, UK, 1968, p. 115.

22  Bretherton, *Holy Scripture and the Trance-State: Old Testament*, pp. 28–29.

23  Palmer (ed.), *NIV Study Bible*, Daniel 8:15–18, p. 1291.

24  Ibid., Daniel 10:7–18, pp. 1293–1294.

25  Ibid., Ezekiel 3:22–24, p. 1213.

26  David Paterson, *The Roles of Israel's Prophets*, JSOT Supplementary Series, University of Sheffield, UK, p. 98.

27  Bretherton, *The Holy Scripture and the Trance-State: Old Testament*, pp. 28–29.

28  Ibid., p. 35.

29  Palmer (ed.), *NIV Study Bible*, Acts 10:9–20, pp. 1629–1630.

30  Ibid., Acts 10:10, p. 1630.

31  Ibid., Acts 11:5, p. 1632.

32  Ibid., Acts 10:3, p. 1629.

33  Bretherton, *The Holy Scripture and the Trance-State: Part 2 – The New Testament*, CFPSS, Kent, UK, 1988, p. 35.

34  Palmer (ed.), *NIV Study Bible*, Acts 22:17–18, p. 1656.

35  Ibid., Acts 9:3–8, p. 1627.

36  Bretherton, *The Holy Scripture and the Trance-State: New Testament*, p. 36.

37  Ibid.

38  Palmer (ed.), *NIV Study Bible*, 1 Samuel 28:6, p. 409.

39  Ibid., Matthew 1:20–21, p. 1412.

40  Ibid., Matthew 2:13, p. 1414.

41    Ibid., Luke 1:9–19, p. 1504.

42    Ibid., Luke 1:26–31, p. 1505.

43    Ibid., Luke 2:8–13, pp. 1507–1508.

44    Ibid., Luke 3:21–23, p. 1512.

45    Ibid., Luke 4:1–13, pp. 1512–1513.

46    Ibid., Matthew 17:1–8, pp. 1436–1437.

47    Ibid., Matthew 17:6, p. 1437.

48    Ibid., Matthew 12:24–25, p. 1429.

49    Ibid., Luke 11:17, p. 1530.

50    Ibid., Matthew 9:4–5, p. 1425.

51    Ibid., Mark 2:8, p. 1465.

52    Ibid., Luke 5:22, p. 1516.

53    Ibid., Luke 6:8, p. 1517.

54    Ibid., Mark 12:41–44, pp. 1489–1490.

55    Ibid., Luke 21:1–4, pp. 1548.

56    Ibid., Luke 19:41–44, p. 1546.

57    Ibid., Matthew 24:1–2, p. 1447.

58    Ibid., Matthew 26:2, p. 1453.

59    Ibid., Matthew 26:21–25, p. 1454.

60    Ibid., Mark 14:17–21, pp. 1494–1495.

61    Ibid., Luke 22:14, p. 1550.

62    Ibid., Luke 22:21–23, p. 1551.

63    Ibid., Luke 22:47–48, p. 1552.

64    Ibid., Matthew 26:45–48, p. 1455

65    Ibid., Mark 14:41–43, p. 1495.

66    Ibid., Luke 2:25–28, p. 1508.

67    Ibid., Matthew 21:1–5, pp. 1441–1442.

68    Ibid., Matthew 10:19, p. 1426.

69    Ibid., Luke 22:34, p. 1551.

70    Ibid., Matthew 26:31, p. 1454.

71    Ibid., Matthew 8:23–27, pp. 1423–1424.

72    Ibid., Matthew 14:25, p. 1433.

73    Ibid., Luke 24:50–53, p. 1558.

74    Ibid., Matthew 15:30, pp. 1434–1435.

75 Ibid., Luke 24:13–30, pp. 1556–1557.

76 Ibid., Luke 24:36–45, p. 1557.

77 Ibid., Mark 16:9–20, p. 1500.

78 Ibid., Mark 16:20, p. 1500.

79 Ibid., John 8:28–29, p. 1580

80 Ibid., John 8:38, p. 1581.

81 Ibid., John 12:50, p. 1590.

82 Ibid., John 14:2–3, p. 1592.

83 Ibid., John 14:16–26, p. 1593.

84 Angus H. Haddow, *The Paranormal and the Synoptic Gospels*, CFPSS, Kent, UK, 1988, pp. 8–9.

85 Palmer (ed.), *NIV Study Bible*, 1 John 4:1–6, p. 1871.

86 Ibid., 1 Corinthians 12:1–11, p. 1716.

## Chapter II The Medium Emanuel Swedenborg

1 J. Klimo, *Psychics, Prophets and Mystics: Receiving Information from Paranormal Sources*, The Aquarian Press, Grafton Books, UK, 1991, p. 93.

2 Rev. Dr Michael Stanley, Lecture: 'Swedenborg, Prophet of the New Age', CFPSS Annual Conference, Stewart-Digby College, Sept 1988, England. Available from The Churches' Fellowship for Psychical and Spiritual Studies, The Rural Workshop, South Road, North Somercotes, Nr Louth, Lincolnshire, LN11 7PT, UK.

3 E. Swedenborg, *Principia: The First Principles of Natural Things* (1727–1734), The Swedenborg Society, London, UK, 1958.

4 E. Swedenborg, *Oeconomia Regni Animalis* (1734–1742), The Swedenborg Society, London, UK, 1958.

5 E. Swedenborg, E., *Regnum Animale* (1734-1742), The Swedenborg Society, London, UK, 1958. (Much was left in manuscript form.)

6 E. Swedenborg, E., Letter dated 1769 to the Anglican priest Rev. Thomas Hartley. (Owned by The Swedenborg Society, 20–21, Bloomsbury Way, London, WC1A 2TH, UK.

7   E. Swedenborg, *Journal of Dreams* (1744), The Swedenborg Society, London, UK. (Commentary by W. Van Deusen: Swedenborg Foundation.)

8   E. Swedenborg, *Arcana Coelestia: Heavenly Secrets* (8 vols.; 1749–1756), The Swedenborg Society, London, UK, 1958.

9   Ibid., introductory page.

10  H.E. Palmer (ed.), *The NIV Study Bible*, New International Version, Hodder & Stoughton, London, 1987, Genesis, p. 8.

11  Ibid., Exodus, p. 88.

12  E. Swedenborg, *The Word of the Old Testament Explained* (1746–1747), The Swedenborg Society, London, UK.

13  Palmer (ed.), *NIV Study Bible*, Genesis, p. 8.

14  Ibid., Exodus, p. 88.

15  Ibid., Leviticus, p. 147.

16  Ibid., Numbers, p. 187.

17  Ibid., Deuteronomy, p. 242.

18  Ibid., Isaiah, p. 1000.

19  Ibid., Jeremiah, p. 1100.

20  E. Swedenborg, *Heaven and Hell*, The Swedenborg Society, London, 1958.

21  *The Swedenborg Society (London) Catalogue*, London, 1994, p. 16.

22  Michael Stanley (ed.), *Emanuel Swedenborg: Essential Readings*, republished by The Swedenborg Lending Library and Enquiry Centre, Sydney, N.S.W., Australia, 1993, p. 24.

23  E. Swedenborg, *The Last Judgment* (1758), The Swedenborg Society, London, 1991.

24  Palmer (ed.), *NIV Study Bible*, Revelation, p. 1885.

25  E. Swedenborg, *The New Jerusalem and Its Heavenly Doctrine* (1758), The Swedenborg Society, London, 1990.

26  Ibid., introductory page.

27  E. Swedenborg, *Apocalypse Explained* (1757–1759), The Swedenborg Society, London,

28  Palmer (ed.,) *NIV Study Bible*, Revelation, p. 1885.

29  E. Swedenborg, *Divine Love and Wisdom* (1763), The Swedenborg

Society, London, trans. 1958.

30  Stanley, *Emanuel Swedenborg: Essential Readings*, p. 24.

31  Ibid.

32  E. Swedenborg, *Conjugial Love* (1768), The Swedenborg Society, London, 1952.

33  *Conjugial Love: The Swedenborg Society Catalogue*, The Swedenborg Society, London, 1994, p. 10.

34  Stanley, *Emanuel Swedenborg: Essential Readings*, p. 24.

35  E. Swedenborg, *Apocalypse Revealed* (1766), The Swedenborg Society, London, trans. 1969.

36  Stanley, *Emanuel Swedenborg: Essential Readings*, pp. 24–P25.

37  E. Swedenborg, *The True Christian Religion* (1771), The Swedenborg Society, London, trans. 1987.

38  Palmer (ed.), NIV Study Bible, Daniel 7:13–14, pp. 1289–1290.

39  Ibid., Revelation 21:2–3, p. 1907.

40  Stanley, *Emanuel Swedenborg: Essential Readings*, p. 25.

41  Klimo, *Psychics, Prophets and Mystics*, p. 93.

42  E. Swedenborg, *Heaven and Hell*, Commentary by Wilson Van Dusen, Pillar Books, 1976, p. 12.

43  David Lorimer, Lecture: 'Swedenborg and Survival Research', 12 Oct. 2000, The Society for Psychical Research, 49 Marloes Road, Kensington, London, W8 6LA, UK. (Lecture dedicated by David Lorimer to Arthur Ellison due to his passing; Ellison had held posts as the president of the Society for Psychical Research and vice-president of Scientific and Medical Network.)

44  I. Kant, 1724–1804: 'German philosopher who believed that knowledge is not merely an aggregate of sense impressions but is dependent on the conceptual apparatus of human understanding, which is not derived from experience' – *The Hutchinson Encyclopaedia*, Arrow Books, UK, 1990, p. 435.

45  D. Lorimer, Lecture: 'Swedenborg and Survival Research'.

46  Ibid.

47  Ibid.

48  Ibid.

49    Ibid.
50    Ibid.
51    Ibid.
52    Ibid.
53    Ibid.
54    Ibid.

## Chapter 12 Major Features of Swedenborg's Teachings

1    Michael Stanley, *Emanuel Swedenborg: Essential Readings,* republished by The Swedenborg Lending Library and Enquiry Centre, Sydney, N.S.W. Australia, 1993, p. 124.
2    E. Swedenborg, *Heaven and Hell,* The Swedenborg Society, London, 1958, para 41, p. 26.
3    Ibid.
4    Ibid., para 47, pp. 27–28.
5    Ibid., paras 178–179, p. 113.
6    Ibid., para 171, p. 109.
7    Ibid., para 173, p. 110.
8    E. Swedenborg, *Apocalypse Explained* (1757–1759) (posthumous), The Swedenborg Society, London, 1969, para 926.
9    Swedenborg, *Heaven and Its Wonders and Hell,* paras 15–16, pp. 11– 12.
10   Ibid., para 292, pp. 195–196.
11   Michael Stanley, Lecture: 'Swedenborg, Prophet of the New Age', CFPSS Annual Conference, Stewart-Digby College, England, Sept. 1988; The Churches' Fellowship for Psychical and Spiritual Studies, The Rural Workshop, South Road, North Somercotes, Nr Louth, Lincolnshire, LN11 7PT, UK.
12   Stanley, *Emanuel Swedenborg: Essential Readings.*
13   Stanley, Lecture: 'Swedenborg, Prophet of the New Age'.
14   Ibid.
15   E. Swedenborg, *The Principia. The First Principles of Natural Things* (1727–1734), The Swedenborg Society, London.
16   Stanley, Lecture: 'Swedenborg, Prophet of the New Age'.

17  Stanley, *Emanuel Swedenborg: Essential Readings*, p. 30.

18  Ibid., pp. 26–31.

19  Ibid., p. 26.(My italics & in bold)

20  Ibid., p. 27.

21  Ibid., p. 27.

22  Ibid., p. 27.

23  Ibid., p. 28.

24  Ibid., p. 28.

25  Ibid., pp. 28-29.

26  Ibid., p. 29.

27  Ibid., p. 29.

28  E. Swedenborg, *Conjugial Love* (1768), The Swedenborg Society, London, trans. 1952.

29  Stanley, *Emanuel Swedenborg: Essential Readings*, pp. 29–30.

30  Ibid., p. 30.

31  H.E. Palmer (ed.), *The NIV Study Bible*, New International Version, Hodder & Stoughton, London, 1987, Revelation, p. 1885.

32  Ibid., Matthew 24:29, p. 1448.

33  Brian Kingslake, *Swedenborg Explores the Spiritual Dimension: An Introduction to the New Church*, Seminar Books, London, Swedenborg House, 1982, pp. 12–13.

34  Ibid, p. 13.

35  The Swedenborg Society, 20–21 Bloomsbury Way, London WC1A 2TH.

# Bibliography

Achterberg, Jean. 'The Shaman: Master Healer in the Imaginary Realm', in *Shamanism*, ed. Nicholson, S., Quest Books, Theosophical Publishing House, Illinois, USA, 1987.

Angoff, A. (ed.). *The Psychic Force*, G.P. Putnam's Sons, New York, USA, 1970.

Audi, Robert (ed.). *The Cambridge Dictionary of Philosophy*, Cambridge University Press, 1995.

Banks, Hal N., STD. *An Introduction to Psychic Studies*, The Seminary of the Church, Alaska, 1980.

Barker, David Read. 'Psi Phenomena in Tibetan Culture', *Research in Parapsychology*, Scarecrow Press, Metuchen, NJ, USA, 1978/9.

Benton, Helen H. (pub.). *Encyclopaedia Britannica: Micropaedia*, 15th edition, vols II, IV, IX, XII, XVII, UK, 1974.

Besant, A. *Man and His Bodies*, Theosophical Publishing House, Adyar, India, 1971.

Blavatsky, H.P. *Isis Unveiled*, Theosophical University Press, USA, 1972 (original edition 1877).

Bohm, D. *Wholeness and Implicate Order*, Routledge & Kegan Paul, UK, 1982.

Bretherton, D.J. *The Holy Scripture and the Trance-State: Part 1 – The Old Testament*, The Churches' Fellowship for Psychical and Spiritual Studies (CFPSS), Kent, UK, 1988.

Bretherton, D.J. *The Holy Scripture and the Trance-State: Part 2 – The New Testament*, The Churches' Fellowship for Psychical and Spiritual Studies (CFPSS), Kent, UK, 1988.

Bretherton, D.J. 'Psychical Research and the Biblical Prohibitions,' in *Life, Death and Psychical Research*, ed. J.D. Pearce-Higgins and G.S. Whitby, Rider, UK, 1973.

Budge, Wallace E.A. (ed.). *The Egyptian Book of the Dead*, Dover Publications, 1985.

Campbell, Holms A. *The Facts of Psychic Science*, University Books,

Inc., New Hyde Park, New York, 1969.

Corbin, Henri. *Mundus Imaginalis: The Imaginary and the Imaginal*, Seminal Paper, Gogonooza Press, Ipswich, UK, 1976.

Cournos, John. *A Book of Prophecy: From the Egyptians to Hitler*, Bell , New York, 1942.

Dobkin de Rios, Marlene. *Visionary Vine*, Chandler Publishing Co., San Francisco, 1972.

Doyle, (Sir) Arthur C. *The History of Spiritualism*, Psychic Press, London, 1989.

Eliade, Mircea. 'Shamanism', in *Encyclopaedia of Religion*, ed. Mircea Eliade, Macmillan, London, 1987.

Eliade, Mircea. *Shamanism: Archaic Techniques of Ecstasy*, Arkana/ Penguin Books, London, 1989.

Eliade, Mircea. *The Myth of the Eternal Return*, Routledge and Kegan Paul, London, 1955.

Elliott, M. *Spiritualism in the Old Testament*, The Psychic Book Club, London, 1940.

Elliott, M. *The Psychic Life of Jesus*, The Psychic Book Club (special edition), London, 1938.

Ellwood, Robert. 'Shamanism and Theosophy', in *Shamanism*, ed. S. Nicholson, Quest Books, Theosophical Publishing House, Illinois, USA, 1987.

Evans, W.H. *Twelve Lectures on the Harmonial Philosophy of A.J. Davis*, The Spiritualist National Union (SNU), UK, 1924.

Evans-Wentz, W.Y. (ed.). *The Tibetan Book of the Dead (Bardo Thodol)*, trans. Lama Kazi Dawa-Samdup, London, 1927 (2nd edn, 1949; 3rd edn, 1957).

Firth, R. *Shamanism: Dictionary of the Social Sciences*, ed. J. Gould and W. Kolb, Free Press of Glencoe, New York, 1964.

Fodor, Nandor. 'The Birth of Spiritualism: The Fox Sisters and the Hydesville Rappings', in *The ESP Reader*, ed. David C. Knight, Grosset & Dunlap, New York, 1969.

Forman, H.J. *The Story of Prophecy, Hildegarde of Bingen*, Farrar and Rinehart Bell, New York, 1936.

Fox, George. *The Journal of George Fox*, ed. Rufus M. Jones, Richmond, Ind., Friends United Press, 1976.

Frederick, S.O. *A Dweller on Two Planets*, Alhambra, Bordon, California, USA, 1952 (first pub. 1899).

Gershom, Yonassan. 'Shamanism in the Jewish Tradition', in *Shamanism*, ed. S. Nicholson, Quest Books, Theosophical Publishing House, Illinois, USA, 1987.

Haddow, Angus H. *The Paranormal and the Synoptic Gospels*, The Churches' Fellowship for Psychical and Spiritual Studies (CFPSS), Kent, UK, 1988.

Hall, Trevor H. *The Spiritualists: The Story of Florence Cook and William Crookes*, Helix Press/Garrett, New York, 1963.

Hallowell, Irving A. *The Role of Conjuring in Saulteaux Society*, Octagon Books, New York, repr. 1971.

Houston, Jean. 'Foreword: The Mind and the Soul of the Shaman', in *Shamanism*, ed. S. Nicholson, Quest Books, Theosophical Publishing House, Illinois, USA, 1987.

James, Fleming. *Personalities of the Old Testament*, SCM Press, London, 1963.

James, W. *The Varieties of Religious Experience*, The Fontana Library, Collins, 1971.

Jung, C.G. *The Archetypes and the Collective Unconscious*, Collected Works, vol. 9, part 1, Routledge & Kegan Paul, London, 1959.

Kalweit, Holger. *Dreamtime and Inner Space*, Shambhala, Boston and London,1988.

Kardec, A. *The Gospel According to Spiritism*, The Headquarters Publishing Co., London, 1987 (original edition, 1864).

King, Serge. 'The Way of the Adventurer', in *Shamanism*, ed. S. Nicholson, Quest Books, Theosophical Publishing House, Illinois, USA, 1987.

Kingslake, Brian. *Swedenborg Explores the Spiritual Dimension: An Introduction to the New Church*, Seminar Books, Swedenborg House, London, 1982.

Kirkpatrick, E.M. (ed.). *Chambers Twentieth Century Dictionary*,

Chaucer Press, UK, 1983.

Klimo J. *Psychics, Prophets and Mystics, Receiving Information from Paranormal Sources,* The Aquarian Press, Grafton Books, UK, 1991.

Knight, D.C. *The ESP Reader,* Grosset & Dunlap, New York, 1969.

Lees, J.R. and E. *The Life Elysian,* Leicester, England, 1905.

Lewis B.P. *Spiritism and the Cult of the Dead in Antiquity,* Macmillan, New York, 1921.

Maynard, Nettie Colburn, *Séances with Abraham Lincoln: The ESP Reader,* 1969.

Metzner, Ralph. 'Transformation Processes, Alchemy and Yoga', in *Shamanism,* ed. S. Nicholson, Quest Books, Theosophical Publishing House, Illinois, USA, 1987.

Moolenburg, H.C. *Meetings with Angels,* C.W. Daniel Co., Essex, UK , 1992.

Moore Garth, E. 'The Frontiers of Religion and Psychical Research', *The Christian Parapsychologist,* vol. 5, no. 6, UK, June 1984.

Moses, The Reverend William Stanton, *Spirit Teachings and Higher Aspects of Spiritualism,* London Spiritualist Press, UK, 1949, 1976.

Myers, F.W. H. *Human Personality and Its Survival of Bodily Death,* edited and abridged by S.B and L.H.M. Longmans, Green and Co., London and Toronto, 1927 (original version edited by R. Hodgson and A. Johnson, 2 vols, New York, 1903; reprinted New York, 1961).

Nicholson, S. 'Shamanism and the Perennial Philosophy', in *Shamanism,* ed. S. Nicholson, Quest Books, Theosophical Publishing House, Illinois, USA, 1993.

Palmer, H.E. (ed.). *The NIV Study Bible,* New International Version, Hodder & Stoughton, UK, 1987.

Peake, Arthur S. (ed.). *A Commentary on the Bible,* Thomas Nelson & Sons, UK, 1952.

Peters, Larry G. 'The Tamang of Nepal', in *Shamanism,* ed. S. Nicholson, Quest Books, Theosophical Publishing House, Illinois, USA, 1993.

Peters, L.G., and D. Price-Williams. 'Towards an Experiential

Analysis of Shamanism', *American Ethnologist*, no. 7, 1980.

Phillips, P. and W.L. MacLeod. *Here and There: Psychic Communication Between Our World and the Next*, Corgi/Transworld, London, 1975.

Plato. *Theagetes, Theaetetus,* Loeb Series, W. Heinemann, London, 1921 (trans. by H.N. Fowler, bound with *Sophist*).

Ray, J.D. *Ancient Egypt in Oracles and Divination*, ed. Michael Loewe and Carmen Blacker, Shambhala, Boulder, Colo., USA, 1981.

Roberts, U. *Hints on Mediumistic Development*, Almoris Press, London, 1980.

Robinson, T.H. *Decline and Fall of the Hebrew Kingdoms*, Clarendon Press, UK, 1944.

Robinson, T.H. *Prophecy and the Prophets in Ancient Israel*, Duckworth, UK, 1967.

Robinson, H.W. *Religious Ideas of the Old Testament*, Duckworth, UK, 1968.

Rogo, D. Scott. 'Shamanism, ESP, and the Paranormal', in *Shamanism*, ed. S. Nicholson, Quest Books, Theosophical Publishing House, Illinois, USA, 1987.

Roy, A.E. *The Archives of the Mind*, SNU Publications, UK, 1996.

Roy, A.E. *A Sense of Something Strange*, Dog and Bone, Glasgow, UK, 1990.

Saint John of the Cross. *Ascent of Mount Carmel*, Image/Doubleday, Garden City, NY, 1958.

Saint Teresa of Avila. *Interior Castle*, Image/Doubleday, Garden City, NY, 1961.

Saltmarsh, H.F. *Evidence of Personal Survival from Cross Correspondences*, Bell, London, 1938.

Shirokogoroff, S. *Psychomental Complex of the Tungus*, Routledge & Kegan Paul, London, 1935.

Silverman, J. 'Shamans and Acute Schizophrenia', *American Anthropologist*, no. 69, USA, 1967.

Stanley, Michael. *Emanuel Swedenborg: Essential Readings*, Swedenborg Lending Library and Enquiry Centre, New South Wales, Australia, 1993.

Stevens, O.W. *Psychics and Common Sense*, E.P. Dutton & Co., New York, 1953.

Swedenborg, E. *Apocalypse Revealed* (1766), The Swedenborg Society, London, 1969.

Swedenborg, E. *Arcana Coelestia*, The Swedenborg Society, London, 1958.

Swedenborg, E. *Conjugial Love* (1768), The Swedenborg Society, London, 1952.

Swedenborg, E. *Death and After*, The Swedenborg Society, London, 1958.

Swedenborg, E. *Divine Love and Wisdom*, The Swedenborg Society, London 1958.

Swedenborg, E. *Heaven and Hell*, The Swedenborg Society, London, 1958.

Swedenborg, E. *The Last Judgment* (1758), The Swedenborg Society, London, 1991.

Swedenborg, E. *The New Jerusalem and Its Heavenly Doctrine* (1758), The Swedenborg Society, London, 1990.

Swedenborg, E. *Principles of Nature*, The Swedenborg Society, London, 1958.

Swedenborg, E. *The True Christian Religion* (1771), The Swedenborg Society, London, 1987.

Talbot, M. *The Holographic Universe*, Harper Collins, UK, 1996 (earlier edn, Grafton Books, 1991).

Taylor, B. John. *Ezekiel*, Tyndale Commentaries, Tyndale Press, UK, 1969.

*The Christian Parapsychologist* (Journal of CFPSS), vol. 5, no. 6, June 1984.

*The Compact Edition of the Oxford English Dictionary*, vol. II, P–Z, Book Club Associates, Oxford University Press, 1979.

*The Hydesville Millennium Magazine, Psychic News*, July 2000, The Spiritualist National Union (SNU), The Coach House, Stansted, Essex, UK, *The Journal of the Society for Psychical Research* (SPR), 49 Marloes Road, London W8 6LA, UK.

'Report by Mrs Henry Sidgwick on the Psychology of Mrs Piper's Trance Phenomena', *The Proceedings of the SPR*, vol. 28, 1915; SPR, 49 Marloes Road, Kensington, London, W8 6LA.

*The Spiritualists' Hymn Book*, SNU, 19th edition, The Headquarters Publishing Co. Ltd, London, 1985.

Ward, Charles E. *Oracles of Nostradamus*, Scribners, New York, 1941.

Wright, G. Ernest. *Isaiah: Layman's Bible Commentary*, SCM Press, UK, 1964.

# BOOKS

O is a symbol of the world, of oneness and unity. In different cultures it also means the "eye," symbolizing knowledge and insight. We aim to publish books that are accessible, constructive and that challenge accepted opinion, both that of academia and the "moral majority."

Our books are available in all good English language bookstores worldwide. If you don't see the book on the shelves ask the bookstore to order it for you, quoting the ISBN number and title. Alternatively you can order online (all major online retail sites carry our titles) or contact the distributor in the relevant country, listed on the copyright page.

See our website **www.o-books.net** for a full list of over 500 titles, growing by 100 a year.

And tune in to myspiritradio.com for our book review radio show, hosted by June-Elleni Laine, where you can listen to the authors discussing their books.

mySpiritRadio